The Poles

The POLES

STEWART STEVEN

MACMILLAN PUBLISHING CO., INC.

NEW YORK

Macmillan Publishing Co., Inc.
866 Third Avenue, New York, N.Y. 10022
Collier Macmillan Canada, Inc.

Library of Congress Catalog Number L.C. 82-9924.

Printed in the United States of America

For my son, Jack Steven,
with Love

Acknowledgments

IT WAS THE SPLENDID NOTION of George Walsh, the editor-in-chief of the general books division of the Macmillan Publishing Company, in the high summer of Solidarity's existence, that a book was needed that didn't seek to compete with the daily headlines on one of the most important news events since the end of World War II. It would be a book that sought to explain the Poles and their country to a world that, throughout history, periodically woke up to their existence and then shamefully forgot them once their immediate crisis was over. I accepted the commission with great excitement.

When I first met my wife, in whose veins Polish blood runs hot and strong, sixteen years ago, I not only fell in love with her but also with Poland. In fact I had little choice in the matter. Polish culture is so strong and pervasive that it was made fairly clear to me that I could not have one without the other. Since then we have traveled extensively in Poland. Each trip has reaffirmed my deep and lasting attachment to this land and its people.

Though these are not adequate qualifications to write a book of this kind, they help. However, for most of my life I have worked in one branch or another of political and diplomatic journalism, specializing principally in Eastern Europe and the Middle East. Several of my Polish trips were made as a reporter—seeing Poland with a reporter's eye. Here, too, I was helped by my wife, Inka. Being a professional artist who has often appeared on Polish radio and TV and who has exhibited, among other places, in some of Poland's leading art galleries, she was able to show me a Poland that few people see. Many of her friends have become my friends too, and most of them—some without knowing it—helped enormously in providing the information to make this book possible.

My wife's view of Poland is not mine, and vice versa. Her emotional attachment to the country is intense. I see it with the colder eye of a professional journalist. Accordingly, many of my conclusions she disapproves of strongly. But, of course, her influence is ever present: Poland and its people, from the men at the very top to

[ix]

ordinary workers and peasants at the bottom of the ladder cannot be judged by their actions alone. They must be viewed in context: Poles are the product of a country that has, down the centuries, been the battlefield of seemingly all the forces of history. This makes them a unique people—destined to be misunderstood and misinterpreted by those who have not shared their collective experiences. So my wife has attempted to instill in me that understanding and then left me to interpret what I found as best as I was able.

It is undoubtedly true that the sheer difficulty non-Poles have in dealing with Polish proper names presents a barrier to understanding which is sometimes difficult to breach. How, for example, can any one who is not Polish deal with a name like Szczawczyński or Leszczynski? In order to ease the burden of non-Polish readers (though by doing so I recognize I will irritate Polish readers), I have decided to leave off all accents with which Polish names proliferate. They are, of course, important, but only if one understands the system. Thus, Walesa is pronounced "Valensa" once the correct accents (Wałesa) have been inserted. Solidarność is pronounced "Solidarnosh" thanks to the dots above the final *s* and *c*. But I am sure that the average reader merely finds all of this confusing and so even at the risk of doing a certain amount of violence to the Polish language I have taken the unilateral, but I hope, ultimately forgiveable, decision to leave accents out altogether.

Recent events in Poland have forced me to omit from the extensive chapter notes I had planned all the names of my sources in Poland—a long, long list of people who freely gave me their time and showed me so much hospitality. It would be unforgivable, however, if this book were to be an additional burden to people who are suffering so much already. I do not even feel that I can name here those friends who opened their doors to me and let me stay in their apartments during the summer of 1981. During that trip I took the view that staying at one of the large American- or Western European-built hotels in Warsaw or Gdansk would cut me off entirely from the Polish experience. How can one expect to understand this strange and extraordinary country if every night one almost literally leaves Poland by going to bed in a Sheraton hotel? However, my hosts know who they are, and I am happy here to express my gratitude.

The young Polish woman who so brilliantly helped me in my research will also not thank me for naming her. She will be able to recognize, however, the fruits of her labor in this book.

Also my thanks to Miss Sultana Javeri, who translated my hieroglyphics and, always against the clock, produced from them an immaculately typed manuscript. Without her I could never have finished in time.

Finally, I must express my gratitude to my wife and all those Poles in Poland, but some in London too, who, in their determination to ensure that Poland and its people were at long last properly understood by the outside world, took it upon themselves to educate me. I do not imagine for a moment that there will be a single Pole anywhere who will agree with every word that I have written. There are 50 million Poles scattered around the globe, with 50 million different notions about Poland, its history, and its current predicament. Unable to take note of them all, I ask for their forebearance.

Prologue

JAN X, A MORDANTLY WITTY SOCIOLOGIST from Warsaw University, had been one of the first members of his faculty to join Solidarity in 1980, but he had resigned shortly afterward on the grounds that "throughout my life I have stood with the minority, I feel uncomfortable as part of the majority." At about 8:00 P.M. on Saturday, December 12, 1981, he received a telephone call from a friend weekending in the country. The friend reported unusual troop movements near his home. Columns of army trucks seemed to be heading for Warsaw. Though it was dark, he was sure that at least some of the soldiers he had glimpsed in the trucks were wearing steel helmets. It looked, he said, ominous. Jan told his friend, a well-known pessimist, not to worry and went out to a small party being given by a colleague for his wife's name day. It was a good party with old friends, but somehow Jan couldn't put the image of those lines of army trucks out of his mind, and after an hour or so he used his friend's telephone to ring someone in authority on the Committee of the Warsaw district branch of Solidarity. He had difficulty in finding anyone at home. Some of the top men were in Gdansk, where Solidarity's National Commission was in session. Others had simply taken a well-deserved weekend off. Everyone knew that the next few weeks and months were likely to be critical, and there would probably not be much chance of a break for some time to come. Eventually he got through to someone, generally acknowledged to be one of the most self-important members of the Warsaw Committee, and explained what his friend had seen. Jan was brusquely cut short.

"Look," said the Committee man, "if anything was going on, you can be sure we'd be the first to know."

"On the contrary," replied Jan mildly. "If anything was *really* going on you would, almost by definition, be the last."

He replaced the receiver and returned to the party, having done, as he saw it, his best to pass on the information. He, and everyone else, might have been more alarmed if he had known that the unmanned Telex room in Solidarity's imposing office block in the center of Warsaw was spewing out similar reports of sightings of unusual troop movements from Solidarity branches all over the country.

Jan left the party about 2:00 A.M. on Sunday, December 13, for his long walk home. He had stopped using his car a few months earlier, when the first of the unending queues for gas began. "If I have to sit in my car for four hours to get some gasoline, then the car ceases to serve me, I am serving the car," he had explained to me in the summer. It was a cold night, and the streets were deserted. Just as he was crossing Constitution Square, his head bent against the cold wind, some instinct suddenly made him look up. The street ahead was crawling with soldiers and military vehicles of all kinds. For some reason he couldn't hear any noise—it was like a silent movie he said. He didn't need anyone to tell him what was happening. A few hundred yards down the road was the Warsaw district head- quarters of Solidarity. He felt only a weary sense of resignation as he stood back in a doorway, watching the sixteen-month reign of Solidar- ity draw to a close.

They came for Lech Walesa, fast asleep at home in Gdansk, at about the same time. He had left the Solidarity National Commis- sion early, complaining of a splitting headache brought on by the endless bickering of his colleagues. They continued talking far into the night until they tumbled out of the old Hotel Monopol—the national headquarters of the movement—opposite the main Gdansk railway station, and straight into the arms of the militia waiting below.

All over the country, with stunning efficiency, the Army and police arrested not only prominent members of Solidarity, but their sup- porters within the intellectual community, the arts, and the sciences. Members of the Communist Party were taken into custody as well, including at least one member of the Central Committee who had proved too accommodating to Solidarity's wider ambitions. Also arrested—in a vain attempt to balance the books—were shamelessly corrupt and incompetent ex-leaders of the Party, who should in truth have been arrested months before, when their malfeasance first came to light.

The country fell into the hands of General Wojciech Jaruzelski and a Martial Council for National Redemption and, from being a beacon of light in Eastern Europe, it fell back into the Dark Ages. So, yet again, a new generation of Poles faces up to the bitter con- sequences of the two-hundred-year-long fight for national freedom and sovereignty. They were marched off to prison camps and denounced as "dangerous fanatics," "extremists," and "reactionaries" because some of them had dared to suggest that only free trade unions, a free press, and free elections would provide the necessary national consensus to cure Poland's chronic economic and political woes. The country was bankrupt, unable to honor its international debts without drawing hugely upon the Soviet Union, and governed by a Party from which the population at large had long since withdrawn even the semblance of support.

Whether Russia had ordered Jaruzelski to act or whether they merely approved his plans is of less importance than why he and his supporters believed that nothing short of martial law could save Poland from what they perceived as its accelerating slide to anarchy and national tragedy. Unnecessarily complex explanations have been put forward for the Polish December. It is surely enough to state that General Jaruzelski and those who encouraged and supported him were gripped by the same illusion that has, at one time or another, taken the fancy of military men through the ages. They compare the order and discipline inside their barracks with the anarchy that exists outside. If an army can be cracked into shape, then so can society itself. The Polish Army under Jaruzelski is not only the largest in the Warsaw Pact but, in the view of Western intelligence, the best trained and most professional. Its officers are highly proficient and motivated, principally because Jaruzelski threw away the Communist rulebook in the early seventies. Political officers exist but are not granted the status they hold in other Warsaw Pact armies. A working class or peasant background is no great advantage to achieving high rank. All that matters, Jaruzelski insists, is professional competence. Soldiers who misbehave in public are severely dealt with. The Army's duty to society (not the Party) is constantly emphasized in officer training schools. Soldiers help with the harvest, lay roads in poor areas, and help in times of national emergency.

It is no wonder that Jaruzelski was tempted to make unfavorful comparisons between this structured military society that he was instrumental in creating, and the larger society that is Poland, and to assume that what he had done for one he could do for the other.

And so the Army, backed by the hated anti-riot police, the ZOMO, the elite corps of the Citizen's Militia, moved against the population of Poland. General Jaruzelski and his Crows (in Polish "Crow" is *"wrona"* and the acronym for the Martial Council for National Redemption in Polish is WRON) clearly believed that after a few days of sporadic resistance Poland would be set on a new course for

the future. It all seemed very simple. Lech Walesa would be persuaded to run a union cleansed of its undesirable elements and even,
perhaps, be offered a position with WRON itself. The Party, which
had balked so long at economic reform, would be forced to come to
heel, and the huge bureaucracy, as responsible as any institution in
Poland for the country's problems, would be purged.

Meanwhile the Church, whose dislike of some of the men who ran
Solidarity was as great as the Party's, would accept a return to "normal-
ity" in return for a guarantee that its freedom would in no way be
infringed.

And the Russians, assured that such unthinkable concepts as free
elections and a free press had been crushed forever, would accept
what had been as unthinkable an idea as Solidarity itself: a military
regime within the bloc with leaders, no longer subordinate to the
Politburo, who would pay lip service to that most sacred ideal, the
"leading role" of the Communist Party. That leading role had been
well and truly captured by the military.

The scenario must have seemed a beguiling one. But something
was forgotten—the traditions, the character, and the temper of that
most ungovernable of people, the Poles.

For sixteen months the Poles had known what it was like to be
part of something like a free society. It had not been particularly
comfortable. The economy had gone from bad to worse. Not only
the Party, but Solidarity itself, upon which a large proportion of the
people pinned so much hope, was riven with discord. No one could
pretend that greater democracy also meant greater material well-being.

Yet, in an extraordinary way, an awesome national consensus
united professors at the universities with shipyard workers in Gdansk,
coal miners in Katowice with writers and churchmen, ordinary men
and women, old and young, queuing so patiently for the bare neces-
sities of life, with members of the liberal wing of the Communist
Party. For all the discomfort of day-to-day life, they agreed that this
Poland, created under the umbrella of Solidarity, was infinitely preferable to anything that had gone before. And so in every factory and
office, in every university faculty, and in most homes, the Poles simply
shrugged off the imposition of martial law as a temporary incon-
venience. They looked forward to the time when they could again
be strong enough to take on the state that had become to so many
an instrument of repression, face-out the Russians (so frequently dis-
comfitted by their unruliness), and step forward to the day that all
Poles *know* will come, when finally after so much bitterness, and

suffering, so much bloodshed, the nation will know what it is like to be master of its own fate.

"Five times, in 1956, in 1968, in 1970, 1976, and in August 1980, the smell of insurrection was in the air," says Jan X. "In June 1956 the workers of Poznan rebelled and clashed with the security police and the Army. Some eighty people lost their lives, and many thousands were injured. In 1968 the students in Warsaw took to the streets, where they were shown little mercy, as the militia waded in with truncheon and boot. In 1970 the Baltic ports blew up, and again Polish workers lost their lives fighting their own countrymen. In June 1976 more deaths and more injured, this time at Radom. But August 1980 we thought would be different. Poland, we believed, had at last learned its lesson. Negotiations between Solidarity and the government were always difficult, both sides were unused to this kind of dialogue, so normal elsewhere, and mistakes and misunderstandings occurred on both sides. Times were difficult, but Pole was not killing Pole. No one was thrown into prison for saying what he believed. Poland became a country, not a prison in which the inmates take out their frustrations on the warders from time to time. But then came December 1981, and it seemed we really had learned nothing after all.

"It will take years to establish how many were killed—we don't even know exactly how many died in Posnan or Gdansk in 1956 or 1970. What we do know is that *our* Army *our* militia, once again, declared war on *our* workers. For the moment, maybe, the military believes it has things under control. But for how long can it hold down a population that has proved time and time again it is prepared to fight for its rights?

"Resistance began on the first day martial law was declared; that resistance will gnaw away at the foundations of this regime as it has every other, until it crumbles and once again we will face each other across the barricades, either that or one day this government will eventually capitulate to the will of the Polish people. No people, particularly the Poles, can be kept down against their will forever. December 1981 was merely an interval in our affairs. Those who know Poland know that it cannot be otherwise. Those who know the Poles know that we will never settle for second best."

Said by the representative of almost any other nation, that would sound uncommonly like braggadocio. Said by a Pole, it is nothing but the literal truth.

Of course, the Poles have often behaved irrationally, taken the wrong options, or hurt themselves by a sometimes fatal inability to agree. They are not, in short, a people without Original Sin. But then where is such a nation to be found? I would say this for the Poles: For every stain on the escutcheon of the nation, I can find a con-comitant act of unparalleled unselfishness and heroism to lay in the balance. This is no ordinary country—Polish history has decreed it thus. A great and enduring people who have become thus against the most extraordinary of odds—there you have the Poles.

1

Drink and Be Merry

✄

The only reason we're short of vodka is because Polish scientists are trying to turn it back into potatoes.

THE AVERAGE MALE POLE, according to official statistics, is 5 feet 7½ inches tall, and the average female 5 feet 3 inches. Though not particularly impressive by American standards these figures do mean that the Polish population has been steadily increasing in stature since the war. During the past ten years, the population has increased in average height by 1½ centimeters, an impressive tribute to the fact that, whatever their problems today, the Polish people, taken as a mean average, are better fed, better housed and healthier than they ever were in the past. This may also be true of the other people living on the continent of Europe, but that should not detract too much from the fact that, whatever problems may be attributed to the regime that has managed the nation's affairs since the war, its achievements, where they exist, ought not to be glossed over.

Poland is, by and large, a well-educated country with over 17 percent of its population completing secondary and postsecondary education and nearly 4 percent achieving an educational status equivalent to an American master's degree. It is also a country whose people have been thrown into a huge melting pot by the system which governs them. Some fairly recent statistics show that nearly half of all those in employment (44.6 percent) belonged to a socioeconomic group other than that of their parents. A third of the current intelligentsia comes from worker families and a quarter from peasant homes. It is a young country—64 percent of the population are under forty years of age; young people between the ages of twenty and twenty-nine constitute the largest single age group in the country. This important statistic means that the largest segment of the population was either not born until the end of the Second World War or else was far too young for its horrors, visited with particular cruelty on Poland, to have made any impact on them.

These figures also mean that the vast bulk of the population had no direct personal experience of the years up to 1955, when the country was ruled by the rigid dogma of Stalinism.

They are the children of the comparatively benign system of Communist control ushered in throughout Eastern Europe on the death of Stalin. This system, though still permitting no real political dissent, sought to ease the strictness of the Stalinist ideology by giving people some access to the consumer market. The bad old days, as every Communist (and non-Communist) in Poland will tell you, have long since been over. Until December 1981, few people would have recognized a secret policeman when they saw one. Although some leading dissidents were imprisoned in the past decade, most people felt free to speak openly among themselves about what they felt. Provided they did not take their dissent into the marketplace, they were untouched and untroubled. With 93 percent of households owning television sets, and large numbers washing machines and refrigerators, many of the older generation, who had led lives of unbearable and poignant deprivation, were justified in feeling that the good life had at last arrived.

And anyone who travels through this most beautiful of countries, the seventh largest in Europe, will be beguiled by its people and entranced by the scenery, and become convinced that for all that has been said and written about Poland, life is not so bad after all.

Go deep into the forests of the great lake country in the Mazurian Lake District in the north, and life takes on a dimension that is both eternal and purifying. It is said that well into our own times, the last vestiges of ancient European paganism existed in these lands, and to see them is to know why. Watch an early mist on any of the thousands of lakes that dot this area, some tiny and almost intimate, others as vast and impersonal as any sea. The bright orange sun slashes its way through the forest like a sword-thrust, sending a myriad shower of birds into the air, which in turn calls forth the primitive sounds of the forest habited still with roe deer and red deer, bison, lynx, wildcats, elk, brown bears, and wolves. One understands why the gentle message of Christianity must have had trouble penetrating a land where the primeval elements of earth, water, wind, and fire still hold sway.

Young Poles have come to these parts for as long as anyone can remember, set up camp, lit their fires, and lived for days and even weeks on end, totally cut off from civilization, demanding nothing more than to be left alone in commune with this ancient wilderness.

The hundreds of foreign journalists who have come to Poland since the extraordinary events of Gdansk in August 1980 ought first to have been put here, to use the Polish countryside as a decompression chamber to acclimatize themselves to the quintessential Poland before going to the cities to do their work. All of Polish history can be summed up by the Polish people's deep attachment to their land and their cultural inheritance. Chopin's music, say the Poles, is an exact evocation of Poland, but the country came before the music. The composer merely had the ability to tune into it and set it on paper. Only those who have not been enraptured by Poland would regard this as a too fanciful notion. To fail to understand this about Poland is to understand nothing.

Poland seems to be a place where the Almighty tried out his geological experiments before building on a grander scale elsewhere. In the south are the Tatra Mountains, a little Switzerland perhaps, but far more exciting than that well-manicured land. To the southwest are the Sudenten Mountains, superb, natural ski areas which, no doubt, one day will be completely developed to look like ski resorts anywhere in Europe. Already it has hotels and chalets, lifts and marked pistes to which Poles and some foreigners flock in the thousands every year. But there still are the old shepherd huts where people stay and remember what it was like to ski before the sport became big business. Every morning they step outside on the crisp new snow and ski all day, never having to repeat a run until they are down to the foot of the mountain. They take a lift up and then walk—and for this one needs to be strong and fit—the last few kilometers back to the roaring fire, to a meal of roast venison and wild mushrooms, and plenty of vodka to wash it all down.

Poland possesses Europe's only primeval forests, now mainly beautiful nature preserves; the Pieniny Mountains, recognized as one of the most interesting natural features in Europe with a deep limestone gorge through which the Dunajec River tumbles and twists its way to the Vistula; even desert—thirty-two square kilometers of sand near Krakow and on top of that the shifting dunes of Laba. It is a most spectacular country.

And Poland's cities add lustre to its magnificent landscapes. In the south there's Krakow, once the nation's capital, whose history goes back a thousand years. When I first saw Krakow in 1965 I was a bit disappointed. Yes, it has many fine buildings—the baroque Church of St. Anne, the Church of Our Lady built in the thirteenth and fourteenth centuries and, of course, the impressive Wawel Castle, which was both the home and the tomb of Poland's kings and now its national heroes. When I returned in 1980, I was stunned. The great square in the center of the city with its ancient Town Hall tower and cathedral, its bustling and colorful flower market was surely equal to St. Mark's Square in Venice, if not in scale then in the quality of its architecture and its overwhelming charm. What I couldn't understand was why I had not been so struck before. "Ah," said my guide, "perhaps when you were here last they hadn't yet closed the square to motor traffic." And, of course, she was right.

It had been the old Market Square. Perhaps in days before cars and modern shops it maintained a unity of design, but in modern times this had all but disappeared. The buildings remained, but one saw them as individual edifices, not as a complete entity, until a modern visionary opened up the square as it had been so long ago, and revealed a magnificence that even Krakovians who had lived there all their lives had not realized existed. From Krakow the road winds upwards to Wroclaw with its superbly preserved old-town district, its fourteenth-century Town Hall, and its thirteenth-century Gothic cathedral.

From there it's an easy trip to Warsaw itself which, compared to the other great capital cities of central Europe like Vienna, Budapest, or Prague, lacks grace but more than makes up for this by the exuberance of its people. Modern Warsaw, typified by the Palace of Culture, Stalin's gift to the people of Poland and a building of such stupefying awfulness that it transcends all concepts of bad taste, is dull and unimaginative. But the word "modern" has a very particular application. Warsaw was utterly destroyed during the war—not haphazardly by aerial attack, but building by building, as the retreating German Army, under the orders of Hitler himself, vowed to leave behind them a desert. It is hard to imagine this devastation when one looks at what appears to be the well-preserved old town today.

Old Warsaw is a living symbol of Poland's extraordinary sense of national pride. This pride was expressed on an almost heroic scale by the entire nation immediately after the war, at a time of great economic deprivation, when the Poles devoted the country's resources to rebuilding the destroyed old city, literally razed to the ground by the Germans. Working from old Canaletto drawings and sketches, and to Corazzi's nineteenth-century plan, which had been hidden from the Germans, Polish architects and historians, builders, masons, artists, and craftsmen, helped by the muscle-power of everyone from students to housewives, put the whole town together again, stone by stone. The result is a triumph.

This cannot be a city built in the 1940s and early fifties, but the organic creation of centuries of civilized life. Poland's Communist regime, and particularly the Communist regime that ruled Poland while Stalin lived, will come in for much criticism in this book. But I do not believe that any other kind of government would have been capable of this prodigious undertaking. Only such a government could have been able to harness the national will for what was, after all, such a magnificent folly. But compare how postwar planners and speculative builders—operating in a democratic, capitalist country—completed what Hitler's bombs began by destroying the city of London, with Warsaw, and see how the strict application of the rules of the marketplace and *sensible* economic decision-making can blight the lives of generations to come.

Once out of Warsaw the road to the north goes through Poznan, past ancient castles that appear like magic out of nowhere, guarding a road that has long since lost any strategic value, and on to the Hanseatic town of Gdansk, whose streets are reminiscent of the charm and atmosphere of old Amsterdam. On the way is the small jewel-box of a town, Torun, home of the astronomer Copernicus, where I stayed in a small Gothic and baroque inn. My room—one of the nicest I have ever stayed in—had fine old paneling, beautiful furniture, and a view over the old university building.

Gdansk is now famous for its shipyard, but it was known for hundreds of years before for its beauty. Charming, winding streets open into squares of tall, multistoried, narrow buildings, the homes of the merchants and the meeting-halls of their guilds. Built during the Renaissance, the city was the greatest port on the Baltic and one of the most important in Europe. Gdansk, or Danzig as it has sometimes been named, has been German, Polish, and once, between 1918 and 1939, a free city to which both Germany and Poland were to have access. It was also the tinderbox that literally set alight the Second World War.

It is impossible to forget the Second World War in Poland. Everywhere there are memorials to its victims—small and touching street-corner shrines to Polish Resistance fighters shot on that spot, or vast, extremely ugly, Soviet-style monoliths whose very size forbids contemplation and reflection. One suspects they were erected for another reason altogether—to be a constant reminder to the Poles of their geography. On their eastern frontier are the Russians, a constantly brooding presence, and a country which subsumed to itself lands that had been Polish and sacred to the Polish tradition for centuries.

To the south are the Czechs, hostile also and traditionally so. To the west, the most unpleasant country in all of Europe, East Germany, whose people like to holiday in Poland, where they point to houses and suggest none too subtly that one day they will be back to claim their own. To the north lies the Baltic Sea, which Russia considers as a lake within its own vast landed estates—a position which Russia makes clear from time to time, by exercising its vast naval strength.

Poland is totally locked in and isolated—a victim of its own geography, as it has been throughout its history. One of Poland's official guidebooks puts it this way: ". . . the decision to build Poland's security on the basis of an alliance with the Soviet Union meant a radical change in the situation in Central Europe. Poland, once a destabilizing factor, now became a mainstay of the peaceful order of Europe . . ." A remarkable phrase, and a splendid example of how, not for the first time in history, the misfeasances of the cat are visited upon the mouse.

But no guidebook ever printed has told the whole truth about the country it describes nor, for that matter, can casual tourists ever get far below the surface charm of the people they meet on their travels. Yet the internal landscape of Poland has been visible for years to even casual observers if they are not willing to be put off too easily by the tones of self-congratulation in the media and the state propaganda machine.

It has been best expressed by that most enduring of Polish minor art-forms—the Polish joke. In America, alas, it has a horrible connotation—a contemptuous and undignified expression of prejudice and bias. The American-Polish joke is the British-Irish joke, the Belgian-Walloon joke—all the same stories, with the same object—to ridicule a people of assumed stupidity. Polish immigrants who came to America became the butt because they were the least educated and had the most problems with the language of any of the groups of immigrants who came at the same time. They were given the most menial tasks, just as the Irish who came to England at the end of the last century were only able to find work as common laborers, a condition of life which both host peoples put down to something close to genetic idiocy.

The indigenous joke of Poland is of a different quality entirely. It is, at one and the same time, a marvelous demonstration of an entire people defeating an authoritarian regime by laughing at it, and a tragic expression of how far the country has sunk into cynicism and apathy.

Polish humor today is the most obvious public demonstration of how the Polish people have withdrawn support from those who lead them. When a nation laughs at everything a government does, ridicules its officers, pours scorn upon its alliances, when jokes spring up within minutes of every governmental decree, then laughter becomes both an escape and an expression of pain and disillusionment. Humor is a defense against the outside world; the more threatening the situation becomes, the more intense must be the humor to combat it.

Someone once said that there are two ways to surmount the triteness and tragedy of existence—heroism and humor. The Poles have frequently been called upon to display both. Poles now claim that humor has always played an important part in the national character, but there is no evidence to suggest this at all. In the nineteenth century when some Polish writers began collecting for the first time the humor and wit of previous generations, they were hard put to establish any qualitative difference between Polish humor and that of any other country. There were jokes, but with little, if any, political, social, or even specifically Polish significance.

After Poland was partitioned in the eighteenth century, the Poles used humor as a weapon against their persecutors and as a means to keep their own terrors at bay. During the Second World War, when Poland was in the hands of the most fearful occupying force the modern world has ever known, Polish humor flowered. Without any armaments to fight the invader the people used humor as a major weapon of self-defense. It was humor that permitted Poles to bear the unbearable. Everywhere there were jokes—even if the penalty for retelling them could be death—funny, often bawdy songs, and illegal posters all helped Poles to overcome fear, apathy, and despair. Humor helped Poland survive those cruel days; it raised spirits, providing new strength to fight the enemy. Graffiti artists were raised to the ranks of national heroes in the big cities of the country where they spread their message of hope, conveyed by means of laughter. Eventually the leadership of the official Polish Resistance recognized the vital psychological importance of what the anonymous comedians were doing and commissioned them into so-called small sabotage groups to knock the Germans at every turn and, by so doing, diminish them.

Warsaw streets during those bitter times were alive with humor. New words, insulting to the Germans, were put to old popular songs and sung in the streets, in buses, and often by children at school. The silliest joke became a revolt in its own right, an assertion of the dignity of a Poland that the Germans were seeking to destroy.

Example: What should an Aryan look like? Blond like Hitler, slim like Göring, and tall like Goebbels!

Example: After the war Hitler and Mussolini are hanged together. Hitler says, "I told you the war would end in the air!"

Example: A man applies for a pass to travel to another part of Poland. The German soldier asks: "Surname?"

"Schmidt."

"First name?"

"Henryk."

"Place of birth?"

"Berlin."

"Are you a German?"

"No, a Pole."

"Where was your father born?"

"In Berlin."

"And your mother?"

"In Berlin."

"Then you are a German?"

"Look," says Schmidt, "if a hen lays an egg in a pig sty, does that necessarily make him a pig?"

Example: Why is pork in such short supply? Because the last pig joined the Volk-Deutsch!

During the Warsaw Uprising, when Poles again felt themselves to be in charge of their own destiny, humor disappeared almost overnight. This was the time for nationalist songs and sentiment, often sickly and sentimental. For humor, especially Polish humor, flourishes when it is the only method of warfare left, so it was natural that after the war, Polish humor reasserted itself as Stalinism gripped the nation in its steely clasp.

Example: Stalin was addressing a group of Polish Communists when suddenly someone sneezed. Stalin looked up sharply and asked, "Who sneezed?" There was a deathly silence in the hall. "Alright," Stalin said, and motioned to his security guards, "take the first row." Trembling, the men were led outside to the courtyard where they were shot. "I ask again," said Stalin, "who sneezed?" Again no one dared speak. "The second row," said Stalin, and they too were led outside and shot. "For the third and last time," thundered the great man, "who sneezed?" This time a terrified little man at the back of the hall raised his hand. "Ah," said Stalin, smiling. "Gesundheit."

Polish humor was now to reach its apogee. As the authorities sought to use propaganda to stop rational, independent thought and to persuade people to be obedient and subservient to the slogans that appeared everywhere, the people fought back.

The fight was no longer for physical but intellectual survival. Humor and wit were essential ingredients in the battle to blunt the powerful propaganda of the regime. The truth could not be published in newspapers and books, so instead it was told in jokes, and the authorities themselves realized the significance. The anonymous graffiti artist who wrote on the walls of a public lavatory in Krakowskie Przedmiescie, "Shit in peace, Stalin keeps vigil," was saying more about the nature of Stalinist propaganda than a thousand political commentators could ever say. This counterrevolutionary propaganda was damaging to the regime's authority and brilliantly mocked the ludicrous pretensions of the Communists seeking to turn Poland into a contented people's democracy. But it wasn't until the 1970s that Polish humor escalated to the point where entire evenings could be spent swapping the latest jokes.

"What you must understand," said a friend, when one evening I mildly suggested that I'd heard enough, "our jokes are not merely our only expression of political opposition to the regime, but these jokes are what passes for political debate in this country. Listen carefully, and you will see that beneath the laughter each joke contains a profound political truth about this country and its economy, about the way it is governed, and most of all, about what the people really think of their situation. Listen to the jokes and you will have the truth about Poland."

Example: Party Secretary Gierek went to a small village incognito to see for himself how people really live. Everyone looked immensely prosperous. There were fine houses and cars everywhere. Talking to a small boy, he discovered that the boy's parents owned a tractor, a splendid combine harvester, and a van to take produce to market. Very pleased with himself, Gierek told the boy, "You know, you have all of this thanks to me. Go tell your parents I am coming to tea." The boy ran home excitedly. "Mummy, mummy," he shouted. "Uncle Helmut came from Hamburg."

There is a lot of information about the Poland of Edward Gierek crammed into that joke. As there is in this one: "Many members of the Party commit suicide. They jump into the gulf between the Party and the masses." Or the bitter, "What's red and eats grass— Poles in five years' time." The average Pole's attitude toward Communism is beautifully summed up in this joke:

A peasant is applying to join the Party and appears before the local Party secretary to answer questions as to his worthiness.

"If you have two cats, will you give one of them away?"

"Yes, I will."

"And if you have two tractors, will you give one away?"

"Certainly."

"And if you have two houses, will you give one away?"

"Absolutely."

"And if you have two cows, will you give one away?"

"No, I couldn't do that."

"Why on earth not?"

"Because I have two cows."

The Poles' feelings for the Russians are summed up by the story of the Red Army officer who arrived at Warsaw Station one day and called a porter. When the porter appeared, the Russian said, "I need more." The porter rushed off and collected his friends. "We're in for a big tip today, he's obviously got mounds of baggage." "No, no," said the officer, when they arrived, "I want more than you." Excitedly they rounded up another ten, but the Russian officer wasn't satisfied until every porter in the station was gathered around his carriage. "Comrades," said the Soviet officer, "thank you for coming. I bring you fraternal socialist greetings from the porters of Moscow."

And about the system: In capitalism man exploited man, and under socialism vice versa. Or about their leaders: Jaruzelski visits Mitterand and boasts about the achievements of People's Poland. "In our country now," he says, "we have no illiterates." "There are still some in France," says Mitterand, "but we don't have any in the government."

Immediately after martial law was declared, Poland's joke factory went into overtime. "Why do the militia travel around in threes?" "One to read, the other to write, and the third to keep an eye on the two intellectuals."

A militiaman shoots a man dead in the street, a quarter of an hour before the start of the curfew. "Why on earth did you do that?" asks his horrified officer. "Curfew hasn't yet begun." "Maybe," says the militiaman, "but I know where he lives, and he never would have made it on time."

A Pole shows a visitor around Warsaw. "Over there," he says, "is a prison currently housing some of our top intellectuals incarcerated on the orders of our Soviet brothers. And there is a fortified camp where the top-ranking Solidarity men are held on the orders of our Soviet brothers. And there is an army barracks where our Soviet brothers have a large army ready to use against us just in case things go wrong." Shocked, the visitor said: "I'm surprised at the use of this word 'brother'—surely 'enemy' would be more appropriate?" "On the contrary," said the Pole. "One is given the opportunity of choosing one's enemies. . . ."

If the constant jokes are the outward expression of a deep-rooted political sickness in this society, then alcoholism is the visible expression of social decay. A report by a committee of the Polish Academy in 1978, which was never openly published in Poland, presented a terrifying picture.

"Alcoholism is the most pernicious of social diseases, as it effectively destabilizes the whole of society. . . . Neither legislation nor the price increases have made any improvement; on the contrary, their frequently inept implementation has brought about the worsening of an already catastrophic situation. . . . While a comprehensive act was passed in 1971 with the purpose of regulating the consumption of alcohol, its implementation led to an increase, rather than a decrease, of the problem."

The report notes that in France or Italy only 10 percent to 12 percent of alcoholic consumption is in spirits, in Czechoslovakia 13 percent, in West Germany 22 percent, and in Sweden 45.8 percent. In Poland 65.1 percent of alcoholic beverages consumed in a year are spirits, and the figure is rising, while falling elsewhere.

It is impossible to visit Poland and not be struck by the inordinately heavy drinking among all sections of society. A bottle of vodka is produced as soon as a visitor arrives and must be finished before he leaves—it is drunk straight, not sipped but gulped down. Those used to Western social-drinking habits need a strong constitution to match the serious drinking of the Poles. There are dozens of kinds of vodka, with different strengths and flavors, as well as 100-percent pure alcohol readily available everywhere, which is drunk either neat or mixed into mind-blowing powerful cocktails. Poles will say defensively that heavy drinking has always been part of their culture, that vodka is even more deeply enshrined in the Polish tradition than it is in the

Russian. Certainly among vodka drinkers, Polish vodka is judged far superior to anything the Russians produce now or have ever produced. Yet the statistics tell a different story.

Doctor M. Tolkarz, a member of Poland's Committee to Fight Alcoholism, has compared prewar drinking habits with the present situation. During the economic boom years of 1928 and 1929, the consumption of pure alcohol in Poland stood at 1.6 liters per person per annum. During the Great Depression this fell by 57 percent to 0.7 liters and rose again to 1.3 liters per head by 1938.

Since the war drinking has grown dramatically. Expressed in terms of pure-alcohol consumption per head, the 1977 rate of growth was twelve times the 1932 rate. The rate of growth in 1976 amounted to 0.9 liters per head—a rate of annual increase that equalled the total consumption in 1932. Professor A. Swieckici, a member of the same committee, using figures supplied by the Central Office of Statistics, estimates that 4 million adult males are habitually heavy drinkers (someone drinking 10 liters of vodka per month and a half-liter at a time). The influential weekly *Polityka* wrote in July 1978 ". . . we drink and we drink more and more, at an ever-increasing rate. We drink nearly seven times as much as before the war and almost three times as much as a decade ago. Estimates suggest that 2 million, mostly men of working age, are habitual drinkers. Teen-agers drink, and they drink to excess. . . . Fifty percent in the 14-year-old age group drink alcohol, and 80 percent in the 15-to-18-year-old age group.

"Among those still in school at that age, the number drinking 100 grams (3½ ozs.) at one time grew eight times during the decade 1962–1972.

"What about drinking at work, disorderly behavior when drunk, and crime? Over 800,000 are drunk every day. Every day 400,000 are detained by the police until they have sobered up. Between 1964 and 1975, the number of those detained increased by 205 percent. There were over 200,000 charges of disorderly behavior in the last year, 90 percent of those were caused by drinking. The number of under-age persons among the detained is increasingly rapidly. It is estimated that 70,000 drink alcohol at their place of work every day. Production losses caused by drinking are estimated at between 10 billion and 20 billion a year."

Desperately and periodically the authorities try to persuade Poles to drink less, but usually unsuccessfully. The very latest official figures (February 9, 1980) show that the intake of pure alcohol now stands at 9.5 liters per head of population, a massive jump from the 1977 figure. These figures also indicate that 15 million Poles drink to excess, that 1 million can be classified as alcoholic, and that a half-million require hospital treatment because of their drinking. It is estimated that 40 percent of the alcohol is drunk at the place of work.

Drinking on a scale far in excess of any other country cannot be put down to "tradition," as some Poles like to do. They explain the country's addiction to vodka as if it were the national sport, no more eccentric than an Englishman's addiction to cricket. It is perfectly true that the Poles are a hospitable people who enjoy nothing more than opening a bottle of vodka with friends. It is an agreeable social custom, but like the French who thirst for the wines and spirits of their land, some are inclined to overdo. In the past vodka was one of Poland's attractions, never one of its problems.

In August 1980 during the sit-in at the shipyards of Gdansk which led to the formation of Solidarity, an order went out that no drink was to be consumed on the premises during the period of the strike. Astonishingly, the order was taken up by the whole city. Journalists arriving at the big Western hotels discovered to their horror that the bars were only serving fruit juice. In a stunning scene in Andrzej Wajda's film, *Man of Iron* (an account of the strike), an alcoholic radio journalist sent by the authorities in Warsaw to spy on the ringleaders discovers to his deep distress that not only is he required to complete an assignment which disgusts him, but he must do so in a city where no alcohol is to be bought at any price! Freedom, the leaders of Solidarity were saying, and Andrzej Wajda understood the message very clearly, meant not only freedom from political oppression but also the freedom to remain sober. As a leader of the Warsaw Solidarity told me: "When a man is master of his own fate, he doesn't want to get drunk, to do so is utterly self-defeating, because then he is no longer his own master. Men drink when they have no control over their own destinies."

But men also drink to have the courage to face up to the intolerable. In the first week of martial law, alcohol was forbidden in Poland, though the order was quickly rescinded—principally because it was unenforceable. "The stills were working the moment the regulation was printed," says a source in Poland during that period. "It was extraordinary that in Gdansk when Solidarity, though it had no formal power, declared prohibition, the public accepted it immediately. When the generals tried, the people just laughed in their faces.

Now, though in theory vodka is in short supply, more is being drunk than ever before. If people can't get it in the shops, they just make their own."

After several weeks in Poland it is not hard to understand why there are jokes and why there is drinking.

"Few people in the West, and certainly very few journalists who came here to report on events since August 1980, know what it is like to live in a Communist regime," says one professor at Warsaw University. "Few people realize the sense of utter frustration at being part of a system which is supposedly based upon scientific foundations, with which there is no argument. This system is unlike the Nazi philosophy which was self-evidently mad, and one could fight back, because one knew that inevitably it would crumble. Lenin was once criticized, long before the Revolution, for not permitting any dissent in the Bolshevik Party. He was genuinely astounded that an intelligent human being could even make such an observation. When a new principle is introduced into science, he said, the old principle is not permitted to run alongside it. It is immediately discarded, not to do so would not merely be ludicrous but it would lead to chaos. And Communism has run on these principles ever since. Communism is not a political platform, such as the Republicans may have in America, or the Socialists in Britain.

"It is a science, immutable just as Archimedes' principle or Einstein's theory of relativity. Hence no argument or rational discussion is possible. There can be no other view. And those who put forward other views are either ignorant or naive, and require correction, or are criminals seeking to go backward in time (reactionaries) before that era when Leninism was able to prove that all societies not based on the lines of Marxism-Leninism were run in the interests of the bourgeoisie and the property-owning classes against the working classes."

Western commentators and politicians who observed the vain attempt by Polish workers to free themselves from the *diktat* of a workers' state saw this as a delicious paradox which finally exposed Communism as a gigantic fraud. They had simply not read their Lenin. Lenin had few illusions about the workers.

"The history of all countries," he wrote in 1902, "shows that the working class, exclusively by its own effort, is able to develop only trade union consciousness, i.e., the conviction that it is necessary to combine in unions, fight the employers and strive to compel the government to pass necessary labor legislation, etc. The theory of socialism, however, grew out of the philosophic, historic and economic theories elaborated by educated representatives of the propertied classes, by intellectuals."

And later he wrote: "Since there can be no question of an independent ideology formulated by the working masses themselves in the process of their movement, the other choice is—either bourgeois or socialist ideology. There is no middle course—for mankind has not created a 'third' ideology; and in society torn by class antagonisms there can never be a non-class or an above-class ideology. . . . *But the spontaneous development of the working class movement leads to its subordination to bourgeois ideaology . . . trade unionism means the ideological enslavement of the workers by the bourgeoisie, hence our task . . . is to combat spontaneity.*"

Lenin was absolutely opposed to creating a mass movement, or jumping on the bandwagon of industrial strikes in pre-Revolutionary Russia. His Party would be a tight group of people at the vanguard of revolution, not tagging along behind. It would lead the workers, not follow them. As the great Polish philosopher Leszck Kolakowski put it, ". . . according to Lenin, the Party with its 'correct' theoretical consciousness embodies the proletarian consciousness, irrespective of what the real, empirical proletariat may think about itself or about the Party. The Party knows what is in the 'historical' interest of the proletariat, and what the latter's authentic consciousness ought to be at any particular moment, although its empirical consciousness will generally be found lagging behind. The Party represents the consciousness, not because the proletariat agrees that it should, but because the party knows the laws of social development and understands the historical mission of the working class according to Marxist theory."

The Party, in short, is completely independent of the working class even though it may require its support in practice. The proletariat is incapable of formulating its own class aims, and therefore the Party does this for them. Every other group in society—artists, writers, scientists—must equally subordinate itself to the *diktat* of the Party, because only the Party possesses the scientific formula which permits it to decide on the historically correct path for each group to follow.

To those who believe—and in Poland there are not very many— this is a comfortable doctrine. It withdraws all responsibility from the individual, who is required only to obey, in order to fulfill his duty to the Party, to the International working class, to his country, and to his history. To those who don't believe, it is suffocating in the extreme.

Says one young philosophy graduate, "It is like being aboard a ship sinking fast from gaping holes fore and aft. When the emergency is pointed out to the captain and the ship's officers, they smile indulgently. They say that there is nothing to worry about because the ship has been scientifically designed so that it cannot sink.

"You try to point out, at first as calmly as possible, that whether or not this is so, water is lapping over the bow, and the ship is indisputably going down. At that point you have only two options. You can try to take over the ship, but since the officers have the key to the arms locker, chances are you will be accused of mutiny and clapped into irons. Or you can eat, drink, and be merry, as you watch the water slowly rising around you."

The mistake made by many liberals in the West—but not by many people in Poland—is to consider that the modern practice of Communism is an aberration of the teachings of Marx and Lenin, which had been perverted by Stalin. If the socialist countries could get back to first principles, then all would be well. In fact, experience shows the contrary to be true—that repression is the sworn handmaiden of Communism. Maybe if Lenin had lived he would have modified his earlier teachings, as the implications of his economic prescription became plainer and plainer to him. This is by no means certain, and there does not seem to me to be anything in Lenin's published works or his actions to suggest anything of the kind.

So the Poles face their day-to-day life under a stern and inflexible ideology which not even those who rule believe in anymore. It is part of the genius of the Poles and their unfailing charm that they face misfortune, even martial law, with an insouciance which is wholly admirable. They go to parties and the coffeehouses of their big cities where they laugh and drink, mocking all those with pretensions to rule them, happily watching, as my friend put it, the water slowly rising around them. They live in a state that is supposed to have bred disciplined robots, and yet they remain among the most poorly-disciplined people on earth, the despair of those who have sought to tie them down.

There is the temptation now to believe that December 1981 spelled the end of a glorious dream. This would be so only if Solidarity, as it was sometimes presented, emerged out of nowhere, a will-o'-the-wisp which could disappear as quickly as it appeared. But Solidarity was an altogether more substantial phenomenon than that. The soil had been well prepared for what was an extraordinary and unexpected explosion of people power in the heartland of Eastern

Europe. It could only have happened in Poland. The fact is that from the moment the Communists took power, the Poles simply withdrew cooperation.

Even powerful totalitarian regimes require some support from their citizens, and save for a brief period in 1956, the Poles have never been prepared to provide this support. During those long periods when the rest of East Europe lay immobilized inside a gigantic deep freeze, Polish men and women in the arts, at the universities, and in the factories were not merely disputing the right of the Party to lead them. More significantly for the long term, they were laying down such a formidable fabric of criticism of the Marxist state that today the Polish Party, in answering its adversaries, has no ideological weapons left to it which will not be laughed out of court by all of Poland. The Party can only appeal for order and calm on the arid, though possibly realistic, grounds that not to do so might prompt a Soviet invasion.

Out of all this emerged a popular movement of reform and renewal which literally changed the face of Poland so that it became unrecognizable. A street in Poznan ceased to be Dzierzynski Street (after Felix Dzierzynski, the Polish Communist who became head of post-Revolutionary Russia's first secret police force, the predecessor of the KGB). The street became, clumsily, June 29, 1956 Street, to commemorate the Polish workers who died on that day when the Army stepped in to quell the first outbreak of workers' resistance to the Communist regime anywhere in Eastern Europe. The same kind of things were happening all over Poland.

When the symbols of state are dismantled, the state itself cannot survive for long.

And yet much of the ground lost by the state during the heady days of the high-water mark of Solidarity have been recaptured by the Army and the militia. The Poles are told in their controlled press by arrogant Party officials, who apparently have learned nothing, that the "excesses" of August 1980 to December 1981 will never be tolerated again. Perhaps not yet.

I asked one well-connected Anglo-Polish friend who was in Warsaw during the military takeover whether there was any sign that Poland's traditional resistance to the conditions imposed upon them had weakened in the face of draconian regulations and overwhelming force. "If it were not for the fact that people had died," he said, "it would have been a farce. It was sometimes difficult not to laugh."

Writers who had been arrested on the first day of the crackdown reported that they had been asked to sign forms pledging their loyalty to the new regime. Without exception they refused. They were then asked to sign forms admitting that they'd refused to co-operate. Again they refused. Apparently the authorities had not thought of the possibility that both forms could go unsigned; they didn't know what to do and so released nearly all the writers. Stefan Bratkowski, one of Poland's best-known journalists, and chairman of the Union of Journalists, was not at home when the security author-ities called for him. Knowing what was in store, he went into hiding. A group of writers appealed to a senior minister on his behalf, asking for the detention order to be lifted on the grounds that it would harm Poland's reputation abroad if such a distinguished figure were in-carcerated. The minister promised to see what he could do; he went to the generals, but got nowhere. "I suggest a compromise," he told the writers the next day. "If Bratkowski remains in hiding he can't be arrested."

The expression "in hiding" is too melodramatic to describe pre-cisely what went on in those early days. One senior academic on the police list was "in hiding," but held court daily in the middle of Warsaw in both private and public places. In the meantime, the most formidable action of the military was to cut telephone com-munications completely both inside Poland and between Poland and the outside world. One English newspaper reported in marvelous detail how this had been done—by a small army of specially trained engineers, all of whom the authorities could absolutely rely upon (itself an unlikely proposition), that had moved into the exchanges and pulled out the fuses. This has proved to be nonsense. The Army burst in and cut the main cables from all the exchanges with a few hefty blows of an axe. This method, though clean and efficient, turned out to be disastrous and from which Poland and the Polish economy suffered the most unforeseen consequences.

Nobody knows how many people died because emergency services like fire brigades and ambulances were not only cut off but could not be reinstated. Directors of enterprises pleaded with the authorities for limited service simply to call their suppliers, but they were told by embarrassed officials that it was impossible. Party officers in the provinces had no communication with Warsaw and were left ab-solutely floundering. The country, with no telephones of any kind, simply ground to a halt. "The generals forgot that the telephone system in a modern industrial state is not primarily an instrument of conspiracy, though it can be that too," said a Polish friend. "It is first and foremost one of the most vital tools of industry and commerce. We were in an economic mess before. Within twenty-four hours of the December coup, one of the prime justifications of which was to cure a sick economy, our factories and offices were in absolute and total chaos, not because of resistance by the workers, but from what the authorities did by cutting lines of communication.

"The West was impressed by the speed and efficiency of the takeover. But no one ever doubted that our Army was the only organization in Poland that really worked.

"But everything that came later, even just twenty-four hours later, proved that while it may be comparatively easy to take over a modern state, it is a very much more difficult matter to know how to run it.

"Poland's problem is that it has been systematically misgoverned for the past forty years, and there is no evidence that anything happening now has improved matters one iota."

If one considers what went before, that's a bold statement. For Solidarity and the spark it lit in Poland was, when all is said and done, simply a natural, human reaction by a whole people to one of the most foolish, incompetent, dishonest, and corrupt governments that modern European history has known. To understand Poland and the rise and fall of Solidarity, that is the first thing one should know.

2

Every Wall Has Its Silver Grouting

❇

A young Pole emigrated to America, and within a short time he made his fortune. After a few years he invited his father over to spend a holiday with him. Brimming over with self-satisfaction he showed off his magnificent ranch, his ten cars, his Olympic-size swimming pool, and his palatial house. But instead of being happy, the father seemed more and more morose as he saw more and more possessions.

"Look," said the son finally, "what's wrong with you? Aren't you proud of me?"

"Proud?" the father exclaimed. "You expect me to be proud that my only son has joined the Party?"

FROM MILES AROUND you can see great chimney stacks belching black smoke into the sky and the untidy slag heaps, manmade mountains of industrial waste, scarring the landscape. You can see the town itself, bleakly gray, an untidy mixture of the building styles of the thirties, when the greatest problem was a poverty of materials, and the fifties, when that was coupled with a poverty of imagination. There are similar workers' apartments all over Eastern and Western Europe, built in the great day of Socialist promise. It is impossible to see them now without believing that, deep down, the men who designed and built them—but who would never dream of living in them—had a profound contempt for the people they were supposedly serving. So it is a grim town made acceptable only by the courage and exuberance of the people who live in it.

This is Katowice, a town that is to Poland what Pittsburgh is to America, Birmingham to England, or Essen to Germany. It is in the wealth-producing heartland of the nation and is the capital of Silesia. Before World War I, under Prussian rule, Silesia was one of the most important industrial regions in Europe. Today Silesian coal is Poland's principal export and its miners the new aristocrats of the country. They earn three times the national average and are always assured that, even in time of food shortages, they will be fed first. To politicians and Party newspapers alike, the Silesian miner holds a special

[25]

place in their rhetoric. To them socialism and the Silesian proletariat are indivisible. Anyone who travels to Katowice cannot help but be impressed by the evident prosperity of the miners compared to other groups of workers, white or blue collar, elsewhere in Poland.

Their homes are larger and better furnished than those found elsewhere, and they have enough spending money to make a night in the miners' club a riotous and momentous occasion. "Poles know how to drink," says one miner cheerfully. "But it was the Silesians who taught the Poles how to drink!"

There can be little doubt that if there had been free elections in Poland, in 1947 Silesia would have voted Communist almost to a man. There are still survivors—old men now, of course—who remember Polish Silesia (part of Silesia was in Germany) as it was before the war and the bitterness of industrial relations then: strikes, lockouts, demonstrations—agitation all fueled by low wages and minimal welfare benefits. It was a time of terrible hardship for this tough and resilient people. Then illegal, the Communist Party might have had few supporters in the rest of Poland, but in Katowice it found no difficulty in attracting recruits.

If, since then, loyalty to the cause has been suspect in the rest of Poland, Silesia and Katowice surely have always remained solid.

It is Katowice which should be the moral conscience of the nation. It was in Katowice that the miners, after the clamp-down of martial law, held out against the generals longer than any other group of workers in Poland. They stayed down the Piast coal mine, one of the most modern in Poland, if not all Europe, over Christmas, and when they eventually came up, dared the authorities to take action against them. There is a great deal of bitterness in Poland today, but nowhere more than in Katowice. The coal miners have resigned from the Party in droves. In the fifties, sixties, and seventies they used to joke that it was impossible to dig any coal because the shafts were crammed with film equipment, yet in the early days they were proud that no Polish propaganda film was complete without shots of happy, toiling miners doing their bit for the nation and socialism. One can't put a date on when it first began going sour. Some miners remember the day in the early sixties when a film crew was actually chased off, and thereafter miners who appeared in close-ups were carefully hand-picked by the mining authorities. Nevertheless, it is probably true that this was an isolated incident, and right into the early seventies the Katowice miners were contented with their lot. So what went wrong?

In the summer of 1976, an official from the office of the First

Secretary of the Party organization in Katowice called on a senior administrator in Katowice's state-owned Coal-Mining Industrial Building Company (PBPW), the governmental agency responsible for all construction work in the mining industry, and was received with the courtesy due a man of his position. He had a request to make, he said. Comrade Zdzislaw Grudzien required a villa to be built—a villa appropriate for a man of his position as First Secretary of the Party in Silesia. The director of PBPW regarded the commission as an honor. Comrade Grudzien not only ruled the province on behalf of the Party, but as a worker and son of a worker and a member of the Politburo, he was someone beyond criticism and reproach. If the miners of Katowice were the aristocrats of the nation, then he surely was its prince.

The plans for the house were immediately drawn up and a project engineer appointed to complete the building. It was, he remembers, a nightmare from the beginning.

"Usually," he recalls, "it takes a year to complete a building of this size. We started in August and were told to complete by December. The villa had to be ready by Christmas . . . it had to be ready."

Poland may be a Communist country, but it is also a deeply religious country, and Christmas is celebrated there with an intensity that has no parallel in the rest of the world.

When the Party first took power, Communist officials made a fetish of pretending not to celebrate Christmas at all, but that didn't last long. Now all of them go through the magnificent ritual of the Polish Noël. So it was natural that Comrade Grudzien should want to be in his new house in time for the holidays, though the pressure that put on the work force was immense.

The project engineer recalls: "You will never understand. That building had to be ready against all reason. We worked day and night, Sundays included. The builders, carpenters, and joiners never left the site. And all the time there were the guards! They were checking every move. I used to finish work at 2:00 to 2:30 A.M. When we reached the end of the project, I was a nervous and physical wreck.

"Those were the most difficult days of my life. We worked as if we were possessed. Every demand had to be met. If they asked for the moon they would have got it. You don't believe me? I can assure you, they would."

By any standards the first secretary's house was magnificent. He had marble walls, with real silver grouting, a feature which even outside Poland would probably be regarded as ostentatious. The floors

were parquet, of the finest woods. All the bathroom fittings, in a
country desperately short of foreign exchange, were imported from
Austria. There were crystal mirrors everywhere, an imported automatic sauna, and larch-wood paneling for the walls. The last caused
the biggest problem of all. By the beginning of December most of the
work was finished, but the plaster on the walls was still damp. Special
heaters were brought in to dry them, but even then an expert said
that if the paneling went up on walls which were even slightly damp,
it would inevitably go moldy. This was reported to the First Secretary.
Nonsense, he said. He wanted the paneling in and the house finished.

By all accounts Grudzien had an excellent Christmas, though later
in the summer of 1977, when he was away on vacation, the now
moldy paneling was removed and replaced. These were the first of
many alterations and improvements. In 1980, for example, magnificent trees, twenty years old, were removed from the local park and
planted in his grounds with an English crane specially purchased for
this purpose. Grilles and larch-wood shutters, reinforced with alu-
minium, were fitted to the windows with special ball bearings ("the
best in the world," says one of the workmen) imported especially
from Japan. So proud was the First Secretary of this magnificent villa,
another worker remembers, that when he painted the shutters, he was
provided with a special cover for the grass in case any of the paint
spilled.

Grudzien was not alone, however. When he organized the building
of his villa he also saw to it that Professor Adam Gierek was provided with an equally splendid villa next door. Adam Gierek is the
son of Edward Gierek, who had been First Secretary in Silesia until,
in December 1970 he became First Secretary of the Party and de
facto leader of the nation. The original estimate for the two houses
was 3.6 million zlotys. By Polish standards that is a huge amount of
money, equivalent then to fifty years pay for the average wage-earner.

The final bill, which included all the furnishings right down to the
bedspreads, actually came to a figure in excess of 27 million zlotys,
which even by Western standards is a remarkable sum of money.
(Taking the average American industrial wage at $20,000 a year, the
villas at the then-current rate of exchange would have cost $7.5
million.)

With annual earnings of no more than 30,000 zlotys a year, the
First Secretary and his partner had to find other means to pay for
this luxurious lifestyle. Those means in Communist Poland were not
hard to find. Three years before he started building, approval had

been given by the Katowice County Council to refurbish, and in some cases rebuild, houses which had fallen into disrepair in Murckowske Street, in a residential section of the town. In 1976, while that work was still going on, the leader of the council simply added an undated appendix to the 1973 documents specifying that a number of private family houses were also to be built in Drosdow and Rosyckiego streets. One of those houses was the First Secretary's, another Professor Gierek's.

But just to ensure that the Katowice County Council was not too out of pocket on the deal, it invoiced the Mining Construction Company and the central government for part of the work. In the meantime, of course, to be fair to the First Secretary and Gierek, the houses did not become their private property. They were entered on the records as the property of the local municipal council and given a book value of 4.1 million zlotys—a sum considerably less than the actual cost, occasioning a suspicion that both men planned subsequently to purchase the property from the council for themselves.

What went for Katowice, of course, went for the rest of the country.

When Professor Gierek's father, the all-powerful Edward Gierek, celebrated his sixty-fifth birthday in 1979, gifts came in from all over the country, but his friend and protégé, Maciej Szczepanski, fifty-two, whom he had appointed as head of the nation's radio and TV system, outdid them all with presents which he was to describe as "modest," but which were subsequently valued at 150,000 zlotys, or roughly the equivalent of four years of Szczepanski's salary.

That Szczepanski was corrupt had been known by everyone of any rank working in television in the country for years. The quite extraordinary lifestyle which he managed to establish for himself was to become headline news throughout the nation shortly after Gierek himself fell from power in 1980. Yet his birthday gifts for Gierek say more about the way corruption in Poland had become institutionalized than any of the other really quite remarkable facts which were to emerge, once the investigation of Maciej Szczepanski was under way—an investigation which was to prove that he and his close associates had taken the state for several million dollars.

Corruption is not something confined to Poland or the Eastern bloc. Corrupt officials exist almost everywhere there is a powerful bureaucracy. But in Poland, and almost by definition throughout the Socialist bloc, the decency of the majority was made a mockery of by the conspicuous consumption of a few top officials, theoretically the keepers of the nation's conscience. How remarkable and how corrupt that Edward Gierek, the most powerful man in Poland, should accept gifts of such value from one of his subordinates. It was, firstly, a remarkable demonstration of how he had simply ceased to wonder at what was going on around him, that he did not order an immediate investigation into how one of his officials had such a fortune to give away and, secondly, it was an astonishing display of confidence by Szczepanski himself that he could display such wealth, sure in the knowledge that no questions would be asked.

These were not the only presents that Gierek received over which questions were subsequently raised. For example, a comparatively minor official was accused of giving Gierek a gift of a greenhouse, valued at 1.5 million zlotys. As the poor man later said: "Do you really believe that this was one of my brilliant ideas? I was called to the office of my minister and instructed to produce the goods. There was no room for discussion, and in reply to my question about finances, I was told to include all the costs in the overall costs of a factory my company was building at the time. What was I to do, how was I to protest, where would I go? I could hardly go to Gierek, could I?"

As for Szczepanski, he had a lifestyle which few, if any, of Poland's great princes could have enjoyed at the height of their power and wealth in the fifteenth and sixteenth centuries. He ran ten magnificent residences scattered all over the country, including a hunting lodge equipped with antiques valued at $1 million, a thirty-two acre sheep farm (enormous by Polish standards), a forty-room palace in Warsaw, six cars (an assistant had seven), and a five-room villa on the outskirts of Warsaw, complete with a glass-walled swimming pool and five concubines permanently in residence. In one of his mountain villas he had $8,000 worth of magnificent hi-fi equipment which he had imported officially for Polish radio, but which he expropriated for himself. He had a swimming pool and sauna installed in his office, together with an attractive masseuse and a special private cinema where he could view his library of some 900 pornographic video cassettes, and a magnificent yacht.

Once an unknown newspaper editor in Gierek's Silesia, he had become friendly with Gierek and climbed high on his mentor's coat-tails, relentlessly stealing everything he could lay his hands on as he moved to the top. Once there, of course, there was no holding him. Some of TV's better executives, directors and producers, were fired as soon as he arrived and replaced with his henchmen. They too were encouraged to steal, and they did so to remarkable effect. It will take a long time and a lot of patient bookkeeping for investigators to get all the facts on Szczepanski. Even if they eventually manage it, it is unlikely that too much will ever be allowed to come out. "Maciej," says a man who knows him, "was very clever. He corrupted everyone he came into contact with. If he kept a little black book and it was ever published, then not too many people in the upper echelons, not only in government but also in society, would remain unscathed."

It has been established, for example, that Szczepanski and his deputy, who had official funds to pay bonuses to directors and producers who had particularly pleased the authorities, used this money to pay people, often totally unconnected with TV, who could prove personally useful to them at some later stage. The Party newspaper in Krakow reported that "the list of beneficiaries includes the names of prominent personalities from the world of arts and entertainments, and such well-known figures cashed over one million zlotys in two years." Estimated value of this fund, most of which was misused, was 15.5 million zlotys.

An Austrian TV agency that used Polish television facilities and studios to make a commercial paid Szczepanski 74,000 Austrian schillings and his deputy 19,000 Austrian schillings, as well as expensive gifts and free holidays in the Alps for "creating a favorable atmosphere for their activities in Poland."

A British TV company went into a co-partnership deal, in theory with Polish TV but in fact with Szczepanski, to make, of all things, a Sherlock Holmes movie with British actors. The film has never been seen, but a wood-and-papier-mâché Baker Street still exists, looking somewhat forlorn in the middle of a Warsaw TV movie lot. By the time Szczepanski fell, the cost of the movie had risen by four million zlotys, much of which could not be accounted for. Official gifts were missing, props brought from Denmark were expropriated, and at the end of it all, a bankbook was found which showed that apart from what he owned in Poland, Maciej Szczepanski had no less than $1.5 million in a Swiss bank account.

Here was a man, a high official in a Communist state, living the life of a particularly unpleasant medieval monarch. No wonder that while men in positions of authority were indulging themselves so grotesquely, ordinary people should in turn find ways of cheating the system and turn to the black market whenever they could, until the whole nation had been, some thought, hopelessly corrupted. No wonder, either, that those who still believed the ideology (so loudly proclaimed on TV and the newspapers) all but disappeared as evidence of the cynicism of the leadership became common gossip in every street-corner café.

I remember, on a visit to Poland in the seventies, meeting at a dinner party a senior official who impressed me by the force of his argument concerning East–West relations. His thesis was that capitalism and Communism would inevitably clash, not because Marx had decreed it but because common sense dictated it. He himself, he said, was nothing other than a state worker who was bound, as a worker, to see things from the point of view of other workers. When he went abroad negotiating on behalf of Poland he met men, equally sincere, who owned capital and the means of production but who, as hard as they tried, could not fail to see things primarily from the point of view of their own class. He said that despite this, negotiations had often been successful, because there were common interests, but these commonalities could not, nor would they ever, disguise the essential "cultural, social, and economic" differences between men like him and the state he represented, and men like the capitalists he met and the countries and interests they spoke for.

Believing him to be an intelligent and sincere Communist, I tried to make contact with him on my most recent trip to Poland. He had disappeared, and it was only much later, after I had returned to London, that I discovered why. He was in prison awaiting trial on a charge of corruption dating back several years. The cultural, social, and economic philosophy he was propounding turned out to be the cultural, social, and economic philosophy of the Mafia.

If Solidarity did nothing else, it forced the Party to embark upon the painfully Herculean task of cleaning out the stables. No fewer than 200,000 Party members were sacked or forced to resign on ethical or moral grounds in 1981. More than 4,000 people were criminally charged. These figures are staggering. It means that about 6 percent of the membership of the Party was forced out because of corruption. But even that doesn't begin to tell the full story. If one assumes, conservatively, that three quarters of the Party membership were at the grass roots, ordinary factory workers, miners, and the like (the figure was a good deal higher than that), then one is left with a figure of about 750,000 Party members in administrative positions from factory foreman and up. That means that among those in some position of power, however small, some 26 percent were found guilty of a serious enough misdemeanor to warrant their being expelled from the Party. If there was corruption on that kind of staggering scale, the question bound to be asked is what were Party leaders, especially those in leading positions in the Politburo, doing about it? The answer is they were doing nothing.

"It is easy to be a hero now that the truth is beginning to emerge," says one senior Party official. "But in those days it simply didn't pay to complain at the way some people were behaving.

"I did attend one Party meeting where the behavior of an official was raised. I can't be absolutely certain what happened, but it seemed to us that the official who was caught with his hand in the till was removed from office, but so was the man who first brought the matter into the open. Certainly both were moved on. In fact, of course, the corruption moved downward like a slow poison, destroying everything in its path. When people saw how the 'bigwigs' were behaving, they thought well, why not me. It was a terrible atmosphere and it was difficult to escape it, but I do assure you that things are no better in neighboring Socialist countries."

The risk of corruption is enormous in a system with an elite answerable to no one but themselves, creating an oligarchy which, in order to preserve its privileges, must police its own activities. The "rotten apple" theory can never be shown to better effect. If one senior official is openly corrupt and is allowed to get away with it, for whatever reason, then others will follow suit, holding him out as both a precedent and a protection. "Every corrupt official in Poland knew someone senior to himself involved in the same sort of thing. It was implicit in the system that if someone lower down the pecking order was picked up, he would blow the whistle on a superior. Everyone was standing surety for everyone else," my Party friend explained.

Indeed, so widespread was corruption during Gierek's years that it is difficult to understand how anyone in any position of power managed to stand up against the prevailing wind. Was there, in short, a single honest man in the higher reaches of the Party anywhere? That is not my question, but one which existed for everyone in the country, then and now.

The prevailing sentiment is, "If they didn't know what was going on, they were fools, and if they knew and did nothing, they are criminals." Looking at the record, I find it hard not to sympathize with that point of view. It is worth considering some of the cases which have come to light, if only because they all beg the question— was it possible that this behavior went unnoticed?

Stanislaw Staruch, director of a scientific institute in Warsaw, a Party post, and the chairman of numerous Polish scientific commissions and technical organizations, had his car stopped and thoroughly searched as he was crossing from Poland to Austria on September 20, 1980. Customs men found in his government car a secret compartment which contained forty-nine blue-fox skins, 50 nutrias (coypu skins), twenty-five silver rings valued at 297,000 zlotys and four amber necklaces.

Mr. Adam Glazur, former Minister of Construction (appointed in 1975), had a house built for himself for which he paid 340,000 zlotys when the value of the materials and labor was 2.5 million zlotys.

The governor of Leszno took bribes amounting to 95,000 zlotys in return for assistance with the purchase of cars. He also took bribes of 20,000 zlotys in order to permit couples to jump the waiting list for housing. The director of the Transport Department in Leszno was also taking bribes in return for helping people buy cars.

A man referred to as Jerzy, who was a high ranking official with the State Planning Commission, took bribes amounting to one million zlotys for assistance with the allocation of private cars. Leszek Z, counsellor to the chairman of the Planning Commission, took 150,000 zlotys for similar services. In all, twenty-eight people in that one department have been taken into custody.

Tadeusz H., former director of the Foreign Trade Department, one of the big industrial centers in the country, took 50,000 zlotys in bribes from foreign firms. Stanislaw Grzybek, chairman of a craftsman's cooperative, embezzled half a million zlotys to refurbish his country house. In Legenica, Franciszek Rawkowski, in charge of state lands, found a brilliant way of making money by simply renting the land in his charge back to its former owners, instead of selling it to small farmers as he was legally obliged to do. E. Pacis, a state governor and a deputy minister for the food manufacturing industry, took 150,000 zlotys in bribes in return for favors in the allocation of motor cars; he used 99,000 zlotys from the public purse to construct his family house.

In Lublin an investigation is underway concerning the construction in the old town, at a cost of 5 million zlotys, of 102 luxury apartments, all occupied by local high-ranking party officials. The investigation had to be conducted by the central prosecutor's office in Lublin, because the local prosecutor was found to be the owner of this complex. Roman Mieloch, former director-general of Predom, a state-owned household-equipment manufacturer, is under investigation for taking "gifts" valued at 740,000 zlotys and for making a gift of two prototype mobile homes to influential friends. Tadeusz Wrzaszczyk, former chairman of the Government Planning Commission, was expelled from the Party for "using his official position to obtain gains." At the same time the Minister of Steel, Franciszek Kaim, was accused of using the resources of state companies for his own personal uses and was expelled from the Party.

Bronislaw Kafel, chairman of the Parish Council of Tyniec, near Krakow, was expelled from the Party for exploiting his public office for private gain; for neglect and mismanagement of the agricultural plant in the area; for misuse of land belonging to the State Land Fund; and for allowing the construction of private houses on land on which development was forbidden. Jerzy Rzessuta, secretary of the Party in Myslennice, also near Krakow, was expelled for the illegal possession of apartments in Krakow and in his own town, and for illegally obtaining a bank loan to build a holiday home for himself elsewhere.

Ryszard Chorobski, leader of the Parish Council in Skata, was expelled for taking bribes in connection with the allocation of plots of lands sold to peasants from the State Land Fund and for making illegal payments for nonexistent work on the town's water storage tanks. Where that money went has so far not been made clear.

The governor of Wroclaw managed to obtain an astonishingly luxurious villa and his daughter a penthouse in ways which were highly questionable. Criminal proceedings are underway in his province against a group of officials for whom fourteen family homes were built between 1975 and 1977. These houses were especially notable for their luxurious appointments, which included oak paneling even in the basements. Invoices to the owners of these homes were only issued by the building contractors after an investigation into malpractice had begun.

Jerzy Olsowski, ex-Minister of Foreign Trade and Marine Economy, committed suicide in May 1981 before he could answer serious charges against him. They were remarkable by any standards. In what is a tight, centrally planned economy, Olsowski managed, with others, to build several office blocks and hotel complexes including the huge downtown Warsaw terminal of LOT, the national airline. He completed eight projects in all, costing $265 million, without Cabinet approval or the approval of the chairman of the Planning Commission or the Finance Minister, an expenditure not included in the national plan or allowed for in any state budgets.

He stated before he killed himself that he operated with the verbal approval of the Prime Minister, Piotr Jaroszewicz, and there is some evidence to support this, for without the help of ministers at the very highest level, this extraordinary program of construction would have been impossible. One can't build several skyscrapers in the middle of a capital city without someone noticing. Olsowski and his associates were clearly intent on making a fortune for themselves from the very beginning.

"These people," say a Polish journalist, with little exaggeration, "committed grand larceny on a scale which must be unique in modern European history. I doubt if we will ever get to the bottom of it all, because too many people in the highest ranks of the government were involved. What they did almost literally was to steal Warsaw!"

Foreign contractors who didn't pay kickbacks were simply excluded from bidding. One British firm with an international reputation put in a bid offer for $10 million less than a Swedish firm's, yet the latter got the contract. Elsewhere in the country, also under Olsowski's control, equally peculiar decisions were beings made. In Katowice another Swedish firm signed contracts to build a hotel, received $7.5 million, and declared itself bankrupt, as did yet another Swedish firm which had won a contract for furnishing several hotels on the Baltic coast, received a down payment of $780,000 and declared itself bankrupt straight away.

Those in with Olsowski were handsomely paid, not only in money, but also in privileges. For example, one of the minister's henchmen was rewarded with a diplomatic passport and an "S" pass, given only to high-ranking officials and ministers, permitting them to park where they wish, and ignore virtually all traffic regulations.

But, of course, Olsowski did best of all. After his death his private bank account was opened. To the amazement of even those who knew what he was up to, he had a credit balance of $205 million. The world has seen many corrupt officials in its time, but Olsowski's nest egg must put him not far below men like Perón and Trujillo, whose records for rapaciousness have hitherto gone unchallenged.

Some argue that not all of this money was destined to end up in his own pocket. Much of it, they say, was there to pay off other government ministers who permitted him such an extraordinarily long leash on which to operate. It is unthinkable, they argue, that Olsowski could possibly have operated on such a gigantic scale in defiance of every known Polish law without having a huge network of silent partners—many beneath him in rank, but some necessarily above. It is difficult to quarrel with that assessment, and it is difficult, too, not to sympathize with those who feel that Olsowski's suicide was, to say the least, convenient.

There is no evidence to suggest that it was anything but suicide, but there are many in Poland, in positions of authority, who believe that if Olsowski had gone on trial he might have named so many people that the Party could never have recovered. It will take years before we ever get the definitive answer to this most fascinating of conundrums.

Olsowski did a good deal of his business through a state-owned company in Warsaw called Minex, famed throughout the country for the scale of the work it was able to undertake, and probably one of the largest firms of building contractors in the Eastern bloc. Its managing director, Kasmierz Tyranski, a state employee, was known throughout the administration for his extraordinary ability to be able to sort out practically anything for anyone. He was, as he subsequently and colorfully put it, given the task of "walking on a nonexistent tightrope." What made it worse was that there wasn't even a safety net. For when Tyranski was finally arrested, all those for whom he had so freely dispensed favors disappeared into the woodwork. He was quite alone but, loyal to the last, refused to name names. During his years of power he lived the good life. Through Minex he bought a flat in London for his girl friend. True to his reputation as a fixer, he saw to it that there was a spare room for the mistress and children of ministers and important officials when they were in London.

Minex set up a special account for those itinerants, so they were all paid living expenses, had their English-language courses in exclusive private academies paid for, and had enough money left over for expensive presents.

Even when he got money directly, he spread it around. He was accused of taking 470,000 deutsche marks and $310,000 from foreign companies, that paid him out of their slush funds in order to get business on favorable terms. An official of the strictly amateur national football team, that had acquitted itself magnificently in two World Cups as well as the Olympics, told Tyranski about the dissatisfaction of players who complained that their European opposition stars were living handsomely on princely salaries. So Tyranski chipped in $3,000 to set up an illegal fund for the players, and there are indications that other state firms did the same. He drove a BMW 320. Interestingly, Warsaw, in the Socialist bloc, where inequalities of income (in theory) hardly exist, is able to support two garages which deal exclusively with BMW cars, among Europe's most expensive. Obviously, the diplomatic corps makes up some of their business, but I was told the majority of customers were Poles. Tyranski built a villa in a fashionable district of Warsaw, had a flat in town, once spent 50,000 Austrian schillings on a dinner party, and kept an expensive mistress in Poland as well as the one in London. He was given a diplomatic passport, permitting him to travel at will without any problems of custom checks and allowing him to import at will all those highly desirable Western goods simply not obtainable in People's Poland. It all came to an end when Solidarity appeared on the scene.

It ended somewhat earlier for Jan Kulpinski, Minister of Mining from 1974 to 1977 and before that managing director of the Mining Industry Corporation. He made his fortune by stealing ideas. He claimed patent rights for technical and scientific innovations to which he had no title whatsoever. From 1972 to 1977 he pocketed 1,068,000 zlotys for supervising scientific research projects which proved to be wholly fictitious. He was known to be in the market for substantial gifts, such as cars, from those who wished favors from him, but he was finally undone when it was reported that he had used state funds to build a one-kilometer-long private road leading to his property.

It is a superb commentary on the morality of the Polish government at the time that he lost his ministerial position and as a punishment was sent as the Polish representative to the International Labor Organization in Geneva where, paid in precious hard currency, he could increase his fortune still further.

Stanislaw Durbacz and Boleslaw Czerniak were both senior members of the Krakow Party Secretariat and members of the city administration. Czerniak, in particular, was known throughout the area as a tough, hard-line Communist who gloried in being known as "The Protector" of Myslenice, a suburb of Krakow, which he ruled with a rod of iron. Between them they organized a scheme whereby 600 houses were built on land which had previously been put under an environmental protection order. This they ignored, and then proceeded to steal it for themselves. Firstly they lowered the value of the plot by ordering a layer of fertile soil to be removed, so making it useless for agriculture. Then they created a special post in the administration of both town and district councils to enforce compulsory purchase orders of peasants' holdings. Finally, when all this had been done, they sold the plots to private individuals. Durbacz, in particular, seems to have done particularly well for himself. He had two flats in Krakow and, when arrested, a house nearing completion on the outskirts. He had managed to have four cars in five years, obtained a job as administrator in a hospital for his cousin, gotten a pied-à-terre in

Krakow for his niece, and obtained a previously nonexistent job for his wife in the town council.

Edward Barszcz, former mayor of Krakow, built a magnificent four-story house for himself with a living area of 234 meters on three floors, plus a ground floor comprising three rooms, hall, and toilet. The internal finishings were so expensive that, even though he was mayor, the building cooperative erecting this imposing mansion protested to the authorities but was overruled. This house and two others built for associates cost the state 7,444,000 zlotys, or 2.5 million zlotys each, but on completion were sold to the mayor and his friends for 2.6 million zlotys or 888,000 zlotys per house. The mayor's family also benefited substantially from his position. In a district where it could take as long as ten years to buy a flat, Barszcz's son applied for membership in a cooperative on June 20, 1978; his membership was formally granted on June 29, and a flat was allocated to him on July 6. This transaction was known as "the miracle of Krakow." Barszcz became a minister but killed himself when investigations began.

And so the catalogue, both astonishing and sickening, goes on. Yet, even if the thousands of cases which are known all go to trial, there are certainly double that number that nobody knows about. The thefts can never be quantified, and the distortions they created for the Polish economy never rectified.

When the minister of mines, Wlodzimierz Lejczak (reappointed as late as June 1980), wanted a villa, he turned to the "Wuyek" coal mine in Katowice to act as the "investor." The records show that the cost of the property was 2.6 million zlotys, though it is known that this did not cover the cost of the original 5.6-million-zloty-estimate paid by the mine. The rest was simply "lost" somewhere in the books. Quickly it was realized that there was not nearly enough money, and another two million zlotys were handed over and recorded in the books as money spent "on the miners' bath house." Nearly a million more zlotys were added to the total to pay for fittings, including bedroom suites, radios, curtains, refrigerators, bedspreads, bed linen, blankets, towels, dinner sets, pots and pans, and other kitchenware. "How is it possible," asked a Polish journalist, "that a government minister in his late middle age did not even possess knives or shoe brushes?"

Lejczak rewarded the managers of the mine by assuring that year after year their mine was at the top of all mines in the country in reaching their productivity targets under the national plan. It was acclaimed in the mass media, held out as an example to other industries as well as to the mining community, and its supervisors and workers received special bonuses. It was all a lie—payment for Lejczak's house.

It was happening everywhere. Directors of state firms, department heads in ministries, and ministers themselves used official funds for their own purposes. They built houses of an ostentation which bespoke of no shame. And it was not only material things that they took. They even devalued university degrees, intangibles maybe, but honors which in every civilized society are not the subject for barter. The diploma examination for mining and steel industry engineers at the mining academy in Katowice is known and respected all over the country, if not the world. It's a two-year course that places heavy academic demands on the students who take it. The First Secretary of the Katowice Party, Zdzislaw Grudzien was, if not a genius, certainly the most talented engineering student this academy, or perhaps any other, ever had. He enrolled on September 1, 1960. He passed an examination in chemistry on September 26, receiving a "good" grade, took and passed an examination in mathematics on September 30 and in physics on October 4, thus completing the first-year course in three months. The second year flashed by as he took examination after examination with grades which were either "excellent" or "good," finishing the two-year course in a mere fifteen months, on December 30, 1961. However, students only receive their diplomas after completing a thesis which normally takes a year to write. Grudzien presented his on March 10, 1962, and it was immediately accepted as "excellent." One mystery about his thesis is that while all others are on file, neither his, nor the title of his paper, is on record anywhere.

There is even a question mark over the degree which the former First Secretary of the Party, Edward Gierek, has always claimed he had, both in conversation with foreign visitors, in his published entry in the Polish Who's Who, and in almost every newspaper article ever written about him during his years of power. According to the Polish Who's Who, he has a diploma as well as a B.Sc. from the same academy at which Grudzien performed so brilliantly. In fact there is no record at the academy of his every having been a student or being awarded anything at all. Gierek himself has sought to explain this discrepancy by saying that, in the 1950s, legislation (which no one had ever heard of before) was passed which permitted a special state commission to grant degrees to people having a minimal-qualification secondary education and "special work experience" with notable achievements. It would be a tedious task to examine the academic qualifications of every senior Party official in Poland, especially those claiming to be engineers, but it is thought that a quite remarkable number boast of distinction they simply do not have.

To be fair to men like Gierek, in the fifties in a country absolutely ravaged by war, there were simply not enough qualified men to go around. Unqualified people did important work, though they were lacking the educational background and qualifications. They had to learn quickly on the job. Some did so brilliantly, but still had reason to fear that when graduates began coming out of the technical colleges they would be put on the scrapheap. Nevertheless, what they did was dishonest. Their dishonesty was compounded when they not only insisted upon being given their academic titles long after they were any use, but they continued to support a system which handed out fraudulent degrees as if they were free gifts in a box of breakfast cereal.

The scale of corruption during the Gierek years was so immense, one newspaper editor told me, that in his view there was not a single member of the entire administrative hierarchy throughout the country who was not touched by it.

"It was a sickness," he says, "which raged through the body politic. It was like smallpox—once you were in contact with a corrupt official, you caught it. It started at the top and percolated down to the bottom, and when the people at the top saw that the people down the ladder were also feathering their nest, they went in for bigger and bigger deals."

One of the reasons—which he obviously could not make public— General Jaruzelski agreed to the imposition of martial law was because he (and everyone else in Poland) was aware that negotiations between the administration and Solidarity could never come to a satisfactory conclusion. There were too many people in senior positions within the government and the ruling apparatus who had too much to lose. Polish officials were more interested in covering up these scandals than they were in exposing them. The Party Control Commission that is charged with investigations has certainly made a wide trawl, but many suspected that those who were politically kosher had been left strictly alone.

"There was a good deal of wheeling and dealing behind the scenes," says one insider, "which left some immune from prosecution while others, against whom there was a political axe to grind, were exposed. But it was very unhealthy and very unstable. An ambitious politician who wanted to knock off a rival merely needed access to the Party Control Commission and then look for material damaging to him. It didn't need to be anything sensational, just organizing car vouchers or passports for friends would have been sufficient to destroy a career once those facts became public."

Though General Jaruzelski may not top any Polish popularity polls at present, in fairness to him, not a hint of scandal has ever touched his name. Someone close to him told me just a month before martial law was declared that nothing disgusted him more when he became Party Secretary than the extensive corruption within the Party. "I doubt if there has ever been a Party Secretary so unpopular among the higher administrative ranks of the Party," my informant told me. "He is chopping down hard—and they're doing all in their power to resist him. That's where the explosion will come—not between him and Solidarity."

In any event, the general decided to take on both at once. I am informed that he feels a sense of injustice because the West has singularly failed to understand his predicament.

Politically, say his friends, it was impossible for him to smash a corrupt Party without also smashing Solidarity. The latter could not have achieved anything while the former still remained in place. One does not have to buy this argument in its entirety to see that a genuine dilemma faced a man who, even his bitterest opponents in Solidarity accept, was personally honest, who inherited a corrupt apparatus that was negotiating with a potentially counterrevolutionary mass movement. Unfortunately, while it may be comparatively easy to deal with Solidarity "extremists," corruption in the Party has probably run too deep to be easily eradicated. The new law promulgated in January 1982, making it mandatory for officials to reveal their bank balances on acceptance of office and again upon retirement (evidence of Jaruzelski's determination to stamp out corruption), is too simplistic a measure to have much impact on a highly sophisticated society that has long learned how to bend not merely rules but the governments which impose them.

Shortly before I visited Warsaw, an astonishing event occurred outside the city in a beautiful forest where top officials own attractive holiday homes. One morning a man who owned one drove from the city to inspect his property, but to his shocked astonishment the house had disappeared, only the foundation betrayed that once a house had stood there.

"I have heard," he told the police, "of people stealing from houses. I have never heard of people stealing houses." An investigation revealed that a very senior official, fearing that he might be asked how he had paid for *his* holiday home, got a group of workmen to go to his house in the middle of the night, take it down, and remove the materials to a location where they could remain hidden until the political atmosphere "improved" and he could rebuild once more. Unfortunately, the workers had taken away the wrong house!

All over Poland, in every province and parish, in every city and town, when the cry for reform became irresistible, corrupt officials of all ranks desperately sought to destroy the evidence which showed that here, in the middle of Socialist Eastern Europe, these servants of the proletariat were living like the robber barons of old.

Today, though the worst of the excesses have been eradicated, first by Solidarity and then by Jaruzelski, the gap between the rulers and the ruled is greater in Poland than in Western Europe or America. Even today, anything is available in Poland at a price. And that price has had to be paid by the rest of the country. No wonder, after seeing how their leaders live, so many otherwise honorable people decided they wanted a slice of the action.

3
The Black Market

*Before the war, you'd see a sign on a shop-front and it would say 'Butcher.'
And you went in and you found meat. Today the same shop has a sign
which says 'Meat.' And you go in and you find a butcher.*

SOONER OR LATER every foreigner visiting Poland, especially if he is
staying with a Polish family, asks the same question: If Poland is so
badly off and its people so poor, if the food shops are so empty and
agriculture so inefficient, how is it that when a guest comes to dinner
there is enough, at least until recently, to feed a regiment?

During holidays such as Easter or Christmas, dinner tables in most
middle-class homes seem to be laden with enough food for an enormous banquet. As for the rest of the year, not a day goes by that the
family is not eating at least one substantial meat dinner. The Poles
take their food, but no one else's, seriously. It is the only country in
the Western world where not only have French and Italian cuisines
made little impact, but are unlikely ever to do so. I took a Polish TV
director on his first trip to the West to one of London's most distinguished French restaurants. The next day I took him to one of the
best Chinese restaurants west of Hong Kong. But his eyes only lit up
when my wife, recognizing a hungry man when she saw one, took him
to a Polish restaurant in London.

To a non-Pole, the food is heavy. Though the soups like barszcz,
beetroot soup, particularly when served as it is at Christmas with tiny
pastry patties stuffed with wild mushroom, cucumber soup made with
pickled cucumbers; krupnik or barley soup; and kapusniak or sauer-
kraut soup are truly magnificent. There is an emphasis on pork and
game, served in huge portions with mountains of potatoes made more
delicious with a sprinkling of dill, an herb without which the Polish
kitchen could hardly exist.

No Pole will thank me for saying so, but the portions that a Pole
regards as adequate are one of the explanations for the nation's constant food crises. If last Easter Poles had been prepared to accept a
few slices of ham per family, and not insist that anything short of a

[47]

whole leg would be an unbearable privation, the nation would have
had enough pork to see it through the summer. However, that is the
Polish way, and nothing, not even stringent rationing, at least as far
as the middle class is concerned, can ever change it. The Poles call
their ability to stock their tables, larders, and refrigerators with food,
when to all intents and purposes there is no food, "The Polish
Miracle." But if it's a miracle, there's little of the supernatural about it.

Poland illustrates the economics textbook thesis that when goods
are in short supply, a black market will arise to provide those goods
to whoever can afford to pay for them. The Polish black market, however, is not the seedy, back-street affair those who lived in war-torn
Europe will remember from the forties and early fifties. Here it has
become a sophisticated and virtually open trading community. The
authorities pretend to frown upon it, but in reality they accept it as
both a way of siphoning off excess purchasing power and of withdrawing from them the onerous function of feeding the whole population.

"Without the black market," says one Polish economist, "the distribution system which is already chaotic would completely collapse. If
between 15 percent and 20 percent of your population gets its food
from outside the system, then the system, already creaking at the
joints, is better able to look after the remainder."

It could be argued, and of course those who cannot afford black
market prices do so vociferously, that if the food eaten by the few in
such large quantities was equably shared around, there would be more
for the many. However reasonable that proposition may look on
paper, the reality, alas, is very different.

If the black market were abolished tomorrow and all of the food
sold there were distributed through legitimate sources, the average
Polish family would probably get one extra pork chop a week—not a
significant difference in the diet. But that assumes the same quantity
of food available on the black market would find its way into the
official system. In practice that wouldn't happen. Indeed, it's possible
there would be less food to distribute overall than previously. The
black market is an important source of income to thousands of small
farmers near every big city. Their plots are too small to be farmed
efficiently. If they had to rely upon state wholesale prices, which are
so low they even beggar the larger units, then the family income
would be intolerably low. However, if they can sell some of their
produce on the black market, their farms begin to make economic
sense.

So, if the black market were to dry up, all incentive to produce would disappear and, as has happened before in postwar Polish history, these farmers would simply grow only enough food to provide for themselves and their families. If the state tried to counter that by raising wholesale prices, it would either have to raise prices in the stores, even more than they were forced to last winter, which politically is impossible, or run the budget into even greater deficit than it is now. So the black market serves the interests of the state. Ministers from time to time may speak out against it, the Martial Council promised to abolish it, the police may occasionally raid the premises of a black marketeer, but everyone knows that the game is played for form's sake only.

Even during the present situation, when there is in some parts of Poland real hunger, the black market serves the government by permitting a dual pricing system in the country—official prices in the shops and black market prices for those who can afford them. There is evidence to suggest that products manufactured in Polish factories by state firms are put directly on to the black market, with only a small proportion of each consignment going into the shops. Thus, for a period, paper was in very short supply through official channels, and yet easily available at four times the normal price on the black market. This appears to have happened to cigarettes, too. Last Christmas a pack of Sport—Poland's favorite—cost officially six zlotys and was in desperately short supply. Yet the cigarettes were easily obtainable on the black market for twenty zlotys a single cigarette or one hundred zlotys per pack.

There have been crackdowns on so-called speculators, but the big dealers seem to have no difficulty at all in operating, prompting the suspicion that they are encouraged by the state, which harasses only the freelance operators. The latters' supply probably comes from sales clerks and the like who sell to friends in order to make some money on the side. These unofficial sources undoubtedly exist, but they cannot begin to explain the sheer quantities the black marketeers seem to have available to them. So the conundrum is this: The government has officially stated that it only has enough raw material to make half the quantity of cigarettes it produced previously. Yet Poles are smoking only slightly fewer cigarettes, and only slightly more cigarettes were coming from outside Poland. If they can't buy in the shops, they buy on the black market. But if the cigarette-manufacturing companies are not producing cigarettes, where are the black marketeers getting their supplies? Like so much in Poland, the arithmetic simply does not add up and only begins to make sense if one presumes that the state is in the black market in a major way. It is, when one comes to think of it, a quite brilliant way of raising prices without actually raising prices—of making those who can afford to pay, pay through the nose and subsidize those who cannot.

It also happens to be a way that free enterprise, which the Polish economy so desperately requires, can be made to operate in a society where the ideology insists it must be officially outlawed.

The black market is one of the few areas of the Polish economy which operates efficiently, which is showing record profits, and where there is genuine growth. Insofar as it also encourages the small farmer to produce, it also has a dynamic effect on the economy as a whole.

The black market operates at a variety of levels, from the simple to the vastly complex. In the early hours of the morning, between 5:00 A.M. and 6:00 A.M., shabby vans seem to be parked all over the city. They belong to peasants delivering goods to their "customers." A ring at the bell and the lady of the household hurries to the door, where she is handed a couple of ducks or a leg of lamb, a shoulder of pork, and some bacon. The buyer and seller have known each other for years, and there is little or no haggling over money. The price will tend to be double the prices in the stores, in winter probably more, but each feels she is doing well in the transaction. The vendor is, in nearly all cases, female, and known by the lady of the house as "her woman." Everyone in Poland knows what you're talking about if you say "I've got to get up early, because my woman is coming," or "I've got problems this week, my woman is ill."

While I was last in Warsaw, taking a particular interest in the black market, although it was a period of officially intense meat shortage, I noticed that so much meat was around that there was a constant problem of storage. One senior official told me of a disaster that had occurred to him. His deep freeze and refrigerator at home were so full that he had taken to bringing meat to work to put into his office refrigerator. It was only at the end of the week when he opened the refrigerator to take out the meat that he discovered the office cleaning woman had turned the refrigerator off and all the meat had spoiled.

Though he was in the midst of this drama when I called, it was interesting that while he was angry—as anyone would be—he was far from inconsolable, and within a few minutes was laughing and joking about the whole incident. There, I felt, was a man who didn't have any anxiety about where his next meat delivery was coming from.

Those who don't have direct deliveries have farms where they are known and where they make their purchases. These days so many people have cars this situation doesn't pose the problem it once did. For a majority, until a few years ago, a weekly trip to the country by public transportation would almost invariably take a whole day. Now things are better, but there are still people without their own car to whom this trip to the country is still a weekly ritual. One woman working in a government office told me that every Saturday she spends in Warsaw in store lines and every Sunday she visits her farmer friends in order to supplement the family diet. "They sent a form around at work from the personnel office," she said, "asking all sorts of questions. Under 'hobbies' I wrote 'shopping,' because that is all I ever do, summer or winter, in my spare time."

The peasant markets in every town and city, open most days and weekends, are the visible side of the thriving black market. Rather than face the problem of even trying to ban them—which happens from time to time—the authorities give them respectability by calling them the free market under the pretense that peasant markets were created by them. It is as if a man found a thief in his house, and in order not to have any trouble, called him a guest and treated him like one.

One doesn't often see meat in the free market, but when the shops are virtually empty of all vegetables, the free markets have them in profusion. Of course, they cost a great deal more than the official price, but that seems to suit both the state and the consumer. The former does not have to pay out vast subsidies from an ever-shrinking treasury, while the latter has a freedom of choice that the centralized-market economy seldom is able to provide. Everyone at one time or another engages in the black market. It has become an accepted part of society and the economic system. "This," says my Polish economist friend, "is true of the entire bloc and nowhere more so than the Soviet Union. The Polish experience is only different in terms of scale. In Russia the black market operates mainly in the big cities and towns. Here it is universal."

Whatever the economic benefits of the black market, it does have brutalizing effects in Poland, something which is rarely acknowledged.

That this is happening, however, there can be little doubt. The whole economic system is based on the principle that while wages may be considerably lower than in the West, fixed costs such as food and housing are also very much lower. For those with the lowest level of income—unskilled workers, office clerks, and workers in the less highly qualified areas of education, public health, and the social services—black market prices are simply beyond them. It would be wrong to suggest that anyone starves in Poland (all places of work have canteens where meals can be purchased at subsidized prices), but malnutrition is prevalent. Illnesses associated with poor diets and vitamin deficiency, such as rickets in children, are reappearing alarmingly. The plight of the poor in Poland goes largely unacknowledged and unrepresented. The regime denies there is any real poverty, and, of course, on paper there is not. Rationing assures, in principle, that there are fair shares for all. But if many stores can't even get their proper quota, inevitably some people go without altogether. As for the middle class, they simply shut their eyes. They know there is a food crisis, but they assume that "everyone" has the resources to make up deficiencies on the black market. Even intellectual opponents of the government are inflicted with a curious malaise about what ought to be regarded as Poland's single greatest social issue. The point is, of course, that most are reasonably affluent and benefit from the black market along with the rest of the middle classes. The existence of the black market, and it goes far beyond food, has created social inequalities in Poland on a breathtaking scale while it has reduced respect for law and for society itself.

"We have all been criminalized," says a sociologist. "When you start to buy meat regularly on the black market in defiance of the law and get away with it, it's not long before you start buying other things too. From there it is a short step to cheating the system in every way open to you. And because so many people do it, the social stigma that such acts might attract in other societies has long since been eradicated here. Cheating the system has become a sport. Some rationalize it to themselves by saying that engaging in the black market is a political act aimed at a Communist government. Of course they fool themselves. It is Poland they attack." Does he buy on the black market? "Yes."

It is also clear that a society suffocated by a web of restrictions will inevitably produce men and women with highly developed skills in twisting, turning, and manipulating the system to their own advantage. The majority will be happy to pay these people dearly for the privileges they are able to obtain. It may not be a particularly desirable state of affairs, but so universally can this rule be applied, it seems to be endemic to human nature. So firmly entrenched is it in Poland, there is no area of national life where the black market does not operate.

It takes three years to get a car through official channels, but if

someone wants a car tomorrow, it can be arranged. There is a twelve-
or fifteen-year waiting list to purchase a new cooperative apartment
in Warsaw, and an older, larger flat is almost impossible to come by.
Yet those with money will have so little difficulty that they'll even
be given a choice.

In theory, Western products like West German kitchen units,
American refrigerators, Italian dishwashers or Swedish stoves are
impossible to come by. They are certainly not available in any store,
and permission would be refused if someone sought to export precious
foreign currency with which to buy them. Yet I walked into several
homes where objects like these, brand-new, were proudly on display.
Western clothes from jeans to Parisian haute couture, Western food
products from Black Label Johnny Walker to elegant Swiss chocolates
are available on the Polish black market.

Many Western products were brought in by Poles permitted to
travel abroad so freely from the mid-seventies until December 1981,
and even more with Polish diplomats and those serving on trade mis-
sions returning home after a tour abroad. But only a small percentage
of what they bring in is used for their own purposes. The rest finds
its way to the black market. It is well known in Poland that anyone
who can get a five-year tour of duty in the West is set up for life
with the goods he is able to bring back. In all the years I have worked
in political and diplomatic journalism, I cannot remember a Russian
or an East European diplomat returning hospitality by buying a lunch
or even a drink. As the Russians and the Poles are among the most
hospitable people on earth, this puzzled me until I learned the work-
ings of the Polish black market. A Polish journalist explains:

"The pressure on Poles sent abroad to save every cent of their
salary and allowances paid in foreign currencies is enormous. Most
aim to buy a foreign car which, if they need an apartment, they are
able to sell on the black market for a huge amount of money. They
send or bring back an enormous quantity of stuff, all of which makes
its way to the black market and ensures that the man and his family
can live comfortably for years. Remember, everytime he looks at a
restaurant bill of, say, $50, he is mentally converting that to the black-
market dollar rate in Warsaw and sees that the meal is costing him
two months' salary. He would be less than human if he didn't think
that all of that money could be put to better use back home. And
he's almost certainly right."

Obviously the black market is so large that it cannot exist entirely
on what travelers bring home with them. The bulk comes through

several well-organized and -financed gangs of smugglers who operate
throughout Russia and Eastern Europe. Comecon, the Council for
Mutual Economic Assistance (the common market of the Communist
bloc), may not be the world's most efficient trading area, but the
smugglers aren't complaining. The route which appears to serve the
whole bloc with illicit goods, from drugs to Dior perfume, starts in
Helsinki and makes it way by boat to Talinn or any one of the many
Estonian ports. From there it winds through Estonia and Lithuania,
assisted by a people who have no more reason to love the Russians or
the system that governs them than anyone else in the area, and then
through to Poland.   .

Poland is the central clearing-house for the whole operation and
its smugglers, the brokers for all Eastern European countries and
Russia. Its relative freedom and sophisticated acceptance of a black
market are two reasons why Poland is the natural center for the
operation, but this would count for nothing if the most important
fact of all did not exist. Poland, unlike any other country within
Comecon, is awash with dollars and, at the end of the day, whatever
happens to the product eventually, someone is going to have to be
paid off in hard currency.

One of the greatest black marketeers in the history of modern
Poland, a man of whom it is impossible to approve and yet impossible
to dislike, operated through the forties, fifties, and sixties. He was
picked up in 1969 less because of his black marketeering than because
he was a Jew. Richard Kowalski's greatest coup in the sixties was to
sell water to the state, for 26 million zlotys, on a contract which
stipulated wine. In a country which forbade the private ownership
of more than 100 hectares (approximately 250 acres) of land, Kowalski owned several dozen 100-hectare apple orchards throughout the
country, always registered in different names. His business principles
ought to appear in every book ever written on how to make money.
On one occasion he lost several million zlotys on a diamond deal
which went wrong. When a friend sought to sympathize, he merely
shrugged his shoulders and said: "In business, losses don't count"—a
remark which, when you come to think about it, has the wisdom of
a true genius.

But Kowalski's classic response, which deserves to be in a dictionary
of quotations, was made to an investigating officer of the militia on
one of the innumerable occasions when Kowalski's obvious wealth
could no longer be overlooked, and he had to be called in for interrogation. Exasperated, the militia man said, "Mr. Kowalski, do us all a

favor. Stop making money. Don't you understand the kind of political and economic system which exists in this country?" Dolefully, Kowalski considered the remark and replied with great sincerity: "I never learned to read and I never learned to write. What else is there left for me to do but make money?"

Kowalski came from a poor Jewish family in Eastern Poland in territories that are now Russian. He had a wife and three children as well as a mother and a sister, all of whom he was supporting as an odd-job man when war broke out and the Soviets came in. One day he was picked up by Russian soldiers and put on a local working party. That evening the group was transferred to a train and, without having the opportunity of even saying goodbye to his family, he was taken to the mines in the Urals. Four years later he managed to escape. He walked through war-torn Russia, through the German lines, and back to his home village, which had been overrun by the Nazis. There he discovered that his entire family had been slaughtered by the Germans. Distraught, he moved on, eventually arriving in Warsaw, his only possessions the rags he wore and an inner rage. His tragedy, he had decided, was due to his poverty. If he'd had money, he would have been able to buy freedom for his family. He saw his abject poverty and not the Germans or the Russians as the principal enemy. He had one ambition—to make money—even though the business environment was now hardly conducive, and he was totally illiterate.

He converted to Catholicism, on the grounds that if he was going to operate in a Catholic country, he might as well have the god of that country on his side. Thereafter, according to friends, he practiced a peculiar kind of religion all his own, but one to which he was deeply committed, praying at least three times a day to a god of his invention. He had never really understood Catholicism and so made do with a curious mixture of Christianity, Judaism, and paganism, and a doctrine that was specifically his own.

"Had he heard," he was once asked, "about the story in the New Testament when Christ threw the money-lenders out of the temple?" "Certainly," he replied. "Christ understood business very well. Nobody in their right mind would do business in a temple—it's far too public a place!"

It wasn't Kowalski who ran the great Warsaw bus racket in the sixties, but it was the kind of scheme that would have met with his complete approval. One day a woman, who happened to be a member of the Party, was rudely turned away by the conductor of a bus operating in the center of Warsaw. In a fury she wrote to the state bus office, complaining about her treatment and demanding that disciplinary action be taken against the conductor. To her astonishment, she received a reply from the manager saying that the company was unable to pursue her complaint because she had incorrectly copied down the bus's license number. No such bus existed. The reply incensed her. She was a methodical woman; she knew that the number she had given in her letter was correct. Determined not to let the matter rest, she bombarded the company and influential friends with letters, demanding an investigation not only of the company, but also the manager, whose behavior she said could only be explained if he was in collusion with his workers and covering up for their deficiencies.

Six months later, by now obsessed, she saw the same tram on the same route bearing the number which she had been told did not exist. She approached some passers-by and asked them to witness the figure she was writing down. This time there had to be a real investigation, of which resulted in a prison sentence for two brilliant operators. Somehow they had managed to get an old bus, clean it up, and hook it on the central system—running it as a free enterprise bus at great profit for themselves for eighteen months.

All of Lodz, a town renowned internationally before the war for the quality of its textiles, was enormously impressed by the genius of a pensioner, who used his skill as a trout fisherman to net a sizeable fortune before he was caught. His small room in a narrow street faced the windows of a factory manufacturing nylon thread. One day, when the windows of the factory were open, he cast a line with a hook attached onto a giant bobbin into the factory and drew a single thread into his room. He then purchased an huge empty industrial bobbin and simply reeled in, until he became Poland's biggest supplier of black-market nylon thread. He kept it up for years because, of course, a single thread coming out of one window and into another several stories high, is going to be completely invisible to passers-by below.

There are hundreds of such stories every year in a country where all private initiative is severely limited by the system. The only area of Polish life which escapes control by the state is the underworld, where the natural wit and talent of the Poles can find their true expression. In a society where so many have their little fiddle, it is hardly surprising that there is little public indignation against those, unless they be part of the apparatus, who indulge in the big swindles.

How much money is siphoned out of the economy through straight fraud is hard to calculate, especially when the government itself shuts its eyes to so much of it. Yet the evidence that it runs into millions and millions is there for all to see. A tourist waiting in a taxi line is quite likely to be picked up by a car which doesn't appear to be a taxi, and yet whose lavish appointments suggest that it isn't a private car either. In fact, it is quite likely to be a minister's driver using the ministry car and ministry gas to do some profitable moonlighting. The scale of thefts from factories is said to be astronomical. Though there is a chronic shortage of spare parts for almost everything, there is absolutely no difficulty in obtaining parts privately from a supply purloined from the place of manufacture. A friend ordered material to have a wooden house built. It was very expensive, but he could afford it and didn't query the bills. It was only when a Western architect friend became interested in the construction and asked to see the lumber orders, that he realized he had purchased enough timber to build three houses. When he remonstrated, the builder told him that he was always forced to order three times the quantity of material that he required on any project, because at least two thirds would be stolen, either on site or before it arrived. Polish people have become so innured to the scale of the problem that the extent to which it degrades them has almost been forgotten.

A part of the economic system to which they belong, the black market is a way of life, and can no more be avoided by the average citizen, than can an American choose to disregard the Internal Revenue Service. In a country where the constitution is so frequently overlooked, as in Poland, institutional instruments assume a far greater importance than they do elsewhere and the Polish black market is firmly established as one of the most important economic institutions in the country. And it works at every level.

The Poles use an eloquent word to describe the people outside the official system they rely upon to survive. That word is "shoulder." A builder may be the "shoulder" of a great many people who need material or labor for urgent jobs. They will call him and explain that perhaps the roof is leaking, and that it will take months going through normal channels to get it repaired. He will send a man or do it himself, charging, of course, three or four times the official rate. But he also takes something which, in some cases, can be more valuable than money. The man he has helped may in due time be *his* "shoulder" when he requires assistance.

Assume that a man who has had trouble with his roof is a doctor. He is a most useful "shoulder" for everyone. Poland, of course, has an absolutely free national health service, and every citizen is entitled to the best medical treatment available at no cost at all to himself. Yet the country is desperately short of hospital beds, of specialized treatment centers, and these days in particular, even the most basic surgical aids. At one point in the summer of 1980 the country ran out of surgical needles and sutures, adhesive tape was in desperately short supply as was X-ray film. There were no rabbits to be used for blood tests in the hematological test centers for the simple reason that, while they had a budget to buy a rabbit for 300 zlotys, the black-market value of rabbits in a country short of meat had shot up to 850 zlotys. To get them the state itself had to buy on the black market. In a country where there are 75,000 doctors, 25,000 work in administration with no clinical function whatsoever, principally because this is the easier option, but also because only a doctor who has worked in the bureaucracy has a chance of getting a coveted position with the World Health Organization and all that means in terms of foreign exchange earnings and the riches which that implies.

For Poland, all of this adds up to a crisis of awesome proportions within the health service. It also means that health is yet another item freely bartered on the black market. "There are hospitals," says one Polish report, "that are so poorly supplied they do not even have cotton, and our relatives die in the corridors; but other hospitals are equipped with private rooms and full medical care for each room."

So no one who can possibly afford it will rely solely upon the state system to see him through should he be ill. The waiting lists for all surgery are huge, and in some areas complex treatment cannot even be attempted. So Poles have their medical "shoulders" to look after them. Surgeons are not allowed to have private consulting rooms, and neither are there any private hospitals in which they can operate. So once they've been paid enough, many will use state facilities to treat private patients, enriching themselves and assuring that the waiting list gets longer still. Fairly recently a senior Warsaw team of doctors saw the minister of health and urged him to permit private clinics which would benefit, they said, not only those who could afford to go to them, but those who could not. The former could do openly what they were now doing secretly; the latter would have shorter waiting lists as the rich moved out of the public and into the private sector. The minister understood the point, but ideology could not permit him to act. But a doctor also needs a "shoulder."

In theory there is no difference between one Polish school and another. They all teach a standard syllabus and have teachers of similar background and qualifications. But outside the world of mathematics, notions of strict equivalence do not exist, and all experience tells us they cannot.

So in Poland, as elsewhere, one school, perhaps because of tradition, or the quality of its principal, or merely because of its geographical location, is academically superior to a school, similar in every way save for those standards which matter most, in the next district. So Polish parents strive to get their children in the better school, and will use all their influence and pull every string they can. The children of a doctor or anyone else with a "shoulder" in the educational world have a distinct advantage over their fellows.

But even that might not be enough. Pressure to get into a university is enormous, and private tutors are not only in high demand but are very expensive. The demand is so great that they will only accept pupils from parents who can be useful as a "shoulder" in some other direction. "It is impossible to take any service for granted in Poland," say a friend. "When I go to my hairdresser, I will always bring a present—a bunch of flowers is the minimum, but in times of general shortage, I am probably expected to bring something which is not easily available on the open market. These gifts are not in place of a tip, which I pay too. They are given to assure that it will be possible for me to get an appointment in the future. If I once forget, the chances of getting back on the list are very slim indeed."

The further up the professional ladder one goes, the more lavish the presents are expected to be. A dentist, whom one will almost certainly have to pay if one wants emergency treatment, will also get a few pounds of coffee before treatment starts. It operates at every level.

As a foreigner unused to the system, I was embarrassed when I was advised to bring presents to some of the extremely distinguished people I was seeing. But my arrival, accompanied by a bottle of whisky or a can of ham or boxes of English tea, was simply taken for granted. They would not have refused to see me if I had turned up empty-handed, and personally I doubt if they'd been any less helpful, but nevertheless arriving without a present would have been a breach of etiquette. "You scratch my back and I'll scratch yours" has become an ugly slogan of Polish life, and there are few people who hold out against it.

Though it is useful, sometimes crucially so, to have "shoulders" in the professions, the most important "shoulder" of all is someone in the country's political or administrative hierarchy. Nothing is impossible for a Pole with influential friends. When most people have to wait three months to get a passport to travel abroad and always

stand the risk of being refused, those with "shoulders" in the bureaucracy get one within a few days. When building permits are hard to
come by, they manage without difficulty. When the car waiting list
is particularly long, they manage to get what they order within a few
weeks. They manage to cross frontiers without being properly checked;
drunk-driving charges are mysteriously waived, and rules concerning
the size of property they are permitted to hold are somehow ignored.
Sometimes this is achieved by bribery, but by no means always. A
comparatively unknown official in government or Party office dispenses
favors with a regal gesture to his friends, because by doing so he is
able to demonstrate the power and position he holds. Very often he
has less of an education and is lower in the social pecking order than
the people he is able to help.

A friend who needed to get his mother into a special Warsaw
clinic but had failed to do so through normal channels was eventually
introduced to a middle-level official in the Ministry of Health. If it
had not been for his mother, he now says, he would have walked out
within minutes of arriving. Though the official knew every particular
of what he was requesting, he was forced to go over the story down
to the smallest detail, and permit himself to be abominably patronized
while he, as he puts it, bowed and scraped, flattered and cajoled, until
the official, having had his pleasure, promised to see what he could
do. He pulled off the trick, but my friend finds it hard to feel much
gratitude towards him.

But if food and services are huge elements on the black market, the
biggest single commodity of all is money.

In June 1981 I gave a dinner for twelve people in one of the better
restaurants of Warsaw. The meal started with some excellent wild
mushrooms in a cream sauce, followed by herring in oil. We had
venison for a main course and finished with fresh strawberries picked
that morning. We drank vodka and a rough, rather heavy, Bulgarian
wine. The bill came to just over 5,000 zlotys. There are four ways
of deciding the real cost of that meal. The average monthly wage in
Poland is almost exactly 5,000 zlotys. The average monthly wage in
America is $900. On that reckoning the meal was very expensive in-
deed. However, when I arrived in Poland I was given thirty-two
zlotys to the dollar by the bank at the border. At that rate of exchange,
the meal cost me just over $156, which by most Western standards
would be regarded as reasonable.

However, if I had given my money to a Pole and asked him to
exchange it, as if it were his own, quite legally, at a local bank, he

would have been given 100 zlotys to the dollar. This meal of four courses, wine and vodka for twelve would only have cost me $50— quite ludicrously cheap. But I could have done better still. If I had exchanged my dollars on the black market, I would have gotten 200 zlotys to the dollar, at which rate of exchange the dinner would have cost me only $25.

As a matter of interest, a month after I'd left, the rate on the black market had gone up to 350 zlotys to the dollar, which would have put a value on my meal to just over $14 and when martial law was declared it was 1000 zlotys, valuing this sumptuous banquet at $5. Just why the dollar was increasing so remarkably in value was clear. In 1968 when the Russians entered Czechoslovakia, they took over all the private dollar accounts held in banks in the country and paid out in Czech currency. The dollar disappeared. So, as fear of Soviet intervention was at its height in the summer and autumn of 1981, everyone who had the opportunity to do so sought to get out of zlotys and into dollars—not to put into a bank account where they could have benefited the hard-pressed Polish economy, but in private caches hidden all over the country. "Drill for oil in these parts," said a farmer in one of Poland's wealthier regions, "and up would come green dollar-bills." (At the beginning of 1982, the zloty was devalued and its official value stood at 100 zlotys to the dollar.)

It is impossible for a foreigner, easily recognizable to any Pole, to walk through a city, town, or village in the country without someone sidling up every few yards and asking, "Change dollar?"

The street rate varies from day to day, and person to person, but there are generally only a few zlotys difference between each approach, just as if there were some central board marking the official black-market rate for the day. How in fact the word gets around setting that day's rate is one of the higher mysteries which, I suspect, will never be wholly understood. No doubt part of the explanation is the astonishing and hitherto unpublished fact that Warsaw's central banks are as deeply into black-market currency speculation as anyone else. Indeed, many of the men who approach tourists on the streets are bank officials. That is an amazing yet incontrovertible statement.

Years ago Poland decided that traditional East European and Third World restrictions imposed upon the import and export of foreign currency were counterproductive. A traveler entering Russia is required to fill in a form which details the amount of foreign currency he is bringing into the country. He is then required to exchange his money at the official rate of exchange in banks or hotels, and he gets a document detailing the transaction. When he leaves the country, it is a simple process to check these documents in order to find out how much he exchanged into rubles, how much he spent, and how much foreign currency he has left. If the figures don't tally, he can be presumed to have exchanged money on the currency black market. The system has the advantage of keeping the black market to manageable proportions, but it forces tourists to pay for their goods and services at a totally unrealistic and artificial official exchange rate. It also has the distadvantage of making Russia so expensive to visit that it discourages a great many people who might otherwise be tempted to make the trip.

Poland used to be just as strict until the country became desperately short of hard currency. Then the government decided to permit Polish citizens to hold bank accounts in foreign currency to encourage relatives abroad to send them money and also to make it easier for visitors to leave behind as much as they could afford. The Polish banks devised a brilliant system which combined hard-headed business strategy with a clear insight into behavioral psychology. So, today, visitors to Poland are still required to fill in a form stating the amount of the foreign currency they are bringing into the country. But the back of the form clearly states that they may, if they wish, leave behind as much money as they like to a Polish citizen. This, of course, is a direct invitation to speculate on the currency black market. When they return with a few hundred dollars short, they have a ready explanation: They left the money with a Polish friend.

However there are several catches. Firstly, each visitor is obliged to change $15 a day at the ridiculous official exchange rate. When he comes to pay his hotel, he will find that they will only accept foreign currency, which is also exchanged at the official rate. If he brings in a car, he must buy gasoline coupons at the same rate. All of that takes care of his main expenditures. Chances are that the visitor will eventually be attracted by the amazing exchange rate being offered all over the city. He changes some of his money and suddenly is rich in zloty bills. The problem now is, what can he do with them?

He will quickly discover that Polish crystal, furs, antiques, works of art, and so on may not be taken out of the country without an export license. All that is left for him to buy are quite attractive mass-produced pieces of "folk art," distinctly superior to most souvenirs one buys on foreign travel, but souvenirs of undistinguished quality nevertheless. I have seen people looking at woven rugs, priced in zlotys, which appear very expensive when converted to the official rate. Only when they are bought with black market zlotys are they cheap. You can see the foreigner's amazement as he works with his pocket calculator, doing both sums. The scale of the "bargain" appears astonishing, and it is the bargain that he buys and not the rug, which he will find little use for at home. What he and most visitors forget is that the price put on the rug in the first place has nothing to do with market value or profit or loss. It is merely a device to part a tourist from his money.

Any town that has tourist traffic has artfully arranged traps for them. Cepelia shops are the nearest thing in Poland in looks and design to Western stores. They are large and airy, beautifully arranged, and their products temptingly displayed. The Cepelia is officially a cooperative of Polish craftsmen and women making their products available to the general public through their own shops. In fact, as the goods in one Cepelia shop are exactly the same as in another, obviously they are mass produced; what craftsmanship there is went into the original design.

No Pole would ever dream of buying in a Cepelia store, even though quality is very high. What puts them off are the prices. An attractive single-bedspread costs 3,000 zlotys, or about $90 at the official rate of exchange. Some tourists, of course, will buy with credit cards or with zlotys exchanged at the official rate. Most, however, will see the Cepelia stores as a remarkable bargain basement in which they can buy things they may not need, but which are extraordinarily cheap once they are using black market currency. Working away with their pocket calculators, they greedily observe that the bedspread, instead of costing $90, costs them only $12. It becomes irresistible, and they rush in and buy. And that is where the psychology has been so brilliantly applied. For the zloty prices make due allowance for the fact that most customers in the shop will be using currency exchanged on the black market. The bedspread is not a bargain at all. Its real value, giving the store a reasonable profit, is $12! Cepelia stores are not there for people who want bedspreads, or candlesticks, or tablecloths, or any of the other things they sell, but for people who like to feel they have made a fantastic bargain.

The point is best illustrated by a woman friend who purchased a silver necklace with an agate drop, beautifully designed, in a Cepelia store. The price tag was 10,000 zlotys, which at the official rate of thirty-two to the dollar, was worth just over $300. She liked it, exchanged money on the black market, bought it for the equivalent of $50, and returned home to England satisfied that she'd made the bargain of her life. But when she showed it to her insurance assessor she had a shock. He valued it at no more than £20, just about the price she'd paid for it, and when she sought to challenge that valuation by trying to sell the necklace, she found that no one would give her even that.

I have still not been able to convince her that the original price was based upon the expectation that the zlotys she paid were black-market zlotys. Even then, of course, she was slightly overcharged, but Poland is not the only country to rook innocent tourists as they pass through. Interestingly enough, anything at all of real intrinsic value, like Polish crystal or furs which the Polish state marketing corporation is able to dispose of in the international marketplace, cannot be taken out of Poland by a tourist without an export license, easily obtainable once proof has been given that the goods were purchased with hard currency and not with zlotys. That means that anything of genuine value is simply not available for zlotys. Nobody is going to risk soft black-market zlotys being used to purchase goods for which hard currency dollars can be readily obtained.

Having got at least some of the black market zlotys back through Cepelia stores, the authorities also want to be sure of getting at least a slice of the action from the original transaction, when the foreign currency was first converted. So its agents are out on the streets with the genuine black marketeers, competing with them for the all-precious dollar. "The first lesson the authorities learned, long ago," says an economist who has worked with the official bureaucracy, "is that it could not kill the black market. It then took the extremely sophisticated point of view that, even if it could, it was perhaps not desirable to do so. Remember that the prime objective of Polish economic policy over the past ten years has been to earn as much hard currency as possible in order to pay for our ambitious plan for high capital investment based upon Western technology.

"Now the central objective is to repay the huge loan we chalked up during that period. Every dollar counts. Consequently nothing must stand in the way of keeping them in the country. As a first consequence of that policy, no one ever tries to prosecute tourists exchanging dollars on the black market. To do so would discourage others, and dollars which might otherwise have been converted would remain firmly in the visitor's pocket. The other consequence is that if dollars are being exchanged in this way, then the government might as well get its cut."

Having exchanged his money with a government agent, using it to buy bargains which turn out to be not bargains at all, the tourist finds that all he can do is to eat. Because he had to exchange $15 per day at the official rate of exchange, he won't end up deriving much benefit from his illegal currency speculation. There is one last catch. When he leaves Poland, he is likely to have a lot of zlotys left. He will not be allowed to take them out of the country or exchange them for dollars. Instead he will be directed to the airport gift shop where the same goods available in Cepelias beckon. The visitor to Poland who believes he's playing the black market might as well forget it. The black market is playing him!

Just one word of warning. Legally it is an offense under Polish law to speculate in the currency. I, for one, have always refused to do so, even though I recognize that what the law states and what is accepted custom and practice, encouraged by the authorities, are two different things entirely. Nevertheless, while the law is what it is, it seems to me to be folly to lay oneself open to the danger, however minimal, of being set-up and compromised.

In a country where the black market is officially acknowledged and unofficially sanctioned, a two-tier currency system is an inevitable consequence. It means that many vital goods and services are only quoted in dollars, and those who do not have access to the latter have no chance of acquiring the former. To a certain extent this is true of the entire bloc, so that a sturdy Rumanian Fiat is available on the Polish market but only for dollars, a situation which says something, though not a great deal, for the Communist bloc's own trading market Comecon.

Those who have dollars to spend have no trouble getting spare parts for their cars or having them serviced. Goods such as Polish washing machines, for which there are an enormous waiting list can be obtained immediately, provided the customer quotes a dollar rather than a zloty price. Every store in the country will keep scarce goods under the counter—from cigarettes to newspapers, from soap powder to books, and from razor blades to clothes, for their customers who are prepared to pay with dollars.

In Warsaw, taxis are hard to come by and so taxi drivers in a buyers' market are not renowned for their helpfulness. But ask a taxi driver how many dollars he wants for a morning's shopping, and he is yours for life. The result is that those who have access to dollars form a monied elite, and are not only insulated against the general hardship which ordinary Poles suffer, but are living a life a good many in the West would envy.

A couple I know long since decided that waiting in line in the stores was not for them, and so every night they eat out at the very best restaurants in town, often taking friends with them. Because they have dollars, the cost is hardly more than eating at home and certainly more enjoyable. They have a large apartment in Warsaw, beautifully equipped with Scandinavian furniture and West German kitchen equipment, and a truly beautiful country home paneled in pine, with fine views from the picture windows set into their vast two-story, cathedral-ceilinged living room. They holiday four times a year, once in the West, and drive a Swedish Volvo that they have no difficulty in having serviced. He is, by any international standards, a very small-scale businessman, yet his lifestyle is enviably remarkable.

The effect of all this upon the morale of the nation is, of course, catastrophic. Though there are wide disparities of income in the West, that can and do lead to social tension, people living in the same area tend to have similar incomes. In the United States, a used-car dealer in a middle-class area is likely to have a larger house, more expensive furnishings, and perhaps an extra holiday a year compared to the salesman living a block away. But in Poland, the spectacle of one man suffering all the horrendous consequences of a siege economy, in a nation which has gone bankrupt, living literally next door to a man who seems to have everything that money can buy is quite common. And what makes it so galling for the Poles and so ironic for the rest of us, is that Poland is a country ruled by an ideology—constantly proclaimed by the mass media—of equality of income and opportunity.

The first is nonsense, the second is questionable. But this dual currency—the zloty and the dollar—has an even more profound impact upon ordinary Poles than merely a psychological one. Nobody could begin to estimate the number of dollars in the Polish economy, but there are certainly enough to distort the whole pricing structure of the state. Thus, when vodka, so essential to Poles of every class, was in short supply in stores, an immediate black market was established for it. A bottle of vodka overnight went up from twenty-one zlotys to 500 zlotys, a price that Poles were prepared to pay, so innured were they to the vagaries of the black market. The amount of vodka available to black marketeers was so great, however, that under the law of supply and demand the price soon fell, settling to about 200 zlotys per liter, about ten times its official retail price. The question, of course, is: How did the black marketeers get such huge quantities, when it was unavailable elsewhere? And the answer is they bought it, with dollars, straight from the state itself.

What the treasury lost in tax revenue it gained by being able to sell large quantities of locally produced vodka for hard currency. If the effect of this were not to place a further burden upon an already hardpressed people and enrich still further the black marketeers (the least deserving members of Polish society), one could applaud the Polish Ministry of Economic Affairs for one of the most creatively imaginative economic concepts in the world. They have established a system where the state exports local produce to its own people.

"Exporting is fun" a British prime minister once told a doubting British business audience that knew the harsh reality of making the rounds of foreign parts, selling goods against international competition. Well, the Poles have made exporting fun. They have devised a system of selling abroad without actually having to go abroad. And if it happens with vodka, if the Poles have set up a local hard-currency market for that, one can be sure they have done so for other products too. In some cases, like cars, they do so without making even a pretense about it. Anyone who has dollars can jump the waiting list and get a vehicle almost immediately. But in most cases, ordinary everyday household objects, obtainable for the most part only on the black market, are there because this is a unique and foolproof method of earning foreign currency. Of course, many suffer because of this policy. Those who are on low pay, with no other source of income, are squeezed helplessly. Their tragedy is that they are paid in zlotys in a country where the only currency worth holding is the dollar. But their greater tragedy is that they live in a country whose internal trading structure is dominated by the black market. And the biggest and most successful black marketeer of all is the state itself.

4
The Art of the Queue

⚜

A man had been waiting in line for five hours. "I've had enough!" he suddenly exploded. "I'm going to kill the Prime Minister." Half an hour later he returned more disconsolate than ever. "What happened?" asked a friend. "No luck," he said. "There they had a six-hour line."

THE LONGEST SHOPPING LINE anyone can remember in Poland is one which lasted for three and a half weeks outside a furniture store in Warsaw. The year was 1978, a period when, officially at least, Poland was enjoying unparalleled prosperity. Those were the good old days —the years of the Polish consumer boom—yet even then, as the great furniture queue shows, the Polish economy was incapable of satisfying the needs of its citizens. It is important to realize that the shortages which cause so much distress to Poles today did not occur, as some Western observers, ignorant of Polish history, claim, because Solidarity wrecked the economy. On the contrary: Solidarity made the sensational headway it did because, among other reasons, Polish people wanted an end to thirty-five years of heart-breaking economic failure. Though most Poles use the black market some of the time, few can afford to do so all the time, and some, Poland's most deprived, none of the time. So everyone at one time or another is forced to rely on the open market for shopping.

The British queue, the Americans wait in line, and the Poles make a way of life of it. And that is not idle phrase-making. Poles have had to stand in lines since the war and by now have established an etiquette and a line discipline which are highly advanced social forms.

To wait for a suite of furniture for three and a half weeks requires organization and tactical skill. No one who doesn't know the art of queuing would stand a chance. Most long lines—and a line is regarded as long if it looks as if it will last for more than a day—will produce a line-general. He or she will establish a shift system so that in effect it is possible to eat, sleep, and even get some work done, even if one is waiting in a three-and-a-half-week line.

As the line forms, the line-general will issue numbers and a schedule

[71]

will be worked out so there is always someone in the line, all hours of the day and night, keeping the places of the remainder. It is up to the people in line to decide how many they need to keep on watch to ensure that a sudden rush of latecomers won't insist that they take preference.

Poles talk about the lines in which they have stood in the manner of a soldier speaking of battles he fought. Indeed, one Polish student in London told me that she actually missed the Polish lines. "They're a wonderful way to meet people," she said. "I've made many friends in lines, the only institution I know of that can regularly bring together, completely at random, a whole cross-section of the population."

Though Poles grumble incessantly about lines—and in 1981 and 1982 when lines for food could be as much as eight hours long, they had much to grumble about—a good deal of evidence suggests that if they were to disappear overnight, they would be missed. A friend of mine—an old lady now—goes out every morning to do the shopping, leaving home at 7:00 A.M. and returning for lunch at 1:00 P.M. Even during comparatively normal times she would have visited about four food-stores, and waited in line an average of an hour and a half at each. When she comes home, she complains about her aching feet, puts on a pair of slippers, settles back contentedly into her armchair, and then recounts an astonishing series of anecdotes, gossip, and half-digested news, all of which she picked up from the people in the various lines in which she stood. Her queues are her contact with the world. She meets people of every generation and has time to get to know them and the circumstances of their lives before she reaches the counter, makes her purchase, and then starts all over again elsewhere.

Even as a foreigner, I found the one line I had to stand in—for gas for my car—begin as an enormous irritant and finish, if not as pleasure, then as a chore with considerable compensations.

As soon as people saw my GB insignia and my English license plates, they would come up to inspect the car and its engine. In nearly every line there was someone who spoke English, and we would while away the time chatting. I learned a lot in gas lines about how people live and what they think. They were the one place where I was removed from the Warsaw intelligentsia and Party officials with whom, inevitably, I tended to spend most of the time.

It may be difficult to understand the positive aspect to standing in line for anyone who has done so in the States or Western Europe during a gasoline shortage, when tempers are frayed and sometimes snap altogether. But we are irritated because we are not used to queuing, we have not made allowances for it, in deciding how we are going to schedule our day and, perhaps most important of all, we don't know how to behave in a line.

An example of the kind of good manners which develop after one has queued for years was very strongly brought home to me one day in a gas line. Observing that the drivers of the other vehicles preferred not to restart their engines as the vehicle in front moved forward, but got out and pushed, I said rather patronizingly, as I gunned my engine to life every five minutes, that the gas crisis was more severe than I thought. "It's not that," said my Polish friend, delicately, "but a lot of people think that if you have to wait in line for gas for two hours, the constant exhaust fumes of cars starting and stopping become rather unpleasant." After that, I always got out and pushed!

A psychiatrist I met on a trip to Poland in the late seventies advanced the theory that reasonably long lines—and he thought a minimum of two hours and a maximum of two and a half hours was reasonable—were the ideal answer to modern urban blues. "People live in big cities," he said, "in little boxes, totally cut off from everyone else. If they walk out of their front door and down the street, it is unlikely that they will meet anyone they know.

"Even if they do, the pace of life is so hurried that all they have time for is a good-morning nod or, at most, a brief pause to ask about the family. They are hermetically sealed into their family, office, or factory relationships. Yet man is a social animal and enjoys nothing better than idly chatting to friends or acquaintances. The rest of the world doesn't have time for that anymore. But in Poland we do. Our queues are our life-line to each other."

Of course, his tongue was partly in his cheek, yet the effect of what he was saying upon his largely Polish audience was remarkable. They reacted initially with fury at anyone even daring to suggest anything favorable about the lines that were such a burden, the existence of which they laid firmly at the door of an incompetent government. Then, without realizing what they were doing, they verified the essential truth of the argument as they told of their experiences. There is not a Pole alive who doesn't have a series of line anecdotes —ranging from the hilarious to the tragic. Lines have become so much part of Poland that when they disappear, as inevitably one day they will, I should not wonder that a remarkably large section of the population will look back at them with something akin to affection.

However, it would be disgracefully insensitive to push too far. These days queues have become so long that they are now a genuine, and sometimes heartbreaking, burden upon an already overtaxed people. There have been some deaths reported all over Poland of old men and old women simply expiring on the spot after waiting for several hours for their minimal rations. Walk the streets of Warsaw at 6:00 A.M., and already sizeable lines have begun to form outside food stores which don't open until 9:00 A.M. In areas outside Warsaw, there have been reports of women standing in line for three days for meat, and then discovering that the meat had gone bad when they got it.

Up till now, discipline mostly still holds, and it is a remarkable tribute to the Poles that it has. In most other countries of the world, there would have been riots; in Poland they accept it all with stoic resignation.

The reasons for the lines are both simple and complex. The simple reason is that there are few goods on the market, while Polish salaries in the past ten years have increased by leaps and bounds; too much money is chasing too few goods. A more complex explanation is that Marxist philosophy has a great deal to say about production, less to say about selling, and nothing at all to say about distribution. The classic "middle man" has always stood high in the litany of Communist demonology. He is the man who takes money from both the producer and the consumer, producing nothing, an unnecessary burden upon everyone. Every farmer in Poland has stories to tell of whole harvests going to waste, milk turning sour and meat spoiling after they had been paid for by the state purchasing company, but before transportation was provided to move the products to the stores. But that is not the whole explanation.

A neurosis built up by years of shortages affects every Pole so strongly that shopping is no longer an entirely rational transaction. Open any cupboard in any Polish home and out will tumble a most unbelievable array of goods. One home I visited had an entire cupboard full of Nescafé, even though everyone in the household hated the stuff. It had been purchased "just in case" during a brief period when Nescafé had suddenly appeared in large quantities on the market. "Just in case" is a phrase every shopper will use two or three times on every expedition. If soap powder appears on store shelves, shoppers will take as much as they can carry and the shop will allow. Inevitably, the next day there is no soap powder.

A government economist told me that a factory making candles for both household and decorative use had decided to do a Western-style market research study of the number of candles that Poles would expect to use in a year. They got a figure and, understanding the hoarding impulse, doubled it, ordered the material from the state purchasing house and went into production. Within a week they had exhausted their supplies for the year. The only conclusion —there were no candles in the shops anymore, but a large number of homes had a huge supply of candles which they were unlikely ever to need.

Poles will line up at a shop when they see a truck unloading at the back. It may sound apocryphal, but I swear to the truth of the following story. I was walking through Warsaw with the director of the city's most prestigious art gallery, and we stopped at a line outside a store. "What are you in line for?" he asked a woman. "I don't know," she said, "but some deliveries have just arrived." Whatever it turned out to be—and we didn't stay to find out—she was able to say to herself "just in case."

Inevitably this hoarding impulse means that Poles always need to carry quite a lot of money around with them, since checkbooks and credit cards for other than foreigners are unheard of. They always need to carry a bag of some sort. One seldom meets a Polish woman without a shopping bag or a Polish man without a cheap black attaché case designed to look businesslike, but which, in fact, is used to carry home anything seen in the stores that day. The really efficient will have two or three string or shopping bags folded up inside the main bag "just in case."

Not all of this surplus shopping is hoarded. I was walking with a friend past a tobacco shop that had a surprisingly short line for a place which actually had cigarettes in stock. He asked if I minded waiting, and we stood for three quarters of an hour so that he could buy half a dozen packs. What was slightly surprising about the whole exercise was that my friend didn't smoke. When he got home all became clear. Immediately he was on the phone to smokers. He had some cigarettes, he said, and was in the market for any reasonable exchange. He managed to get two ducks, which were our dinner that night.

Bartering has become part and parcel of everyday life. As soon as they get home from their shopping, people telephone friends all over town reporting upon their purchases that day. Soap, toothpaste, and detergent were the hottest items on this unofficial market while I was in Warsaw, because they were in the shortest supply and, I am told, still are. But, of course, speculators in any commodity, can be caught by unexpected shifts in supplies.

"One never gets any warning, that's the peculiar thing about the Polish economy," said one woman. "For weeks there won't be, let's say, any adhesive tape in the whole of Warsaw. Suddenly, overnight, every shelf in every store is crammed with it."

"I'm into toothpaste futures," said another friend sardonically. "I take the view that in the whole history of the world there has never been a recorded case of a nation rioting over a lack of toothpaste. Accordingly, toothpaste must have a low priority in the office of the planning ministry. So I tell everyone who comes to see me from the West 'bring me nothing else but toothpaste.' With toothpaste I live like a king. It has proved to be a much more solid and reliable currency than the Polish zloty!"

But it's not merely the distribution system which is at fault. The obligations imposed upon Poland as a member of Comintern are also onerous.

While I was last in Warsaw, I noticed that in every department store in the city the only counters not blocked by struggling humanity desperately trying to get at the goods were those selling peculiarly repellent knickknacks—a white dried fish on a black base from the Republic of Vietnam. Though these may have been immensely desirable in Vietnam, they were not going very well in Warsaw and yet, from the number I saw, it had to be assumed that some Polish purchasing mission had ordered a vast quantity. Though Poland was short of many things, I have no doubt the members of that mission knew perfectly well this was one commodity the country could well do without. Nevertheless, there they were on display in Warsaw. Where once there had been a shortage, now there was a glut, and no one, but no one, was buying. The question is: Which of Poland's scarce resources—cash, food, or minerals—did it have to part with in order to honor its obligations to the bloc and purchase these. I pointed the knickknacks out to a Pole. "I'll have one," he said, "if you can eat it or wash with it." And then, he added bitterly, "If I found the minister responsible for buying them, I'd lock him away and feed him with his Vietnamese dried fish until they were all gone. At least during that period Poland would have one less mouth to feed."

Constant shortages have an effect on the way people think and behave. "It's extraordinary how obsessive you can become about the most trivial things, if they are no longer available," said one university student. "Suddenly there were no matches in the stores, and I found myself traveling all over the city on rumors of sightings. The fact is, you don't realize how important matches are, until you face the risk of not having any."

The absence of apparently trivial items from store shelves causes the most anguish. While I was in Warsaw, there were no cotton balls, no matches, no soap, no soap powder, no razor blades, no lighter fluid, no powder or liquid detergent, no floor wax (most Polish homes have wooden floors), no coffee or tea, no ordinary household flashlight or radio batteries, no writing paper, and, worst of all, no toilet paper. These are all, of course, things which it is possible to live without, but try doing so, as one Pole put it, and you will discover that modern society has many "unnecessary" conveniences without which life is simply not bearable.

Even the Polish language has subtly adapted itself to the situation. Someone walking past a line will not ask "What are they selling?" but "What are they giving?" They hardly realize they are doing it, so ingrained has this usuage become. In other words, a normal commercial transaction, the handing over of money in return for an object, has absolutely no meaning anymore. Everywhere else in the world, the most important aspect of shopping is price: in Poland, price is one of the least important considerations. Neither does it really matter what the product is, provided it can be bartered immediately or kept for exchange at some unspecified later date. My friend, who has four brand-new hair-dryers, is not really buying hair-dryers, but getting out of currency. Hair-dryers, she reasons, will go up in value, the zloty down. Most middle-class Poles always keep several thousand zlotys readily at hand to purchase some unspecified article which may suddenly appear in the stores. Whatever they see, whether the item costs fifty or a hundred zlotys doesn't matter nearly as much as whether there's a quarter-of-an-hour line or a one-hour line waiting for it. So the verb "to sell" becomes the verb "to give."

Some of the older generation take a grim amusement from the current predicament. "I lived through the war," said one. "I saw my father shot by the Gestapo before my eyes; I saw my mother foraging for food in dustbins; I lived in a country where nothing, including life itself, was ever taken for granted.

"Don't expect me now to regard the absence of soap powder as a national disaster." This point of view, which has occasionally been given official backing by articles in the press reminding Poles what real deprivation means, misses the point. Poland is not at war despite Jaruzelski's "state of war," and has not been at war for nearly forty years, and yet its economy is still on a war footing.

The shortages have produced a unique skill—professional shopping. In every big city there are a small number of middle-aged to elderly women who appear to have nothing else in their lives to do but exercise a quite extraordinary knack of finding on the market goods that everyone believed had disappeared long ago. They travel far and wide within the city limits (once outside, they are in new territory and as lost as everyone else), sniffing out new deliveries or buying up the last of the old, always, one step ahead of the game. Like any skill, shopping depends upon a high level of expertise. These women know every store in the city. They work out for themselves or eventually are told vital information. For example, a store may have a special relationship with the state importing company, another storekeeper may have relatives who own a large farm which sometimes uses the shop as an outlet for spare produce. One store may simply be fortunately placed at the start of a delivery run and can always be sure of full shelves for the first three hours of opening. In another, the reverse may be the case—getting its goods only at 4:00 P.M., two hours before closing. The permutations and the possibilities are endless, but the professional shopper will have them all at her fingertips. Some do it simply for the pleasure of it—they have acquired a skill and they enjoy using it. Others offer to shop for families in their block and will be rewarded by presents, perhaps some meat or chocolates. A really good professional shopper should be able to get along, by never having to pay for anything herself, relying at all times entirely upon presents from her grateful customers.

Professional shoppers have had plenty of time to practice. The current shortages and rationing of all basic foodstuffs and household supplies, as stringent as any in wartime Britain, are new phenomena. Certainly there have been periods in recent times when the shops were full, but the good years have always been followed by the years of reckoning, when consumerism designed to placate a hostile public has, once again, given way to the urgent need for Poland to pay its way in the world. As a nation it has singularly failed to do both contemporaneously.

It is in consumer durables that the Polish economy has most singularly failed to meet the aspirations of the people. Walk into a department store in Warsaw and you will see Polish-made automatic washing-machines and, to my surprise, dishwashers. Try to buy one, however, and you will find that you are on a three-year waiting list.

And the price will, in any case, put it out of reach of most ordinary people. Simple washing-machines cost 20,000 zlotys—the equivalent of four months' average pay—well out of reach for the ordinary family. A tiny Polish-made Fiat, the Poles call it "the little one," costs 500,000 zlotys—the equivalent of eight years' pay. But that is only part of the problem in buying a car. There is no such thing in Poland as car showrooms. If a Pole wants to buy a car, he puts his name on a list and then expects to wait up to three years for delivery. To make the process even more unattractive, a prospective buyer had to put down the full purchase price on ordering the vehicle, handing the government, in effect, 500,000 zlotys or, for a larger car, over 1½ million zlotys, interest free, for up to three years.

In the late seventies, even the government realized the injustice of the system and sought to ameliorate it by introducing throughout the Communist bloc an imaginative and quite unique system that helped assuage the sense of injustice suffered by potential car purchasers. If they couldn't get a car straightaway for their money, they were given a lottery ticket. And if their number came up, they got a new car immediately, free.

The chances of winning, like in any lottery, are small, but at least people who have their money tied up so unproductively for so long feel a sense of excitement every month as the draw—which must be the most expensive in the world to enter—is made.

And there have been other, and perhaps more significant, changes recently. People can now pay in monthly installments from the moment they order a car, but the system differs still radically from Western credit sales. The whole purchase price must be paid before the car can be delivered. There are Communist theoreticians who make this an ideological point. Western workers, they say, are enslaved by their debts to banks and finance institutions. Freedom is only illusory if a man is forced to work not only to maintain his wife and children but also his interest payments. This is not entirely hypocritical, for there are many Poles, particularly among the intelligentsia, who find Western society's obsession with material goods purchased on credit to be obscene. Yet the fact remains that Poland has not gone down the same road, principally (though to be fair, not entirely) because its industries have been unable to keep up with the demand—never mind the explosion which would follow the introduction of any kind of credit sales. Color television sets, for example, though available at a cost of 45,000 zlotys or nine months' average salary (twenty-one-inch models only) are beyond the means of almost everyone, and yet it is still impossible to buy any off the shelf. "Even when you get one, there's no guarantee it's going to work," said one Pole. "To get it repaired is another story altogether."

Though some Polish design is unbelievably old-fashioned, this is certainly not true of all products. I bought an electric floor-polisher as attractive-looking as any I've seen elsewhere. Its motor appeared to be sturdier and more powerful than I would expect from a similar machine in the West, and a noteworthy design feature was the way it could be easily folded up and put away in a small closet, and not take up as much space as machines of this kind normally do. This excellent product was totally spoiled by the weak and unreliable small plastic clips that were supposed to keep the polishing pads in place. This otherwise well-conceived and well-made machine could not perform its function because of slovenly attention to the one detail which mattered most—keeping three fast-spinning pads securely in place when the polisher moved over a parquet floor. Hearing the pads as they scrape across the floor is not the best advertisement for Polish workmanship. Such problems are compounded in Poland by the almost total absence of any back-up service for appliances and the near impossibility of finding a repairman capable of doing the simplest household jobs.

"What I envied most in the West," said one Polish woman, recently returned from London, where she'd stayed with relatives, "was not the supermarkets, but the sight of a man coming in to fix a washing machine that had gone wrong. My machine has been sitting for over a year, and I can't get anyone in even to look at it."

"The trouble with a centrally planned economy," said one economist, "is that it always breaks down at the most basic level. Contrary to what one is taught to expect, planners will inevitably overlook something absolutely fundamental. When they realize what they've done, it is too late to change course without disrupting the plan itself. Thus, when our planners decided that Poles ought to have access to TV sets, washing machines, and so on, they simply forgot the need for the army of men required to service them.

"When this became evident, it was felt that nothing could be done. There were already too many people working in the so-called nonproductive sections of the national economy." In other words, the planners decided to manufacture washing machines, some of which could be earmarked for export to increase the nation's wealth. But, at the same time they made no provisions to repair machines bought for use in Poland, on the grounds that it would require skilled labor that would be better employed elsewhere. The fact that the Polish consumer not merely *feels* cheated but *is* cheated is apparently a matter of little consequence. Inevitably, however, shortage creates opportunities. A new aristocracy of skilled self-employed artisans, able to charge extraordinary sums of money for the simplest of repair jobs, has appeared on the scene. TV repairmen in Poland can earn ten times the national average wage, putting them among Poland's new rich. The success of the private repairman has meant that those who *were* employed in the state sector have all but disappeared. Where once a Pole could have a household appliance repaired eventually, if he were prepared to wait long enough for a reasonable sum, now he is absolutely at the mercy of whatever his electrician, plumber, or the like feel the market can bear.

However, what may be good news for the private repairman is part of an unhealthy trend in Poland. Economic inequalities are, according to most Polish observers, actually on the increase rather than the decrease. As the economic levers at the disposal of the government increasingly rust over, due to years of incompetent management, the pricing structures based upon a framework of egalitarianism are breaking down with quickening pace. The tragedy, as far as the Marxist experiment is concerned, is that these economic levers were simply found not to work. The government itself implicitly recognized this in the mid-70s, when it established a two-tier pricing system for meat —good cuts at high prices for the rich, poor cuts at low prices for the poor. It may have made economic sense, but it wasn't Socialism.

It all went back to the day in December 1970 when Edward Gierek came to power, determined to go all out for a massive expansion of the economy at whatever cost. These were fat years for Poland. Wages rose between 1970 and 1975 by 40 percent, while prices remained frozen. Only Poland's farmers didn't share the general prosperity. Not only did they suffer from two bad harvests, but also, in order to keep the general population happy and prices down, the government simply couldn't afford to pay the farmers more without this increase being reflected in increased prices in the stores. The farmers dropped their yield in protest, and the government was forced to start buying food abroad. The moment of truth came in 1975, when the balance of payments were critical. The Polish economy could no longer pay the vast bill for imported food, while the treasury could no longer stand the strain of food subsidies, so vital if consumer prices were to be kept down. So on June 24 the Prime Minister, Piotr Jaroszewicz, announced price rises which put meat up by an average of 69 percent and butter by more than half.

Denied the right to the ballot box in which to express their opinion about government economic policies, the Polish workers used the only method open to them, they put down their tools and took to the streets. At the Ursus tractor factory in Warsaw, the workers stormed out and formed picket lines on the main railway lines, forcing the cancellation of most trains in and out of Warsaw, including international express trains. In Radom, a large industrial town south of Warsaw, in the province of Kielce, workers from virtually every factory marched on Party headquarters, where they submitted the deputy secretary of the Party (the Party secretary refused to meet the mob) to wholesale indignities. He was stripped to his underpants by workers, insisting as they did so that his expensive suit, sold in the open market, would just about cover the cost of the extra money they would require to buy food. As the day progressed the workers became angrier and angrier. The headquarters was stormed, and the huge surplus of food and drink they found inside was first put on display and then distributed to the demonstrators. What began as a peaceful demonstration ended in tragedy. Security forces were eventually brought in and put the demonstration down with the utmost brutality. At least seventeen men died, and many, many more were beaten senseless. The repercussions were to reverberate throughout Poland for years, and Gierek himself was never forgiven. Price rises, however, were shelved. Twenty-four hours after announcing them, a shamefaced Premier Jaroszewicz was back on television saying that "as many questions had been raised," the parliamentary bill legislating the increases would be withdrawn for further study. What emerged at the end of that study was a compromise which was not only economically inefficient, but also ideologically highly questionable. Indeed, it's doubtful that the compromise solution would be tolerated in any Western country facing problems similar to Poland's.

It was announced that in every town and city in the country new stores would be opened, to be called "Commercial" stores. The old stores would continue as before, offering the same produce at the same prices. At the Commercial store, however, prices would be commercial and not subsidized to the same degree, hence the name. They would be designed for shoppers who didn't want to bother standing in line and were prepared to pay for the privilege. This concept of first- and second-class marketing, surely unique anywhere, proved to be a more subtle instrument than it first appeared. Gradually the better cuts of meat began disappearing from the ordinary stores, until the Commercial stores had a virtual monopoly, forcing more and more people to pay the higher prices. Today, save for very rare occasions, the ordinary butcher shops sell only the poorest cuts of beef, from which a traditional Polish soup is made. The beef is very cheap, well within the means of everyone.

In theory, better cuts are not much more. But that is theory only, for the better cuts are available only in Commercial stores, where the meat will cost considerably more than three times the official price. However, because of the existence of this dual system, the government has found a convenient way of raising prices without being forced to admit what is happening. In their negotiations with workers, they can claim that the cost of living is much lower than it actually is. Thus, when a Polish official told me that the best cuts of beef in Poland cost only thirty-five zlotys, he was speaking nothing but the truth, but that is the theoretical price. The fact that no meat is available at that price, or at least only very occasionally, is another matter altogether.

More divisive than the existence of the Commercial store is what is known as the PEWEX or the Polish Savings Bank, in which Poles can deposit any foreign currency. The PEWEX also functions as a store at which Poles can buy most things, but only with Western currency. In June 1981, when the country was going through a particularly severe period of shortages in every sector, the PEWEX stores in every city had a sale, offering 15 percent reductions on all their products. While it was almost impossible to buy Polish cigarettes or even vodka in other stores in Warsaw, the city's various PEWEX stores were offering a huge selection of foreign-brand cigarettes and drinks at prices well below those which Americans, English, French or Germans would expect to pay at home. When my brand of English cigarettes cost ninety pence in England, they cost only fifty pence in Warsaw, as good a deal as any offered by a duty-free shop. Those with dollars in Poland are able to buy all the things that are in such short supply in the real economy; duty-free detergent may seem an odd concept in the West, but it's real enough in Poland. From a strictly economic point of view, PEWEX stores are probably necessary. Foreign-exchange earnings are vital to the national economy, and PEWEX stores encourage members of the Polish community in the West to send dollars home to their families, who know what a significant difference a few dollars can make in their everyday lives.

Socially, however, the PEWEX stores are a disaster. People who can't get dollars, and they are the vast majority, can only stare through the windows of stores where their fellow Poles seem to be luxuriating in some extraordinary treasure trove, access to which is forbidden to them.

Even more extraordinary than the PEWEX are the Pekao stores. These are huge supermarkets or warehouses where Polish citizens can purchase Polish products, anything from food to building materials, household appliances to farm equipment, and clothing to cars, all of which have disappeared elsewhere but available here for dollars, or other hard currencies. If the black market is a disguised way of Poland's exporting its own products to its citizens at home, then the Pekao stores are the visible monuments to this uniquely Polish system of "internal export." Western entrepreneurs have gotten into the act too. Around most big cities are warehouses full of Western produce —purchasable with hard currency only. Western entrepreneurs, mainly European, but some American firms as well, export Western goods to Poland and then share the hard currency profits with the Polish government. Personally I was confident that martial law would bring an end to these institutions that have caused so much bitterness to that section of the population, mainly the peasants and the working classes, who do not have access to hard currency and who suffer extreme privations while others live in comparative luxury. So I was astonished when I received a telephone call from a London businessman who operates a warehouse in Warsaw. He told me that his exit-entry visa had been renewed, and business was booming. If anything, he told me, the new administration seemed keener than the old one to permit his business to run smoothly.

"We are always being told," says a Polish friend, a polytechnic lecturer on a very low income, "that in the West there is rationing by price—though a lot of products are on the market, the ordinary person cannot possibly afford them. This rings very hollow in Poland, for not only do we have genuine rationing, we have rationing by price and then rationing by dollars as well. If anyone had told me in the forties that, after forty years of Socialism, the only store in Poland with a decent selection of goods would be stores that refuse our own currency and accept only the American dollar, I would not have believed them."

Struggling along in the wake of the ordinary stores and the Commercial, the PEWEX, and the Pekao stores is another type of store— one becoming more and more significant—the stores owned by private people, mostly in Warsaw or Krakow, but in other big cities too. Until recently, all food stores were state-owned, but so desperate has the food crisis become that the authorities welcome anyone who thinks that he can ease it. Now there are private fruit and vegetable marketers and semiprivate grocers—people who rent their stores from and share their profits with the state. Their prices are higher even than the Commercial stores, but their produce is better quality and available in greater quantity. That too will be denied by the authorities, but the truth was explained to me by a Warsaw greengrocer. He complained that in order to make a profit and provide a service which the state stores don't, he has to drive to the country every day at 5:00 A.M. to buy his produce. Then, of course, he has to sell for a higher price to make the trip worthwhile. When I told him that a good London greengrocer will be up at 5:00 A.M. to get to Covent Garden, he answered simply: "Well, they wouldn't do that if they worked for the state and not for themselves." It is making no particular point to say that he is certainly right.

But most private store-owners are in the clothing business, owning the boutiques that dress the fashionable women in the country. Sometimes the quality can be very low and the price shockingly high, but as one fashion-conscious woman told me, the boutiques are bound to do good business. Though clothes made in state factories and sold in state shops can sometimes be of high quality and pleasantly, if unadventurously designed, the production run is so big that everyone can tell on the instant where someone has bought a dress and how much it cost. "Of course Western chain stores also sell thousands of copies of the same dress," said my friend. "But because the market is much wider and the choice much bigger, the chances of meeting someone wearing exactly the same clothes, though always possible, are not likely to be a daily occurrence. Here, if you buy a new dress in a state store, you are almost certain to see someone wearing exactly the same dress that day." Private stores also sell goods from the state factories, particularly boots and shoes, but prices are likely to be as much as double those in the state store. If women wish to pay more for the convenience of not standing in line, that is their right. But if certain products, unavailable in the state stores, are quite plentiful, though at a price, in private stores, then that is quite different, and it seems easy to believe that the state is once again manipulating prices without actually admitting it's doing so.

The Poles, as a friend observes, have been reduced to the point where most of their time is spent either shopping or thinking and talking about shopping. The direct, measurable effect upon the economy has now reached a catastrophic stage. The entire Ursus tractor factory in Warsaw came to a standstill recently because of a rumor that some cigarettes had appeared in the kiosk outside the main gates. All over the country, managers are reporting that whole departments of workers are walking off the job in order to do their shopping. And one senior civil servant told me that he was close to a complete breakdown, trying both to hold down his responsible job and fit in his share of the family marketing as well.

"I have noticed," said one Polish friend, "there is a cumulative effect of so much hardship during times of peace, when the enemy is ill-defined and the issues intangible. The danger of moral disintegration is very real indeed. Only the most committed opposition activists or the most rigid Party hard-liners have it easy. For them everything is so simple—the solutions to our problems so self-evidently obvious. For the rest of us, standing in line for the bare essentials, scrabbling around for that little bit extra, just getting by, hoping that we'll make it through the next winter, are really all that concerns us. When a proud people begin to feel like that, there is no knowing what they may do next to alleviate their sense of grievance."

Of course when the martial law authorities increased prices by, in some cases, as much as 400 percent (at the expense, it must be said, of the poorest sections of the community), they did a great deal to correct some of the distortions in the economy which had resulted in daily shopping becoming like, as one Pole put it, an applied course in adventure training. Undeniably, the price hikes of spring 1982 were as painful as they were necessary. But that such draconian measures were essential shows the culpability of previous Polish governments for the collapse of the economy.

"Don't look just at the lines, look at what lies behind them," says a young Pole. "They are the evidence of years of incompetent management, corruption, and greed. When Western newspapers 'tut, tut' at our violent reaction to price increases of say, tobacco, they display total ignorance of our situation. We are not protesting about price increases, we are protesting against those men still in power, who remain unpunished, who led us to this pass where a simple cigarette becomes a luxury.

"Our bankruptcy humiliates us in the eyes of the world. One day there will have to be a reckoning. That is something every Pole understands: And that is why the nomenklatura is so desperately fighting its rearguard action."

5
The Bureaucrats

A peasant entered the imposing office of the Party Secretary of his agri-cultural cooperative. "I'm a loyal member of the Party and I've got a problem," he began. "Ah!" said the official. "I can't help you. Problems are handled by the town's Party Secretary." After some difficulty the peasant secured an appointment with the local Party Secretary and entered his even more splendid quarters. "I'm a loyal Party member and I've got a prob——" he began. "Before you go on," said the official, "problems are dealt with at regional level." After many months he saw the Regional Party Secretary in his huge office suite. "I've a problem . . ." "Can't help you," said the Re-gional Party Secretary. "Problems are dealt with in Warsaw." And so it went on. He was passed from bigger and better offices, from Vice Ministers to Deputy Ministers to Ministers to members of the Politburo until finally, three years later, he arrived at the door of no less a man than the General Secretary of the Party. "Comrade," said the great man expansively, "I under-stand you have a problem, and as General Secretary of the Party it is my duty to help you solve it. Don't be afraid—speak." "My problem," said the peasant, "is that as a loyal member of the Party, what do I do when I learn that my father is on his way to shoot the Party Secretary of my agricultural co-operative for making my sister pregnant?"

To most Western perceptions, all of Poland's ills can be laid at the door of Communism. Poles who think about these matters only wish that it could be so simple. Leaving aside the military for the moment, there are 100,000 people who rule present-day Poland. They are all Communists, it is true, but, in most cases, Communists in name only. They pay lip service to the ideology and in so doing, pervert it. These people represent an entirely new social class. Like all socio-economic groups anywhere in the world, they possess common interests, sub-scribe to rigid hierarchical structures, have their own coded language not properly understood by the rest of the population. They con-gregate at work and also socially, a process made easier by the fact that (again like social classes everywhere) they live in the same dis-tricts, streets, and apartment buildings. In thought and behavior they conform to a common ethic which lays down rigid social rules—

observance of which is obligatory to all. The price of nonobservance is, at best, severe disapproval or, at worst, expulsion by their peers.

According to a group of Polish intellectuals, this elite, at the pinnacle professionally, "seeks not only to preserve its numerous, almost feudal, privileges to the end of its days, but also, in keeping with the rules of the feudal order, to pass on these privileges to its descendants."

If Poland is bankrupt today, then the responsibility for this state of affairs rests squarely not upon the abstract notions of Marxism but on these top 100,000 people, real flesh and blood.

Marxists believe that the abolition of private property will lead to the disappearance of the class system. It is ironic, therefore, to observe that while the sequestration of property led to the impoverishment of the old aristocratic class, it has merely been replaced by a new class, more powerful, more estranged from the rest of the population and, in some respects, wealthier than the class it replaced. That class is the bureaucracy, or as it is known throughout Russia, Poland, and the rest of Eastern Europe, the *nomenklatura*.

Nomenklatura is a Russian word meaning "to be named to a position." The *nomenklatura* is a huge army of men and women "named" by the Party to take up important positions within society. The *nomenklatura* exists everywhere a Communist government exists. It is the *nomenklatura* rather than the Party (though its members are, by definition, members of the Party) which makes it possible for a centrally organized and planned society to operate at all.

It is the Party, or rather its highest organ, the Politburo (literally the political office), that decides which positions within the state bureaucracy are so important that they need to be staffed by a man or woman whose political credentials and loyalty are beyond question. Nothing is left to chance. Like some gigantic corporation, the posts and the personnel are carefully matched. The *nomenklatura* posts fall into three basic categories: those under the control of the Party Central Committee, the regional Party committees, or district Party committees. The most important, of course, come under the first category. The Central Committee has issued three directives; the first in 1972 set out, in great detail, the *nomenklatura* posts which are in its gift.

It is an astonishing list. It includes, among hundreds of others, the heads of Central Committee departments, and their deputies; the first secretaries of the Regional Committees; the rectors and vice-rectors at the Academy of Social Sciences; the editor and deputy editors of the main Party newspapers; the directors of the Party schools; the president and vice-president of the Polish Parliament; the presidents of the Supreme Court and of the Polish Academy of Sciences; the commander-in-chief of the police force and his deputy; the president and vice-president of the National Bank; the commander-in-chief of the Fire Brigade; the president of the National Women's Council; the president and vice-president of the Polish Academy of Sciences; senior officers in the Army; the editors of all national circulation dailies; the president of the Higher Lawyers Council; the full-time presidents, vice-presidents, and secretaries of social and cultural associations; and the directors and deputy directors of all key industrial and business enterprises throughout the country.

Of course, this is but the tip of the iceberg. All these *nomenklatura* appointments also make their own appointments, always seeking out those who will precisely fill the mold they themselves have squeezed into. In the end, all owe their positions and therefore their loyalty, in theory, to the Central Committee, but in practice to the Politburo. Small wonder then that during the period that all of Poland was caught up in the revolutionary fervor inspired by Solidarity, the *nomenklatura* almost without exception stood icily aloof. It is not socialism which was most at risk, it was the lifestyles which their jobs gave them.

The *nomenklatura* literally controls everything. It is, as a body, omnipotent. I have met some outstanding men and women who are members of the *nomenklatura*—ambassadors, diplomats, journalists, members of the staff of the central committee, university rectors and businessmen. But anyone who knows Poland and the *nomenklatura* system as it operates there and elsewhere, also knows that by and large it is a system seemingly designed for the mediocre by the mediocre. It cannot be otherwise. As one of the few members of the *nomenklatura* who voluntarily opted out said to me: "In a pluralist system a bright young man who joins an organization at the beginning of his career has no great expectation of still being there at the end. He will keep moving on, always testing himself against greater and greater challenges. Right up to his mid-forties all kinds of options are open to him and, if he is particularly bright, for long after that as well. He can afford to quarrel with his boss at almost any stage of his career because, if he loses out, there will be other jobs elsewhere.

"He can afford, and indeed is encouraged, to take risks. If he fails, he can pick up the pieces; if he succeeds, the rewards can be incalculable. But a member of the *nomenklatura* has only one boss. . . . He dare not quarrel with him; he must constantly play safe; he cannot take risks. His life is dominated by the absolute need to keep faith with the system which nurtures him. For if he comes a cropper, there is absolutely nowhere for him to go."

Like everyone making a point, my friend exaggerates. There are innumerable cases in Poland, particularly in the senior ranks of the *nomenklatura*, when men quarreled with the policies they were asked to adopt, or took the wrong side in a political battle, and were simply moved sideways. For example, Stefan Olszowski (rather too easily caricatured as a hard-liner in the West) quarreled so bitterly with Edward Gierek when he was Party secretary that he was removed from the Politburo in February 1981 and sent off into exile as ambassador to East Germany. As soon as Gierek fell, he was recalled. It is probably fair to say that something like half of all Polish ambassadors abroad are there because they took the wrong side in a political battle and were removed out of harms' way. In fact, the trend at the very top is very much designed to see that the *nomenklatura* looks after its own. I have already mentioned the minister, indulging in corrupt practices, who was sent abroad as Poland's delegate to the International Labor Organization. In this respect, at least, the system is surprisingly benevolent, if also highly inefficient.

All kinds of senior positions—museum directors, managers of transportation systems, editors in publishing houses, senior directors of state corporations, chairmen of high technology institutes—are currently held by people totally unsuited in temperament or training for the position they hold. They are members of the *nomenklatura* who, for a wide variety of reasons (personal, political, ideological, or sometimes plain inefficiency), have fallen out with their masters, but, in compensation, were given other jobs where they can, and do, wreak great damage.

"The trouble with trying to climb to the top in Poland," say the cynics, "is that one's path is constantly being blocked by people coming down."

The classic illustration of an unsuitable job being found for a member of a *nomenklatura* occurred in Russia in 1957. George Malenkov, who was briefly appointed Premier and First Secretary of the Soviet Union on Stalin's death, was deposed by Khrushchev and named manager of a hydroelectric plant in the Urals.

"There is no reason why an expert in hydroelectrics should not become Prime Minister," they said in Russia at the time. "But there's every reason why a Prime Minister should not go into hydroelectrics."

One Polish intellectual had this to say about the *nomenklatura* in a work recently published in the West: "Because of their status they (or their parents) do not have to pay for the disorganization that surrounds us. The authorities give them access to the second economy for goods, apartments, health care, and so on. Moreover, the more inefficient the national economy, the more trumps the authorities hold to gain supporters by handing out privileges."

Another says: "Inequality and injustice are everywhere. There are hospitals so poorly supplied they don't even have cotton, and our relatives die in the corridors; but other hospitals are equipped with private rooms and there is full medical care for each room. We pay fines for traffic violations, but some people commit highway manslaughter while drunk and are let off with impunity. In some places there are good stores and lavish vacation houses with huge fenced-in grounds that ordinary people cannot enter. People see all this, and they know that high-ranking officials drive luxurious cars, although they have also heard stories about prime ministers riding buses.

"These days in Poland people cannot excuse the injustices associated with anyone who has any connection with power. It is not a question of money so much as a whole range of informal benefits that accrue from having a share in power. This state of affairs is totally at variance with the basic principles of our system, yet it is painfully common knowledge. Worst of all is the feeling of helplessness, the impossibility of changing the system that produced all this."

Still another: "Conflicts of group interests are indeed a major issue. . . . Doing away with private ownership of the means of production does not eliminate conflicts of group interests; in Poland there is a relatively large group of people who have a lot to lose and *are capable of doing anything to preserve their privileges* (italics added). The real reason for stagnation is that an economically privileged group hold a de facto monopoly on political action."

Members of the *nomenklatura* when tackled about the power they wield and the privileges which accrue from it, will say that they are no different from civil servants in any country in the world. There are many reasons to show that this is simply not so. The most crucial difference is that unlike non-Communist countries, the political leadership of the nation emerges from the *nomenklatura* and not from the population at large. In all Western nations the administrative, executive, and judicial functions of the state are kept firmly apart. In Communist countries they are one. Almost as important is that people may join the Civil Service of Western powers for many reasons, but not many do so believing they will be rewarded with a standard of living significantly higher than that of the rest of the population. They may believe they are joining an elite, particularly those entering the higher echelons of the service, but by withholding from them high material rewards society indicates they are regarded with no special worth.

Even those who reach the top ranks of the Civil Service know that the electorate will impose upon them a minister or cabinet officer who is either personally elected by popular mandate or appointed by a man who has been so elected. However incompetent or ignorant the minister may be, his officials are obliged to defer to his judgment.

None of this is true within the Communist bloc. Every member of the *nomenklatura* can be regarded as a member of the government capable of climbing to the top of the ladder, receiving no mandate from anyone and answerable only to his peers within the *nomenklatura*. Members are given special privileges to underline their status and to cut them off from the rest of society both as a reward and, perhaps more significantly, as insurance that their loyalty to the group remains intact. A middle-ranking member of the *nomenklatura* who joined Solidarity (though I understand he now regrets his impetuosity) told me that from the moment he left his university he had never had a conversation of more than a few minutes with a Pole who was not also a member of the *nomenklatura*. "I remember," he says, "reading an article in *Newsweek* about food shortages in Warsaw, and I was disgusted at what I thought to be the biased and untruthful reporting of the Western media. I mentioned this to a colleague and he remained oddly silent. A few days later he called me to one side and said 'we live like foreigners in our own country. We know less about what's really going on than a foreigner who flies in, talks to ordinary people, and leaves again.' I was shocked at what he said, but I decided to investigate. I called a cousin I hadn't seen for years and casually invited her to dinner. I asked her about food shortages, and I was frankly shocked at what I heard. Of course I knew things were not very good, but I had simply no idea how bad they had become."

The remoteness of members of the *nomenklatura* from the rest of the population—and the more senior they become the more remote they are—explains so much about Russia and Eastern Europe that it is astonishing that more research has not been done in the West on the governing elite of the Communist countries. Western specialists on Communist affairs appear transfixed by the ideology. They seem unaware that, of the many forces at work in the modern Communist state, Marxism has become merely a system of philosophic inquiry, and it is not thought to have much practical importance as a guide to day-to-day decision-making. The Communist leaders are certainly not unique in the present-day world in leaving their ideology at the starting gate as they proceed to gallop down the course, but it doesn't do therefore constantly to judge them by their own self-image as men constantly weighing their precepts against a Marxist analysis.

What is of greater influence on their method of government is Leninism. Examine the *nomenklatura* and you find a structure for which Lenin's writings were the blueprint. Only a professional, centrally disciplined party with a newspaper of its own would "introduce into the spontaneous labor movement definite socialist ideals" is what he said. The *nomenklatura*, taken out of the pre-revolutionary situations he was writing about, is the precise model of that disciplined Party he had in mind.

Professor Alain Besançon puts this point brilliantly when he argues that Lenin insisted that "all moral, religious, political and social phrases, declarations and promises" are a facade for the interest of some class that is the enemy of Marxism. It therefore follows that they must all be ruthlessly suppressed. The consequences are as follows: First, "the yawning gulf between the Party and society, between the world as seen by the Party and the world which society knows, is a constant threat to the legitimacy of the government's power." Secondly, a direct result of this problem, which naturally surfaces when an ideology is seen to have no basis in reality, is a special language of prescribed lies.

"The use of this language has two advantages; it provides a protective carapace which shields the Party from the gulf between ideology and reality by making real discussion impossible or at all events illegal. And it provides a ready test of the loyalty of the individual to the ideology, since any departure from the ideological language is immediately recognizable."

It also has a more prosaic virtue that Besançon has overlooked. A member of the bureaucracy observing the chaos around him has any number of acceptable explanations to make his own failure more bearable. Thus, when I gave a dinner party in London for a visiting Pole, one of my English guests had the "bad taste" during the meal to suggest that it was a pity my friend wasn't a camel, because he could then eat enough during his stay in Britain to sustain him during the first month of his return to Poland. To everyone's mild embarrassment at this attack on the Communist system, my guest launched into an astonishing explanation why Britain was "apparently" [his word] a more prosperous country than Poland. Britain, he said, owed its present wealth to a huge armaments program that gave the people an illusion of prosperity. The sale of the Hawker Siddeley jump jets to America was proof of this. He had at his fingertips a number of statements made by British Conservative politicians. He said, for example, that the Conservatives, in answer to proponents of unilateral nuclear disarmament, maintained that if Britain went unilateralist and left NATO, the country would suffer heavy unemployment and its prosperity would be threatened as defense-based industries became inoperative. By contrast, he said, Poland was a "peace-loving country," something he was not ashamed of, even if as a Pole he suffered the economic disadvantages that position entailed. There was a desultory attempt to argue with him, but it quickly petered out as everyone realized that my friend simply had no intention of moving from his elaborately constructed system of falsehoods. The question all Westerners inevitably ask after such confrontations is: "Do they themselves actually believe what they are saying?"

In my view it is an irrelevant question, one that can only be answered by "some do some of the time, some do none of the time, and some do all of the time." What does matter, however, is not whether they believe, but how successfully they can suspend their disbelief.

It is my experience that the Poles manage that very successfully indeed, so much so that the entire *nomenklatura* is able to base its entire decision-making process on the premise that it does believe—if only in itself. An individual within the bureaucracy who does not speak the language of the system opens himself up to the most intolerable pressure from his peers, ending in possible, if not probable, expulsion from the group. But a pressure more subtle even than that exists. It is hard to imagine working day by day and living cheek by jowl with others whose language and system of thought one despises and yet be forced, because of a desire to retain membership of the group, to swallow all of one's doubts and uncertainties, to live, in short, a permanent lie. Obviously some have an infinite capacity for self-deception, but few are quite so fortunate. It is easier to sublimate all critical faculties until they are buried beneath that gross mound of intellectual falsehood. Again, I must repeat that I realize that such a phenomenon is not unique to Poland or Eastern Europe. Every political party anywhere in the world has some members that are prepared to swallow every dot and comma of the party line, to believe because their leaders tell them to believe. In Poland such people make up the entire administration of the nation. The effect upon the management of the economy is clearly disastrous. A society, run by people who are terrified of any lapse from the orthodox and who build a mental ghetto from which there is no escape, must lead to chaos. A friend who is an engineer told me that every Thursday for years the furnaces vital to the manufacturing at his plant had to be turned down because of a shortage of coal, causing severe loss of production.

The managing director of the factory was, of course, a member of the *nomenklatura*. When his senior employees raised the problem with him he told them that nothing could be done. The country was short of fuel, and the plant was not of sufficiently high priority to be given more coal than had originally been allocated. He had, he said, raised the matter several times with the ministry, and had been able to achieve nothing. This situation went on until he retired and a new man took over. Within a fortnight the factory received double its previous fuel allocation and was able, at last, to go into full production. When the new man was asked how he managed to achieve the impossible, he looked surprised and said that he had noticed that the factory had run short of fuel and had simply asked the ministry for more. But, he was told, his predecessor had written on countless occasions and had got nowhere. A check in the files showed that no request had ever been made. Furthermore, the fact that the plant had always operated under capacity had been skillfully fudged in the montly production reports. In other words, not only had the man not asked for more fuel, but he had successfully disguised the effect that this shortage had upon his plant. The question is, why? Few Poles will quarrel with my friend's explanation: The old managing director had simply been too frightened to ask for more coal. To do so, he thought, would imply criticism of the National Plan under which the original coal allocation had been made. It would also call into question the competence of the senior official or minister responsible for this particular factory, and perhaps, most important of all, earmark the managing director as a malcontent, the kind of man who explains his failures by blaming others. Better, therefore, to keep quiet and doctor the books.

The ironic tailpiece to this story is that the new managing director, by virtue of writing one letter, got the increased fuel allocation, and was able to report that production in his plant had gone up almost from the day he arrived. He has been moved to a senior position in the Ministry of Economic Affairs with the reputation of being a management genius. "Yet," says my friend, of someone destined now to reach the very top, "every other decision he made while he was with us was disastrous. The only reason he wrote his famous letter is because he lacked the imagination to understand that the outcome might have been his own downfall."

"You must understand," said a Warsaw sociologist, "that anyone with real flare and imagination working within the system is going to be crushed by it. By definition an idea designed to improve the way things are done is critical of the old way and those who designed and operated it. They have a vested interest in maintaining the status quo and will rally as many influential friends as they can find to defend it. Obviously this happens elsewhere too, but members of the *nomenklatura* can always fall back on politics as the last line of defense. In the West an innovator may find all kinds of people standing in his way, but in the end, provided he can show that his ideas will objectively lead to greater efficiency, he has some chance of seeing them adopted. Here, even when he gets to that point, his enemies, as a last resort, can call upon Marx or Lenin to show why his plan must be rejected, as antisocialist or what have you. When an ideology is set in a mold it is inevitable that any new dynamic force is going to bounce off it. Ideology and dynamism are quite simply incompatible."

Because there are no objective criteria, like profit, in the end all decisions tend to be subjective. This can and does have catastropic consequences.

Edward Gierek plunged Poland into debt through huge borrowings in the West in order to modernize Polish industry and to create a high-technology economy capable of competing with the best in the world. It went disastrously wrong for a wide variety of reasons. One of the most significant was the failure of Polish management properly to utilize this sudden huge influx of Western capital. Another reason was the incompetence of the central planners, who consistently made incorrect decisions based upon faulty analysis of the kind of investment they required. For example, the Polish Ursus tractor factory had for years made a tough little tractor, unsophisticated by Western standards perhaps, but nevertheless one ideally suited for Polish farms, which tend to have small plots, and Polish farmers, who lack much in the way of technical education. This tractor was phased out in order to permit Ursus to manufacture, under license, the far more sophisticated British Massey-Ferguson. This decision cost the Polish economy millions and produced a tractor which Polish farmers don't like and don't want. There were hundreds of similar decisions made at the time, and Poland today is littered with half-finished factories, or huge idle plants designed to manufacture sophisticated products which the country simply doesn't have the infrastructure to support.

But Poland is in danger of learning the wrong lessons from the Gierek disaster. Gierek is now being criticized not because he or his ministers failed to exercise sufficient control over the investment program, but because he initiated the program at all. If officials can put the blame upon the investment program itself, then they can be absolved of all responsibility and blame only Gierek and his few close associates. But if the concept of drawing huge investment from the West was soundly based, then those who administered the program must shoulder responsibility along with Gierek for its subsequent failure. The *nomenklatura* is not prepared to do that, as it has now become Holy Writ that foreign investments are dangerous and should be regarded with the deepest caution. It is a view from which Poland will suffer greatly in the years to come.

Any foreign businessman who has ever operated in Poland knows that the country both desperately requires capital investment and yet lacks the means to harness it properly. A director of a large British construction company that won a profitable order in Poland told me that he was forced to deal with a Polish businessman who not only knew virtually nothing about construction or budgeting, but consistently overruled his subordinates, who knew a great deal. One of the Poles, says the Englishman, was a brilliant engineer who had built vast power stations in China, and yet he was being treated like an office boy by this ignorant buffoon. Eventually the engineer didn't even bother to turn up on the site, which seemed to delight his boss who found his superior knowledge so very irritating. "In the end we got out, having made a nice profit on what we all knew to be a substandard building. That all happened before the present crash, and now we feel a bit guilty about having ripped off the country. But there was nothing we could do at the time but take our money and run."

A visitor to a factory producing oil from rape in the Mazurian Lakes reported the following incident to me. He discovered that the plant had stopped production altogether because it had run out of the fuel required to run its generators. The factory's own tankers did not have enough gas to reach the depot, while the depot refused to deliver to the factory because it had its own tankers. The depot manager told the factory manager over the telephone, "If everyone who had tankers asked me to deliver oil to them, then people who didn't have tankers wouldn't have any." The manager replied as calmly as he could, "Though I have tankers, I have no gas, therefore I am in the position of having no tankers at all." "That," said the manager of the depot, "is not my fault. You have tankers and that's all there is to it." The visitor left before the issue—unsolved for a week—had been settled.

A man trying to buy shirts in a Warsaw store learned that large sizes were no longer being made. The explanation turned out to be that the national plan, which called for X million shirts, only allotted Y million yards of material to make them. The factories honored the plan by producing the right number of shirts, but in order to do so they were forced to make small sizes only.

It will surprise most Westerners that, for politically aware Poles, the debate about Jaruzelski's coup is not whether it was inspired by the Russians, but whether Jaruzelski was acting on behalf of *nomenklatura* or against it. Initially, nearly everyone was convinced that the latter was the case, now they are not so sure.

Though it was the Party that created the *nomenklatura*, the *nomenklatura* grew into a hydra which even the Party feared. A Polish politician who did not take it into account, who did not recognize that it was his only constituency, could not be expected to go very far. The police and the ubiquitous security services, the Urzad Bez-pieczenstwa, known to every Pole as the UB or Bezpieca, with their special shops, splendid country clubs and innumerable privileges, became the praetorian guard not of the Party but of the *nomenklatura* with which it is inseparably bound. If Poland were to become a democratic state tomorrow, the Communist Party would remain and no doubt continue to be a major influence in the country. It would be the secret police and the *nomenklatura* that would suffer. It has been calculated that no less than 200,000 people at every level of the administrative apparatus would lose their jobs if there were genuine industrial reform, transferring decision-making from the central planning body to the factories. Nobody quite knows how many people work for the Bezpieca, but it certainly runs into thousands. Their jobs and the good life which goes with them would largely disappear too. Small wonder then that every attempt by the previous government to meet Solidarity halfway was frustrated by a powerful group within the apparatus reaching up high into the Politburo, managing successfully to sabotage the proposals. No wonder that television, upon which the *nomenklatura* has always had an extremely firm grip, was always more hostile to Solidarity than the government itself. No wonder that there was evidence of numerous provocations by police agents designed to show Solidarity and its supporters in a bad light at the very time that its leaders and the government seemed to be coming to some kind of accommodation.

It is hardly surprising that they should have reacted so strongly to change. Like any separate social class, in any country in the world, whose status is under assault from below, they will fight with all the weapons at their disposal to protect themselves and their privileges. Equally like any ruling class that is perceived to have exploited the general population, they came under immense pressure from below once the gloves were off.

Says a Polish report: "One hears complaints about unfair appointments to leadership positions and administrative posts. But how, indeed, can it be otherwise, if the ability to pursue a career depends on obedience rather than independence of mind, on readiness to shift positions quickly rather than firm convictions. To obtain a top job where decisions are made, one must know how to do one thing: carry out the orders of others, although they may contradict themselves from one day to the next. There is an almost universally shared belief in society that the road to promotion and successful careers is most open to the obedient: a kind of negative selection is operative from the outset." The contempt implicit in that statement is shared by the entire population.

Inevitably it is the middle rank or junior officials—those who come in day-to-day contact with the rest of the population—who receive this hostility head on and who answer in kind. These are the directors of enterprises, junior local Party or administrative officials—people responsible for allocating apartments, cars, licenses for buildings, passports for foreign travel, foreign currency accounts or any one of the many "permissions" without which life is impossible.

"You have no idea of the arrogance of some of these officials," I was told by a young mother who had led a delegation to a Party headquarters to complain about the lack of reasonable play areas for children in her locality. "At first they treated us as if we were dirt. But then one of our mothers was the wife of a Party member, and he saw to it that we met the Deputy Party Secretary for the whole region, and he was a human being."

One of Poland's small army of private entrepreneurs admitted to me that he had bribed an official to get early delivery of a truck he desperately needed for his business. "I hated myself as I bowed and scraped before this little Napoleon," said the businessman. "During our negotiations I had constantly to say to myself 'the truck is important, the truck is important,' because otherwise I think I would have throttled him with my bare hands."

Of course, the obdurate petty officials have their own problems too. They work within a tight set of rules, leaving no room for initiative. "There is nothing more galling than to be suspected of corruption when one hasn't been corrupt," says one official wryly. Those who bend the rules, those who use intelligence rather than regulations have always risked falling out of favor if things went wrong. They risked accusations of favoritism or corruption. The safe thing has always been to play it by the rules, however ludicrous or counterproductive they may be.

"I was once refused a passport to travel abroad even though I was seeking to do so in order to win a worthwhile export order for Poland," says a Polish businessmen. "I knew why—because I was still on the blacklist as a result of my political activities while a student. But the really frustrating thing was that there was no one to whom I could reasonably appeal. As far as the officials were concerned I was on the blacklist, and that was that. Eventually, through a friend, I got to a minister who overruled the local office immediately, but if I hadn't had that introduction I would never have succeeded."

Every Pole has a story of some petty regulation and some small-time local official who helps to enforce it. Every Pole, too, knows of men appointed to senior positions within the *nomenklatura* who simply lack the necessary qualifications or experience, and every Pole has stories of how that situation has led to a new autocracy, operating in a style alien to the ideology to which they supposedly subscribe.

There is one example I like, coming as I do from a country where occasionally a minor scandal erupts because a town has lavishly refurbished the mayoral lavatories in preparation for the visit of a minor member of the Royal Family. It concerns the projected one-night visit to a small town called Zamosc, east of Lublin, by the then-First Secretary of the Party Edward Gierek, in order to attend a harvest festival. An apartment was taken for him in an ordinary building, but the standard of comfort was judged to be unsuitable.

So a team of workmen and craftsmen went in to make it fit for a king. They either paneled or handpainted the walls in the decorative style of the locality, and imported gilt ornaments and expensive furniture until no finer apartment existed in all of Poland. The cost to the municipality was no less than three million zlotys. Unfortunately, the visit never took place because the festival was cancelled. The apartment with its wonderfully lavish decorations, designed for this great panjandrum for one night's stay, but which he was never to use, is as good a monument to the folly of the system as we will find anywhere.

Whatever General Jaruzelski's position when he staged his coup, when he became First Secretary of the Party in October 1981, he did so without the support of those members of the Central Committee who were most committed to the *nomenklatura,* those who had based their career on orthodoxy. For the first time in any Communist country, the position of Party Secretary was not granted by acclamation. When his predecessor, Stanislaw Kania, (whose simple failing was his utter lack of charisma) resigned, it was accepted only after a vote, 104 to 79. The *nomenklatura,* surprised by Jaruzelski's move, voted for Kania to remain, to be in a better position to push their own candidates later. Jaruzelski, they knew, was the only senior politician in Poland who owed nothing to the *nomenklatura.* Moreover, because of his Army training, he was the most likely to be sympathetic to Point 13 of the Gdansk Agreement, which pledged the government to "introduce the principle of cadre selection on the basis of qualifications, not on the basis of membership of the Party." As far as the outside world was concerned, more glamorous provisions in the Gdansk Agreement—such as those relating to press freedom or the right to strike—were what mattered. In Poland itself it was the anti-*nomenklatura* Point 13 that was the most controversial, and the most difficult to apply.

During the Gdansk negotiations that led to official recognition of Solidarity, what seemed a comparatively simple pledge to which everyone might agree proved to be the biggest single stumbling block in the way of the government's honoring its part of the Gdansk accord. From the government's point of view, it was quickly realized that a centrally planned economy can only operate if down-the-line officials obey their instructions to the letter.

It is an illusion to imagine that politically neutral appointments can run an apparatus based on authoritarian political principles. The truth is that the system cannot operate without ciphers running it.

But as long as ciphers continue to run it, the system will not function. It is a paradox for which no solution is in sight.

From the *nomenklatura's* point of view the concessions made to Solidarity were disastrous. Having served the Party for so many years, they expected the Party to protect them in turn. Yet, every compromise the government effected seemed to be evidence of the Party's unwillingness to stand by its servants who worked so loyally. From this sense of grievance a powerful new political movement grew up in Poland. Called the Grunwald Patriotic Union, an organization, according to its chairman, the chubby and affable Zdzislaw Ciesiolkiewicz, was opposed to "cosmopolitan tendencies" and represented 50 million Poles throughout the world "linked by the White Eagle and a thousand years of common history." Grunwald took its name from the famous Polish battle, in 1410, when the Polish Army defeated the Germans at Grunwald. This victory ensured the continued existence of Poland itself and at the same time kept German ambitions in Central Europe in check for three hundred years, thus decisively affecting the history of all nations bordering Poland, including Russia itself.

The Grunwald Organization—officially not a political but a "sociocultural" society—was the *nomenklatura's* answer to Solidarity. By shrewdly pitching its appeal to the patriotic instinct of every Pole, by emphasizing law and order, and by drawing attention to the "cosmopolitanism" of some of Solidarity's intellectual advisers (a none too subtle code for Jewish), it sought to draw upon the natural conservatism of the Polish people, and turn them against Solidarity and the revolutionary social experiment with which it was flirting.

Grunwald openly backed the Party hardliners against the liberals whom it sees as the enemies of Poland. It supports what used to be called the "police wing" of the Party, those politicians, connected in some way with the security forces, whose real power and influence has always rested on their willingness to back the *nomenklatura* and represent its interests in the administration.

In its own weekly magazine, which mysteriously got enough paper to enjoy one of the widest circulations in the country, Grunwald played down Marxism, which its leaders knew to be unpopular and at odds with Polish nationalism. It skirted around Poland's uneasy relationship with the Russians by presenting them as the nation's only protectors against "West German militarism," while appealing to the deep-seated need of the people for a life of peace and tranquility.

Grunwald never received the attention it deserved. While I met no one in Poland who accepted Grunwald's own membership figure, given to a Western journalist, of 250,000 people (100,000 is nearer the mark), it certainly has as many if not more sympathizers throughout the country. Stefan Olszowski, inside the Politburo, and Zdzislaw Bek, the influential editor of *Trybunu Ludu*, Poland's *Pravda*, spoke out in favor of Grunwald. So did the Ministry of Defense's daily paper, *Zolnierz Wolnosci* ("Soldier of Freedom").

What I found disturbing was that the demoralized elite of a Communist country should have sought its salvation in a movement appealing to patriotism, authoritarianism, xenophobia and anti-Semitism. It ran too close for comfort to Fascism to be dismissed lightly.

Not many political historians who predict the eventual break-up of the Soviet empire have considered the possibility that, should it fall apart, it could be replaced by something even more unpleasant. The political consequences of the collapse of Marxist-Leninism, a process which is hastening upon us, is incalculable. It is a profound folly, however, to imagine that what follows must inevitably lead to systems of government that represent the values of freedom and democracy of the Western world.

There is no evidence to suggest that General Jaruzelski initially supported or even approved of Grunwald. His political appointees were absolutely opposed to everything it stood for. Yet there can be no doubt that some of the generals behind the scenes saw in the Grunwald program the means of salvation for the nation. With the most influential section of the *nomenklatura* on their side, the pressure upon Jaruzelski either to bend or be bent was enormous. Today the spirit of Grunwald has seized the very apex of the executive and administrative machinery of the country. Its natural opposition in the Polish Communist Party—so divided when Solidarity ruled the roost, and now in no fit state to take a stand on anything—has been crushed. Many on the liberal wing of the Party, those who welcomed reforms, have been purged. These Party liberals knew that Solidarity, with its basis in socialism, was not necessarily to be feared. They knew the real enemy was within. Hopelessly compromised, their leaders out of the way, they have opened the door wide once more to the old *nomenklatura*. To win the victory it had not only to destroy Solidarity but also the Communist Party. Who can doubt that it has gotten perilously close to success in achieving both objectives.

6
The Party

QUESTION: *"What proof is there that we have already taken a gigantic step on the road to Communism?"*
ANSWER: *"Once we have Communism, everyone will have everything. And we've had quite enough, already."*

IT IS THE VULGAR ASSUMPTION in the West and, it must be admitted, almost everywhere in Poland itself, that all members of the Party are either time-serving careerists at best, Soviet agents at worst or quite likely, in a large number of cases, both. There is, of course, a group of Party members who do fall into these categories. In any one-party state, membership in the ruling elite is an advantage. It would be foolish to deny—and certainly the Party doesn't—that in Poland, as in Russia or elsewhere in the Warsaw Pact nations, many join to secure the material advantages and job opportunities available to Party members. Because of Poland's strategic importance and also the endemic conspiratorial nature of the Russian ruling elite (which stems from its prerevolutionary history), the Soviet Union has consistently placed a significant number of agents in senior positions in the Party to influence governmental policies and to keep an eye on those tempted to stray from the orthodox Moscow line. Though these people exist—and any Party member will give you his list of those he believes fall in this category—the majority are sincere and honest men and women, as upset as any Pole by the way the careerists took hold of the nation in the seventies and corrupted it. These people are as powerless as the rest of the nation to control the "police wing" of the *nomenklatura* and were as genuinely determined to rescue Poland from its predicament as were any of the activists of Solidarity.

If this were not so, the *International Herald Tribune* would not have been able to print a headline on April 16, 1981, which ran "Rank-and-File Communists Ask Change in Polish Party." The story reported that a conference, organized by Communist activists in Torun, called for sweeping changes in the leadership of the Party and large-scale democratization—including direct elections to the Party Congress.

Yet less than two months later, June 8, 1981, the same paper ran a headline contradicting the earlier one. Directly confirming Western misconceptions about the Polish Communist Party, it read "Polish Communists Gird for Showdown on Party Authority," over a story accurately reporting the government's determination at that stage to crack down on Solidarity radicals. This story clearly implied what the first headline was unable to, that the Polish Communist Party and the Polish government are synonymous. They are not. Neither, in fact, is the government or the Politburo a monolithic organization open to only one point of view. It is quite a normal state of affairs, say Warsaw politicians, for half the Politburo not to be on speaking terms with the other half for weeks on end.

Today there are some 2 million members of the Party in Poland. Since December 1981, thousands who supported Solidarity have been purged, and many thousands more, in factories, mines, and offices, resigned in protest against the military takeover. One of the periodic purges that afflict every Communist country from time to time, as one group in the Party organization gains dominance over another, has been underway for several months. We have heard a lot about the "loyalty tests" applied to ordinary workers, but these are very mild compared to the grillings to which lifelong members of the Party are currently being subjected by Poland's new Thought Police.

It is not surprising that this is happening. While Solidarity was still active, the Party had 3 million members—a third of whom were actually members of Solidarity, while probably another third were active sympathizers.

The 1981 special Party Congress was the first Congress in any Communist country where delegates were democratically elected by the rank and file of the Party. They, in turn, democratically elected, by secret ballot, the Central Committee, the Politburo, and the First Secretary of the Party. About 10 percent of the delegates were also members of Solidarity. Only Westerners were surprised by the fact that so many members of the Party embraced the radical reform movement, even though Czechoslovakia had proved in 1968 that the concept of "socialism with a human face" could emerge from the bowels of even the most authoritarian of Marxist regimes. Indeed, it is possible to argue that by paying so much attention to the genuinely courageous, outright opponents of Communist governments in Eastern Europe and

Russia, the West has gravely weakened the position of liberal elements seeking reform from within.

As one member of the Party put it to me in June 1981: "It has always been a comparatively easy option in Poland to remain outside the Party and criticize its leaders and make jokes about the system. Some of us, however, tried to be rather more constructive than that—and it cost many of us our livelihood. In the past, to stand up at a Party meeting and criticize the leadership took courage. Many of us, denounced by outsiders as Party hacks, did that and suffered for it. If the Party is now opening up, it has much to do with *our* battle from inside to see that Solidarity was not crushed from the outset. I can name you men who one day will be regarded as martyrs within the socialist calendar of saints, who today are reviled in and out of the Party. For years we have carried the torch for socialism, and for that we have been discriminated against by unworthy Party leaders at home, and attacked as Communist lackeys abroad. At least our dissidents have had the comfort of the plaudits of the Western press.

"What I say of Poland is true of everywhere else within the bloc. If one day Russia reforms—and it will—it will come about not through the activities of the Sakharovs or Solzhenitsyns hawking their consciences to Western publishers, but through Party activists who are even now risking careers and reputations by calling into question not the tenets of Marxism, quite the reverse, but by arguing that the philosophy has been distorted beyond recognition by a *nomenklatura* led by Leonid Brezhnev."

One does not need to buy the entire package to have some sympathy with this position or even the less lofty, idealistic viewpoint of a distinguished editor of a popular magazine whom I have known for many years. He recognizes the flaws in his society, he knows how the system has led to corruption, he is aware of what he would describe as the economic and political distortions of Polish life, and he is sufficiently well traveled to know that whatever the propaganda may say to the contrary, by and large a worker in the capitalist West is considerably better off than a worker in the East.

Yet he would regard it as philosophically idle to reject the teachings of Marxist-Leninism because of these "distortions," rather in the manner of a Catholic rejecting the view that the Spanish Inquisition negates the whole doctrine of Christianity. Furthermore, he believes it is folly not to recognize that Poland's geopolitical situation obliges it to remain within the Soviet orbit. This fact alone imposes an obligation on the people of Poland to accept a Communist government and the economic system which that entails. Those in Poland who refuse to cooperate are either naive or treacherous. In a country which equates Communism, for which it has little love, with Soviet power, for which it has even less, this bleak assessment of what this group regards as "our ever-present realities" is hardly popular. Yet it is from this very group that reform-minded members of the Party have sprung. That the Russians, rather late in the day, came to realize that the Polish Communist Party was as ideologically "corrupt" as the Czechs in 1968, was shown in the subtle shift of Russian press commentaries on Poland from the early autumn of 1981, when not only Solidarity was under attack, but also the Party's acceptance of the concept of "renewal" was severely criticized.

It does no Polish Communist in the present government a favor to single him out as someone who offers any hope for the future. I will name an exception: the nation's Deputy Prime Minister, Mieczyslaw Rakowski, on the grounds that he has proved, among his other virtues, that he is able to look after himself. Rakowski has recently had a bad press in the West. Correspondents who had met him before he became a member of the government remarked upon his Westernized manners, his open mind, and his willingness to argue without recourse to the stultifying pseudo-scientific language of Marxism. As I remarked in my diary after having heard him talk to a group in 1979, "he was a thoroughly modern man, so unlike the fossils around him." These same correspondents who now see him defending this unpleasant government against Solidarity feel that he has sold out, compromised his liberalism in return for high office.

But Rakowski has never changed; it is the perception held by so many from the West who met him previously which was violently at odds with the truth. A peculiar form of Western arrogance assumes that every Communist in Eastern Europe who seeks to liberalize the Party is a Social Democrat in wolf's clothing. Rakowski is a committed Marxist-Leninist who went along with Solidarity. He regarded it as an essentially positive force as long as it did not seek to take over what he regarded as the prerogatives of Government or change the political system which has existed in Poland since the war. Communism, he will argue passionately, is well able to subsist alongside an independent trade union movement and, indeed, benefit from such an association. The Party needed purifying and who is better equipped for that task than the organized working class. But, and it is a big but, the Party is also protector of the interests of that same working class, and those who sought to subsume its function would, in the end, betray the proletariat even while they believed, perhaps even honorably so, they were defending it.

To a Russian ideologue, the concept that the Party can benefit from the existence of an independent watchdog is heretical in the extreme, not to say utterly illogical (which, as a matter of fact, it is, for how can the working class be organized against itself!). Nevertheless Rakowski's position (and those who thought like him) represents a decisive intellectual break from the rigidity of the old system, which has proved so incapable of organic life without a secret police apparatus to sustain it.

Mieczyslaw Rakowski, now fifty-five years old, worked as a teenager in a railway repair workshop in Poznan during the German occupation and joined the Party immediately after the war in 1946. It wasn't long before his intelligence led to a place on the influential secretariat of the Central Committee. There he quickly made his mark by taking the turgid and boring language in Party documents and pamphlets and giving the old words a new contemporary significance. Language is not just an instrument of thought, it eventually comes to influence it. Eventually the old guard found his activities disturbing, and he himself began to question, if not the Communist philosophy itself, then at least the way it was being applied. In 1958, during an exciting and exhilarating period when discussion became possible and new ideas, if not new ideologies, were actively being encouraged, he was made editor-in-chief of the political weekly, *Polityka*, which was to become the most influential voice for progress and reform throughout the Party. In 1971 he wrote: "Among the millions of non-party people, there are many individuals superior in intelligence and performance to many Party members. . . . A wise cadre policy must strictly observe the principle of equal opportunity for Party and non-Party people alike." Language like that would be unlikely to endear a Washington Republican or Democrat to his Party workers back home; in Communist Poland it was dynamite. In February 1981, after writing a trenchant critique of the way the government was handling its negotiations with Solidarity, the prime minister, General Jaruzelski, called him in and told him that if he felt he could do better, then perhaps he should join the government and take over the talks himself. From that time until the tragic breakdown, never budging from the principle that the Communist Party must have the leading role in the nation, he has proved to be a flexible negotiator, acknowledging the need for renewal, admitting the mistakes of the past and putting forward concrete proposals how these should be corrected. The man who was to tell the July 1981 Party Congress that the Party should forget its "naive utopian programs," has constantly sought to shake up the Party, of which he is a loyal member, from the inside.

Though he would be unlikely to use such language publicly today, Rakowski spelled out his philosophy in October 1981 in an interview he gave a Western Marxist journal. The interview is remarkable for its lucid and jargon-free analysis of the Polish scene. Poland's new leaders, he says, "have gained their positions as a result of criticism of the former establishment. Now they, themselves, are experiencing criticism from the same people who hoisted them into position. This, in essence, is one of the guarantees for the reconstruction of the political strength of the Party. The majority of the Central Committee is composed of workers and peasants, and they are not going to make political careers in the sense of gaining new positions. For instance, a railwayman who belongs to the Central Committee will continue to be a railwayman in four years time. He's not going to be put on the track that formerly led to the emergence of a ruling elite, which lost its contact with the rank and file, because he is stuck with the rank and file. When he comes back from the Central Committee he has to explain himself to his colleagues. . . . Onto the political scene has walked a new generation free from the fears that my generation has coded in its brain. A liberated generation is making an assessment of the developments in Poland ever since 1945. This is one of those great guarantees that this time the process of renewal will not be shunted into a blind alley. This generation now has a completely different idea of what democracy is and of how to participate in governing the country. The enlightened part of the Party, regardless of age, knows that you cannot, this time, stop and feel satisfied with cosmetic changes. At the turn of the seventies and eighties the old structures had outlived their time and everybody knows it. . . . If we don't carry through deep-seated structural modifications, there will be a great catastrophe for socialism in Poland."

The trouble is that Rakowski's assertion that "everybody knows it" is simply not true. The so-called hardliners, the police wing of the *nomenklatura*, desperately seeking to reverse the trends Rakowski spotlights, certainly do not. "Rakowski's head has been on the block for sometime," says one insider. "His presence or absence in the government can be taken as a sure sign of the way things are moving."

"Just as the Catholic Church has traditionally reserved its greatest enmity for its own heretics, so does the Kremlin, with very good reason, fear reforming Communists more than it does any outright opponent of the system," says a friend of Rakowski's. The block is already in existence and there is no shortage of people prepared to use the axe.

But, of course, many ordinary members of the Party found the political situation in Poland up to December 1981 perplexing. As one old gentleman put it to me: "The Party is there to protect the interests of the workers. That's what the revolution was all about. How then is it possible for a loyal Communist to support another body who also claims to represent the interests of the workers? It is simply impossible to be a Communist and a member of Solidarity, as it is simply impossible to have an organization like Solidarity within a Communist state." The logic is impeccable for those who believe that the Party does represent the interests of the workers. But what the Party still has to face up to, is that very few of the workers actually believe it themselves.

Certainly the old comfortable certitudes have gone forever. These were best expressed by Professor Jan Szczepanski of the department of sociology, Warsaw University, leading theoretical exponent of what has been described as the school of "political realism" in Poland.

Poland, he said in 1971, is a nation of "insurgents and anarchists." Thus no Polish government has an easy life. Poles should think "logically and rationally." If "every Pole, in every post, honestly and scrupulously fulfilled his duties," than all would be well. He should not bother about politics but leave this to "those who are accomplished at it." "Poland," he said, "needs a strong government resolved to execute power resolutely."

It is comfortable doctrine which few medieval princes, or those exercising power in modern Poland, would quarrel with.

For a long time the privileges which went with power were enshrined in the system. Up till the late 1950s, senior Party members had access to special shops—dubbed "Yellow Curtains" by the general population—because, with a touch of shabby gentility, that is how they were all decorated. These were swept away in one of the periodic bouts of reform which the Polish Party, unlike any other Party organization in Eastern Europe, was forced to accept under pressure from a resolutely non-Communist population. The fact is that despite all the years of propaganda and effort, the Party has never had anything remotely approaching a mass base. Recent figures are hard to come by, but 1973 Party statistics show that of a total Party membership of 2,322,500 (in a population of 33,500,000), 39.6 percent were blue-collar workers, 10.1 percent peasants, 43.9 percent white-collar workers, and 6.4 percent classified as others. While it is certainly true that a large percentage of the white-collar workers are first-generation children of blue-collar workers and peasants, the picture these statistics show is a remarkably unhealthy one. From 1945, when white-collar workers represented only 10.7 percent membership in the Party (blue-collar workers represented 61 percent), to today's figures which, I am told, reveal an even higher proportion of white-collar workers than in 1972, the working-class base of the party of the proletariat has been eroded to the point where it is no longer compatible with its historic origins. These figures appear even more damaging when it is realized, as Party members themselves accept, that a third of the so-called working-class list are Party employees at the shop-floor level who owe their livelihood and careers to the Party itself. Probably one half of the white-collar membership are careerists through and through. Among ordinary people, Party membership is so low that it is almost unquantifiable.

In September 1980, *Paris Match* had the bright idea of employing eight Polish interviewers to conduct a full-scale public opinion poll in Poland. Out of a sample of 510 people interviewed across the nation, only 3 percent said they would vote Communist in a free election, 34 percent would vote Christian Democrat, 27 percent Socialist, 19 percent Liberal, and 18 percent didn't know.

Though there is no way that *Paris Match* could verify the accuracy of these findings, and their validity seems questionable in view of the smallness of the sample and the fact that the kind of Pole who would assist in such an enterprise would be unlikely to be as "coldly objective" as *Paris Match* insists they were, the figures are unlikely to be very far off. Party members with whom I spoke about these results seemed more interested in pouring scorn on the high score shown by the Christian Democrats than in disputing their own poor showing. One Communist did admit that he thought it highly unlikely that in any such elections his party would poll more than 10 percent. Oddly enough, it has been almost a source of pride among many Party members that throughout the long difficult years since the war they have worked like missionaries in hostile territory, unappreciated and misunderstood by the local population, actively fighting off counter-revolutionaries in their midst, earning the enmity of the bourgeoisie and their allies in the Church.

A leftists socialist, Boleslaw Drobner, a member of the original

Central Committee after the war, dependent upon the Communists though not himself a Party member, has written how, in 1944, he spoke to a group of Polish teachers. "Their eyes burned with hate for us. We answered: 'You can hate us. . . .' In August 1944, I found myself before the doctors of Lublin where the same scene occurred. Again we answered: 'You can hate us. . . .' "

No one knows exactly how large the Party was when, riding in with the Russian tanks which liberated Poland from the Germans in 1944, it took power in a remarkable Stalinist coup. Some sources put the figure as low as 1,000—no one claims more than 10,000. Whatever the figure, Party membership represented a tiny fraction of the Polish population. Of course, it quickly consolidated and drew considerable support from all sections of the population. Despite the outbreaks of violence among certain sections of the Red Army that engaged in an orgy of rape and pillage of a population still dazed from the devastation of the war, the Russians were the liberators. A most savage and terrible war in which the Polish population had suffered so hideously was over. Subsequently, Russian behavior was to come under closer scrutiny, but for the moment at least, among ordinary people unconnected to politics, Polish feelings toward the liberators were guardedly optimistic. The optimism didn't last long.

It quickly became apparent that an organization known as the Committee of National Liberation, or the Lublin Committee, created on Soviet soil and made up of Polish Communists, some of whom were actually released from Stalin's camps and put straight onto the committee, was not going to hand over power to the legal government in London, recognized by all Western powers, or even to a coalition of national interests which would recognize the legitimate interests of the Soviet Union in a way in which the staunchly anti-Communist London Poles were never likely to do.

There is no one in Poland today—inside the Party or out—who does not admit that the Communist seizure of power was brought about only by the presence of the Red Army. This process began immediately upon the liberation of Poland in 1944 and was completed during the fraudulent elections of January 17, 1947, when the so-called Democratic bloc (controlled by the Communists) won 80.1 percent of the vote. The ballot at the election was so rigged that probably in fact only 20 percent of the country voted the Democratic bloc. Of those, probably well over half and perhaps as much as three quarters, according to one professor of history at Warsaw University, did so because they had been effectively terrorized. Interestingly, the

Party never felt confident enough in its own appeal to the masses to call itself what it was, the Communist Party. Instead, initially, it was called the Polish Workers' Party or PPR (*Polska Partia Robotnicza*) and then in 1940 the Polish United Workers' Party (*Polska Zjedno-czona Partia Robotnicza*) PZPR, and to this day, despite all that has happened, the Communist Party has no official existence.

Former United States Secretary of State James F. Byrnes reported in his memoirs that during the Yalta Conference, President Roosevelt said to Stalin: "I want the election in Poland to be beyond question, like Caesar's wife. I did not know Caesar's wife, but she was believed to have been pure." To this Stalin replied: "It was said so about Caesar's wife, but in fact she had certain sins."

As a prominent member of the Polish Communist Party, Wladyslaw Wolski, said to a Polish-American writer, Alexander Janta: "Was anyone so naïve as to expect that a revolution carried into this land on bayonet points would yield before a ballot box . . . ?"

Neither is there any question that the principal qualification of the then-government was not that its members be Marxists (though they certainly were), but that their principal loyalties be to Russia and Joseph Stalin rather than to Poland and the Polish people. From the revolutionary Marxist point of view this did not make them entirely contemptible.

One splendid old Communist of that era told me that though he knew that at least half of the Politburo were active Russian agents with ranking positions inside the NKVD, and he knew full well the elections were rigged, and that the vast majority of Poles not only hated Communism but had good reason for their hatred, he had believed that the arrival of the Red Army was the only opportunity the Communists in Poland were likely to have to stage a successful revolution. "We acted," he now says, "out of an historic imperative. The eventual success of the revolution, the prosperity both material and spiritual which would result from it, was to be history's answer to the charge that our hands were not entirely clean." Unfortunately, as he now reluctantly accepts, history has not been quite so obliging.

The new Polish government had to move quickly to establish authority throughout the country. Five distinct groups of people came to its assistance. The first was composed of army officers and professionals who had some way or other compromised themselves in the past and who could be blackmailed; they could be given a new lease of life under the new system.

The best known of this group was General Michal Zymierski, a former Deputy Minister of National Defense, who had been sentenced to six years' imprisonment for corruption before the war and was now appointed commander-in-chief of the Peoples' Army and Minister of Defense.

The second group consisted of prewar civil servants, many of whom genuinely believed that the best and only hope for Poland lay in the fullest cooperation to the only government likely to win the approval of the Soviet Union.

The third group came from the prewar socialist parties, most of whom were prepared to accept the assurances given them by the Communists that democracy would be maintained, but the shattered nation needed a popular-front government while it got back on its feet. Of this group, as in all the groups of course, most were simply opportunists, men who saw the way the wind was blowing and were determined to be wafted along with it.

The fourth group consisted of those Poles with totalitarian proclivities, such as members of the prewar Polish Fascist Party—the Falanga.

The fifth group, also prewar socialists, were politicians who, because of the experiences of the war, had been won over by the Communists and were prepared ideologically to throw in their lot with them.

It is clear, looking back, that if there had been a single politician of stature within the opposition, the postwar history of the country might have been very different. There was a brief period when the prewar socialist party and peasant party appeared to be gaining enough ground to challenge the Communists. There is evidence—albeit slender—that Joseph Stalin would have accepted such an outcome. A British journalist and politician reports a story which I, too, heard in Warsaw. A Polish general who had fought with the Russians was called in to see Stalin during the war. Fearing the worst, he arrived trembling. Stalin at first complimented him on his military successes and then asked his advice about the kind of government Poland should have after the war. Telling Stalin what he believed Stalin wanted to hear, he proposed a Communist government backed up by a substantial Soviet occupation. Stalin is supposed to have replied: "Though you may be a very good general, you are a very stupid politician. I do not much care if Poland is a socialist, a Catholic or a democratic state, or even a kingdom, so long as a pro-Russian party is in control. Poland's importance is not ideological, it is strategic and geographic."

Whatever Stalin may once have thought, as soon as the world

pitched into the Cold War Poland was very definitely drawn into the Soviet empire. But as a result, the Communist Party itself was split right down the middle from the outset into two factions, the "natives" and the "Muscovites." Without an understanding of what happened then it is impossible to understand the current battle between "nationalist" Polish Communists and pro-Soviet Polish Communists that is being fought as bitterly as ever. To understand today's battle, it is necessary to learn a little about the long history of the Polish Communist Party. For many years, up to 1918, while the Eastern half of Poland was part of the Russian empire, the Polish Communist Party was an important section of the illegal Russian Bolshevik Party. It accepted the leadership of Lenin and sent delegates to the Party congresses being held all over Europe, took part in the great debates and schisms which racked the movement and then glorified in the triumph of the 1917 revolution. Many of its members saw themselves as much Russian as Polish. More importantly, they considered themselves as members of the international proletariat, contemptuous of what they regarded as the bourgeois concepts of nationhood. They took part in the revolution and then joined the administration which Lenin established to take control of his country. Felix Dzierzynski, for example, a brilliant underground organizer in Poland, and certainly one of the fathers of Polish socialism, stayed in Russia and became chief of the secret police and the architect of the Gulag Archipelago. There is a statue of Dzierzynski in Moscow in Dzierzynski Square opposite Lubianka Prison, the headquarters of the KGB, and another in Dzierzynski Square in Warsaw. In Russia he is colloquially referred to as "that fucking Pole." In Poland he is known as that "fucking traitor." It was indeed precisely with such as Dzierzynski that the idea the Polish Communist Party was both an alien and a traitorous body first firmly took root.

All of Poland saw the First World War and its immediate aftermath as the opportunity to restore Poland's long-lost sovereignty. The Polish Communist Party, for reasons which may have been entirely understandable, opposed independence. Recognizing that an independent Poland was bound to be a Catholic and, in their eyes, reactionary country, Party members saw the only hope for Communism and the proletarian revolution, was if Poland continued to be part of Russia.

To an intensely patriotic people like the Poles, this campaign against independence was not merely incomprehensible, it was treasonable. Eventually, of course, the Polish Communists, recognizing the political inadvisability of maintaining their stance, shifted ground. Secretly, few of its leaders could forget the mainspring of their early beliefs—a world revolution in which nation states would disappear. In the late thirties, Stalin, who by then had firmly committed himself to the concept of revolution in Russia alone, had tired of the squabbling Poles. He expelled the Polish Party from the Comintern, the International Organization of Communist Parties; arrested those Polish Communists living in exile in Russia; executed hundreds; and sent the rest to the Gulag.

The Party was broken, but habits die hard. Polish Communists still looked to Russia for their spiritual leadership and when, in 1939, the Red Army marched into Eastern Poland as the Nazis advanced in the West (under a secret agreement of the Ribbentrop-Molotov Pact), Polish Communists emerged to greet the Russians as brothers and liberators. That, too, has never been forgotten in Poland.

The fortunes of the Polish Party changed dramatically on June 22, 1941, when the German Army invaded Russia. Suddenly Poland became, for the first time in its history since the days of Peter the Great, an ally of Russia. Hundreds of thousands of Poles from the Eastern territories, rounded up by the Red Army and sent to Siberia in 1939, were released. They were permitted to leave Russia and to form an army fighting under British command against the Germans. Another army of Poles was formed in Russia, the Polish Kosciuszko Division under General Zygmunt Berling, to fight on the Russian front, and the old Polish Communist Party was rehabilitated.

But too much had happened to permit the Party to adapt easily to the pace of current events. In Moscow, Stalin established a Communist front organization which he called the Union of Polish Patriots, headed by a famous prewar Polish Communist named Wanda Wasilewska. This group soon found itself at odds with the rump of the old Polish Communist Party. These survivors had been lucky enough to have been arrested by the Polish police before the war and sentenced to imprisonment—thus making it impossible for them to flee into exile to Russia, where they would have been victims of Stalin's great purge. The wartime battle between these two groups —those living in Moscow under Stalin's benevolent patronage, and those heroically fighting in Warsaw against the Nazi invader—proved to be a titanic struggle for power. Marceli Nowotko, the first Secretary-General of what was known as the Workers' Party (the Communist Party in yet another guise), was assassinated in November 1942. A year later, his successor Pawel Finder was captured by the Gestapo in circumstances which suggest that he had been betrayed. The Party today, on one hand, desperately seeks to avoid any serious examination of who was responsible. To do so would be to rattle too many skeletons. On the other hand, the Party is haunted by the realization that somewhere among its first leaders stood traitors and murderers. Neither the heirs of the Moscow or the Home groups have ever forgiven each other for that bleak chapter in their shared history. Beneath the surface of the Polish Communist Party now lies the knowledge of Pawel Finder's betrayal.

Once the war was over, there was little hope that the two groups could ever work happily for long. The Home group was led by the stern, unsmiling Wladyslaw Gomulka. Son of a locksmith, he would have been an American citizen if his parents, who had emigrated to the States, had been able to make a go of it. They had found the New World even harsher than the old and had returned home in time for their son to be born on Polish soil. The Home group believed that it understood the Polish situation in a way those who had been out of the country for so long could not. Gomulka, though never anything but a hardline Party member, spoke of the Polish road to socialism which would owe as much to Polish history as it did to Marxist-Leninism. The Moscow group, the Muscovites, headed by Boleslaw Bierut, an active NKVD agent from the early thirties, accused the "natives" of being "radishes," red on the outside, but white within. The Muscovites gloried in being "beetroots"—red all the way through. They sought to establish a Stalinist regime from the outset, taking Poland by storm with the repressive power of the Red Army.

Both sides battled for positions of power and influence inside the first provisional government. Gomulka became Secretary-General of the Party and a Vice Prime Minister as well as Minister of the Recovered Territories, an influential position giving him authority over the new lands in the West taken from Germany. His friend Marian Spychalski became Vice Minister in charge of political affairs in the Ministry of Defense as well as Deputy Commander-in-Chief of the Armed Forces. But Gomulka was naïve if he believed his wing of the Party had done well in the apportioning of portfolios. Bierut became head of state and his close friend and ally, the sinister Jacub Berman, a Vice Minister, tracking every Gomulka move, in the Praesidium where he was to be the eminence grise of the regime, while another ally became Minister of Security. The pattern for the future was set as the "police wing" of the Party was firmly established. Even while a member of the Politburo of the Polish Workers' Party was specifically denying that "this new party" was a Communist Party, Stalinist repression of dissent, organized or otherwise, became the norm, as Bierut and his henchmen tightened his grip on the country. In 1948 he was strong enough to move against the natives, expel Gomulka, and put him under house arrest, where he remained until he came back to supreme power, in the most dramatic of circumstances, eight years later.

This, in brief, is the early, unhappy history of the Party. It came in as an alien presence with no popular mandate, absolutely dependent on the Red Army. It has desperately tried but failed to live down those beginnings ever since. It has always been on the defensive; its members have never known anything but antagonism from the rest of the population.

Some Party members have tried to keep membership secret from their friends and workmates. Most have long since given up any idea of normal relations with non-Communists. "It is impossible to be a Communist in a Communist country," says a professor of sociology in one of Poland's leading universities, quoted before in this book. "It must be apparent even to the most naïve simpleton that the system doesn't work and cannot be made to work. It therefore follows that anyone with a modicum of intelligence who is a member of the Party is so for quite other motives than ideology and is therefore not worthy of respect."

However unfair this characterization, it is how Party members are seen by all sections of society throughout the nation, and Party members themselves know it. The psychological effect has been profound. Drawn into tight little circles, having little intercourse with non-Party members, the best of them see themselves, as one put it to me, "like a religious order" and the worst of them like "an elite."

An elite group is above society and does not have to conform to the rules of society. An elite is composed of special people deserving of special privileges. So it is hardly surprising that corruption spread like a plague until the Party was virtually destroyed by it. In fact, two thirds of all Party secretaries, national, regional and local; thirty vice-ministers; thirty heads of civil service departments; and 100,000 Party members have been expelled from the Party in the past two years for corruption.

"But it all depends upon what you mean by corruption," said one long-standing Party member whose California-style kitchen indicated an access to funds which did not quite square with the job he holds.

"Of course, some people disgraced themselves and the Party by, in effect, stealing from the state, but there are crooks in any society. If the state had legitimate favors to distribute, why should Party members not receive first pickings? The spadework is ours, so why not the rewards? In any case, there is no one in Poland, in or out of the Party, who does better than his American or Western equivalent. Even if some people have done well for themselves, we are still a more equal society than is found elsewhere, and it's equality that we are striving for." This argument is dishonest, and such Party members are now finding the new conditions imposed upon them by society almost impossible to come to terms with.

And the higher they are, the more difficult it became for them as Solidarity took hold. May Day, a world-wide socialist festival, has always been celebrated in Warsaw, as in other Communist countries, by the Party leadership high on a flower-bedecked rostrum reviewing the armed forces and groups of loyal citizens marching by. In 1981, for the first time ever, that was changed. The leadership themselves took to the streets and walked through Warsaw, a mark of extraordinary humility which didn't sit too well with many of the old-time Party members.

"We are being made fools of," said one official. "We represent authority in this country and unless we behave accordingly, people will walk all over us." To a degree that was certainly happening. Unable to distribute favors anymore, Party bosses found their authority crumbling. Free and secret balloting in the Party for the new Party Congress not only knocked out an incredible number of men previously regarded as sacrosanct, but turned, almost overnight, great Party chieftains into ordinary ward politicians who, instead of issuing instructions, were reduced to canvassing for votes. While rank-and-file Party members, denied the rewards which membership in an elite previously gave them, began exercising power in another direction, making their voices heard and insuring that their opinions matter.

"We had the local Party Secretary down for a question-and-answer session the other day," one Party member told me in the summer of 1981. "He used to be completely unapproachable. We only saw him twice a year in the local congress hall, delivering a long and boring speech that we all had to attend. Now here he was, being forced to justify his existence and explain what he had done for the region since he took office. I tell you we had him sweating."

For ten years, Jerzy Zasada was Party Secretary of Poznan, one of the biggest industrial cities in the country. Zasada, a man who ruled his region with an iron fist in an iron glove, was one of the first Party secretaries to fall when first Solidarity and then local Party members demanded his removal from office. Warsaw agreed, but still believing it possessed the absolute power of *nomenklatura*, sought to compensate him with the job of deputy director of the prestigious Poznan International Trade Fair. But to the astonishment of the whole country, the fair staff simply refused to have him, on the grounds that he was neither a linguist nor a trade expert and so had nothing to offer. Other jobs also fell through for similar reasons. Zasada was unemployable. Even when he eventually applied for a job as a taxi driver in Poznan, the other taxi drivers threatened to go on strike if he were given a license.

Only one job was available for him: Factory workers at the huge Cegielski Engine Works said they wanted to see this representative of the proletariat working on the shop floor. A notice stood on an old engine, a museumpiece by the factory gate, saying simply: "We are waiting for you Comrade Zasada." Comrade Zasada, who had his Party pension to fall back on, of course failed to show. There is not a Party Secretary or a politician in all the land who did not shudder at the story or, remembering it, greet the military coup with great relief.

But the Party's problem of destroying the old system and replacing it with something more acceptable, while retaining control and authority in the end proved too great a burden. Senior Party officials were closely scrutinized, as one explained at a recent meeting: "I feel I've got to go around without shoes on my feet just to show that I'm an honest man."

It is little wonder, then, that this pressure, personal rather than political, brought about a kind of collective psychosis within the Party. This psychosis took two forms. Some party activists outdid even extreme elements in Solidarity in their demand for reform. "What we are doing," said one, "is going back to first principles, back to Karl Marx, and in doing so we must reject Lenin, who was an organizer rather than a philosopher. There is nothing wrong with the philosophy, it is the organization which has proved to be at fault."

On the other hand there are those who, like the so-called Katowice Forum, demanded a complete reversal of policies so that Poland once again became the country it was before Lech Walesa and Solidarity had ever been heard of.

These groups, and there were more than ever were acknowledged, are routinely described as Stalinists in and out of Poland. They were not. They merely represented the views of a large cadre of middle-ranking members of the Party who equated their own loss of prestige and power with the evident disorganization of the economic and social structures of the country. They were bitter men who had been betrayed by their own leadership. Encouraged to take a hard line against Solidarity activists when the Free Trade Union first began to get a footing in the country, they discovered that on virtually every issue on which the Party leadership stated it would stand firm, it eventually capitulated. Their view was starkly simple: "Our Party," one told me, "was created in order to serve the interests of the working people of Poland. Suddenly, along comes Solidarity claiming to represent the working people of Poland against our Party. That is a paradox as complete as any portrayed by Lewis Carroll. But this is not Wonderland. This is a modern, industrial, socialist state. Solidarity only makes sense if it is seen as a new political party. But as this is a one-party state, it can have no legal existence here. Our leaders will rue the day when they come to realize the nature of the monster they have helped create. Of course, the Party needed reforming . . . it didn't need to be destroyed, however. And that is now in danger of happening."

Tadeusz Zareba, a top staff member of the Central Committee, represented the other school of thought. "In this country," he said, "the authorities will have to get used to spending much of their time answering criticism." "Criticizing the government, even without basis at times, has become a lasting element in Polish political life. It is not the most rational method of spending your time or ruling the country, but it is necessary after this eruption of democracy.

"The Party had become passive before the total criticism that blamed the Party for everything. The Party is rebuilding itself from the ground floor up through democratic means that we did not use much before. Reasonable people in Solidarity know they need a strong party trusted by the people."

Alas this process of "rebuilding" the Party which could in the long term have had an even greater influence than Solidarity throughout Eastern Europe was brutally halted in its tracks. But it had gone surprisingly far.

So much so that it is difficult to see how military discipline can reintroduce into the Party the old notions of blind obedience to central authority. For instance, the Politburo which Jaruzelski inherited had been directly elected by the Party itself, rather than merely being appointed by an existing oligarchy. One or two Politburo members who, even if they are now keeping their heads down, by virtue of their election rather than appointment still retain a unique moral authority that cannot be lightly brushed aside.

As for ordinary Party members, they will be unable to forget the times when, instead of just listening, they were actually listened to. "I don't know if democracy actually works," one Party activist (who has not been purged) told me before the takeover, "but it's certainly more fun. In the past we accepted instructions; we were supposed to believe in the near infallibility of our leaders; policy for us to implement came down from above. I used to listen to our leaders telling us how wonderful our system was and what incredible economic progress we were making, and I would look out my window and see with my own eyes that it really was all so much nonsense. But I never said so, not because I was afraid, but because somehow I believed that they must know things that I didn't. They asked us to suspend our disbelief and most of us obliged. But then the whole pack of cards came crashing down, and we could see that they were all empty words after all. Now we insist on making our voice heard—we insist on policy decisions which have direct application to the problems of the Polish people. And this time we're serious. We not only ask for changes, we ask for guarantees that those changes will be implemented. We are aware that we had been manipulated in the past, and this time we keep our eyes constantly open to ensure that we're not manipulated again. Yes, it is more fun to be part of the process of change than merely the sounding board for the voices of others. But it's deadly serious fun."

"Guarantees" and "manipulation," were the two words very frequently heard in Party meetings in 1981. Poland had been through so many false dawns since the war, that this time its people, as represented in the Party, seemed determined not to be fooled again.

To this end the Party began a process not only of changing its leaders, but also of changing its methods, and a new word, which sent shudders through every Communist Party in the bloc, suddenly became fashionable—horizontalism.

In Poland, as in the rest of Eastern Europe and Russia, according to Lenin's very precise blueprint, policy decisions come down from the Politburo to the Central Committee, to regional Party offices, and finally to local Party cells in offices and factories. At each stage the decisions are discussed, almost always approved, and then sent back up the ladder again. This system has permitted these countries to call themselves democracies. Government may be centralized in the hands of a few, but Party members throughout the country have the opportunity of debating and having their say on Party policy.

In practice, of course, it has never worked out that way. The policy decisions come down, and it is the function of the Party at all levels to approve them overwhelmingly before sending them back up again with a wholehearted endorsement of all Party workers. In the 1970s the Polish Party leadership itself felt that the old ways needed reforming and approved a system of horizontal contacts between Party branches. It envisaged Party organizations from different towns and regions meeting together, debating policy, passing resolutions, and sending these up for consideration to the Central Committee. But again it was a charade. Tough local Party bosses took charge. Debate was restricted to subjects which they knew in advance the Central Committee would approve. Any resolutions that were adopted simply reinforced the leadership in its current positions. So farcical did horizontalism become, that it had virtually fallen into disuse. In August 1980, when Solidarity took the country by storm, for a period of several months the Party was virtually paralyzed at the center. In a genuine crisis, the Party machine, which had for years bombarded local offices with daily instructions, resolutions, and exhortations (mostly of a totally inconsequential nature), remained silent as its leaders desperately sought a way through the quagmire.

At a time when revolution was in the air, when the Party itself was being rocked to its very foundations, as factory after factory reported mass resignations of long-term loyal Party members, during that period, the Central Committee had no advice whatsoever to offer its beleaguered rank and file. No wonder that the first instructions it issued at the time of Solidarity's first warning strike ordered Party members to remain at their post. It is estimated that no less than three quarters of Party members disobeyed instructions. Then local Party offices took matters into their own hands and revived the horizontal structures, but this time without asking for Central Committee permission. They called meetings and congresses among themselves, occasions of great historic importance, at which were heard the first genuinely free debates among ordinary Communist Party activists anywhere within the Eastern bloc.

Realizing what was happening, and the implications for the future, the Central Committee tried to put a stop to it. Zbigniew Iwanov, a thirty-three-year-old clerk and Party Secretary of a factory on the outskirts of the beautiful thirteenth-century town of Torun, who had organized the first of such meetings, was expelled from the Party by local officials. The workers were asked to elect a new Party secretary. They overwhelmingly reelected Iwanov, who thus held the unique and quite improbable distinction of being Eastern Europe's only Party secretary who did not hold a Party card. "I want to save the socialist system, not destroy it," he said. "If we could vote and speak freely, I am absolutely certain we would have socialism in Poland. But it would be a *Polish* version of socialism."

The Iwanov heresy, so directly at odds with Lenin's hallowed principle of democratic centralism, was perceived to be more dangerous to the Soviet Union than even Solidarity. Soviet hegemony exists because democratic centralism has made it a comparatively simple task to ensure that the satellites don't stray. Provided those at the top are pro-Soviet, the Party itself automatically falls into line. But if that system is destroyed, if the Party itself starts laying down policy, then all the old certainties are gone forever. What kind of Party the Communist Party would become once it is directed by its own membership is something no one can know, but for certain it will be nothing like any Communist Party anywhere in the world today, and, one may argue, it could be considerably less desirable.

The extraordinary battle within the Polish Communist Party, virtually ignored by the Western media, absolutely fixated by Solidarity throughout 1981, will one day make a book in its own right. Every week for a whole year somewhere in Poland, political scientists and Party members were holding seminars for Party activists to educate them in the doctrine of horizontalism. These activists were seeing how they were deceived in the past and how, by the manipulation of the media, attempts were being made to deceive them then. False reports designed to create either panic or disillusionment were circulated by government agents or published in the government-controlled press. A classic illustration came during the crisis months at the beginning of 1981, when the spectre of Russian intervention appeared very real indeed. In the press and on radio and TV alarming crime statistics were produced, seemingly pointing to a virtual collapse of law and order. At the same time the newspapers began publishing police reports and court cases in lurid detail although the Polish press has never taken much interest in crime. For a short period it worked. People blamed Solidarity as the nation seemed to be slipping into anarchy, but the accusation didn't hold up. It was soon pointed out that previous crime statistics were almost certainly doctored—no socialist country has ever been honest about its crime statistics, to do so would tend to quarrel with the thesis that crime is one of the suppurating sores of capitalism.

Manipulation became such a popular catchphrase that the authorities were blamed for it even when they were innocent. During the worst of the food crisis in the summer of 1981, everyone I met was convinced that the shortage had been artificially created to discredit Solidarity and that in warehouses throughout the country there was quite enough food for everyone. I pointed out, in vain, that this was unlikely on the grounds of pure logistics if nothing else. Where are the warehouses that could store so much food, I asked? Wasn't Solidarity so deeply entrenched that if such warehouses did exist, knowledge of their contents would eventually leak out? You don't know the Party, I was told. We know the kind of tricks they are up to. It quickly became apparent after the coup, when rations had to be cut still further, that nothing had been held back.

Today, of course, the old Party conservatives, if not exactly back in the saddle, have for the moment beaten off a radical left wing that was making massive inroads into Party organizations in the out-lying provinces. Campaigning on a platform that stood for anti-bureaucracy, anticentralization, and local democracy, the leftists were gathering increasing support, especially among young Party members. It is only the Western world's ignorance of Communist doctrine which persuaded those few commentators who noticed these developments to applaud them, almost wholly uncritically.

"Western politicians like President Reagan believe that the world is divided into Communists and non-Communists," one historian told me in Warsaw last summer. "But the difference between some of our young radicals in the Party and the traditional Polish Communist Party is considerably greater than the difference between the Republican and Democratic parties in the United States. Should the radicals ever come to power inside Eastern Europe or Russia itself, then Western Europe would have a great deal to worry about. The traditional party is in favor of the status quo and an ordered, disciplined society. The radicals are in favor of a system of perpetual revolution, an extreme form of Trotskyism, and what is more, would wish to export that revolution elsewhere. This was a very worrying development for all Communist Parties within the bloc, even more so in some ways than Solidarity itself. Some of the warnings issued by *Pravda* to the Polish leadership were often hopelessly misconstrued by the Western press. When the Party was told to put its house in order, it was not warned about Lech Walesa, about whom it needed no reminding, but the dangers posed by Zbigniew Iwanow, and his friends.

"Open up Communism to democracy and you cannot be sure what kind of cat you let out of the bag." As one British writer put it: "It must be emphasized that the ideas behind the rank-and-file movement were not liberal, but close to those of the Soviet workers' opposition in the 1920s. It was sensed that, in becoming a gigantic universal administration, the Party had almost completely lost its political character. "These rebels wanted a lean, highly political revolutionary Party of the working class, which would give ideological leadership and leave the drudgery of administration to the government."

Whether such a Party would, for all its pretensions to democracy, be kinder to the aspirations of the Polish people than the present Party, or more comfortable a bedfellow for the Western world, is something that I would gravely doubt. Be that as it may, the opening-up of political debate in the country during 1981 and the demand for *Odnowa* (Renewal) which the cynics split up to say *Od Nowa*, meaning "all over again," had as profound an effect on the Communist Party as it did on the rest of the population.

As will so often happen when great principles clash, the center, that section most open to compromise and representing the best in the Polish Communist Party, was inexorably squeezed out of existence. Stanislaw Kania, who took over from Gierek as Party Secretary and who genuinely sought to find a middle way, was eventually worn down by both left and right, leaving only the largely nonpolitical Jaruzelski to hold the balance.

But just as he could not govern with a *nomenklatura* stubbornly refusing to accept reforms, nor could he work with a Party that was so hopelessly split.

"Solidarity," one Party man told me, "accepted its membership from anywhere and everywhere. It didn't realize that many of the people it took in were merely using it to advance their own ambitions, which were to destroy one form of government and put in its place a revolutionary party whose first act, if it ever came to power, would have been to destroy Solidarity."

If Solidarity activists were locked up when martial law was declared, so were the Party horizontalists. And even now it is too early to say which of these two groups General Jaruzelski and the Russians regarded as being the more potentially dangerous.

Lenin declared, "For an outbreak of revolution, it is not usually enough that people at the bottom don't want to carry on as before, it is also essential that at the top it is no longer possible."

The military coup, say its apologists in Poland, was carried through because precisely such a situation existed in Poland.

The country had become ungovernable, not just because a free trade union was making political demands unacceptable to the leadership and to the Russians, but also because the Communist Party, the standard-bearer of the proletarian revolution and the only legitimate political power in the land, had been broken perhaps beyond repair on the wheel of onrushing events.

Communism, as it is practised in those nations where it holds power, has been based upon an extraordinary fabric of half-truths and falsehoods. It is hardly surprising therefore that nowhere in the Eastern bloc is anyone prepared to acknowledge the most shocking truth of all—that the Communist Party in Poland, momentarily at least, has fallen from power. The leading role of the Party, the most sacred of all of Lenin's texts, has been dismantled, not by the extremists of Solidarity, but by the Polish armed forces. They, and not the Party, for good or ill, now rule Poland. The revolution which Solidarity ushered in in August 1980 came to a logical conclusion in December 1981 with the collapse of Communist rule.

The pretense that nothing has changed is assiduously maintained. Yet the Party in Poland and the Russians know full well that thirty-seven years of uninterrupted Communist rule built upon Leninist principles has come to an end. To Russian ideologues what has occurred is an extraordinary scandal. To Russian pragmatists, whether or not they approved—which, of course, they did—or assisted in organizing Jaruzelski's coup, it is a frightening development. They may have been afraid before that the germs spread by Solidarity were contagious, what must they think now, every time they see one of the military leaders take his place, with increasing confidence, in the midst of their most earnest deliberations?

7

The Neighbors

✿

QUESTION: *"Why are Polish cows of such a peculiar shape?"*
ANSWER: *"Because they're fed in Poland and milked in Russia."*

IN THE MIDDLE of the Municipal Cemetery in Warsaw, there is a neat, cobbled square—a piece of landscape gardening, placed there for no particular reason other than it looked attractive. This is the cemetery where modern Poland buries its great men: Party notables, generals of the armed forces, and senior politicians. Most people who go there hardly give these tombstones more than a glance. It is to the cobbled square that they pay homage. Go there any day of the year— but particularly on All Saints Day in November, when Poles traditionally go to the cemeteries to place little candles at the foot of the graves of their loved ones. You will see in the square flowers and wreaths, often draped by a red and white ribbon, the national colors of Poland. Ask a passerby the significance of the square, and chances are that he will shrug, smile secretly, and walk on. But dare step on it, and someone almost certainly will sternly ask you to move away. This little plot of ground was for many years one of the best-kept secrets in Poland—one that every Pole shared, but no one ever passed on to an outsider. To the Poles it was known simply as Katyn Square —a memorial adopted by a people who were officially forbidden one for the 4,253 Polish officers killed by the Russians in the Forest of Katyn in the spring of 1940.

Without exception, all the victims had been shot in the back of the head. About 5 percent had their hands tied behind their backs with a rope. Some had their heads wrapped up in their overcoats and their mouths stuffed with sawdust. Some of the bodies on exhumation were shown to have bayonet wounds in the back and stomach, or their jaws smashed by blows, presumably from the butts of rifles.

Of the bodies exhumed, 2,914 were positively identified. They included three generals and one rear admiral, 100 colonels and lieutenant-colonels, 300 majors, 1,000 captains, 2,500 first and second lieutenants and more than 500 officer cadets.

[135]

About 50 percent of the group were reserve officers, who included among their number twenty-one university professors and lecturers, 300 surgeons and physicians, 200 lawyers, and 300 engineers, as well as teachers, journalists, writers, and industrialists.

All of them had been taken by the Russians at the outbreak of the war when, under the secret provision of the Ribbentrop-Molotov Pact, the Russian Army moved in on a Poland shattered by the Nazi *blitzkrieg*. As the Gestapo in the West rounded up Polish intellectuals and herded them into concentration camps, so did the NKVD in the East. Of these, 14,500 were taken to three Russian prisoner-of-war camps, Kozielsk, Starobielsk, and Ostashkov. Most of the officer prisoners sent to the latter two camps have simply disappeared without trace, and all we know is what happened to the inmates of Kozielsk—their bodies were found in Katyn Forest.

It was certainly one of the great and terrible ironies of the Second World War that the Katyn graves were found by the Germans in the spring of 1943. The Germans, who had so cold-bloodedly exterminated so many Poles, invited in an international medical commission composed of doctors from the nine countries of German-occupied Europe, one from a neutral country, Switzerland, and one from Italy. These men of unquestioned distinction in forensic medicine examined the corpses. The commission concluded unanimously that the bodies they examined had died in March and April of 1940—when the Russians, and not the Germans, were in possession of Katyn. However, the Bulgarian expert, Dr. M. D. Markov, subsequently revoked his signed statement when arraigned before a now-Communist Bulgarian court, in 1945, on a charge of collaboration with the enemy. He declared that it had been "materially impossible for the Russians to have committed the crime," and the prosecutor, honoring his part of a disgusting deal, withdrew all charges against him.

This is not the place to tell the story of Katyn. Suffice to say that the Russians have always claimed that the Germans committed this terrible atrocity in 1941. No one in Poland, and hardly anyone in the rest of the world, believes them. The evidence is as conclusive as any evidence can be—everything points to the fact that the Poles were murdered by a special execution squad of the NKVD and that some of Poland's finest sons died at the hands of a nation who now claims it has a moral obligation to protect the Polish people from themselves.

The cobbled square is Poland's silent tribute to the men who died. That is remarkable, because Katyn itself can never be mentioned in public; no official book or newspaper article has ever appeared in Poland discussing it. The memory of Katyn, despite or perhaps because of the official silence, lies like a fetid swamp between the Russians and the Poles. Until it is drained, it will ensure that Polish hatred of the Russians will never be assuaged. It is impossible to write about Poland without also writing about Russia; the two countries are linked not only by treaty but by what is much more important, a thousand years of mutual enmity.

A Polish historian: "The Germans committed many more atrocities against the Poles than the Russians ever did. But at the end of the war there was a kind of national catharsis. Germany was defeated; Poland was given German lands to settle in, and German war criminals went to the gallows. Many Poles will never forgive the Germans for what they did to their country, and yet they reserve most of their bitterness for the Russians, the people who finally liberated them. The Russian crimes have not only gone unpunished, but we have not even been permitted properly to mourn our dead at their hands. If the Russians were intelligent, they would admit Katyn and the deaths of thousands of other Poles. It would not be difficult for them to do. These people died at the hands of men who victimized the Russian people as much, if not more, than they did the Poles. If the Russians were to pay some compensation and admit to the terrible crimes of Stalinism, not half-heartedly but wholly, then that would cause a sensation, yes, but it would immediately lay the ground-work for Poles and Russians to start learning to live together, just as all enemies do once mistrust is replaced by trust. That is something which has been true from the most ancient of times."

But the Russians have seldom applied any intelligence in their dealings with Poland, and the Poles have reciprocated by finding every means available at every opportunity to disparage and humiliate their Russian "friends." It is said that when the Russians at last heard about the meaning of the Katyn Square in the Cemetery, their ambassador in Warsaw called upon Party Secretary Edward Gierek. Despite the publicity he received in the West as a new breed of East European politician, Gierek was always very much Moscow's man, trained and prepared for high office at a comparatively early stage in his career by the Russians. The ambassador described the square as an insult to the Soviet Union and demanded that it be dug up immediately. Gierek, who seldom stood up to any Soviet pressure, this time did so. He replied mildly: "If we remove the square, they will choose a piece of pavement in Warsaw; we dig that up and they will choose another. We will have to bulldoze all of Poland, and still the Polish people will find a place to commemorate Katyn."

If the ambassador left that exchange spluttering, imagine the anger in the Kremlin only recently when they realized why it was that every time a senior Russian delegation, from Party Secretary Brezhnev down, laid the obligatory wreath at the Tomb of Poland's Unknown Soldier, the crowd that came to witness the event appeared to be more deeply involved in the ceremony than is customary at what are the usual diplomatic courtesies extended on every state visit. What they learned was that the soldier interred there died in 1920, when fighting under Marshal Pilsudski—who withstood and then broke the Russian line pressing on Warsaw and then chased the Red Army deep into the hinterlands of Russia—and not during the 1939–1945 war.

For years now, Poles of every rank have enjoyed the secret of their Unknown Soldier and flocked to see the Russians pay tribute to this representative of a Polish Army which so soundly thrashed the Soviets.

Enmity between Russia and Poland goes back centuries. For two hundred years the Russia of the czars had a hand in the partition of Poland and treated their preserve with callous brutality. The Polish language was forbidden to be taught. Yet it not merely thrived but gained a new vibrance of expression as hardship and persecution gave Polish writers a subject matter which transcended the drawing-room concerns of so much European culture of the time. If Polish Communists schemed and plotted alongside Lenin and Trotsky for the revolution which they assumed would engulf not merely Russia but also its province Poland, Stalin repaid them by imprisoning and murdering many of their leaders in the late thirties. When war broke out in 1939 he swallowed up half of Poland and murdered the intelligentsia of the area he annexed on the cynical grounds that, as a Soviet note to the Polish ambassador in Moscow dated September 17, 1939, put it, "the Polish state and its government have, in fact, ceased to exist." Even before Warsaw itself had capitulated, V. M. Molotov, the Russian foreign minister, wrote to the German ambassador in Moscow: "I have received your communication regarding the entry of German troops into Warsaw. Please convey my congratulations and greetings to the German Reich government." In a speech on October 31, Molotov put the situation more colorfully: ". . . one swift blow to Poland first by the Germans and then by the Red Army and nothing was left of this ugly bastard of the Versailles Treaty . . ."

After Germany attacked Russia, Poland and the Soviet Union became uneasy allies—and have remained thus ever since. But the Polish wish to be a truly independent nation and Russia's determination to have a buffer at its border have never been compatible.

Neither are the Poles much moved by Russia's constant and continuing reference to the sacrifices it made for Polish independence. During a press conference given by Solidarity spokesman in August 1981, a Russian journalist eventually exploded in irritation at the insistent questioning by Western correspondents about the possibility of a Soviet intervention. "Soviet armies are here already," he said, "buried in Polish soil, for which they fought and died in order that Poland may be free." That may well be true, but it is also true—at least the Poles believe it to be so—that, having assisted in Poland's rape, Russia permitted Poland to hemorrhage uncontrollably until it suited them to help.

Every Pole is convinced, just as they are convinced that Katyn was an example of Soviet bestiality, that the Warsaw Uprising showed the Russians to be supremely callous to Polish, and indeed human, suffering in the furtherance of their political ambitions. In that supremely gallant action, the people of Warsaw tried to liberate themselves from the Germans and fought with virtually no weapons against the Wehrmacht for sixty-three days. When the city rose, the Soviet Army was already on the outskirts, having established a bridgehead for their assault on the city. But there they unaccountably stopped, while Warsaw lay burning before them and 200,000 of its citizens were butchered in a terrible engagement which Poles claim the Red Army could have brought to a rapid conclusion, thus saving the lives of thousands of their brave allies.

The Russians say in their defense that the troops were exhausted and had outrun their gasoline and ammunition. While there may be more basis for that argument than anti-Soviet historians have generally been prepared to credit, it cannot be denied that Russia failed to grant its beleaguered ally the minimum aid that any civilized country in similar circumstances might be expected to give. For example, until it was too late to affect the outcome, Russia refused to grant landing rights behind Soviet lines for British planes to fly in relief supplies, although its own air drops were so haphazard that it's hard to escape the conclusion that they were designed more for propaganda than for effect.

The Poles believe they know why: for the same reason the Soviets killed those men at Katyn—in order to destroy the very best of the nation and make their own eventual takeover that much easier. The small Communist resistance movement that fought with the utmost bravery in Warsaw had no doubt that the Russians could have helped, if they'd wanted. Very early one morning in the fourth week of the uprising, five soldiers—four men and a girl—emerged from the smoke of burning houses in Old Town, carrying the body of a dead soldier. Their white and red armbands with the letters AL identified them as members of the Armia Ludowa (the Communist insurgents). They were looking for a piece of ground free from rubble, and that was not easy to find. Eventually they succeeded and dug the grave. After a little while the girl reached into her blouse and brought into the daylight a beautiful white carnation. With great delicacy and composure she kissed the flower and put it beside the dead man's face. And then the composure broke. She turned to the Eastern shore of the Vistula, toward the Soviet forces, and exploded with an eerie high-pitched scream of an intensity unexpected from such a small body. "You sons of bitches—you haven't come!"

But, of course, they did come—eventually. They came with a ready-made government of men whose loyalty to Poland was always in doubt and who imposed a Stalinist-style, slavishly pro-Russian government on the nation.

As the Cold War began in earnest, Stalin strengthened his grip on Poland until this sovereign state was, in all but name, a Russian province, its leadership twisting and turning in any wind that Stalin sent in their direction. The Kremlin became an ever-present reality in Polish political life. Though over 500 miles away from Warsaw as the crow flies, Moscow was the place where the big decisions were made. A Polish leader without the approval of the Russian Politburo could not hope to remain in office for long. Polish economic decisions were sent to Moscow for endorsement before they were promulgated. Any sign of independent thinking by Polish Communists was ruthlessly suppressed by a Russia determined to hold the nation in its iron grip. But many Poles, Communist and non-Communist alike, never forgot how Russia, parading itself as the country's ally, had so brutally and cynically exploited the war to destroy Polish sovereignty and self-respect.

In 1956 the suppressed fury of the people exploded. It began on June 28 when a peaceful march, led it is often forgotten by Party members in Poznan, moved toward the local Party headquarters, demanding higher wages and an improvement in general living standards. The workers from the ZIPSO factory (the initials stand for the

Stalin Metal Plant of Poznan) were greeted enthusiastically by the local population as they arrived in the center of town. The demonstration quickly turned into a riot lasting two days and was only quashed when police and the security forces, backed up by tanks, opened fire on the mob. More than fifty people died and at least two hundred were injured, but their memorial proved to be a lasting one.

The Polish Prime Minister went on the radio to warn that the "provocateurs" would have their hands chopped off—a statement so deeply offensive that even if the Poznan riots and their terrible consequences had not stirred the Polish nation from its slumbers, that one remark would certainly have done the trick. For the first time ever in the history of a Communist country, the people rebelled. In factories, in the universities, in every home in the country, the age-old Polish tradition of national independence asserted itself, and by autumn the national will for change at the top had become overwhelming. The Central Committee and the Politburo met and decided that only one man matched the mood of the country, a man who until then was in official disgrace, Wladyslaw Gomulka.

Gomulka is an important figure in the history of Poland and Eastern Europe. In many ways a great man, he eventually came to grief because he lacked sufficient intelligence and imagination to capitalize upon his strengths—his enormous reserves of courage and honesty. Those latter qualities came into play in 1956 and had a fundamental role in changing significantly Russia's hold over its satellites. Gomulka had been drummed out of office as Deputy Premier and out of the Party in the forties, when he led the nationalistic wing of the Party against the Muscovites who, once he was ousted, were able to take total control. It is to the credit of the Party leadership, headed by Boleslaw Bierut, that, unlike what happened in the rest of the satellites, there were no Polish Show trials. Gomulka was never badly treated, but was held under house arrest in a pleasant villa in the country. It would be going too far to suggest that others didn't suffer or that prisons were not full or that there were no executions, but as far as they were able, Polish Stalinists managed to save their country from the worst of the excesses of the Stalinist terror machine. With the country in ferment, it was clear to the leadership that only Gomulka could save the nation from insurrection. Released only six months earlier and living in retirement, Gomulka was summoned and offered the General Secretaryship of the Party. That in itself was extraordinary. General secretaries of every Communist Party in Eastern Europe held office because the Russians had willed it. Here were the Poles appointing their own. To the Kremlin that was an unthinkable act of independence. As soon as they heard, they decided to act.

Marshal Rokossovsky was appointed commander-in-chief of Russia's Polish forces by Stalin after the war. Though Polish-born, he was a Russian citizen and a creature of the Kremlin. He was ordered to put the Soviet troops stationed in Poland on the alert, ready to take control of the nation on the night of October 18–19. Unbeknownst to the Polish Politburo, of which he was a member, he was given orders to march on Warsaw. But these troop movements were observed by Polish officers, who informed Rokossovsky that the Army supported Gomulka to a man and would fight if necessary to protect his position.

In the meantime General Komar of the Internal Security Corps pledged his support to the new leadership and occupied all the key buildings in Warsaw, while throughout the factories, schools, and offices of the capital, the people put down their working tools and picked up arms, ready to fight if called upon to do so.

Shortly afterward, the Polish Politburo received the dramatic message that a Soviet airliner was circling the capital, asking permission to land. On board was the entire top Soviet leadership—Nikita Khrushchev himself—not the avuncular peasant leader whom the West had almost taken to its heart, but the tough Kremlin bully, brutal and evil-tempered, who had been drinking ever since he left Moscow and was determined to put his house in order. With him was Marshal Konev, commander-in-chief of the Warsaw Pact forces, in full-dress uniform, medals gleaming on his chest; General Antonov, the Red Army chief of staff; Molotov; Mikoyan; and Kagnovich. This was the first team, deliberately chosen to put the maximum psychological and political pressure on these recalcitrant Poles.

Khrushchev refused to shake hands with anyone as he alighted, shouting and abusing everyone in sight. "We shed our blood for this country," he said to no one in particular, "and now they want to sell it to the Americans."

The initial meeting in Warsaw's Belvedere Palace, the official residence of the Polish head of state, did not go smoothly. A messenger came in to inform Gomulka that the Soviet Army inside Poland was quite definitely on the march. In a hard, controlled voice, the new Party Secretary turned to Khrushchev and said, "Unless the troop movements are halted this instant, I will go on Polish radio and tell the people what is happening here. There will be no negotiations. We will not talk while cannons are pointing at Warsaw."

That afternoon while *Pravda*, unable to conceive of the possibility that the Poles could confront the Soviets and win, was still accusing Gomulka of being anti-Soviet and anti-Marxist, Khrushchev was forced to accept the inevitable. He shook hands with Gomulka and wished him well. The Soviet forces were halted, and Marshal Rokossovsky was removed from his post and returned to Moscow; Poland had won back some measure of its lost freedoms.

Encouraged by the Polish experience, the Hungarians rose against their Communist masters a few days later. But they had no Gomulka to stop the Russian tanks. The Hungarian Revolution was a glorious but ultimately ineffectual expression of the people's will to fight totalitarianism. From this period the phrase was coined: "The Hungarians have behaved like Poles, the Poles have behaved like Czechs, and the Czechs [who sent troops into Hungary] like swine."

The importance of what occurred in Poland is well summed up by a historian who wrote: "When the Central Committee elected Gomulka First Secretary, it was perhaps the first time in the history of the Communist Party that the general public had directly imposed its will upon a Central Committee in the election of a leader. It was also, perhaps, the first time that a Central Committee had submitted to the will of the masses. Two events without precedence in the Communist world. Herein lay the greatness of the Polish October."

The Polish October had a wider significance too. For the first time in the history of Eastern Europe a ruling Communist Party had stood up and defied the Kremlin and emerged victorious. The tragedy of the Polish October was that in order to save everyone's face, both the Russians and the Poles pretended that nothing untoward had occurred at all. Accordingly, though relations between the two changed de facto, de jure there had been no change at all. The press of both countries never referred to the matter again in anything but the vaguest of terms; academics and political theorists excluded these events from their analyses; and the politicians, as if by some mass frontal-lobotomy, simply pushed the October events from their minds, never to refer to them again in public and hardly ever in private.

Tomasz X, then a member of Gomulka's Secretariat, remembers being part of a briefing session for a team of Polish ministers, headed by Gomulka, before a visit to Moscow to negotiate a new trade deal. One of his colleagues presented a paper which set out the strength of the Polish position—namely, if Russia had been forced to acknowledge the events of October, it certainly would have taken a considerably less rigid line than it had in the past on economic relations between the two countries. Polish ministers, he concluded, instead of merely listening, as they had in the past, could now do a good deal of the talking. His presentation was listened to in pained silence. The atmosphere, Tomasz recalls, reminded him vividly of a book he was then reading, set in the early nineteenth century, telling the story of the son of a middle-class family who brings a prostitute home to dinner. The man who presented the paper was fired a few days later.

So, instead of embarking on a new era of cooperation between the two countries, Russian-Polish relations stumbled forward haphazardly and uncertainly until the moment had gone, and the new era of Leonid Brezhnev brought back so much of the old interdependence. "Both Russia and Poland have paid a great deal by their unwillingness to be honest with each other or with their own public," says a Polish politician, who happens not only to be a member of the Party, but who would be regarded in the West as very much a Marxist hardliner. "October 1956 should have provided the occasion for our relations to be put on a sound and secure basis.

"In fact, it was the Poles, perhaps because they could hardly believe they had got away with what they had, who somehow seemed to insist upon all forms of the old relationship, while Russia was already ready to dispense with them. I know that the Russians were genuinely astonished that within eighteen months of becoming Party Secretary, Gomulka outdid everyone else in the bloc, both publicly and privately, in accepting the supremacy of the Soviet Union in all matters, both external and internal."

A member of his staff explains why: "Gomulka became convinced from the moment he took power—perhaps it was something Khrushchev had said when he arrived in such a rage—that Russia was prepared to settle the continuing problems of European security and Germany at the expense of Poland. His constant nightmare was that Poland's Western territories, which he had administered when they fell into Poland's hands at the end of the war, would be returned to Germany under an overall general peace settlement. He believed that if he stepped out of line again, then that would be what the Russians would do."

Certainly I was told by a senior source that, in 1958, Khrushchev told Gomulka that Russia should admit its guilt for Katyn and pay compensation, laying all the blame on Stalin and the evil Lavrenti Beria. Thus, he hoped the Polish people would be more ready to accept, by this act of contrition, Russia's honorable intentions for the future. Gomulka, fearing such an avowal would have the reverse effect of what Khrushchev intended, demurred and persuaded him to remain silent. Today, under the more rigidly orthodox Leonid Brezhnev, such a proposal is almost unimaginable, but the consequences for Soviet-Polish relations are little short of catastrophic.

In the forties and early fifties, the Russians treated the satellites like colonies, stripping them of scarce resources for little or no return. For a time things were better.

Thus Poland and the rest of Eastern Europe were shielded from the worst of the catastrophic rise in international energy prices following the Yom Kippur War, because for years Russia kept the price of its oil deliveries down. Only when Russia began running short of energy itself did it renegotiate oil prices to international levels, and even then, for a long period, permitted payment in local currencies, though oil is always priced in dollars. It is true that when the Russian Navy ordered boats from Polish shipyards, they paid in nonconvertable rubles, although the Poles had to purchase sophisticated electronics in the West and pay in hard currency, thus making the deal hopelessly uneconomic. Yet some Poles argue that even this deal could have been properly renegotiated, if the minister responsible had had the courage to approach his Russian opposite number and not leave the matter, as he did, to frightened officials, who behaved as if they were operating in the climate prevailing in the forties and fifties.

There is a great deal of evidence to suggest, however, that from the mid-seventies on Russia contributed directly to the collapse of the Polish economy, either because of greed, negligence, or a particularly unpleasant form of real-politik. In 1975, Polish ministers accepted payment from the Soviet Union for goods exported from Poland in what were called "transfer rubles." Transfer rubles were valued at 62 kopeks to the dollar, an administrative currency value which bore no relation whatever to reality. Poland might as well have been paid in Monopoly money for all the good the transfer rubles did to the Polish economy. She bought high-technology components from the West, incorporated them into manufactured products which she then sold to Russia for transfer rubles. The trouble: these transactions were to plunge the country deeper and deeper into debt. To buy with real money and sell for pretend money is the shortest way to bankruptcy known. The advantages to Russia were, of course, considerable. As a Polish economist, a Party member, explained to a Party meeting in May 1981, Russia began drastically cutting down its purchases from the West—for which it had to pay in precious hard currency—and bought the same goods from Poland instead, using transfer rubles and thus getting them cut price. For example, Russia became Poland's largest customer for high-voltage equipment and complete transformer stations, at the same time ceasing to buy this equipment on the international market. According to a Polish minister, Poland had to borrow $11 billion in 1981 in order to guarantee production of equipment for the Russians. Many Polish factories exported 90 percent of their output to Russia and all for a currency unacceptable anywhere in the world outside the bloc, and even within the bloc Poland's creditors preferred dollars.

Obviously many Poles knew what was going on. Professor Witold Trampczynski, an ex-Minister of Trade sacked in the late sixties when he began questioning the basis of Soviet-Polish trade, managed while ambassador in Washington in 1971 and even before the transfer-ruble came into being, to have a clause inserted into a trade deal between International Harvester and Poland that any re-sale of equipment received by Poland under that agreement could only be conducted with hard currency. But in the mid-seventies men like Trampczynski were out of favor. So Russian trade delegations began pouring into Warsaw. The Minister for the Chemical Industries arrived, and Polish farmers were suddenly without fertilizer. The Soviet Health Minister called, and pharmaceuticals disappeared. The Minister of Agriculture arrived, and the shops emptied of food. In the meantime, Polish power stations began receiving low-grade coal as the best went to Russia, reducing their productivity by 15 to 17 percent (exactly the current deficit in energy). And for all of this the Poles were paid in a worthless currency. Mieczyslaw Jagielski, a Deputy Prime Minister when challenged about this, said on Polish TV in March 1981 that no one could be sure of the facts because for the past five years, "we have not prepared proper accounts." It was an astonishing statement but one which might well bear out the assertion that Poland's annual losses during that period are almost exactly equivalent to losses Poland sustained in its transfer ruble deals. Thus Poland directly and the international banking community indirectly have been heavily subsidizing the ramshackle Soviet economy for the past few years. Recently, probably because of the catastrophic consequences of this policy, both economically and politically, there has been a considerable rethinking in Moscow and perhaps, too, Polish ministers have learned how to be tough with their senior partner.

It is hard to understand why Russia behaved as badly as she did, until one realizes that for all the shortcomings of the Polish economy, the Russians were even worse off. It must have been genuinely galling for Russian ministers to accept that somehow a situation had come about whereby the colony was better off than the colonizers. Until the recent troubles, Russians would travel to Warsaw with the same sense of excitement and expectation that a provincial European might regard a trip to Paris. To a Muscovite, Warsaw was a city of bulging shops, superb choices in food, and consumer goods simply not experienced back home. In Russia, a Polish shirt, or better still a Polish-made pair of jeans, is regarded as the height of elegance and luxury. Poles not only know this, but speak of it with pride. They regard themselves as the Athenians to the Russians' Sparta. When they return from Moscow, they speak with the same smug awe of shortages and lack of variety in Russian shops as a Westerner does when he returns from Warsaw. The transfer ruble was obviously designed to "correct" this imbalance. But the effect of it was to sour Russian-Polish relations almost beyond repair.

At the beginning of last year (1981), Poland successfully negotiated a four-year debt moratorium with Russia, providing for deferment until 1985 of repayments of credits grabbed in 1976 to 1980, including a $1.1-billion hard-currency loan in October 1980 and an additional $465 million in January 1981—not an inconsiderable sum from a country chronically short of hard currency. The existence of the loan itself, let alone its deferment, is surely evidence that Russian-Polish economic relations have not all been one-sided.

For years no Russian soldier has been seen in uniform in Warsaw or any big city, though occasionally they can be glimpsed in the countryside. Both governments have been forced to accept that the presence of a Russian uniform in a Polish city would be provocative and lead to the kind of incident that both countries dread.

A friend of mine married a Russian woman who, though she lived for ten years in Warsaw, was never made comfortable by the Poles she met. But when Solidarity came into being, when the barriers to free speech broke down, she began to understand the hatred that Polish people felt for the Russians. Given ration cards, she was nevertheless refused food in some shops by clerks who roughly suggested she return to Russia. Eventually, cut off entirely from any contact outside the family, reluctantly and tearfully she went home to Moscow in the summer of 1981.

Of course there is an element of the "Yankee go home" syndrome in all this, and it can be taken too seriously both in Russia and in Warsaw. The desecration of Red Army graves and occasional attacks on Russian soldiers, which occurred during 1981, are as deeply and genuinely deplored by most Poles, who regarded most if not all of these events as provocations, as they are by Russians.

"I don't need to love the Russians to tell my children that one of the greatest days of my life was when I saw Red Army tanks in the middle of Warsaw, coming to liberate us from the Germans," says one Warsaw journalist. "Neither do I need to love the Russians to acknowledge that the burden of their war effort against the Nazis was unimaginably greater than the Western powers have ever given them credit for. So those who now spit on their graves, spit on all of us who fought the Germans." But the same man added: "Of course, if the Russians threaten us, if only by implication, with armed invasion, then one should not be surprised if Polish citizens become angry when they see a Russian uniform."

No one doubts anymore that three times—in December 1980, in April 1981, and then in June 1981—the Russians had actually embarked upon the preliminaries of an invasion of Poland. Throughout November 1980, twenty Soviet divisions and several Czech divisions were in place, and the Polish Army was effectively neutralized with positions assigned in a Warsaw Pact exercise that kept it well away from where it could effectively mobilize resistance. Senior Soviet officers had been placed in key positions throughout the Polish Army, some wearing Polish uniforms; a separate Russian communications network and independent transport arrangements had been established throughout the country; fuel dumps had been established, and reservists in key specialist roles, particularly medicos, had been recalled. In December the invasion force got no further than the jump-off point, but in April, in what was called "creeping intervention," they actually entered Poland in the guise of a military exercise, and they did the same in June.

What is not known is why, at the last minute, on all three occasions the Russians pulled back from the brink. Evidence is hard to come by, but senior sources in Warsaw suggest that on no occasion could the Russian persuade any Polish politician who would make a convincing-enough figure (if only in the eyes of their own propaganda machine) to take over the reins of government and invite them in.

The first man on their list was unquestionably Stefan Olszowski, a fifty-year-old professional politician who has been destined for high office for many years. His ability and intelligence have never been in doubt, but he's someone who has consistently been misunderstood by

Western observers. For years he was described as a "liberal," on the grounds that during the 1976 food riots in Poland he sided with those who blamed economic mismanagement for the problems of the country. In fact, he has always been a Party man in the classic tradition, believing that it is the Party's function to rule. However, as he told the Politburo in 1976, when he was Foreign Minister (he was later shunted off in semi-exile in disgrace to East Germany as ambassador), he believed the Party's right to rule the people implied a compact between the two, and that the Party should rule efficiently. Now he is regarded as a hardliner, because efficient government, in his book, does not permit the kind of freedom granted Solidarity by a government with little to offer save for a willingness to buy peace at any price.

Brezhnev is presumed to have asked Olszowski to take over when the two met in Prague in April, but to his credit Olszowski refused to do so. "What the Russians discovered then," says a man close to Olszowski, "was that there is no one of any substance left in Poland who is prepared to buy the Russian ticket to power. No one is prepared to be Moscow's tool. Olszowski has made it clear that, though he is ambitious to take over, he will do so on his own terms, as a Pole, not as a surrogate for the Russians."

Whether General Jaruzelski was simply a Russian tool when he took over, is a question the historians will be arguing over for years. What is sure is that the issue is not as clear-cut as the State Department would have the world believe. The Russians must have been informed, and probably were asked for logistical support. But it is a long way from that position to assume that the Russians, with a convenient pawn at hand, ordered the Polish general to act. While it is impossible to be dogmatic either one way or the other, Jaruzelski wears a uniform that presents a deep commitment to Polish nationalism, and those who believe he sold his nation to the Russians need to put up stronger evidence than they have hitherto. Jaruzelski (as most senior Warsaw Pact officers) completed most of his military training in the Soviet Union; does that experience outweigh the deep and instinctive patriotism of the Polish Army of which he is a member? The answer, I suggest, is still very much an open one.

Of course, direct Soviet intervention—especially if things start going wrong again—can never finally be ruled out. Indeed, many people still believe that this is the only possible solution to Russia's Polish problem. "Don't worry," a member of the Russian Politburo is supposed to have told his Polish opposite number recently. "When we come in, we won't hang you. We'll hang the people who hanged you." And a jocular East German leader recently defined a Polish optimist as someone who thinks he'll be taken to Siberia by train, while a Polish pessimist believes he'll be made to walk.

What is for sure is that Russia could never allow Poland to slip out of its orbit. Russia's lines of communication to East Germany, on the Western border of the empire, go right through Poland. The population of Poland is the largest in any Eastern European country and its armed forces, after the Russians, numerically the strongest and probably the best trained in the whole of the Warsaw Pact. Yet this country, so strategically vital, is bedevilled, and always has been, by "counterrevolutionaries," by a Party that has been virtually neutered and by a population that is endemically anti-Russian.

Yet there are very few Poles I have spoken with who do not recognize that the only real future for Poland is within the Soviet Pact, and that this is the will of the people, provided the Soviet Union accepts a free association between the two countries, not one based, as at present, upon duress.

"If we Poles are anti-Soviet, it is because the Russians have made us so," says one prominent university professor. "They believe they liberated us and gave us socialism, and so we owe them a debt of gratitude. We believe they killed many of our people and took away from us our independence of thought and action, and so we have nothing to thank them for.

"Yet, if ever there was a time to end the hatred of the past, that time is now. Solidarity gave us back our self-respect. If they will come to us as an equal, put forward their legitimate interests and listen to our legitimate grievances, they will find that all of Poland is prepared to listen. From such a dialogue both sides will emerge stronger."

One day that will have to happen—but it will need a more imaginative and probably younger man in the Kremlin than Leonid Brezhnev before a start can be made.

8
The Church

※

Poor Cardinal Wyszynski, when he went to heaven and met the Virgin Mary, he found that she was wearing a lapel badge with a picture of Lech Walesa.

"I WAS ON A BUS in Warsaw and someone came on and just shouted —just shouted as loudly as he could. 'I just heard on the radio that Karol Wojtyla is the new Pope.' Everyone thought he was joking, and then saw that he wasn't. And we laughed, and laughed, and hugged each other, and laughed again. I have never known anything like it. We were all complete strangers, and suddenly we behaved as if we had known each other for years, as if we were all members of one family." A Warsaw secretary.

"I was out of the country attending an international seminar in Prague. And a Czech came up to me, knowing I was Polish and told me the news. My first thought was this means trouble; my second thought was this means very big trouble." Communist journalist.

"I was walking down a street in Krakow on my way home, when suddenly all around me windows and doors opened, and people came pouring out on the streets, singing and dancing. Wojtyla is Pope. Wojtyla is Pope. People were crying, and I began crying, too, I just couldn't stop myself. Then suddenly someone began singing the national anthem. And we all just stood there and sang it over and over again. In no time there were hundreds and hundreds of people in the street, and then we walked to the cathedral to be joined by thousands upon thousands of others. As we walked, I remember thinking quite consciously that no event in my lifetime was ever likely to move me quite as much as this moment, and so I kept my eyes and my ears attuned to every single detail so that I would always be able to remember." A Krakow student.

"I put my right hand before my eyes and looked at it in some wonder. 'This was the hand,' I thought, 'that has shaken hands with a Pope.' You see, only a year before I'd met him when he came and

[153]

visited our parish. And I called the whole family together and I said to them, 'Always remember and tell your children and your grandchildren that your father shook hands with the Pope.' " A factory worker in Nowa Huta.

"Mother Superior announced it over supper, and there were tears running down her cheeks. And we all silently filed into chapel, and we stayed there all night, praying. No one told us to, no one said we couldn't go to bed. Speaking for myself, I just didn't want to leave. That night, for the first time in my life, I finally achieved a total communion with God, and to this day my soul still glows from the experience." A nun.

"I was watching the television news and suddenly the announcement came. I couldn't believe it, I didn't want to believe it. Obviously, I am not a Catholic, and neither do I believe that Catholicism has been anything but a brake upon the social progress of this country. But I have to admit it, I was moved. Call it irrational Polish pride, if you like, that well-known chauvinism of ours, but I was proud of Poland that night and was on the 'phone to my friends, and I could tell even as they talked about the problems this would inevitably bring, they felt proud too." Staff member of Polish Central Committee.

"Well, that's one in the eye for the bastards, I thought, and I brought out some very special vodka and we drank to the Polish Pope." Peasant.

"I heard it on television. The expression on the announcer's face was wonderful. Those people could announce World War III and the latest harvest figures, and if you turned the sound down, you wouldn't be able to tell which was which. But this time you could see how astonished and how happy he was. Well, we all had a party and we said 'now things will be different.' We had often said that, but this time we really believed it. And we were right weren't we?" Polish factory worker.

Just as most Americans remember what they were doing when the news came about the assassination of President Kennedy, so can the Poles remember the moment when the news was announced that Karol Wojtyla, cardinal, archbishop of Krakow, had been elected the supreme pontiff. Neither is it surprising that those in the Party and government who predicted trouble got it exactly right.

No Pole I have spoken with has doubted for a moment that Pope John Paul II's accession to the throne of St. Peter was the trigger for the mechanism which set the events of August 1980 into train. "We would probably have had isolated strikes and maybe won some concessions from the government," says one member of KOR who has spent as much time fighting the Church as the Party. "But a Polish Pope united the Poles in a way I personally never imagined possible. When he came to Poland, the air was electric. It was not primarily a religious event, it was a nationalistic one. Here was a Pole, head of a universal Church, and here were the Polish people, cut off from universal experiences by being members of this narrow, claustrophobic pact. He opened the windows of the world for us, and all Poles were determined never to see them shut again."

But the funeral of Cardinal Stefan Wyszynski, in June 1981, says more about the power of the Church in Communist Poland than the national celebration that followed the election of Wojtyla. His funeral compared with those of Winston Churchill, John F. Kennedy, and Charles de Gaulle in modern times. They were statesmen—two of whom had embodied the full expression of their people's yearnings in their darkest hour, while the third had died still rich in promise. Cardinal Wyszynski, in a secular age in a Communist country, was a prince of the Church. Yet the people of Warsaw in the hundreds of thousands filed past his coffin. Dignified and grief-stricken, they waited hour after hour, shuffling slowly forward to see a coffin bedecked with flowers, the purple of his calling, the red and white colors of Poland, and the blue and white of the papacy. Throughout the country flags stood at half mast. The state radio broadcast only religious and solemn music. Theaters and cinemas were closed as the country went into official mourning. More than a quarter of a million people attended his funeral in Victory Square before an altar dominated by a forty-three-foot wooden cross, the symbol of Christianity towering over a square more typically used for great demonstrations of Communist power. There, to pay him homage, was the President of the country, Henryk Jablonski, and three Deputy Prime Ministers.

The man who in the 1950s was sent into three years internal exile for refusing to compromise on the issue of the independence of the Church, knew on his death-bed that the final victory was his. For, remarkably, the ancient privilege of the primate of Poland to stand for the people before the king, to serve as regent during periods that there was no king, had been tacitly acknowledged by his old enemies in the Party.

At the beginning of 1981, when Poland seemed to be ungoverned and ungovernable, First Secretary Stanislaw Kania, who once had been in charge of the Politburo's relations with the Church, turned to Cardinal Wyszynski in desperation and asked for the Church to use its good offices and act as mediator between the state and the workers. Wyszynski moved quickly and skillfully. His basic proposal to both sides was that if they could reach an agreement, the Church and the Episcopate would act as guarantor. Solidarity, led by Lech Walesa—whose Catholicism is more important to him than his political activities, and who always wears a portrait of the Virgin Mary on his lapel—needed no persuading. Ministers for their part, while not exactly liking the situation, could not doubt Wyszynski's integrity. The titanic struggle, waged since the people's republic came into being, to separate Church from state had finally been resolved, but on terms which astonishingly place the Church at the political heart of the nation. The Communist government found it could not rule without the Church, and the Church, for its part, agreed, for the sake of the nation's integrity, that it would be prepared to compromise with a Communist government.

If the army, the *nomenklatura*, the Party, and the Russians are the rulers of Poland, then the Church, the spirit of Solidarity, the farmers, and the country's intellectuals, in that order, are the opposition. Pre-eminent among the latter is the Church. From the day the Communists came to power the Church has stood not only for the right of religious freedom, but for other freedoms, too. Freedom to worship, the Church's leaders realized, was meaningless if its parishioners did not also have freedom of speech and political conscience.

Some Western leftists find it hard to understand why the Church had such a powerful influence on Solidarity. The answer is that it could not have been otherwise, because for many long years only the Catholic Church kept the bright flame of freedom alight. The Polish Catholic Church is unlike any other Catholic Church in the world. It is closely identified with Polish nationalism and deeply committed to its Marian tradition that proclaims the Virgin Mary as the queen of Poland. "There are aspects of Polish Catholicism which have an almost pagan ring to them," says one Catholic intellectual.

"The Polish Church has always encouraged some of our ancient myths and enshrined them into the canon. Polish Catholics are reluctant to believe that Mary and Jesus speak any other language than Polish. A Polish priest once told me quite seriously that he believed Poles in heaven would act as the armed guards of the Lord. When I asked why God should require heavy security, he reminded me of the story of Michael the Archangel casting Lucifer into the outer darkness. As far as he was concerned, God faced the perpetual prospect of a military coup, and it is the function of the Poles in this life and the next to preserve and protect him. For his part, in this divine contract, God and the Virgin Mary have agreed to preserve and protect Poland and its people."

The cult of the Black Madonna, the Blessed Virgin of Czestochowa, shared by Pope and people, is a celebration of primitive Catholicism and nationalism which has no equal in the world. The madonna is a rare and precious icon, encrusted with jewels, which has been scientifically dated back to at least A.D. 500. As far as Polish legend is concerned, however, it was painted by St. Luke and somehow found its way to the vastness of the great fortress of Czestochowa. And it was there, in south-central Poland, that a motley collection of Polish soldiers in 1656 fought off 9,000 crack Swedish soldiers laying siege to the castle, the Swedish army then being regarded as one of the most powerful in the world. King John Casimir vowed then to dedicate himself and his country to this icon, blackened by age and known by all Poles as the Black Madonna.

Countless miracles have been attributed to her, and annual pilgrimages to the shrine are among the most impressive and awesome sights in the Catholic world. Two miracles in particular are remembered now, and both produced tangible results, though whether the miracles were wrought by the Virgin or the Polish people themselves is a matter of debate.

The first such occasion was on August 11, 1956, the 300th anniversary of the day that, according to legend, the Swedish troops stood with cannons aimed, ready to destroy the monastery of Jasna Gora where the Black Madonna was on display. The attackers were confounded as the entire monastery rose from the ground in a mass of clouds and levitated above them. Three hundred years later, the Russians and their Polish puppets were the enemy. The Church was under immense pressure. Cardinal Wyszynski was under house arrest. Bishop Kaczmarek of Kielce had been tried and found guilty of treason and sentenced to twenty years imprisonment. Eight bishops and a thousand priests, including Archbishop Baziak, the apostolic administrator of Krakow, had been imprisoned. Well over a thousand nuns had been taken into custody after raids on convents all over Poland. A group of so-called "Patriotic Priests," who were prepared to support the government and denounce Wyszynski, had put in an appearance. The final drive by the Communist leaders to destroy the authority of the Church once and for all was well underway.

Children were taught at school how the Church had traditionally exploited the peasants by keeping them in ignorance and fear. Jacek Kuron, who subsequently became leader of KOR (the Committee for the Defense of the Workers), the forerunner of Solidarity and its intellectual powerhouse, remembers life as a young Marxist at a Warsaw academy for young Party members.

A well-known writer whose books were based upon the principles of socialist-realism addressed the students one day on the splendors of Marxist-Leninism.

At the end of his talk, a young man at the back of the room, whom nobody had seen before, got up and hobbled on one shriveled leg to the front of the class. He was a pitiful sight. Ill-dressed and under-nourished, he was slightly hunchbacked as well as lame. He had, he said, a statement to make. Though only twenty years old, he knew he looked as if he were forty, and he explained the reason why. Ever since early childhood he had worked as a virtual slave for his parish priest. Fetching and carrying for him, working his plot of land, never a day off and never any leisure. One day, by chance, he said he had picked up a book by the author now addressing the class. He had read only a few pages before he realized that not only had he been en-slaved physically, but spiritually, too. By the time he had finished the book, he resolved to leave the priest and his false gods and work in order to become a member of the Party and for the betterment of mankind. Kuron says that so moving was this speech, and the sight of this poor man, that he felt tears pricking the back of his eyes, and he joined the whole school, led by the celebrated writer, more moved than anyone, as they rose in tribute to applaud him.

A week later, however, when another author came to speak to the school, exactly the same thing happened. The only difference was that the hunchback's inspiration to break with the priest and join the Party came not from the writer who had spoken the week before, but this new writer. And, says Kuron, every Party writer who visited the school was granted the same tribute for his influence on this one poor, misbegotten, and utterly fraudulent "slave" of the Church.

Such scenes were being repeated all over Poland. For younger children the most exciting outings of the year were arranged on big Catholic holidays, forcing their parents into the uncomfortable posi-tion of denying their children the pleasures that the authorities had in store for them in order to send them to church. Older children found they faced crucial examinations on the same day or, if that were not possible, Party events which they were told (none too subtly) would affect their chances of entering university and their subsequent prospects if they didn't attend. The screws were tightening daily on the Church, and few outside observers, even those who understood the extraordinary hold which the Church had on Polish life, believed it could survive for long in anything but a truncated form—in rather the manner of the Orthodox Church in Moscow, where priests and prelates are acknowledged to be servants of the state before they are servants of God.

So nobody knew quite what to expect on the 300th anniversary of the miracle of Czestochowa. Workers had already rioted in Poznan the previous months, had been bloodily suppressed, and the mood of the nation was explosive. The authorities were careful to ensure that the anniversary celebrations received no publicity. They were quietly confident, in any case, that Catholics would not dare make too noisy a demonstration. What happened astonished even the Church itself. Exactly how many joined the pilgrimage to the monastery no one can possibly say, but the most conservative estimate puts the number at one and a half million, traveling from the farthest corners of Poland, often on foot. Cardinal Wyszynski's empty throne was carried high in procession with a vast bouquet of red and white roses lying on it. Rather than face what could have turned into another anti-Government demonstration, the authorities, caught short by this overwhelming expression of religious fervor, were forced to cooperate with the Church to handle this vast congregation. Special trains were hurriedly laid on, refreshment facilities hastily arranged, and police called in to marshal this huge assembly.

The event, almost totally unnoticed in the West at the time, was not only the greatest religious demonstration ever seen in a Communist country, and perhaps even in the world, but also it was a rude shock to Russia and all of Eastern Europe. Most importantly, it served to arouse Polish patriotism, which had lain dormant for so long, as the people, wearied by the war years, had tried to come to terms with the alien philosophy imposed upon it. Within months a new spirit of hope flooded through Poland. Wladyslaw Gomulka became Party Secretary, and Cardinal Wyszynski was released from his place of incarceration.

That October when Gomulka, in spite of Russian resistance, came to power is remembered also for the appeal that Wyszynski broadcast to Polish Catholics, calling for "loyalty to the republic." It was a time that brought together, not for the last time, cardinal and commissar in a remarkable alliance in the face of grave danger for the whole nation.

For pious Catholics, the mass pilgrimage to the Black Madonna by the people of Poland and the events of that October when the iron grip with which Russia held Poland were gravely weakened, were not unconnected. And the same Catholics date Gomulka's downfall from the moment he grappled with the Black Madonna and Cardinal Wyszynski almost exactly ten years later. Relations between Church and state had once again come to a breaking-point, as the battle for soul of Poland was fought in public between these two old antagonists. The Catholics were celebrating their millennium—one thousand years of Christianity in Poland. The government countered by inventing its own celebration—one thousand years of nationhood. The cardinal told his people that Poland could "often be without a king, and without a military commander, and without superiors and without prime ministers and without ministers, but this nation has never lived without a shepherd."

To which Gomulka replied: "This irresponsible shepherd of shepherds, struggling against our people's state, who proclaims that he will not grovel before the Polish raison d'état, places his illusory claims to spiritual leadership over the Polish nation higher than the independence of Poland. What blindness this must be which makes him forget the lessons of history, to forget who has brought Poland to ruin, and who has liberated it. . . ." Although it was an astonishing battle for the minds and hearts of the people, there was never much doubt who would win.

The state did everything it could to snatch victory for itself. When the Church had special celebrations to mark an event, the authorities answered with their own parades. For example, in Przemysl on the Russian border, the cardinal came to celebrate Mass and take part in a religious procession through the town. On the same day the local Communists organized a military parade. The bells of the basilica were partly drowned by the noise of blank shots being fired from cannons and aircraft, flying low in salute overhead. But again the Black Madonna was the focal point of the religious celebrations. Hundreds of thousands went to Czestochowa for the celebrations, and even more people turned out for processions organized in every town and city in which a replica was paraded by local bishops. The government panicked. The madonna, destined for Warsaw, was forcibly removed from the hands of a bishop and returned to Jasna

Gora under a "not to be moved under penalties" act which Wyszynski branded as a sacrilige, unmatched since the days of the Swedish invasion itself. Thousands of Catholics marched on Party headquarters in Warsaw in protest and were attacked by riot police. Wyszynski and other bishops were refused passports to Rome to attend the Vatican Council, and the Pope, who had wanted to come to Poland for the celebration, was told by the Polish government that he would not be welcome. Not only that, but the government went to the extraordinary, unprecedented lengths of closing the border between April 15 and May 22, neatly flanking the May 3 celebrations, just to make sure that if the cardinal did score a triumph, there would be no foreigners to witness it.

Addressing the people at Jasna Gora, the archbishop of Poznan rubbed in the true meaning of these extraordinary events:

"Ten years ago," he said, pointing to the cardinal's seat, "this chair was empty. You," he told the cardinal, "were persecuted for the sake of the Virgin and you still are. For us, you are the true father of the people and the nation.

"We have been prevented from having the Holy Father among us. But in your person, Saint Peter is with us. The Pope's absence was to humble you, but it has exalted you, for he has named you to represent him. We Catholic bishops believe in you and have full confidence in the way you lead us. You are the personification of the Church. The more you are insulted, the more we love you. . . . We, the Polish bishops, jointly and severally, are united with you as one body. The bishops and the nation are united with you as never before, and this solidarity is our strength." It was the first time that the word "solidarity" as an expression of Poles acting in unison against the state had ever been heard. It was not to be the last.

Gomulka, who lost that particular argument, was never to recover ground. He had four more years in office, but they were years of mounting frustration among the people, which he met with increasing repression until he was forced out of office in December 1970. And the people of Poland looked knowingly at each other and spoke again of the intervention of the Black Madonna.

However, many commentators around the world, not necessarily left wing, and a good many foreign Catholics, including some high officials in the Vatican, didn't put all the blame for the problems of the sixties on an obdurate Gomulka.

The Polish Church may have had continuing problems with the regime, but the worst days of Stalinism were over. Religious instruction may have been banned in schools, but there were thousands of special Sunday schools attached to the churches. There were actually more priests and bishops in Communist Poland than there had been in pre-war Poland, and church attendance was certainly far higher.

The cardinal had written to the German bishops, offering to forgive Germany's sins and asking forgiveness for Poland's sins. The Eastern territories, the area ceded to Poland after the war in exchange for the land lost to Russia in the East, were still in dispute, and this letter was both undiplomatic and mischievous. When the cardinal's letter called Poland a bulwark of Christianity, there could be no doubt he meant that it was a bulwark against militant atheism as expressed by the Soviet Union. That Gomulka felt the cardinal had gone too far was not surprising.

What the cardinal's critics in the West failed to take into account was why Catholicism in Poland was so enduring, and why, after early attempts to crush the religion, the Communist regime had been forced to accept it as an unpalatable fact of life.

"In Poland," said one of the cardinal's closest advisers, many years later, "it simply makes no sense to say that the Church should remain out of politics. The very act of going to Church is a political act. The man or woman who wears a crucifix is making not merely a religious but a political statement as well.

"The Church is both above politics and at the heart of politics. When all opposition to the state was being rigorously suppressed, the Church became, whether it wanted to or not, the true opposition party. The Church spoke out in 1968 when Jews were being thrown out of the country; the Church spoke out in 1970 when troops were used to quell the food rioters; the Church must always speak out where there is injustice. That is a universal truth, but it is more true in Poland than it is elsewhere, because the Church in Poland has become synonymous with the Polish nation. The two are seen by the people as indivisible, he who harms one harms the other. Cardinal Wyszynski understood this completely, so do the present Pope, Archbishop Glemp, and most, if not all, Polish bishops. So those who criticized the Church in the past, and do so today, for meddling in politics, fail to understand that in Poland temporal politics have imposed themselves upon the Church, and not the Church on politics. To understand Poland, you must understand that."

Catholicism in Poland has its roots deeply embedded in the countryside, and though this means that the Church has sometimes seemed to have lost its way in the Middle Ages, it is also a Church that always possessed a deep and abiding sense of nationhood. Before the war, Polish priests were badly tutored in primitive dogma and superstitions long since abandoned elsewhere in seminaries where, it was said by Western clerics, the "unbelievable was taught to the unprounceable." Some priests in country areas, barely literate themselves, opposed education. They felt that all a Catholic needed to get to heaven was take his turn at the plough, go to Holy Communion on Sundays, attend the confessional and be shriven of his sins, and produce enough children to keep the parish register healthy. The Church was rich in property and land. Many priests were against Marshal Pilsudski, the virtual dictator of Poland from 1926 until his death in 1935, because he attacked the Church for its backwardness and sought to redistribute some of its lands to the peasantry.

The war changed the Roman Catholic Church as it changed so much else in Poland. "I suddenly found," one old parish priest told me, "that my parishioners were looking to me for leadership, not the kind I dispensed so readily before—who should marry whom, who was at fault and should pay compensation in a dispute between two peasants, and what to do with little Anna who was believed to have lost her virginity at the age of thirteen. Now I was being asked to decide matters of life and death affecting the whole community, coupled with the kind of moral and ethical questions which I had previously never even thought of. I became immediately a better man and therefore a better priest."

Monsignor Marceli Godlewski, parish priest of All Saints in Warsaw as well as a Nationalist politician and parliamentarian before the war, was famous throughout the country for his virulent anti-Semitism. When war broke out, Father Godlewski's church was in the heart of the Jewish ghetto that was created by the Germans. All Saints was one of the biggest buildings in the area, and Father Godlewski turned it into a clearing-house for food supplies for starving Jews, especially children. He helped hundreds to escape, devoting himself entirely to the Jewish cause. Professor Ludwik Hirszfeld, a bacteriologist and immunologist of international reputation who was in the ghetto for a period, wrote later:

Monsignor Godlewski. Whenever I pronounce this name I feel deeply moved. Passion and love combined in one soul. Once a militant priest, professing anti-Semitism in sermons and in writing. But when fate made him an eyewitness to the abysmal depths of Jewish oppression and squalor,

he cast away his former attitudes and dedicated the whole ardor of his
priestly heart to the Jewish cause. Human heads would bow in love and
humility whenever his beautiful gray-haired head appeared among us. . . .
All of us loved him dearly: the children and the aged. All of us were rivals
for his company and a moment's talk. Nor did he spare himself. . . . He
visited us frequently to console and fortify our hearts. . . . I should like to
communicate to posterity what the chairman of the Judenrat . . . thought
of him. . . . The chairman told us how the monsignor had broken into tears
in his study when they talked about the plight of the Jews; and also how he
endeavored to help Jews and alleviate some of that terrible suffering. Father
Godlewski saved hundreds of Jewish lives—particularly children, as did
other priests of the Church.

After the war the Church, which could not have survived for 1,000
years if it had not learned the art of adapting to changed circumstances, realized that the advent of Communist government be-
stowed upon it not merely grave dangers but unique opportunities.
The seminaries were the first to change. Young men who had barely
completed a secondary education were gently discouraged in favor of
those capable of taking full degree courses.

The Church militant was preparing to go on the defensive, but
the new government was busy as well. Knowing it could not abolish
the Church at a stroke, it tried to infiltrate it instead.

The man chosen for the task was Boleslaw Piasecki. Before the war
he had been leader of a small right-wing party, the Falanga. Although
it is probably unfair to describe it as the Polish Nazi Party, it was
unquestionably Fascist. Poland being Poland, Piasecki, unlike home-
grown Fascists in other European occupied countries, did not collaborate with the invaders but fought against them as a member of the
Underground. Exactly how he came into contact with Poland's new
Communist leaders after the war is not entirely clear, though it has
been suggested that he was arrested and told that unless he co-
operated with the regime as an ex-Fascist he would be shot. Exactly
why he was chosen, and not a more suitable candidate, is not too
clear either. Most likely the Communists were victims of their own
propaganda. If the Roman Catholic hierarchy was Fascist, as all good
Communists believed, who better than a Fascist to deal with them.

This controversial figure set up, with government money, an organization called "Pax," whose principal purpose was "to neutralize
the Catholic Church in Poland." While the Church itself had almost
no paper or printing facilities, Pax became a prosperous publishing

house disseminating what appeared to be Catholic Christian theology, but with a strong underlying theme termed by them "state instinct," which forbade any challenge to the Party or the government as a danger to the state itself. The Church hierarchy quickly recognized Pax as a force to be reckoned with, appealing as it did to the old virtues of patriotism and Christianity, and with ready access to the media. But if the Church had problems from the outside, it also faced criticism from within. Catholic intellectuals, dismayed by the autocracy of Cardinal Wyszynski, were also denied a voice in Church affairs by most of the bishops of Poland. The intellectuals set up their own organization, called "Znak," independent from both Church and Party. Znak, though always suspect by both sides, was to have a unique and extraordinary role in Eastern European politics. In 1956, during the reforms which followed the election of Wladyslaw Gomulka, a Znak group became members of the Sejm, the Polish Parliament, and became an independent voice at the heart of the legislature. They were not immediately acknowledged for fear they were puppets of the regime, but this notion was quickly dispelled, as Znak became an embarrassing thorn in the side of the government, which may have imagined that having given Znak status, it would be able to manipulate the group. In 1968 Jerzy Zawieyski, a writer and a Znak MP, resigned from the Council of State, to which he had been elected, because of the increasing "Fascism" of the government. It was one of the truly courageous acts in modern East European politics.

At the same time the five Znak members, as a group, wrote to the prime minister complaining about the "brutal action of the militia and the national guard against academic youth." The letter spoke of an "outraged society," and went on, "We request the prime minister that the government should undertake steps to relax the political situation. This requires putting an end to brutal police action. Not all those who protest against the brutal act should be regarded as enemies of the regime. . . . Stifling demonstrations is no way out. But one should not forfeit the opportunity of talking with the public. That is the solution we propose."

The experiment of bringing lay Catholics into partnership with the government, a risky maneuver for both sides, came to an end in 1976, when the Party pushed through a new constitution which caused an uproar in the country. Three clauses in particular were bitterly resented and resisted. One established the Polish United

Workers' Party constitutionally as "the leading political force in the building of socialism." Another stated that "the rights of citizens are inseparably linked with the thorough and conscientious fulfilling of duties to the fatherland," and a third constitutionally linked the Polish Peoples' Republic "with the forces of freedom and progress . . . based on strengthening friendship and cooperation with the Soviet Union and other socialist states." It was the Church that led the successful campaign against this outrageous document.

The most bitterly contested clause was the one implying that citizenship depended upon the good behavior of the individual, as defined by the authorities. This was finally amended, and it now states that citizens "ought" to conscientiously fulfill their duties to the country, but not before Stanislaw Stomma, leader of the Znak group, had abstained from voting in the Sejm and then dropped from the list of candidates at the forthcoming elections, his career and the independence of Znak simultaneously coming to an end.

Stanislaw Kania, in charge of Church-state relations, used the administrative machine to disperse the group. He gave new and favorable publishing contracts to those members of the group that had voted for the constitution. For a time there were two Znak groups. One was hostile to the regime and close to more progressive members of the Catholic hierarchy, especially the cardinal archbishop of Krakow, Cardinal Woytyla, and to the majority of Catholic intellectuals. The second Znak group had little support in the country as a whole, but had aligned itself with the government. If this presented a confusing picture to outsiders, especially journalists who came to Poland, and were granted interviews with members of Znak, and then went away to report that Church and state were in remarkable harmony, it also confused, as it was intended, the Poles themselves. As far as they were concerned, the Church was speaking in four voices—the voice of the episcopacy, the voice of Pax, and the voices of the two Znak groups. For intellectuals who knew the score, this didn't pose a problem, but for ordinary devout Catholics looking to the Church for leadership, there was a confused cacophony.

As for Pax, it had one moment of true glory. To his everlasting credit, its new leader, Ryszard Reiff, was the only member of the Council of State (ironically, he was appointed to it in February 1981 in place of the disgraced Edward Gierek) to vote against the imposition of martial law and was instantly sacked to be replaced by Zenon Komender, Minister for Internal Trade. No doubt he has been charged with returning Pax to first principles as the State's propaganda arm in its never-ending struggle against the Church. What is difficult to say is whether the ordinary, decent people who are its members have had their eyes opened at last.

This confusion over who genuinely represented Catholic opinion came to a head in late 1980. With much fanfare (eagerly reported in the West anxious to observe genuine change at the top in Poland), a leading Catholic layman, Jerzy Ozdowski, was named as Deputy Premier—on the surface, a remarkable appointment in a Communist country. In fact, his appointment was not quite as significant as it then appeared. Ozdowski was a leader of the Znak faction which split away from the main body and aligned more closely with the Party. As a reward he was made a member of Parliament and then placed on the Council of State. That he is a Catholic there can be no doubt, but that he represents Catholic thought in Poland, or any significant section of Catholic life, is another question altogether. The fact is, says one Catholic intellectual, the Church was neatly outmanuevered. The Church didn't want to attack Ozdowski, because then it would appear that the Church was as badly split as the Party. On the other hand, by not doing so, it seemed that the Church had a voice in the higher reaches of government and so was in some measure responsible for what was going on. The fact is, though there were Catholics in Parliament, the state made it almost impossible for Catholic charitable organizations to operate effectively; it refuses nuns the right to work in social welfare institutions, such as hospitals and homes for the aged, and denies the right of priests to hold services in hospitals, prisons, and the Army.

Ironically criticism of the Church is now louder among ordinary Poles than it was in the days that it stood in outright opposition to the regime. "The moment," says a Catholic writer, "that the Church took the view (both before and after martial law) that it should adopt the role of mediator between Solidarity and the government, it was forced into the position of urging the workers to moderate their demands. Suddenly it became part of the system and not the sole opposition to it. It may never recover."

Many intellectuals feel now that the Church, having entered the political arena openly, is content to trade political concessions to the workers for religious concessions for itself. "If we're not careful," one Solidarity member once remarked sourly, "we'll find that all we achieved through our struggle are licenses to build more churches. That is not the reason why we dared challenge the system."

The Catholic Church in Poland remains as it has been for centuries

—the force that binds the nation with a mixture of religious and nationalistic ecstasy that has no counterpart elsewhere. To be in Poland in August on Corpus Christi Day; to see in every city, town, and village in the country the sacrament carried in solemn procession to small altars on every street corner; to see the congregation, women of all ages and the children, too, often dressed in their first communion clothes of white, is to witness an event that would be intensely moving anywhere, but that it should still be happening here, in the heart of Communist Europe, is almost painfully poignant.

Even a nonbeliever would be bound to take heart from such a demonstration, proving as it does that people are not just puppets to be manipulated at will by governments imposed upon them. Despite years of official discrimination, despite the fact that people know that regular Church attendance is entered on the record against them, and is sufficient reason to exclude them from senior positions, churches are so full on Sundays that there is no hope of getting a pew unless one arrives early. Party members and officers in the Army, virtually forbidden from going to Church, will frequently go to small, out-of-the-way villages where no one knows them, to have their children baptized. A priest told me how he was called to the bedside of an ex-minister to administer the last rites and hear his confession (he wouldn't name him). I told him that this struck me as a good example of a man hedging his bets—insurance in case there is a God, no harm done if there isn't. Not so, said my informant. I know from what he told me that he had never lost his sense of religion.

This "sense of religion" in a largely secular world has not endeared the Poles to everyone. They are seen as the last guardians of a primitive religious impulse that stands in the way of progress, and that the Church's caution and innate conservatism hold back the Polish people from their true potential. If there is some truth in that, it is because the Church has to balance its religious function and its (no less real, even if largely symbolic), role as guardian of Polish tradition and the moral authority of the Polish state. And it is worth remembering, it is from that soil that Solidarity grew.

I see the Church in Poland as representing for that country precisely what the monarchy represents for Great Britain. Neither the Church nor the monarch has any real power, but nevertheless each is immensely powerful. They both fulfill a need, however irrational, for people to have an institution to which they can look and which is the depository, perhaps illusory and imaginary, of an atavistic and collective national will. Such an institution must, by its nature, be conservative, always one step behind, rather than one step ahead. Cardinal Wyszynski once told a visitor that when the episcopate has ever involved itself in politics, it has been because the political process itself had broken down. Only then did the Church see itself as leading the nation rather than representing it. It would be a definition of constitutional monarchy that Queen Elizabeth II would find hard to fault.

But it would be wrong to consider the Catholic Church in Poland in purely abstract terms. Over the years its priests and nuns have comforted the people, supported them through every trial, and fought with them on the barricades. The Catholic Church, through its cardinals, acknowledged that truth when they honored Poland's Catholics by electing a Polish Pope. At the time it seemed astonishing; looking back, one sees they could have, in all justice, done nothing less.

The first full day of Pope John Paul II's pontificate, October 17, 1978, was the anniversary of the official beatification of Father Maxmillian Kolbe, a Fransciscan priest whose influence on the Pope and Catholicism throughout Poland cannot be underestimated. It is hard to remain cynical in the face of this man's story and the philosophy which motivated him—love of God must lead to a greater love of mankind.

Father Kolbe was in every way a remarkable man. In the twenties he established a monastery which, with its 762 inhabitants, was the largest in the world. It was completely self-supporting, with not only its own farmers and cooks, but also its own doctors and dentists, printers and shoemakers. From there Father Kolbe published a daily newspaper that became the best-selling paper in the country. He had his own radio station beaming out a mixture of religion and entertainment, a forerunner of the many bible-of-the-air stations in America. In the thirties he left Poland to propagate the faith in Japan and India, and he returned to Poland at the outbreak of war in 1939. He was arrested on February 17, 1941, for publishing attacks upon the Nazi philosophy and also for his work in helping refugees, particularly Jews.

"Our mission," he had told followers, "is among them."

He was taken to the notorious Pawiak Prison in Warsaw, where he was beaten and tortured before being deported to Auschwitz on May 18. Prisoner 16670 became a man venerated by all the other prisoners he came into contact with; he was living testimony to the truth that even in such a hell, man can and must hold on to his essential humanity.

Picked upon for specially onerous work—he once received fifty lashes for collapsing under a huge pile of timber—kicked and beaten, Father Kolbe nevertheless shared his pitiful ration of soup and bread with others. When asked whether this was not carrying his religious faith too far in a place where everyone was struggling to survive, he replied: "Every man has an aim in life. For most men it is to return home to their wives and families. For my part, I want to give my life for the good of all men."

He did what he could to comfort the dying and give hope to those still alive. Then, one day, after a prisoner had apparently escaped, the camp authorities decreed that as a reprisal ten men should be starved to death in the bunker. Among those picked out at random was a Pole called Francisek Gajowniczek. As he was being led away with the others, he called out in despair, "My wife, my children, I shall never see them again." Suddenly Father Kolbe stepped forward. "I will take this man's place," he said. "Who are you?" asked the SS commander. "I am a Catholic priest," replied Kolbe. Gajowniczek was taken out of the line, and Father Kolbe walked to his death. He and the men with him died well—praying aloud during every waking hour. It took a fortnight to kill the majority, but Kolbe still hung on to life until he was finally killed with an injection of carbolic acid. Gajowniczek survived Auschwitz to attend the ceremony of his benefactor's beatification.

When Cardinal Wojtyla spoke at a press conference after the beatification ceremony, he referred to Father Kolbe's reply to his captors, "I am a Catholic priest." "So it was as a Catholic priest that he accompanied his wretched flock of nine men condemned to death. It was not a question of saving the life of the tenth man—he wanted to help those nine to die. From the moment that the dreadful door clanged shut on the condemned men, he took charge of them, and not just them but others who were dying of hunger in cells nearby, and whose demented cries caused anyone who approached to shudder. . . . It is a fact that from the moment Father Kolbe came into their midst, those wretched people felt a protective presence, and suddenly their cells, in which they awaited the ghastly final denouncements, resounded with hymns and prayers. The SS themselves were astounded: "So *was haben wir nie gesehen*" (We never saw anything like it before.) And neither had anyone else in that most fearful of places.

Father Kolbe, now canonized, Pope John Paul II, Cardinal Wyszynski—three shepherds of men from one country who have put their mark on this century. That is not a bad record for a church which many believed has long outlived its useful purpose.

9
Solidarity

"Well, what do you think, Lech?" asked the Pope after he showed the leader of Solidarity around the Vatican.

"It's nice, but I won't take it. I still think I'd like something a bit bigger," replied Walesa.

WHEN THE PARISIAN MOB, half starved and deprived of justice and any sense of civic decency, stormed the Bastille on July 14, 1789, many of them were astonished by their own courage. "The attack," wrote the French historian Jules Michelet, "was in no way reasonable. It was an act of faith."

When the workers of the Lenin Shipyards, in Gdansk in August 1980, proclaimed their intention of remaining where they were, inside the gates of the yards, on a sit-down strike until they were granted by the authorities an independent trade union, they too were performing an act of faith. Reason ought to have told them their demands were impossible. Jacek Kuron, more than any other man in Poland, had worked for the day when the Polish workers would rise as a united movement to force changes from the government, but he was close to despair as the shipyard workers patiently listened to his arguments, and then rejected them.

Kuron was leader of KOR, the Committee for the Defense of the Workers, a group of ex-Marxist intellectuals who had come to the conclusion that the dissident movement in Russia and Eastern Europe, including Poland, was condemned to impotence. It might provide readable copy for Western newspapers but had little or no influence upon events in their own country.

Changes in society could only be brought about if the working class so willed it, and so it was to the working class that Kuron and his friends turned in order to seek salvation for Poland. A tough, short, barrel-chested man, Kuron was forty-five years old. His gravelly voice betrayed the only luxuries he permitted himself, Scotch whisky and French Gitane cigarettes, as he toured the country with his "Flying University," giving crash courses to factory workers in politics and philosophy. Kuron emphasized that workers' demands for more money and better conditions would only be met if they took up the demands of the intellectuals for free speech.

Polish workers had been betrayed in the past, he said, and that was only possible because writers and journalists were not allowed to publish the betrayal.

So, when August came around, the workers in Gdansk and those watching their progress all over the country were well prepared. This time, bread-and-butter issues ranked second in importance to the central demands for fundamental political change.

They insisted on an end to censorship and the release of all political prisoners. Above all they demanded, and it was the first article of the list they prepared for the government negotiators, a free trade union. This was "in no way reasonable." Kuron, their intellectual guru, had told them that it was impossible. Insisting on something that the government could not possibly accept, would either lead to total humiliation or a complete catastrophe, for certainly the Polish or the Russian Army would come in to disperse them. The workers listened to Kuron politely, and ignored him.

Patiently Kuron tried to explain. This was a workers' state. The Communist Party's only legitimacy rested on its claim that it represented the higher interests of the proletariat. It stood to reason that the Party could not possibly accept a free trade union, because it would imply that the proletariat required an independent organization to protect it from the Party.

By then, there were thousands in the shipyard and hundreds of thousands more outside, singing patriotic hymns and bringing food and bouquets of flowers. Lech Walesa, on August 14, had to climb over the factory wall in order to join the workers and he was very much in charge. At 9:00 A.M. on that hot Thursday morning, when it was touch and go whether there would be a strike at all, Walesa had emerged as if out of nowhere, pushed himself to the front of the crowd, and addressed the manager. "Do you know me? You should—you fired me. But I've worked here for years, and I've got a mandate from the crew. I proclaim," he said simply, "a sit-in strike."

Throughout the second half of August, the main gates to the yards looked like a strange mixture of a religious revival meeting, a gigantic political demonstration, and a pop music festival. At one stage the committee was prepared to settle for only half a loaf after negotiations with Tadeusz Fiszbach, the powerful First Secretary of the region and a man known for his moderation and reforming zeal. Walesa admitted afterward that he misjudged his people. He had called off the strike, but as he moved out toward the gate, someone shouted out: "You can't let us down, Lech." Walesa's extraordinary political antennae sensed that the whole workforce was prepared to go for broke. He turned around, went back to the committee, and said "The strike is still on; we haven't got anything yet."

Still the KOR activists desperately sought to defuse what they and everyone else could see was a desperately dangerous situation. Kuron had never mentioned the need for a free trade union, and yet here were the workers, telling the government that everything else was negotiable, but not that. It probably wouldn't have made any difference anyway, but with supreme irony, Jacek Kuron, the man who began it all, now ended up almost fighting in the government's corner on the strike committee. He was picked up at his home in Warsaw and, not for the first time in his life, taken to prison. He was released every forty-eight hours in order to save anyone the bother of charging him, and then re-arrested immediately. The dangerous rebel who was now (unknown to the security forces and the government), preaching moderation, had been effectively neutralized. Kuron was in his cell on August 31, in despair at the intransigence of the Gdansk workers when he was called to the office of a major in the UB, the Ministry of Public Security. The major stood up when Kuron entered and held out his hand for Kuron to shake. "Mr. Kuron," he said. "Congratulations, *we* have an independent trade union. You, of course, are free to go."

The totally unthinkable had happened. By sheer bravura, the Gdansk workers had changed the face of Poland forever. Whatever happened next, if Russia intervened or not, Poland and the Marxist-Leninist system of government could never be the same again. The strikers had compromised on only one point—that famous first article of what became known as the Gdansk Agreement. They struck out the word "free" because of its Western connotations, free world, Radio Free Europe, and so on, and agreed to "independent and self-governing" instead. So there it was NSZZ *Solidarnosc*—the independent, self-governing trade union, Solidarity.

In the excitement no one could even remember how the word solidarity came to be adopted, though the claims of authorship are now multiplying by the day. Those members of the strike committee who do not claim it for themselves say it was an accident. A graphic designer was called in to design a masthead for the daily strike sheet issued by the committee for the thousands sitting in and also for outside consumption. The designer had heard the workers talk about the need for solidarity, and so, asking no one, he designed what was supposed to be a symbol, with the Polish flag rising out of the "n" of *Solidarnosc.* Those who got the paper prepared on a factory duplicator assumed that its title was also the title of their organization, and so with the tail very much wagging the dog, that is how it turned out to be.

Those heady days in Gdansk, in view of what has happened in Poland since, seem a long time ago. Solidarity was a force in Polish life which nothing can erase. Even though the union was crushed, its achievements will outlive its persecutors and become a weapon of awesome power for the generation to follow. Its achievements were spectacular. The farmers got a free trade union, the students got a free students' union, the intellectuals had free speech, and the press became more independent than any other in the whole of the Warsaw Pact. Real forms of democracy were practiced for the first time in generations, even within the Communist Party. Nobody was afraid of speaking out, of saying exactly what they thought. It was an unnerving and an uplifting spectacle.

But however important all of that, what mattered a great deal more was that in Solidarity Poland possessed a legally recognized center of power outside the Party or the government. Of course Poland, like the rest of Eastern Europe, in theory at least had the outward appurtenances of a democratic state. There was a trade union movement, a judiciary whose independence was guaranteed by the constitution, local government bodies known as the Peoples' Councils, a Parliament and a Council of State to execute the functions of head of state, sometimes known as a "collegiate presidency," and a Council of Ministers, the supreme decision-making body in the country, and, finally, the government Praesidium, a kind of inner Cabinet of the more important ministers. School children were taught the various functions of these important sounding bodies and the press reported their deliberations at enormous length. This whole complex structure, employing thousands of people and using up whole forests of paper as reports shuffled back and forth, insofar as it exists today, is a ludicrous charade. There has been only one center of power in Poland, and that is the Politburo of the United Polish Workers' Party. The Politburo decides, they say in Poland, and everyone else jumps. It is difficult for any westerner to understand how debilitating it can be to work and live within such a system.

One example will suffice. A lecturer at Warsaw University in the mid-seventies (for understandable reasons, he does not wish his name to be used, so let us call him Karol) drew attention to the huge disparity between Western economies and the East. Karol suggested that one reason for this could be that Communist countries tended to reject a considerable body of work by modern economists all over the world on ideological rather than scientific grounds.

He was called before his dean and told that his view was "unacceptable" because Marxism was itself a science, and therefore all theories that differ from it must be pseudo-science. Though a Marxist himself, he rejected this analysis, continued teaching his courses, and was fired. Because there is no such thing as unemployment in a Communist country, there is also no such thing as unemployment pay—something of a catch-22 situation for Karol and many others like him. He quickly discovered that he was on the blacklist, not only of Warsaw University, but every university in the country, and so he began writing letters. He asked a lawyer to act for him against the university, alleging wrongful dismissal, but he was advised that no court could possibly uphold his case against the dean. His trade union referred the matter to the dean who had dismissed him for adjudication. When Karol demanded more positive action he was told that if he persisted he would be expelled from the union. He wrote to a member of the Polish Parliament whom he knew and was told that "your complaint appears to be a further example of the unhelpfulness which the dean has referred to. . . ." He wrote to the Minister of Education himself, complaining about his "illegal" dismissal and received a telephone call from an official who told him that his letter constituted a slander against the university and the educational system, and if he did not withdraw, he would be charged.

"I cannot begin to explain my sense of helplessness," Karol told me. "There was no one to whom I had any right of appeal at all. Because I was undesirable to one, I was undesirable to all. I discovered, what they no doubt had discovered years before, you don't need Stalinist methods of repression in order to repress."

To Karol and people like him Solidarity meant salvation: an organization that spoke for the individual in a way unheard-of in Communist Europe. A somewhat arid debate in Poland still centers on whether Solidarity should have contented itself with merely being a trade union in the Western tradition, fighting for such traditional rights as wages, working hours, factory safety, and so on, or whether it should have been a great deal more—a citizen's movement for the renewal of the whole nation. It is a question hardly worth talking about. Whatever the Communist Party or some people in Solidarity would have wished, Solidarity became so much more than a trade union, that retreat back into the old traditional forms was unthinkable. That this happened was a twentieth-century miracle. It seems unbelievable that a whole people, acting in coalition, without recourse to violence of any kind, mobilized themselves and destroyed the political structure of a totalitarian regime so thoroughly that it could only be saved by military intervention and virtual imprisonment of the entire nation. To describe Solidarity as a trade union is like describing Coca-Cola as a soft drink. Both descriptions are true. Yet they tell so little of the real story that they could not be more false.

Solidarity was a national crusade, a revolutionary movement of both political and spiritual renewal, the like of which I doubt the world has ever seen. The effect upon the nation was electrifying and heartwarming. "We may not have too much to eat," said an old lady who had just returned from queuing uncomplainingly for four hours for meat rations, "but it is possible to be proud to be Polish again."

"Man lives not by bread alone," it says in the Bible, a phrase which comes easily to a man not actually starving. They were not starving in Poland either in 1981, but the humorous forebearance of the average Pole to the extraordinary difficulties of day-to-day life was remarkable testimony to a people prepared to sacrifice a great deal for their dignity.

Out of a working population of 14 million, 10 million Poles joined Solidarity. That mass membership in itself, of course, caused trouble. "It would be a mistake to imagine," said a leading member of Solidarity's Warsaw Committee, "that Poland had ten million saints and they all joined Solidarity. But as we are a democratic organization, the membership is able to deal with those who misuse the new power they possess."

Sometimes that power was amusingly expressed. During a series of early negotiations between Solidarity and the government at the offices of the Council of State in Warsaw, the doors were pushed open by an army of tea ladies. They placed before every member of the Solidarity delegation a cup, poured the tea, and walked out. They were summoned back and asked why there was no tea for the ministers. "You look after our boys," these great men were told, "and then you'll get your tea."

Sometimes power was expressed crudely. A director of a factory outside Warsaw that has always had a good production record was constantly browbeaten by the local Solidarity leader, a young man still in his twenties and very much feeling his oats. "I am a Party member," the director told me, "but only because I had to join. I am the most qualified man in Poland for this job, but it couldn't be given to me unless I at least nominally agreed to join the Party. I used to have some problems from the local Party office before, but I was able to deal with them quite brusquely, and there was not much they could do. They knew I knew my job, and they would have difficulties in finding anyone to replace me. But Solidarity, which I'm much in favor of, as represented by this young man, doesn't seem to understand that. What I'm having to go through is a form of persecution. I shall leave soon, the situation has become intolerable."

A director of a theater told me that in the forties he was forced to accept a workers' committee, consisting of every one from the cleaning woman to the stagehands, sitting in judgment over his productions. "When that period came to an end, I thought we'd never see the like again in Poland. But now some Solidarity members at my theater want to have exactly the same kind of control over my work. They call it democracy, well if that is democracy, you can keep it."

Poland's Union of Artists appeared to be moving back, without recognizing the implications, to a Stalinist, conformist art by insisting that they alone had the right to decide what exhibitions should hang in the galleries and museums of Poland, instead of leaving such decisions to the individual judgment and taste of the galleries' directors. They called this democracy, but the effect would inevitably have been that a Central Committee of Artists would have decreed the artistic tastes for the whole nation. The time would have come, as I myself warned a member of their executive committee in Warsaw, when an artist who did not go along with the prevailing wind would never have been shown.

There was rarely any acknowledgment in Solidarity and this was a great weakness, that danger lay in exchanging one kind of orthodoxy for another. "Already," said one journalist, in August 1981, a year after the Gdansk Agreement "you have got to be a bit careful about criticizing Solidarity in print, because immediately you are accused by colleaguges of 'selling out.' Remember we have been ruled by a totalitarian government for the last forty years, and totalitarianism can be a difficult habit to kick."

The truly astonishing thing about Solidarity was the way it reached into every corner of society, which is why, now, it cannot be simply wished away. While in Warsaw I was invited to meet some of the leaders of the new independent students' union. They were charming young men and women, looking exactly like their Western counterparts—bearded, rather scruffy, and very intense, working in a rundown office building, every wall of which was covered with posters or political graffiti.

Most of the talk was of the official students' union, which had dominated Polish student life since the war. Not knowing that my wife spoke fluent Polish, they argued in Polish, in my presence, about the number they should give me of their membership. The student leader who proposed telling me the truth—about half the student population—was shouted down by the others.

"We're bound to have 90 percent eventually," argued one, "so let's tell him 90 percent." So that was the figure I wrote down in my notebook, as well as their long catalogue of complaints against the "vicious neo-Stalinism" of the rival organization. When I discovered I had not always been told the truth, for reasons which did not seem to me to be good enough, I insisted on going to see the official students' union. I had been well conditioned in advance to expect to find a nest of young, hard-eyed, Communist fanatics in Stalin's last redoubt. Instead, as I entered the pleasant modern office building, the first thing that caught my eye was an enormous Solidarity poster on the bulletin board, announcing a forthcoming meeting and then, elsewhere, any number of Solidarity election posters for the Warsaw region. I expressed my surprise to the twenty-six-year-old head of the union's cultural department, a member of the Party, certainly, but far from being the sort of ideologue I had expected to encounter. Yes, he said, nearly everyone here, including every single member of my department—the largest in the organization—is a member of Solidarity. But, I persisted, don't they realize that the independent union backed by Solidarity would like nothing better than to drive you out of business? He shrugged his shoulder. "That's Poland," he said.

Because of Solidarity, throughout 1981 Poland was in political turmoil, an experience as exhilarating as it was exhausting. One Western journalist likened the atmosphere at a Solidarity meeting to watching an Eisenstein film of Lenin addressing the workers on the factory floor. The first Congress of the Warsaw District Branch of Solidarity (the largest in the country) reminded me of how I had always imagined it must have been in St. Petersburg after the czar had been overthrown, when Kerensky was addressing the Duma and everything desirable seemed possible.

Wherever one went, it was impossible to escape the heady atmosphere of hope that the mere existence of Solidarity had created. The first thing that anyone who knew Poland or any other Eastern European country, noticed was the astonishing willingness of people to talk about everything. The Poles were always, from the mid-fifties onward, considerably more outspoken than their neighbors, but nevertheless a prudent reserve always existed between ordinary people and foreigners, and it only lifted when they became good friends. That reserve completely evaporated, affecting not only opponents of the regime but seemingly the whole country. A distinguished Communist journalist I have known for years, and whom I met both in Poland and when he visited the West, was a changed man when I saw him in Warsaw in 1981. Before we were friends, but I was always aware of a barrier between us. I felt there were certain subjects I ought not to broach, and sometimes his answers to questions I asked were not only untruthful, but known to him to be untruthful. Inevitably this imposed a distance between us, probably not discernible to an outsider who didn't know us both well, who might have observed the effusiveness of our greeting, but it was there, and we both recognized it. This time he was a different man. His opinions had not changed one iota. A hardliner, he was impatient with the government's inability to do anything about the "anarchy" he saw around him. Yet he spoke with freedom and a candor that astonished me. He talked about ministers and Party officials he knew exactly in the way a Western journalist might, indiscreet, savagely funny, and extremely well informed. Well, I said at the end of a marvelous evening, if Solidarity has achieved nothing else at least it has loosened your tongue. "Yes," he replied quickly, "they've got an awful lot to answer for," and with a chuckle he disappeared into the night.

Inevitably, however, this being Poland, where for every two Poles you find three political parties, Solidarity itself was always a far from united organization. Realistically, it would have been hard to expect otherwise. It sprang into being overnight and in no time at all had absorbed 80 percent of the working population into its ranks. If there were a unifying theme, it was vague: an overwhelming desire by the Poles to reform their system of government and way of life.

But how this should be done produced almost as many answers as there were members of Solidarity. As the first flush of enthusiasm passed, hard questions were put to the national leadership, and there were no easy answers.

The biggest problem existed from the beginning and was never resolved: Should Solidarity have remained an outside pressure group, a kind of permanent Opposition Party which eschewed all desire for office, or should it have taken some responsibility for helping to run an economy as ramshackle as one could hope to find? There were traps for Solidarity in either course. If it had remained simply a pressure group, then the view which was already quite commonly expressed even outside the Party that it was time the Polish worker stopped talking and began working again, would become more strident. If Solidarity became part of the process of government, then it risked sharing the blame if things did not pick up quickly enough.

The size of the organization produced tensions. While I was in Warsaw, Solidarity printers were threatening strike action against their employer for more pay, which eventually they got, but it was an event with great potential for embarrassment. Later there was an enormous row in Gdansk where Solidarity has its national headquarters. Solidarity had outgrown its premises, and the Town Council offered the Hotel Monopol, opposite the main station, which, it said, could be easily converted and would be ideal for the purpose.

Solidarity agreed, but found itself in direct conflict with the Monopol's 300 workers, who would lose their jobs if the hotel closed. A member of Solidarity's Praesidium reported how uneasy he felt when, together with the hotel's management, he met the workers. Suddenly, he said, I found myself sitting on the wrong side of the table. At a meeting with government representatives about the state of the economy, a minister turned to the Solidarity delegation and said: "Most Western observers believe that many of our industries are hopelessly overmanned and inefficient. What could Solidarity's position be if we were to propose large scale lay-offs?" He received in reply what he later described as a bout of coughing so severe that he was concerned about his visitors' health.

At the same time, some members of Solidarity were impatient at the slow pace of reform and the willingness of the national leadership to accept compromise solutions when the strike weapon, which has been so extraordinarily effective, could have been wielded more frequently to introduce the sweeping changes they were after. These men are a new breed. They wholeheartedly despise the European

New Left, which believes it has found in them blood brothers. "They come here with their bright shining eyes and their ludicrous Trotskyist-Marxist theories, believing that they are on our side. We let them take us out to dinner and buy a few vodkas and politely agree with everything they say. They send us the articles or books they have written, based on their conversations with us, and we have an evening of light entertainment at their expense. We have so far outgrown their jejeune syndicalism or Trotskyism that to us they are but school children. Marxism is really only taken seriously anymore in the West. Still if these people want to support us, why not."

Nevertheless, it is easy to see why the New Left should find echoes of Trotsky's theories of permanent revolution in some of the activities of Solidarity's non-Communist left wing.

Impatient and aware of the structural flaws in Polish society, which Solidarity has not even gotten around to discussing, they wanted, as one student put it to me, to make one gigantic bonfire and then start all over again. "Solidarity talks about the renewal of the nation. But you can't have renewal without getting rid of the old. That is what we must address ourselves to."

"What we must create," said another, "is revolution by election. We have seen how much a mass movement has achieved in this country. Now we must go forward by harnessing that mass movement to a democratic rebirth of the nation. If everyone, from members of the Politburo down, who has an official position in the country, from factory managers to trade union chiefs to local party secretaries right down to foremen on production lines, made themselves availabe for election, then a new nation would emerge with powerful leaders, sustained by the knowledge that they had the people's support and able to call upon them, as their representatives, to make sacrifices for the common good. This process is beginning. It is astonishing how well the electoral process works. In my region the Communist Party had its first free elections for delegates to the 1981 Party Congress in its history. I'm not a Party member, but I wrote down on a sheet of paper the candidates I would have chosen, from the point of view of their qualifications, their track records, and their honesty. Everyone of them was elected. You see, people if trusted do not behave stupidly. The trouble is, they are rarely trusted."

At the opposite extreme were Solidarity's conservatives—men and women who don't want to rock the boat. They seized the opportunity that Solidarity presented to press for internal liberalization, but who quickly felt things were getting out of hand. Zofia Grzyb (they made sure that the West couldn't find a Polish heroine to sit beside Walesa by finding someone with an absolutely unpronounceable name, said the Warsaw wits), though a member of Solidarity, elected to the Politburo of the Communist Party, was typical of many.

She saw distinguished service in the Party for years when, unaccountably, she put her head on the block and joined Solidarity soon after its formation. It is said that she was disgusted by the corruption of Party officials and saw in Solidarity a unique opportunity to clean house. Nevertheless, shortly after becoming a member of the Politburo she attacked Solidarity for not being the same organization it was when she joined. What she meant was that Solidarity had ceased to be a trade union fighting for workers' rights but was taking on an increasingly political function. As a Communist, she could not approve of that.

Many internal tensions came to the surface at a private meeting of the Solidarity Praesidium in the Spring of 1981. At the center, chewing his pipe, intervening rarely but with telling effect, sat Lech Walesa, the very embodiment of Solidarity not only in Poland but also the outside world. Leading the case against him was Karol Modzelewski, who in 1964, together with Jacek Kuron, had been imprisoned for publication of "The Open Letter to the Party." Few documents as significant as this have emerged from Eastern Europe. Written by two young men, both research scholars in philosophy, both well versed in Marxism, it was one of the most damning indictments of Russian and Eastern European Communism ever written by insiders. Not only was the letter a formidable critique of the system, it also foretold with remarkable percipience and extraordinary accuracy the course of events which led to the formation of Solidarity. State ownership of the means of production, in practice, meant that ownership was exercised by those who influenced the state's decisions on economic matters, said the authors. This political power was connected with power over the process of production and the distribution of the product. This led to the power of the bureaucracy. To whom did this power belong in Poland? To one monolithic party, the United Workers' Party.

"All essential decisions are made first by the Party, and only later in the offices of the government; no important decisions can be made and carried out without the approval of the Party authorities. This is the so-called leading role of the Party. But did the Party guarantee the interests of the working class? And what opportunities did the working class have to influence the decisions of the state apparatus?

Outside the Party—none. For the ruling Party is monopolistic. It is impossible for the working class to organize itself outside the Party, and to formulate, propagate, and struggle for the realization of their programs, other ways to divide the national product, or political concepts other than those of the ruling Party. The monopoly of the Party in organizing the working class is guarded by the entire state apparatus of power and force; administration, political police, the attorney general's office, the courts, and also the political organizations led by the Party, which unmask and nip in the bud all attempts to undermine the leading role of the Party."

The conclusion was devastating and extraordinarily prophetic. Just as the economic crisis could not be overcome on the basis of the current production relationship, so also the general social crisis could not be overcome within the framework of the prevailing social relationship. The only possible solution was the overthrow of the prevailing system. *"Revolution is a necessity for development. Since it was the working class that entered into direct conflict with the central political bureaucracy in the sphere of production relationships, it had to be the working class that was the chief and leading force of revolution. By the nature of things, the revolution that will overthrow the bureaucratic system is a proletarian revolution. However, this revolution would not necessarily mean that the working class would take up arms.*

"Revolution is the act of an enormous majority of society directed against the rule of the minority. It is accompanied by a crisis of political power and by a weakening of the apparatus of coercion. That is why it does not have to be carried out by force of arms."

This tract, written seventeen years previously, could be taken as the bible for Solidarity. Yet, Modzelewski, the man who was coauthor and had been imprisoned for it, along with Kuron, and who had all those years worked until his predictions came to pass, turned on Lech Walesa and scathingly accused him of leading a movement that had come to resemble a feudal monarchy with Walesa as its king.

It was a bitter moment for Modzelewski as he tendered his resignation, complaining that too much power was concentrated in the hands of the king and the king's men. At the same time, Andrzej Zielinski, a founding member of the Flying University who had been dismissed from his teaching job at Warsaw University in 1976 for political activities, was now dismissed by Solidarity as the Secretary to the Committee. Suddenly, and with savagery, the men who had worked and suffered most over the years to create the conditions which brought Solidarity into being were being squeezed out. Said one KOR activist, not without bitterness: "My wife and children were not too well looked after in the years that I fought for workers' rights. It now looks as if they are not going to be too well looked after because of workers' rights."

Sitting above the commotion, imperturbable and apparently unassailable, remained the remarkable Lech Walesa. Walesa, one Pole said to me, is a bit like Winston Churchill. The further away from him you are, the more attractive he appears.

For a man who, if he is to be believed, has never read a book, he has all the virtues and vices of the peasant stock from which he comes: a family man (he has seven children), he also enjoys a night out with the boys; a man who can combine both humility and boastfulness in the same sentence, he is surely one of the most remarkable figures of our time. Every one of Solidarity's intellectual advisers, whether or not they get on with him personally, has been astonished by his brain power. He remembers everything anyone has ever said to him, said one bemused university professor, and he seems to analyze and synthesize on the run.

"One of the reasons some people think him arrogant is that because he has had no formal education, he has never been obliged to take an examination, and he really has no idea quite how brilliant a mind he has. Consequently he believes that everyone thinks as quickly as he does, and he is simply driven mad with frustration when he comes across what he regards as unnecessary stupidity."

That he is arrogant there can be no doubt. Despite his protestations to the contrary, there can be no doubt either that he enjoyed and encouraged the personality cult that built up around him. The only thing astonishing about either is that anyone should be surprised.

Lech Walesa is usually portrayed as "the unemployed electrician pitchforked overnight into power and the world's headlines," which makes good copy, but is less than accurate. A man with charismatic personality who is also superbly articulate, he believed in the fight he was waging and did not need Solidarity to propel him to the front. Years ago he was already well known in Gdansk as a powerful labor organizer. His and the Polish workers' baptism of fire came in 1970. It politicized him and a whole generation of Polish workers. With political ineptitude stunning in its arrogance, the government, without warning, imposed a large increase in food prices the week before Christmas, at a time when every Polish family buys huge quantities of food to prepare the traditional feast of twelve courses on Christmas Eve, without which Christmas is impossible to imagine.

The workers of the Lenin Shipyard, including Walesa, were already in ferment because they feared a cut in real wages due to new piece-rate premiums that were being introduced. The new food prices proved to be the last straw.

On Monday, December 14, in the huge shipyard employing 50,000 people, though there was no prearranged plan, marched as one man out through the main gates and to the local Party headquarters, the center of power and decision-making in the region. Singing revolutionary songs and patriotic hymns, they were met by a junior official who was unable to promise them anything. By nightfall a peaceful demonstration, fueled by reports that some of the strike leaders had been arrested, had become violent. Fighting broke out sporadically throughout the town as small groups of militia tried unsuccessfully to break up the crowd. By Tuesday, the situation was completely out of control. Workers from neighboring shipyards joined in and Gdansk, the ancient Hanseatic city, was in the grip of revolution. By 11:00 in the morning the authorities gave permission for troops and police to use firearms and bring in tanks and armored cars. It was an astonishing scene. A helicopter had to be brought in to lift Party officials from the roof of the Party building, rescuing them from the hands of Polish workers who, it was feared, might seek personal retribution from their hated masters. Eventually, the building was set alight, and as heavy armor cleared the area, the glow of the bonfire of the Communist Party itself could be seen from miles around.

On the next day, Wednesday, troops surrounded the Lenin Ship-yards where 5,000 workers, still demanding a reply from the management to their demands, were warned by loudspeaker that anyone who tried to break the cordon would be shot. Several did and were killed.

Attention now shifted to nearby Gydnia, a port and a seaside resort. Workers at the Paris Commune Shipyard issued a three point ultimatum—recognition of the strike committee, release of those arrested earlier in the week, and the acceptance of their economic demands—but they too were answered by the authorities sending in troops to occupy the yard.

On Thursday morning, December 17, tanks and troops were on alert in the middle of Gdynia as the men arrived by train for work. If this show of force was supposed to frighten them, not only did it not work, but it had the opposite effect of that intended. Infuriated, the crowds turned on the soldiers, and after a six-hour battle, hundreds lay wounded and several dead on the cobblestones of the city. Helicopters hovered above, tossing tear gas grenades, tanks fired mixtures of live and blank ammunition, it was full-scale civil war. On the same day the workers of Sczecin, Poland's seventh largest city, hundreds of miles away from the main action and close to the East German border, joined in. They too marched on Party headquarters, after breaking through a cordon of militia at the factory gates, and, like their colleagues in Gdansk, set fire to the Party headquarters. Again, the death roll was high and the number of injured—often men taken by the militia into small side streets and viciously beaten—was horrifyingly large. Wladyslaw Gomulka proclaimed a state of emergency and, it is said, asked Leonid Brezhnev for help to put down the insurrection. For whatever reason, Brezhnev refused, and on December 18, four days after the disturbances began, while defending his policy of armed repression before the Politburo, Gomulka, who had come to power fourteen years earlier with the hopes of the entire nation resting upon his shoulders, suffered a cerebral hemorrhage. The next day his support crumbled, and he was asked to resign his post as First Secretary and was suspended from the Central Committee. On December 19, Edward Gierek, tall and good-looking, with the appearance of a Western businessman rather than a Communist *apparachik*, was invited to take his place. Food price rises were temporarily rescinded, the Politburo was completely restructured, and talks began immediately with the workers on the whole range of their grievances.

Lech Walesa, one of the top leaders of the Gdansk workers, was not the only Pole to grasp the significance of what had occurred—namely that workers in a workers' state possess a moral authority that if they care to exercise it, can overwhelm the government itself. In the years that followed, Edward Gierek, slowly at first and then increasingly, went back on the promises made following the Gdansk explosion. Lech Walesa and his associates began analyzing how the lessons of Gdansk '70 could be applied to the future. Initially, he tried to work within the system by becoming an official delegate of the shipyard to the government-sponsored trade union. But when he behaved like a Western trade unionist and presented a list of genuine workers' grievances, he was peremptorily fired from both the union and his job at the factory. By then, however, he had built up a considerable personal following. Here was one trade unionist, the workers saw, who took the function of trade unionism seriously. In 1978, with help from the Flying University, he helped to establish an illegal organization called the Baltic Free Trade Unions. He was sufficiently trusted by rank-and-file workers to be able to proselytize his concepts at large gatherings and small, in workers' flats, and in meeting halls under the noses of the authorities, and sometimes even in the woods surrounding the city. Thus, the prevailing view that Solidarity was a spontaneous explosion of workers' grievances is wide of the mark. While no one involved guessed that it would take off like brushfire, nevertheless the confrontation, the strike that sparked it, and the demands the men made were mapped out in advance by KOR and leaders like Walesa. It stemmed directly from the experience of Gdansk '70, which produced no long-term solutions for the country because the workers were not properly organized. The demands they made on the authorities had not been thought through, and the nation's intellectuals, unprepared, had stood aloof, and a previously disciplined work force was so provoked that it became a mob. One of the first of Solidarity's demands was a memorial to the men who died in the earlier riots. This memorial, a massive indictment of Communist rule, now stands at the gates of the Lenin Shipyards. The men were Solidarity's first martyrs, and the movement was determined that they should be honored by all of Poland.

Things were different in August 1980. Initially, the authorities believed the Gdansk workers could be bought off with more money. What they failed to understand was the significance behind the initial demand: the reinstatement of Anna Walentynowicz, a tough crane-operator in her mid-fifties—Pani Anya (Mrs. Anya) to the crews—a woman who was described as possessing the outward charm and gentleness of a Polish granny and the inner strength of a Polish hussar. Pani Anya had been a member of the original 1970 strike committee and had subsequently been fired for membership in the Baltic Free Trade Unions. Management hastily agreed to reemploy her in order to avert a strike and even sent a car to pick her up. It was a significant moment in the history of trade unionism in Eastern Europe, for the authorities were acknowledging for the first time ever an employee's right to be a member of a union other than the official one. This was of more than symbolic importance, for Pani Anya immediately joined the strike committee headed by Lech Walesa. The Polish August, and the events that stemmed from it, had begun.

People in the factory and then in the country who had not heard about Walesa, were soon to be made aware of him. When Vice Premier Mieczyslaw Jagielski came to negotiate with the strike committee, the workers insisted that the talks should be broadcast to the strikers outside. For years everyone in Poland had deferred to government ministers. When they appeared on radio and television, journalists fawned over them, never daring to ask any pointed questions, always content with bland replies to questions agreed to in advance with the minister.

If Walesa never did anything else but break that suffocating tradition, he would deserve to be remembered for that and that alone. And that is what he did. First to whistles of astonishment and then to cheers from the workers outside, he tore into the unprepared Jagielski, who, according to friends, has never completely recovered from the shock. Jagielski insisted on calling Walesa "Mr. President," apparently to disarm him, said: "These strikes must be terminated." Replied Walesa, "They should have been stopped a long time ago, but we have been waiting for you. What is your position on our twenty-one claims?"

Jagielski sat back and began with all the smugness of his position: "Allow me to begin by making some general points. . . ." Walesa interrupted. "No, I want a concrete answer, point by point." Jagielski again sought to bring the discussion around to generalities, but again Walesa cut it sharply. "What sort of man are you, Mr. Minister, to come here telling us such rubbish?" Here was the leader the Polish workers had been looking for, and they rallied around him.

There were complaints that the Western media had concentrated on Walesa at the expense of able men elsewhere, many of whom were even more deeply involved in pre-Gdansk agitation than he. Indeed, around the country one met a number of highly impressive and extraordinary young men. The leader of Solidarity in the Mazowsze region (which includes Warsaw and seven surrounding counties and is the largest in the Union), Zbigniew Bujak was only 27 when he evaded arrest in December 1981 and became leader of Solidarity underground. Even in his own region of Gdansk, during the days of the old Baltic Free Trade Union, Walesa was inclined to sit and listen, not involving himself too much in the discussions that raged night after night. There were others, more powerful and active than he. Yet even his critics were forced to acknowledge that Walesa was an original who got his way by a judicious mixture of charm, toughness, resilience, and ease of manner, whether he is addressing Pope or peasant, ordinary Polish workers or recalcitrant members of his own committee. He is a bad speaker, but a great orator. He seldom, if ever, used notes, and his speeches were badly constructed, tending to grind gears as he switched from topic to topic, yet for all that, he was a spellbinder. He used humor, sustained by a natural working-man's lyricism that summoned up extraordinary images apparently at will. It is difficult to analyze what qualities make a natural leader, but in Walesa's case there was no such problem. For all his faults, and he will be the first to admit he has many, he is an honest man and is perceived to be so by his fellow countrymen. He was never seen in public without a badge of the Virgin Mary on his lapel and a crucifix around his neck. Wherever he was, he made sure that he attended Mass in the morning. In the early days, some of his intellectual advisers and some of his closest colleagues were embarrassed by these outward displays of piety, and Walesa was advised to tone it down. "People may think you are a reactionary," he was told. "But I am not a reactionary," he said simply. "Yes, but people will think it." "If I am not, does it matter what people think? The trouble with this country is we have too many people pretending to be something they are not. I am a religious person and I am afraid of nobody but God."

There can be little doubt that when Lech Walesa had his own time of trial, taken into custody, and facing daily attempts to persuade him to go on television to lend the regime his unique authority, it was this faith, so often mocked, that saved him.

Lech Walesa was seriously at odds with his own Praesidium when the generals clamped down upon the country. During the first weeks of December, he was warning anyone who cared to listen that disaster loomed. A more "flexible" man might have been able to persuade himself that, having been overridden by his own people, he would be justified in seeking new alliances elsewhere. Many people, especially in the top echelons of Solidarity, believed that Walesa's commitment to democracy was skin-deep. He has shamed them all by his stubborn insistence that without his Praesidium around him he cannot speak for Solidarity, the leadership of which was democratically elected by its membership.

For all the faults of his organization, Lech Walesa has stood firm on one sacred principle—democracy. His strength provides hope for the people of Poland and ensures for him, this uneducated working-man, a place in the pantheon of those through the ages who have fought and suffered for the rights of man.

10
The Countryside

✂

QUESTION: *"Why don't the peasants produce more meat?"*
ANSWER: *"They're moving so quickly down the road to Socialism that the cattle can't keep pace."*

YOU CAN SEE the spire of the church from miles around as the countryside flattens out on the drive from Warsaw. The road, off the highway, is narrow and bumpy. In every little hamlet, chickens seem to be everywhere, pecking nervously at the ground as roosters march imperiously around them. Geese and ducks are much in evidence too —the former in line of march on military exercise around every bend, and the ducks wallowing in small, manmade ponds typical of the larger farms of the region. There is plenty of wildlife too. A buzzard hovers menacingly above, looking for field mice amidst the corn. Suddenly a partridge, followed by its young, scuttles across the road, head bent forward in fevered concentration, and disappears into the undergrowth. But it is the extraordinary range of colors of the Polish countryside that truly astonish. The fields are a riot of blues, purples, and pinks, and red from the poppies that grow everywhere, and a lot of yellow, bright and vivid. You see women at work, often taking a single cow to pasture, pulling the reluctant beast on a halter, or bending down sowing, weeding, and digging. Wherever you look, a Millet painting comes to life. Your car slows down behind a horse-drawn cart taking a family to the nearest town for shopping. A similar cart comes the other way, this one full of animal foodstuffs. It will be hosed down later, so that it too can double as family transport, probably on Sunday to take father, mother, and children to the church toward which we are driving.

A hundred years ago, before the tractor, the combine, fertilizers, before weed-killers and insecticides, before battery farming, and the hundred and one other things that have turned modern farming into an industry, this is how the European countryside looked. Western European and American agriculture is immensely more efficient, and less labor-intensive, and produces yields five times more per acre than the Polish farming community. No one who lives in countries where food is super-abundant and comes to Poland, where it is desperately scarce, would wish it any other way. Yet it is well to admit the price we pay for modern agriculture. To drive along the Berlin corridor to West Germany from Poland is to travel forward in time from a world of savage and dazzling beauty to a land where nature has been tamed and homogenized.

The beauty of the Polish landscape is little consolation (though it is some) to the people in the cities who don't have enough to eat. It is as well to go and see now, for it is assuredly doomed as modern agricultural techniques take over from the horse-drawn plough in fields where only natural fertilizer has ever been used and the hedgegrows have never tasted modern chemicals.

Compared to the gentle purity of the landscape it dominates, the church built only a few years ago is vulgar in its excessive showmanship. It is enormous—the largest building for miles around—built on two stories with a bright red roof, white bricks, a separate metal belltower, a larger-than-life-size crucifix in a grotto by the entrance, and a huge multicolored fresco over the porch. Inside it has shining new, brightly polished marble floors, beautifully built wooden pews, and a simple altar whose clean lines belie the unnecessary fussiness of the exterior.

That a church is here (in Zbrosza Duza, about twenty miles outside of Warsaw) at all, is something of a miracle. When Father Czeslaw Sadlowski arrived here in 1969, at the age of thirty-one, there was nothing. The primate of Poland, Cardinal Wyszynski, came down from Warsaw to consecrate a cow-shed to use for saying Mass. But the local authorities forbade it on the grounds that a cow-shed is for cows. If Warsaw had wanted Mass to be heard here, then it would have agreed to have built a church. The priest got around the ban easily.

Father Sadlowski rode around his parish holding services in people's homes, most frequently by horse-drawn vehicles, but occasionally on the back of an old motorbike. Because the distances were vast and the method of travel slow, he was forced much of the time to stay overnight with his parishioners in their dark, dank hovels.

He discovered that many of the houses were rat-infested and had no electricity. Most of the homes didn't have running water, and sanitary conditions were deplorable. There were only one or two stores for the whole area, selling only the most basic of commodities, and there was no public transportation to take people to the nearest town thirty kilometers away. There were no cars at all, and even if there had been any, they would have been of little use in a parish that had not a single hard-surfaced road. The doctor would come occasionally from the town, but in winter the journey was simply impossible. There was a dentist in the town, too, but he was known as a butcher, and in any case, he never left his office. The children had to walk miles to school and didn't bother once the snows began. In the whole of the parish there was no mechanized farm equipment and two TV sets provided the only organized entertainment for the whole community. In short, here in a modern European state, a significant proportion of its citizenry lived in precisely the way their ancestors had a hundred years before.

Sadlowski, the son of a small farmer (more prosperous than most), had never been interested in politics, although his teachers at school had encouraged other children to denounce his father as a "Kulak" (a usage, borrowed from the Russians by Polish Communists, meaning a wealthy peasant landowner), because he owned fourteen hectares of land. But his experience with his parishioners, living in their homes and sharing their lives, politicized him to a remarkable degree.

In the years to come, Father Sadlowski ran into trouble with the local militia, the government, and the ecclesiastical authorities, who first advised and then warned him that the Church did not look kindly on priests who dabbled in politics. He defied them all, and started a revolution that altered the face of Poland, and rocked the entire Communist world to its foundations.

Father Sadlowski's Polish farmers are, after the Party, the Russians, and the Church, the fourth major power bloc inside Poland. This is not only because over 20 percent of the population still live on the land (before the war 60 percent did so), or because one of Poland's main export trades has traditionally been agricultural produce. It is because, of all sections of Polish society, the farmers represent the great traditions of the past. With no organization of their own until recent times, the farmers have most consistently, courageously, and successfully fought and then defeated the Party's attempt to socialize Polish society. Their efforts have exceeded that of every other section of the population—the intellectuals and writers, the university professors and journalists, the factory workers and the industrial proletariat, even the young reformers.

The Lech Walesas of Poland receive the sole credit for defeating the ancien régime. Yet their victory was only possible because Poland's farmers refused to be collectivized, battled against forced sales, and maintained the old traditions. The farmers kept alive the spirit of non-cooperation during the long periods when most Poles were prepared wearily to acquiesce with a regime they knew to be incompetent, to possess no moral authority to rule, and in whose fundamental philosophy the large majority did not agree. As long as the Party could make no progress in its frequent attempts to collectivize the land (a goal quickly achieved elsewhere in the Communist bloc), the road to Socialism was hopelessly blocked. The Russians understood this perfectly well, and from Stalin onward have put immense pressure on the Poles to bring their agriculture into line with the rest of Eastern Europe. For their part, Polish Communist leaders—and they all tried—promised to act, but always came up against the farmers' implacable will, and every Polish government with collectivization in mind was eventually forced to retreat. Because of the farmers' courage, the speed of Poland's development along Communist lines was seriously abated, and it is from that, that all else has followed.

Poland is the last great peasant country in Europe. The process of migration from the countryside to the cities, which was completed in northern Europe at least a hundred years ago, has still far from run its course in Poland. An English academic wrote in the seventies of watching "the unforgettable, medieval scene of a harvest-making near Krakow where black-robed nuns had tucked their skirts into their garters to wield a flail and help with the threshing before a gathering storm." Wherever you go in Poland, you see the earth being turned by an iron plough pulled by a horse. Cows graze in ones or twos, staked out on the roadside by an old woman. You see seed planted by hand, and the harvest cut by sickle (which many Polish peasants still insist is more efficient than a combine). Many of the people, we don't know how many, still live in the kind of log cabins whose methods of construction would be recognized by any American pioneer of the Old West. In the poorest homes, chickens, goats, and other domestic animals live in one room, while the family lives in another.

However, the casual use of the word "peasant" to describe Poland's huge army of small-holders is not only misleading but also misses the point why Polish small farmers have proved to be so obdurate in their dealings with their government. Few observers seem to be aware of the existence of an entire social class that is still there, but has completely vanished everywhere else, that once was of immense social, political, and economic importance for the whole of Europe.

In Poland today, there are whole villages, especially in the eastern part of the country, where the last genuine survivors of the medieval European gentry can be found—the knights and squires who rode out to battle with their lords, and in return were granted small parcels of land. Impoverished now, of course, they still cling to their semi-noble heritage and their allegiance to Church and land. Since their king was withdrawn from them, they do not easily accept any other temporal authority.

Most Polish names ending in -ski (ska in the feminine), also -cki and -icz, denote a member of the old gentry class. In Norman French they were the esquires, shortened to esq. In Polish that became -ski. One cannot now be absolutely certain that every "ski" is genuine, because in the nineteenth century many families added the suffix for reasons of snobbery. But in the countryside, where a change of name could not have gone unobserved, every "-ski" can trace the origins of the family's name back well into the fifteenth century. In the rest of Europe, the old gentry was remorselessly swallowed up by the rise of the city bourgeoisie, a class they quickly joined. This never occurred in Poland.

Up to the fifteenth century, Poland served as the granary of Europe —wheat was the source of wealth of the nation and its great landed estates. As cities and towns began to grow in size and attract young men from the countryside everywhere else on the continent, Poland feared that similar movements off the land would beggar the nation. Laws were passed to stop this happening. At first it was decreed that only one son of a gentry family could leave the country and go into trade in the cities. Then these laws were made even more Draconian, and only one man from each community could leave for the city every year. Those who broke the law lost their status as members of the gentry and all privileges, such as the vote. The effect in the long term was to be catastrophic for the development of the country. With the gentry excluded from trade, it was taken over by foreigners, especially Germans and then by Jews. By the time of the first great partition in 1772, when Frederick the Great of Prussia proposed to divide the Polish lands among Prussia, Russia, and Austria, the Poles themselves had to realize that wealth, as represented by the new cities through trade and manufacturing, had gone to outsiders, leaving the Poles increasingly pauperized in their own country. The law was changed, but too late, for the country was partitioned. If this had not been the case, custom, practice, and tradition would still have ensured that the gentry of all rank remained in their rural backwaters, having nothing to do with the social and financial dynamite of industrialization. Dealing in money was regarded as beneath contempt, leaving the land as surrendering one's birthright. The gentry became the last defiant champions of medievalism, confronting the modern world. The gentry remained where they were, becoming poorer and poorer every succeeding generation. Those who did leave the villages did so as members of a poverty-wracked intelligentsia, writers or poets. Although they provided the country with one of the most vibrant intellectual elites in all of Europe, nevertheless they were as guilty as those who remained on the farms in ensuring that the rise of an urban middle class, so important in political and social development elsewhere in the industrialized world, did not happen in Poland.

In the rest of Europe the minor gentry joined and usually prospered in the new middle class. In Poland, alone in all of Europe, they retained their identity. One can see the effect everywhere. The manners and customs of medieval Europe and the age of chivalry are still evident in Poland. When a Pole meets a woman, he will lightly kiss her hand. They will always address each other formally. In this people's republic, the old styles of address and manners, the customs and traditions that were once common in all of Europe among the gentry, are still strong and show no sign of passing away.

"In the rest of Europe," says a Polish sociologist, "the rougher style of the bourgeoisie pushed out the old customs of the gentry. The so-called age of chivalry produced an almost stylized form of conduct between people of the gentry class. It has long disappeared everywhere else but here in Poland."

Some 15 percent of Polish villages are today gentry villages. In outward appearance they are no different from peasant villages. The same grinding poverty is evident in both. The old gentry and the peasants wear the same clothes, live in the same kind of houses, care for the same area of land, use exactly the same techniques. The sociologist quoted above spent some time in a gentry village to see if he could discern any difference between the two cultures—and came away with three. Gentry women wear gloves when they work in the fields and hats when they go to church on Sunday. They call each other "sir" or "my lady," (as now do the inhabitants of the big cities, who take their customs from the gentry), but are careful to call peasants in the next village by their surname only. And, finally, to this day, though there is absolutely no economic or intellectual difference between them, a girl from the gentry village will hardly ever, and then only under pain of being cut completely out of the life of her family, marry a peasant.

All of this is of more than mere curiosity value. It goes a long way in explaining why the Communists have had such difficulty in collectivizing Polish agriculture, a process accomplished with comparative ease in the rest of Eastern Europe. For they had to deal not just with a peasantry, and all the innate conservatism of peasants everywhere, but with people who, though living like peasants in poverty, are proud of family origins that go back to a long forgotten history. Their land represents their heritage and is as important to them as the signet rings they so often wear that bear a coat of arms as significant to them today as it was on the day its was granted by a long-forgotten king on behalf of some long-forgotten cause.

"This land," says one farmer, his arms sweeping the few hectares which he manages with a few primitive implements and an almost savage sense of commitment, "belonged to my father, and his father, and his father before him. For me it is not just a means of livelihood, but a sacred possession."

This sense of being part of the soil is as important to most Poles as their religion. It harks back to a way of life that has an atavistic hold on the Polish collective imagination. It is the ambition of everyone to have a small cottage in the country. Many people have bought the old peasant wooden homes and transported them to their own plots, while the peasants build for themselves brick establishments more desirable in every way. But, one peasant told me, the new house was never as warm during the bitter Polish winter as the single storey house he had before, with its thatched roof and thick wooden walls all tightly packed with mud, that was built without a single nail.

Many hundreds of thousands still live in the old ways, that only now are beginning to give way to the steamroller of modernization. With them will go the last vestiges of a way of life that dominated Europe for so many centuries. It is part of the glory of Poland that it exists there still today. But to many young Poles, impatient for modernization and change, the old ways are a barbaric remnant of a Poland that ruined itself on the altar of its own proud, but ultimately self-destructive, traditions. No wonder, then, that Marxist-Leninism made so little impact on such a fiercely independent people who had a record of routing reformers long before Marx was even born.

There can be no doubt that revolutionary land reform was needed at the end of the war. Indeed, ever since the rebirth of Poland in 1918, successive governments had tried, without great success, to solve the problem of a largely agricultural country in which no less than 60 percent of the people derived their living from the land. In 1921 there were three million farms in Poland. There were huge estates and tiny uneconomic holdings, as well as a large landless peasant community that scratched a living where it could. Nearly 65 percent of farms measured ten hectares (2.47 acres) or less. And of these, more than half were less than two hectares (five acres). These tiny farms often had to support large family units, that grew more and more poverty-stricken as the depression years of 1930–1935 reduced their already low standard of living to near starvation level. In 1937 the peasants of Poland went on strike by withholding food deliveries to the towns. The strike was suppressed, but not without bloodshed—an event that to this day is not forgotten in peasant villages throughout the country, where the people mistrust not only Communist governments, but all governments, of whatever complexion.

After the war only Poland's old Peasant Party really stood courageously against the Communists as they sought to win total power. A participant at a congress of the Polish Peasant Party, held in Warsaw in January 1946, and attended by 1,158 delegates from all over the country, recalls that Boleslaw Bierut, the Communist head of state, was invited to the congress as an honorary guest. When he arrived, he was met by the deathly silence of delegates who pretended that they had not noticed his arrival. When their leader Stanislaw Mikolajczyk arrived, he was greeted with a standing ovation. Bierut stood up to speak, and the delegates were seized with such uncontrollabe fits of coughing that the chairman felt obliged to explain that they had all traveled hundreds of miles by train and had all caught cold. Bierut, intolerably humiliated, cut his speech short and left the congress immediately.

During the fraudulent 1948 elections only the Peasant Party posed a genuine challenge to the Communists, but they stood little chance against their intimidatory tactics. About 100,000 Peasant Party members were arrested and interrogated, and some were held for considerable periods of time. Elsewhere, people were terrorized into not putting up candidates at all. In one Silesian constituency a Peasant Party organizer was collecting the hundred signatures necessary to qualify as a candidate. However, wherever he went, security officers followed him. As soon as he left a house on his list, a security man would enter and tell the owner that if he did not remove his name he would be treated as though he had committed an act of sabotage against the state. The candidate thought he would never get his signatures until he received a call from a peasant, saying that he represented more than a hundred people who had fled from that part of Poland which was now Russia and they were determined to vote against a Communist candidate. He collected the signatures, but forty-eight hours later these too were withdrawn. The security forces had found out what had happened, and had taken all the wives and children of the men into a farmyard, refused them food or water, and said that they would not be permitted to leave until the signatures were withdrawn.

It was just before Christmas, the nights were icy cold, and fearing for their children's safety, the men gave in. The official result of that election was that the "Democratic bloc," which consisted of all the pro-Communist Parties, obtained 80.1 percent of the vote, and the Polish Peasant Party 10.3 percent, with the smaller parties making up the remainder. In fact, it is now clear from indications within the Communist Party itself that, despite the intimidation, the Polish Peasant Party received no less than 68 percent of the vote and the "Democratic bloc" and all other parties between them received 32 percent.

After the election the Peasant Party was outlawed and replaced by a puppet Peasant Party, and the process that the peasants believed would lead to the total collectivization of Polish agriculture began. In fact, the government, recognizing that the Polish peasant would not give up his land easily, hoped to achieve collectivization in gradual stages. Initially they only took a third of the land then available for distribution, 9 million hectares or so from both the new territories and the break-up of the old estates. All land of fifty hectares or above in the old territories, and 100 hectares in the new, was taken over without compensation. Only later, from 1949 to 1955, were individual peasants forced to surrender their land and join "cooperatives of producers" that, despite resistance, grew from 243 in 1948, to 10,513 by 1955. If that looked good on paper, in practice it proved to be disastrous. Instead of agricultural productivity increasing, as surely it ought to have done, as farms became more efficient under the economy of scale, in fact it fell. The peasants simply went on strike.

"In the fifties a man from the city came and told us about the

Socialist transformation of the countryside. In the sixties another man came and told us about the benefits of collectivization, and in the seventies yet another man came and told us about the wonders of Socialist reconstruction. And we always listened politely. And at the end of his little speech, the man in the fifties and the man in the sixties and again the man in the seventies, asked if there were any questions.

"And I stood up and I said 'Can you plough a straight furrow?' And each man started to say 'No, but . . .' We never heard the rest because we were out of the door."

The government tried one device after another to bring private agriculture into the Socialist economy, but it was always defeated by the implacable resistance and hostility of the farmers.

Initially tax was to be the weapon. In the forties a heavy tax burden fell on private farm-owners, while cooperative farms were only taxed at 3½ percent of their income and their members were freed from the onerous obligation to pay into the national agricultural savings fund. The peasants hit back by planning and executing acts of sabotage against the state farms. Then the government introduced compulsory purchase of grain, meat, and milk at ridiculously low wholesale prices. The effect of this was that peasants simply hid surplus produce which they sold on a rapidly burgeoning black market. The collectivization program, which had done tremendous harm to the economy, came to a shuddering halt in 1956, when Wladyslaw Gomulka went into reverse gear and dissolved collective farms up and down the country. Then he undid all the good he might have achieved by channelling virtually all agriculture investment into the state farms at the expense of the private farmers.

"I read a Party newspaper, which defended this policy by saying that as we wanted to be private farmers, it was right that we should buy our fertilizers and our machinery privately. On the other hand, as the state farms were owned by the state, it was right that they should get their investment from the state," one farmer told me. "To someone living in the town that might have made sense," he went on. "But to us it was sheer lying hypocrisy. The writer of that article knew perfectly well that, even if we had the money to buy these things, they were simply not available. There was no open market where we could buy them. He also knew that most private farmers were so undercapitalized that they had no hope of raising the money, for example, to buy a tractor, especially as no credits were made available to us at all."

Though this policy was subsequently modified, the Party's own statistics show the folly of pursuing, for ideological reasons, the concept of state farms.

The official 1978 statistics revealed that although the private sector held 68.4 percent of the land, it contributed 77.7 percent of the total agricultural production, 79.4 percent in crops and 75.7 percent in livestock. Yet in that same year, the private sector received only 30.2 percent of the total agricultural investment program. There is every reason to believe that the private sector could have done considerably better still, if wholesale prices had been reasonably based. The government, instead of facing up to the immediate prospect of higher food prices in Poland, preferred to buy grain and fodder on the international market, using precious hard currency—much of it borrowed, and now has to be paid back. Many of Poland's problems today stem directly from the government's refusal, up to as recently as the late seventies, to see that a prosperous private agricultural sector was vital to the nation's well-being and prosperity.

As far as the Communist bloc was concerned, Poland's private farmers were an ideological eyesore that successive Polish governments were asked to remove. Every government tried, and every government failed. And like so much else in Poland, even when the government acted out of the best of motives, it was mistrusted. In some cases old farmers, whose children had left the countryside and gone to work in cities, were offered state pensions in return for their land in order to create larger, more efficient units. Many villages pressured those seeking to sell out not to do so, fearing that the so-called larger units would make it easier for the government to collectivize later. And why should small farmers give up the holdings that, to many families, were their lifeline to a reasonable standard of living? Many of Poland's small holdings are worked by a special breed, unique in Europe—the worker-farmer.

During the day he works in a factory, while his wife looks after the land to which he returns in the evenings and weekends. Keeping the farm means that whatever else may happen, the family eats. If wholesale prices are too low, as one worker-farmer put it, "we eat more or sell on the black market." If the farmer is caught in one of the periodic drives against black marketeers, then he simply doesn't produce. As there are something over a million such farms in Poland, their influence upon the economy is momentous. Yet this country which, in the middle ages, was the granary of Europe, has been beggared by the need to import millions of tons of grain and animal feed and food. At the same time, a bottle of milk in the stores sells for six times less than it costs to produce, an illustration of the fact that food subsidies to the consumer now amount to a quarter of the whole state budget. How this remarkable program has not produced an immensely prosperous agricultural industry must rank as one of the great mysteries of modern-day economics. Still, it must be said, rural poverty is not nearly as great as once it was, and certainly its consequences are not as tragic now as they were before the war. Nevertheless, poverty exists and does so on a bewildering scale, and it was that poverty that the aforementioned Father Sadlowski saw and felt ought not to be tolerated. As he rode around his parish in the early 1970's, he not only preached the gospel of God, but the gospel of humanitarian Socialism. He told his parishioners that conditions would improve only if they themselves took active steps to see that conditions should improve.

During a period that Western newspapermen were coming to Poland and being fed lines like "Growth Industry—Polish Agriculture," *Guardian*, October 4, 1974; "Suddenly, peasants are in" *Guardian*, April 12, 1973, or "Land Reform without tears," *Financial Times*, March 13, 1977, the lot of the small farmer was in reality in decline. Indeed, almost to the day that the "Suddenly peasants are in" article was printed, no less than fifty police cars had converged upon Father Sadlowski's tiny hut that still served as his church. The police shut it, saying that Father Sadlowski was actively campaigning on behalf of those very peasants who, a great British liberal newspaper was telling the world, "have never had it so good." Like most Poles, Father Sadlowski had heard of KOR, the Committee for the Defense of the Workers, set up to the great scandal of the authorities by a group of intellectual dissidents. He traveled to Warsaw to see their leaders. Poland is nothing, he told them, without its farmers, yet those farmers have been shamelessly treated by the authorities and ignored by the intelligentsia. If KOR was really serious, he said, then it should change its statutes to bring Poland's peasants and small farmers under its umbrella. Class distinctions between town and country should disappear; the living conditions of the people should be improved, education guaranteed; basic hygenic conditions must be insisted upon, and last, but in Father Sadlowski's eyes very far from least, religious life guaranteed. The KOR leadership listened to this quiet-spoken, deeply intense young man. Few, if any, of them were or are religious or, for that matter, had much feeling for the land, but they could not help but be moved by the fervor of Father

Sadlowski as he told them straightforwardly of his faith. There and then they agreed to broaden their struggle to include the farmers as well.

Overnight, Father Sadlowski's parish became the center of a massive campaign by Poland's farmers to improve their lot. Father Sadlowski's life was divided between his religious and political duties. On occasions the security people came for him, but somehow word would get out in advance. When they arrived at his house, they would find it surrounded by groups of very tough and very resolute-looking farmers protecting their priest. Frustrated, the authorities sought him en route back from Warsaw where he consulted with KOR activists. But he was always tipped off, stopped before the road block, and continued his journey on foot, across the fields and the woods, skirting the ditches, through the backs of farms until he was safely home.

In the meantime he made sure that the message he had for farmers went to all parts of the country. His parish was in the middle of a fruit-growing area, particularly apples that were packed into trucks and delivered all over the country. His people placed in almost every consignment duplicated newsletters that reached farming areas all over the country. He used the apple trucks as clandestine mail trucks until on September 9, 1978, when it was possible to announce that, as an offshoot of KOR, a Committee of Farmers' Self Defense had been established on a countrywide basis. A small village priest had established an organization that, even more than its parent KOR, was a deep affront to the Marxist philosophy.

But if the temporal authorities were unhappy, so were the ecclesiastical. They had come to an uneasy accommodation with the Party, particularly in important country areas where, away from the prying eyes of foreign observers, it had been difficult to get permission to build churches, where religious instruction of any kind was rigorously discouraged, and where the grip the Church had upon the peasantry was such a cause of concern that everything possible had been done to try to loosen it. The authorities had proved more accommodating in recent years, and here was Father Sadlowski rocking the boat. Accused of neglecting his religious duties, he set about building his church, persuading a rich Polish emigré to put up the money. The church, described at the start of this chapter, is an extraordinary edifice in the middle of literally nowhere. But it's not just a church. The young people of the area have a discothèque to go to every Saturday night in the basement of the building. The pastor insists on prayers before the music starts, but no one complains. In another small room a primitive dentist's chair has been set up for a visiting dentist from Warsaw who comes, on Father Sadlowski's urging, one day a month to look after villagers who have no dentist of their own. On Saturdays, entertainers from Polish radio and TV come down; institutes in Warsaw send books and magazines for the reading room; mechanics and technical experts from a variety of walks of life come either to repair farm machinery free of charge or to teach the people how to do it themselves. When asked why they come, for no payment or reward of any kind, they all say simply "because Father Sadlowski asked me to." The authorities have used subtle and non-too-subtle methods to intimidate him. Once he was arrested and interrogated for twelve hours before being released, which he would not have minded, save for the fact that at the same time his precious duplicator was confiscated. The authorities even sent lunatics to harass him. One came armed with a dagger, another with a rope. Each had the same message—they had been sent by God to kill him. Local farmers were detained and told they would only be released if they made incriminating statements against their priest.

When Solidarity sprang on an astonished world, and an even more astonished Poland, in August 1981, the farmers were once again forgotten. But this time they would not be left out. In what were to be the most moving demonstations of those extraordinary first six months, they paraded in their traditional costumes (still worn on great religious feast days in their own communities to demonstrate pride in their history and culture) through the streets of Warsaw, demanding their rights. To many Communists it seemed that this was the last straw. The First Secretary, Stanislaw Kania, said in January 1981: "We register our categorical opposition to all attempts at inciting the countryside, at sowing anarchy or creating a political opposition. There is no room in the Polish countryside for a political opposition because there is no room for a struggle that is not in the interests of agriculture or farmers or workers."

It was not long after that Rural Solidarity, or to use its official title, Self-Ruling Trade Union for Individual Farmers, was officially registered. The Communist world had seen nothing like it before. The statutes of Rural Solidarity specifically recognize the right of farmers to own the land they work.

In the past, successive Polish governments were forced to accept the existence of private farms but they didn't like them and always wanted to do away with them when they were in a stronger position. Here finally was a Communist government, enshrining the right of private ownership of farmland by statute, and at the same time giving those farmers the strength to fight any attempt by future governments to renege on these agreements by permitting them a union to represent their interests.

As Tadeusz, a small farmer, told me: "For the first time in my life, I feel free of the constant threat that my land will one day be taken away from me. So I and my friends can start thinking of the government in Warsaw not as an enemy, but as fellow Poles who, if they ask for help from us, deserve to be listened to."

As for Father Sadlowski, he could not, of course, take an official position in Rural Solidarity, but when its leaders were invited to the Vatican to receive the Pope's blessing, Father Sadlowski was specifically invited to attend along with them. Ironically, it was the episcopate in Warsaw, and not the government, which showed its disapproval by not letting him travel with the delegation but making him go a day later. Nevertheless, he was there on June 17, 1981, just after the assassination attempt on the Holy Father, to spend five minutes with him, five precious minutes, in the Pope's bedroom in the Vatican.

Afterward he told a high Vatican official of the problems he had with both Church and state in Poland. Don't worry about either, he was told. What you are doing serves man, and therefore serves God. Father Sadlowski has no doubt that it was the Pope who asked that message to be passed on to him.

So the small farmers of Poland, those staunch people who have suffered much deprivation, who had come to believe that their plight mattered to nobody, whose interests were constantly overlooked, have finally broken through to the consciousness of the nation. That romantic ideal which all Poles have of their countryside is matched at last by a hard-headed realization that if the countryside is not looked after, the people won't eat.

It is said that an East German politician remonstrated with General Jaruzelski after Rural Solidarity was officially granted legal status, saying that such a movement was anti-socialist in character.

Jaruzelski thought about it for a moment and replied: "That may be so, but what is the greater anti-socialist element—Rural Solidarity or hunger? If socialist policies lead to hunger, then there is something wrong with those policies."

11
The Intellectuals

An expressionist is a painter who paints as he feels. An impressionist is a painter who paints as he sees. A social realist is a painter who paints as he hears.

In 1969 on a visit to Warsaw I met a well-known Polish intellectual (who has been a good friend since), who shocked me when he spoke of his country with something close to despair. During the previous year Poland had been in ferment. The students of Warsaw University had staged sit-ins and demonstrations against the regime. More than a third of the Warsaw branch members of the Union of Polish Writers signed a petition condemning government interference in the arts. Intellectuals throughout the country gathered under the banner of "No bread without freedom." To all of this the authorities had responded with a massive and vicious display of physical and political force. The police arrested the ringleaders, and the Party found a convenient scapegoat to blame for all the troubles—the Jews, many of whom had led the anti-state agitation. The effect upon the country was saddening as thousands of Jews, many of whom had special skills desperately needed by the country, emigrated, and a particularly unpleasant group of authoritarian right-wingers rose to the top of the Party apparatus.

Yet despite this reaction there seemed grounds for hope. If the intellectual elite of a country withholds its support from a ruling apparatus and its own system of government, history shows that, despite temporary setbacks, the system is ultimately doomed. My friend disagreed. Poland, he said, would never be a free nation again. The Communist authorities had succeeded in what they had set out to do when they came to power—to turn the country into a workers' state from which intellectuals would be rigorously excluded, unless they conformed absolutely with the new regime. As for the workers, they were content and would remain so as long as the Party ensured they had a full bread basket. They had become an acquiescent mass and would always remain so. Intellectuals and workers had been

[215]

turned against each other. "As a thinker," said my friend, "I am an alien in a nation of nonthinkers." It was difficult at the time to fault this gloomy analysis. While the intellectuals and students had been fighting (often physically), for the soul of Poland during the previous year, the proletariat had stood by with apparent indifference and, in some cases, hostility. When the police organized groups of workers from surrounding factories to come into Warsaw to express their support for the authorities, there had seemed to be no shortage of volunteers. Rather pathetically, the students at the Gdansk Polytechnic had announced in banners ten feet high: "We stand united above all with the Polish working-class." The Polish working-class walked by its gates and merely smiled. "You see," said my friend, "the workers are alienated from us, and without their muscle our attempts to change the system are doomed to permanent failure."

The great food price riots in December 1970, which led to the fall of Gomulka and the rise of Gierek, were notable for the fact that just as the workers had stood aloof from the intellectuals' battle in 1968, the intellectuals had remained firmly ensconced in their ivory towers while the workers took to the barricades. What very few people saw was that, while the intellectuals had only succeeded in strengthening the repressive power of the state, the workers had managed to frighten the authorities so that they ushered in an era of unparalleled liberalism in the history of People's Poland. Yet the indifference of the intellectuals was understandable. Why should they support the workers, if the workers had failed to support them in their struggle? And had not the workers in any case chosen to fight on an issue that, to say the least, was far from clear-cut? Maybe the government had been insensitive in choosing the pre-Christmas period to launch a new economic policy designed to bring prices nearer to the real cost of production, but few doubted the reforms themselves were vital for the whole Polish economy. "They are prepared to die because the price of ham goes up, but then live in a society in which their basic freedoms have been taken into pawn," contemptuously said one of the 1968 student leaders then living in exile in London.

The nation, in short, was divided by a gulf so deep that it seemed unbridgeable. Those aware of the gulf gave their sympathy to the intellectuals. It is not my intention to denigrate these brave people when I say that one of the most important by-products of the sixteen months of Solidarity's strength was that for the first time in the history of Soviet imperialism, outside observers such as myself were able to enjoy prolonged access to the industrial working-class of a Communist country. Those of us who have traveled extensively throughout Russia and Eastern Europe had, till then, met either Party officials or much publicized literary dissidents. The working-class was unknown to us. But in Poland, between August 1980 and December 1981, all of that changed, and so did our previous misconceptions. There had always been antagonism between workers and the intellectuals, but that antagonism was based upon a very different set of assumptions than the intellectuals, when they were the sole voice of dissent, had allowed. It was not the workers who had betrayed the intelligentsia, I came to realize, but rather the other way around.

Many who know Poland and particularly those with a line into the intelligentsia will find this to be a harsh judgment. After all, there were innumerable cases in the forties of men and women, poets and writers, or simply ordinary schoolteachers and academics, who refused to acquiesce and who were persecuted accordingly. One Polish journalist told me, "In the forties and early fifties the choice was stark— accept the system or go under." It is impossible to believe that such a fine poet as Wladyslaw Broniewski, though a Party member, willingly wrote lines like these:

> How beautiful to know that Stalin lives,
> How beautiful to know that Stalin thinks, etc.

but that he did write them there can be no doubt.

The position of the Polish intelligentsia has been wondrously summed up by the great Polish playwright Slwomir Mrozek in his play *The Emigrants*. The play is a conversation between an unnamed intellectual and an unnamed worker. The intellectual says:

It's an astonishing thing, but a man who is otherwise quite sensible, like me, does not want to see the most obvious truth when it hurts his pride. At first I jumped around like a monkey in a cage. I swung on my tail, leaping with great speed from the bar to the wall, or from the wall to the bar; or when given a nut, I tried to crawl into the shell, to feel myself lord of limitless spaces. It was a very long time before I really escaped from my illusions and convinced myself that I really was a monkey in a cage . . . when I finally decided that I was a monkey, I began to laugh at myself, and I kept on laughing until the tears ran down my face. Then I realized that my clowning was not so hilarious, although it amused my audience and my keepers enough for them to throw me extra nuts and sweets. But the sweets made me sick, and I could no longer climb into the shells. It was then that I understood how for a monkey there was no other way but to admit that he was a monkey. . . .

The intellectual then explains that he decides to write a book on
Man even though the worker protests that monkeys can't write books.

"I agree, especially in a cage. But that point was only proved later on.
For the time being, I was crazed by the prospect of writing my life's work.
. . . As I told myself, we may have nothing, but we have slavery. That's our
treasure. What do other people know about such a theme? . . . The entire
literature of slavery is either phoney, or irrelevant; it's written either by
missionaries or by liberators, or else by slaves longing for freedom, that is
to say by people who have ceased to be complete slaves. . . . What do they
know about integral slavery, turned in on itself, self-perpetuating with
no thought of being transcended? What do they know of the joys and
sorrows of a slave, of the mysteries of slavery, of its beliefs and customs,
of its philosophy? . . . They know nothing, and I know it all. That's why
I decided to write about it."
"And did you write it?" asks the worker.
"No."
"Why not?"
"I was scared."

To be scared is a painfully human predicament. Who can say how
they would behave in similar circumstances? But what is also true is
that many entered the "cage" with their eyes wide open. But, of
course, that is not a uniquely or peculiarly Polish phenomenon. It is
remarkable how even today such a sizeable segment of the intellectual
community, especially in Europe but also in America, despite all
experience, despite the political history of our times, are at this very
moment intent upon making the same mistake. Like the Polish
intelligentsia, they will not lightly be forgiven by the same working
class they claim to speak for, should the politics they espouse ever
come to pass.

A factory worker on the Ursus production line near Warsaw is
speaking: "Don't talk to me about the intelligentsia," he says. "They
were all right. They had nice comfortable flats and plenty of money,
could travel abroad and read foreign books. And they never once considered the plight of the ordinary workers. They wrote manifestos
about free speech, while what concerned us was that sometimes we
barely had enough to eat."

Working-class suspicion of the intelligentsia has a long history. Said
another worker: "The so-called intelligentsia were the only socialists
in the country. They would talk about Marxism and socialism as if
they were abstract sciences. But they never came down to the factory
floor or into the coal mine to see how socialism was being directly

applied. We knew soon enough that Communism was a fraud. It took our brainy friends a little longer to work it out."

More than any other segment of the population, the intelligentsia welcomed, in some cases loudly, the advent of the Communist regime after the war, and continued to support it after the rest of the country had discovered its shortcomings. That collective guilt of the Polish intellectual community has still to be properly acknowledged by them. Listen to another worker: "Czeslaw Milosz is a lucky man. He starts by giving the Party if not his blessing then his acquiescence by representing Poland as a diplomat abroad, finds that it does not work out to his liking, and so goes off to live in California. But I knew that the Party would be disastrous from the very beginning, told as many people as I dared that it would be catastrophic, and today I live in a very small flat in Poznan, scratching for my living. So I didn't exactly dance in the streets when I heard Milosz received the Nobel Prize for Literature."

There is no doubt that a significant portion of Poland's intelligentsia not only accepted the Stalinist takeover of Poland but even welcomed it. As Milosz himself put it, "The intellectual's eye twinkles with delight at the persecution of the bourgeoisie, and of the bourgeoise mentality. . . . The peasants, burying hoarded gold and listening to foreign broadcasts in the hope that a war will save them from collectivization, certainly have no ally in him." Or, "Parliamentary methods were discredited in the eyes of my generation." To those who felt like that, Stalinism produced immediate rewards. Writers, artists, and musicians found themselves among the nation's elite as part of the great cultural offensive that Russia and its satellites launched around the globe.

Any artist prepared to toe the Party line could expect immediate rewards in the way of priorities with housing, foreign travel, tenure at universities, and, most important of all to a writer, publication.

In the early days the Party could also guarantee good reviews! A classic illustration is the well-known Polish composer, Andrzej Panufnik, who, in 1954, fled Poland "guided by my national and artistic conscience." Invited by the *Times* of London to write an article about Poland, he learned it was rejected because it was too anti-Communist. Today he has married into one of the richest families in England and lives in considerable luxury. He composed on arrival in Britain the beautiful "Song to the Virgin Mary." Although today he loudly condemns the present government in Poland, he is the same man who wrote in the forties the stirring "Song of the

United Party" celebrating the merger of the Polish Socialist Party
with the Polish Workers' Party (the Communist Party) in 1949, with
these inspiring lyrics:

> As one close family,
> From factories, foundries, and carpenters' benches,
> We march beneath the banners
>   of Marx and Lenin
> Toward the happiness of the proletariat!

He also composed "Pledge of the Youth" and "Symphony of Peace."

It was not only the promise of material reward that attracted so
many members of the intelligentsia to the Party in the first place. It
was, as one writer put it, a mixture of intellectual vanity, greed, and
slothfulness that infected virtually the whole of the artistic and intellectual community. Vanity persuaded them that somehow they, as
individuals, would be able to escape the proscriptions of a political
system which they knew was hostile to free thought. Greed permitted
them to exchange their conscience for what has been described as the
"thirteenth-month pay," those vital extras like a decent flat or car
which came to those who lived with the system. Finally, it was
slothfulness which let them embrace the Marxist-Leninist philosophy
without their applying the austere intellectual criteria they would
normally use to evaluate any other philosophical system.

More subtle processes were at work too. The intellectuals emerged
from the same class as the majority of the ruling elite. Each tolerated
the other to an extent that was intolerable to people several rungs
down the social ladder. I am bound to say, it seldom, if ever, occurred
to me on my trips to Warsaw why so-called dissidents lived in pleasant
apartments, drove cars, and had access to goods only available in the
dollar shops. It seems a paradox now, that though these dissidents
were genuinely persecuted by one wing of the Party, they were well
nourished by another. "Our version of the British old-school tie was
always at work," says one university professor. "You do what you can
to look after your own." If the Party and the intellectuals clashed—
as they often did—it was like a family fight with everyone else rigidly
excluded. Both groups were isolated from the population at large.

Of course many did understand their own impotence. That great
Polish writer and author of *Ashes and Diamonds*, Jerzy Andrzejewski,
whom I met in the beautiful Old Palace given to Poland's Authors'
Association outside Warsaw, where writers go to work in idyllic sur-
roundings (or just for rest and relaxation), found solace in the bottle

(though now he doesn't drink). Kasimierz Brandys, another internationally known writer, has written of how so many fooled themselves by writing "for the bottom drawer," secret work that one day they planned to spring on an astonished world, all the while knowing that it would never happen. He tells the story of the man who became a mountaineer, tackling ever more difficult peaks, displaying great physical courage, but sublimating his moral cowardice in facing up to the local Party Secretary of whom he was mortally afraid—"an eagle in the mountains but like a dish rag down below." Brandys himself joined the Party in 1946, and left it twenty years later, in 1966, to become a writer only published unofficially. As late as 1978, he still could describe the masses (a hideously dehumanizing expression that can only be used without irony by a writer inside the Communist bloc) on whose behalf presumably he once joined the Party, as the barrier to liberalization.

"A person who disassociated himself from the masses," he writes, "will become suspect. He will be suspect in the eyes of the masses, because the masses want to have food, clothing, and an automobile, to be entertained with films and songs. Average people prefer good eating and entertainment to thought. Thought represents an effort; it means anxiety and risk. The masses are made up of millions whose heritage is the memory of poverty, war, and fear. The present level of development—the satisfaction of material and cultural needs, the feeling of physical security—has bred in them an entirely new sense of property. . . . So they are afraid to express doubts or to ask questions. . . . When one speaks of freedom or justice, they only listen with reluctance. Those are threatening words, they interrupt the humdrum of daily life and the consequences they entail are unforeseeable. Nor do the masses like to hear talk about moral courage, because they see it as an expense beyond their means and which could ruin them."

These words were written in *samzidat* form in Poland in 1978, two years before those same masses took the future development of Polish society into their own hands, showing a moral and physical courage beyond compare, and facing great dangers on behalf of the freedom and justice Brandys believed they were unconcerned about. It was a form of arrogance in the forties that made men like Brandys pledge their considerable talents to the Stalinist dictatorship and assist, in a not inconsiderable way, in its victory. The same arrogance led to the despair that forced writers like Milosz to emigrate and others to go into a kind of internal exile, living in small ghettos, speaking and writing only for each other.

It was the Polish authorities (perhaps because they were the most literate of all establishments in Russia and Eastern Europe) that discovered the chilling truth that it isn't necessary to imprison or even harass so-called dissidents. All that needs to be done is to ensure that their work does not spread out to the population at large. The dissidents can be left alone, as one Pole crudely said to me, "intellectually masturbating," having no influence on anyone, luxuriating in their own sense of independence, and being totally irrelevant. Denied by the authorities the glory of martydom that gave many Russian, Czech, or East German intellectuals their international reputations (which, in some cases, are hardly deserved), Polish intellectuals were gradually sinking into total and abject obscurity. A regime which certainly never lacked subtlety was always available to any writer or artist prepared to bend, on the theory that a man who first gives way on little matters, will eventually betray great ones. Never was this more clearly shown than in 1956. The workers in Poznan rose in defiance of the state, and the intelligentsia picked up the banner of revolt and forced the dismissal of the old Stalinist leadership, which brought in the reformist government of Wladyslaw Gomulka. Only two years later, the social advances that the Poles believed would follow Gomulka's appointment were nullified one after the other. The Workers' Councils, though never outside Party control, did represent the interests of ordinary people at their place of work, yet they were dissolved. Popular workers' leaders were dismissed, and the absolute authority of the Communist Party over every aspect of life was reinstated.

Poland's intellectuals who had supported Gomulka were nurturing a fantasy, one that Polish workers already knew was a fantasy: that there was nothing wrong with the system, only the people at the top had subverted it and had caused the problems. It was left to Jacek Kuron, variously described as an anarchist, Trotskyist, eccentric, Marxist, Social Democrat, and American imperialist (depending on who is doing the describing), to expose the moral torpidity of the intelligentsia. Kuron is an individual who truly fits only one label— Kuronist. He castigated Poland's intelligentsia for blindly accepting Gomulka, without realizing they were also confirming the right of the Party, to which Gomulka had always been totally committed, to rule over every aspect of their lives. In 1956 with quite extraordinary timidity, Polish intellectuals, instead of demanding freedom, and seeing no further than their noses, decided that their hangman should be a nationalist rather than a Stalinist. The intellectuals have never been forgiven by the rest of the population—while Kuron has never been forgiven by the intellectuals for making their responsibility so clear.

Jacek Kuron is without doubt the most fascinating and, consistently, the most intellectually challenging of so-called dissidents inside the Communist bloc. Kuron began life as a Marxist. His father, still alive at the time of this writing, shares his son's small flat. He was a local organizer of the prewar Socialist Party, himself a worker and son of a worker. Kuron was a political activist from his earliest memory. He joined the Young Communist League as soon as he could, and by the age of 18 was Secretary of the Warsaw District of the Young Communist League and accepted nationally as one who would go far in the Party.

"I had no doubt at all that he would one day rule Poland as Secretary General," says one friend from those days. "He had an incredible personality and was a natural leader, but he was also absolutely ruthless. He was a dangerous fellow to have around, because he was always seeking out class enemies to denounce; he permitted not the slightest deviation from the Party line. He was a rabid Stalinist, though one couldn't help liking him despite all of that."

Kuron's break with the Party came at precisely that time when his preeminence as a member of the Young Communist League was about to take him into the stratosphere of Polish politics. He was asked to help organize a nationwide opinion poll seeking the attitudes of the Polish people toward Germany. The year was 1951, memories of German occupation were still fresh, and the Poles were being told in the press that West Germany was still bent on winning back the Western Territories given to Poland under the post-war settlements. Hatred of Germany was the one issue in Poland in which the majority of the population backed the Government, yet, so demoralized was the government by the hostility of the general population, that even on this issue it feared a true test.

The relief and even exhilaration in the government after the poll was published showing how widespread was the people's support can only be imagined. A bulletin issued by the Politburo singled out Kuron for praise. Still only eighteen years old, he had been drawn to the attention of the ruling elite, and it seemed that nothing could stop him from moving to the top. Kuron then announced his next poll. Having tested Polish public opinion about the Germans, he would now do the same about the country's other powerful neighbor, the Russians. Poland's leaders knew that this time the answer would not be to their liking and ordered Kuron to cease. Stubbornly he refused. He was threatened with expulsion from the Young Communist League, and still he would not back down. The darling of the Party only a few months previously, Jacek Kuron was on the way to becoming one of the most dangerous rebels in all of Eastern Europe.

"The incident," says a friend, "is a classic illustration of the Kuron style. He himself at the time was pro-Stalin and pro-Russian, and I believe he honestly thought that most of Poland agreed with him. He was naive then and he is naive now, finding it hard to conceive that people of goodwill can ever disagree with him.

"But he is also hopelessly stubborn. He did not intend a confrontation with the Party authorities and the whole incident came as a great shock to him. But once it occurred, there was nothing on this earth that could have got him to change his mind. His one besetting sin is his incorrigible honesty."

When Kuron realized that the Party was only interested in a truth that suited its needs, he became as fervent a member of the opposition as he had previously been of the Party. Every Polish intellectual had similar moments of truth, but most believed some form of compromise or personal accommodation was possible, and desirable. Kuron was not unique in believing otherwise, but the number of intellectuals sharing his position can be counted on the fingers of one hand. It has not been a posture that has provided him with an easy life or won him ready popularity. One of the least edifying spectacles of post-Solidarity Poland was the sight of men and women who had served the system well, rallying to the banner of freedom, justice, and renewal, pausing to hurl a jibe at Jacek Kuron, dismissing him as irrelevant or condemning him as an extremist. Yet it was Kuron who, unlike them, had never taken the easy options; he had helped bring to life the movement that, when once it seemed safe, they embraced so eagerly.

Jacek Kuron's importance as a philosopher-politician has been consistently underrated by everyone but a few Marxist ideologues in the Kremlin, who have the education to understand that everything he has ever written or said is part of a large body of work that (using the Marxist dialectic in which he was trained), is one of the most magnificently sustained critiques of Marxism that has ever been produced. The authorities in Poland have accused Kuron of advocating revolution. He never has. What he has done is to predict events with such astonishing accuracy that the accusation seems correct because he describes events years before they actually occur. Kuron's greatest sin has been to force himself out of the intellectual ghetto, to insist that writer speaking to writer, or artist to artist, must in the end produce a barren seed.

Kuron was sentenced to three years' imprisonment for his "open letter to the Party" in 1965, an event which was to lead indirectly to that intellectual revolt with which this chapter began. Kuron's trial led at last to an explosion of protest by the intellectual community. The Party responded by expelling those very writers, historians and philosophers—including the great Leszek Kolakowski—who had given it intellectual dignity. Finally, the intelligentsia, that had sustained the Party for so long, began withdrawing its support.

The comfortable illusion that it would be the catalyst to lead the reformation of the Party and the gradual opening-up of Polish society was destroyed once and for all. No one could have any excuses left anymore. The stage was set for the next chapter in the Polish tragedy.

In November 1967, a play, *Forefathers' Eve* by Adam Mickiewicz (1798–1855), Poland's most revered literary icon, was staged at the National Theatre in Warsaw to mark the fiftieth anniversary of the October Revolution. *Forefathers' Eve* (*Dziady*) is an epic drama of nineteenth-century Russian despotism and the Polish struggle for freedom. Because it was Mickiewicz, a name revered by all Poles, it occurred to no one, not even the director who staged it, that the play was potentially explosive. But the first night audience heard lines like, "Moscow sends only rogues to Poland," or "Am I to be free? Yes! Where this news came from I do not know, but I am alive to what it means to be free under the hands of a Muscovite. These scoundrels! They only take the fetters off my hands and feet, but crush my soul." At every performance the audience cheered and clapped. Demonstrations became rowdier and rowdier until, on January 30, 1968, the government did the unthinkable: they announced that Adam Mickiewicz's play, one of the most enduring monuments of Polish literature, was banned, and the theatre closed. There can have been no theatrical occasion in our time to compare with that last night. At the end of the play, for nearly two hours the audience was cheering and clapping or breaking into patriotic songs as well as the national anthem. After that, most of the audience, headed by students, marched to Mickiewicz's monument in the center of the city, but police were waiting. The first clash of the many that were to occur in the next few months ended with thirty-five students in prison. Even today no one can say why subsequent events evolved the way they did. Throughout the country universities rose in revolt. Writers who had been keeping their heads down signed petitions demanding the reinstatement of academics already fired from their jobs and the acceptance of creative and artistic tolerance. In a magnificent and moving speech at a meeting called by the Union of Polish Writers, attended by 431 out of the 600 members, Leszcek Kolakowski declared, "We have reached a shameful situation where everything written for the stage from Aeschylus to Shakespeare, to Brecht and Ionesco, has become a collection of allusions to People's Poland. . . . The theaters are rendered unfit out of necessity, when it appears that nothing is neutral, for where it is necessary to return to the most elementary values, everything becomes suspect. . . . We are getting to a point where our buffooneries shall become dangerous material for subversion. . . . Let us consider the degradation of the Polish film, let us consider the appalling and miserable system of information in the press, let us consider the restrictions and harrassment practiced in Poland in the humanities, in current history, sociology and political science, and law. Let us consider the deplorable discussions in which no one ever dares say what is really the matter, for everything leads to the forbidden fruit. . . . We want the abolition of such a situation in the name of socialism, not against it."

But that was not the way the Party saw it, and so began one of the most shameful episodes in the history of Peoples' Poland. Desperately seeking a scapegoat, a section of the Party lit upon the survivors of the Holocaust, a small though influential Jewish community. It was true that many of the students who began the protests were Jewish and came from comparatively privileged backgrounds (their parents were senior Party officials who had prospered under the system). They were given the nickname of "The Commandos," as they brilliantly assaulted one barrier after another of Party ideology. To some other students, however, they were known as "bananas," because their lifestyle enabled them to afford a fruit that was virtually unobtainable in the country. Because there was a genuine resentment against some of these students and their parents already, the Party's anti-Semitic drive did not fall on deaf ears. Says my friend Maciej, who left Poland soon afterward and now lives in London, "I feel ashamed of it now, but at Warsaw University while I didn't actively join in demonstrations against Jewish students, I didn't help any of them who asked for assistance either.

"I was the son of a worker living on a student's grant so small that I had to consider very carefully every time I wanted to buy a cup of coffee. But the 'bananas' rolled up to the gates of the university in chauffeur-driven cars, wore the smartest Western clothes, and always had money to do anything they liked, and we resented them. We were envious, and they were the sons of leaders of a Party that we hated. Because of that, though I joined in the demonstrations, I did not object when the Jews were expelled from the country."

The events of March 1968 have been among the most curious in the history of Eastern European Communism. One view holds that the riots were deliberately provoked by a section within the Party, calling itself the Patriotic Party Cadre, to seize power by discrediting a group of senior politicians close to Gomulka who happened to be Jewish. General Mieczyslaw Moczar, then fifty-four years old, was Gomulka's Minister of the Interior, probably the only politician with that position in the Eastern bloc to rise through the ranks from a provincial chief of police. Moczar very much represented the police-wing of the *nomenklatura*, deeply anti-intellectual and anti-reform. In his favor, he was a courageous man with a decent war record; he had commanded a group of Communist partisans on a series of daring raids against the Germans. After the war he was one of those—in his view—pushed to one side by the Communists who came from Russia, many of whom were Jewish. Wladyslaw Gomulka objected to the Muscovites because they were seeking to impose Russian ideology on Poland, when he believed Poland ought to follow the "Polish road" to Communism. Moczar regarded matters in an altogether simpler form. His enemies were simply those people who stood in his way— regardless of ideology. He had always, like his father (by all accounts a considerable figure), been a Communist, but he was also a chauvinist of the old school, who now used the old weapon of anti-Semitism to clear the country of his enemies. The Jews of Poland, many of whom were in leading positions, were subjected to a vicious campaign of harrassment and humiliation.

They were abused, often by name, in the press and in public speeches and Zionism was the acceptable code word under which all Jews could be attacked. The Party organization in the Ministry of Foreign Affairs declared, "We express our solidarity with the general demand for an unconditional purge of Zionists from the Party ranks and particularly from the foreign service." The Army paper, *Zolnierz Wolnosci* ("The Soldier of Freedom") called Polish "Zionists" a "gallery of traitors." The journal of the Socialist Youth Movement argued that "all Jews spread over the world constituted one nation, the core of which was Israel. . . ." And that the chief aim of the Polish Zionist group down the years was to poison Polish youth with the "venom of cosmopolitanism." All over the country Jews were dismissed from their posts, sometimes in extremely unpleasant scenes, and others were expelled from the Party. Gomulka, married to a Jewish woman, was never an anti-Semite. Now sick and exhausted by his incarceration, he no longer had the strength to go against the tide. He put his considerable authority behind Moczar in a speech implying that Poland's Jews were a "Fifth Column" operating in the country. Thousands of Jews, most of them reluctantly and tearfully, boarded the Chopin Express at Warsaw for Vienna, clutching the few goods they were permitted to take; and the historic Jewish community of Poland, save for a few survivors clinging on today, virtually ceased to exist. Was all this a carefully planned provocation? It seems most unlikely. It is unthinkable that any politician, however ambitious—and Moczar was certainly that—inside the Communist bloc would deliberately create such disorder. The leaders rely on an acquiescent population. Once the people are aroused, then there can be no way of knowing where they will halt. It is true that Moczar and his cronies seized the moment to launch the attack that would put them into power.

It has always been assumed that they were successful. In fact, they were not. Though Moczar was allowed into the Politburo, he was dropped two years later. Most of his extremist supporters, who hoped to ride in on his coattails, have disappeared into total obscurity. What ought to be acknowledged is that there were enough people (apparently powerless to resist him at the time), who behaved with supreme dignity during this national crisis, and they made the rest of the Party quickly feel ashamed enough to refuse advancement to those who had been Moczar's henchmen and eventually to Moczar himself. Edward Ochab, Chairman of the Council of State, who had briefly been First Secretary of the Party on the death of Beirut in 1956 and who intriguingly possesses, to this day, an absolutely unique distinction—the only First Secretary of any Communist country to have voluntarily resigned his position—resigned once again, this time to express his disgust at what was going on. Adam Rapacki, Poland's Foreign Minister, and probably the only Eastern European politician before or since genuinely to rank as an international statesman, was presented with a list of Jews he was told to dismiss from the Foreign Office. Rapacki, not a Jew himself, read it, wrote his own name at the top, cleared his desk, and walked out never to return. The editorial board of *Polityka*— that curious hybrid, an independent Party weekly—in the absence abroad of its editor-in-chief, Mieczyslaw Rakowski, was ordered by his deputy, a Moczar supporter, to print an overtly anti-Semitic article.

The editor refused, saying they would resign en masse if the article was printed. Rakowski hurried back to face this crisis, read the article in question, supported the staff against his deputy, and went to Gomulka himself, demanding the support which Gomulka gave. *Polityka* came under attack from the rest of the Polish press as "national nihilist" or staffed by a group of "low grade patriots," to which it replied in measured tones: "Is it necessary to conduct a verbal auction on the subject 'Who loves my country most?' Should one measure a man's patriotism by the loudness and frequency with which he talks of it? I doubt it. The touchstone is whether one's love of country is creative and wise. . . ."

The country was in intellectual and physical turmoil, but the workers remained aloof, even joining government-sponsored rallies to denounce "Zionist" and "intellectual" adventurers. Writers and artists were demoralized as their impotence and, even worse, irrelevance, became apparent. They had been humiliated; their cry for intellectual freedom had not only been firmly rejected by authority, but ignored by the rest of the nation. Never in the history of Poland had Polish intellectuality been at a lower ebb. The nation, whose greatest artists, from Chopin to Mickiewicz, had found their inspiration in the most powerful nationalism, appeared to have deserted its artistic community just as that community appeared earlier to have deserted Poland.

During all this time Jacek Kuron was in prison, powerless to affect in any way the tragic course of events, though earning a special education that included the underworld argot which was to make him a compelling and colorful speaker and lecturer later on. During his incarceration, he was shocked to learn that the prison population regarded Polish intellectuals with as much mistrust and dislike as they regarded the Communist authorities. Intellectuals were held responsible for the situation in which Poland found itself. Intellectuals, more than any other segment of the population, had sided with the Party when it first took over. They had convinced themselves and others that the Party required their backing in 1956, when all the reforms then promised proved to be an illusion. And now in 1968, when the living conditions of the working-class could not be worse, the intellectuals had at last taken up the cudgels, but had done so on behalf of a long-dead playwright, not on behalf of the modern Polish nation. This view was, of course, unfair to the many courageous Polish writers and artists who had, over the years, courageously upheld the basic principles of human rights which the authorities were so reluctant to grant their people. Nevertheless, there was sufficient truth to make

Kuron realize that even his "Open Letter to the Party," which detailed the plight of ordinary people, and had earned him his imprisonment, could be criticized on the grounds that it offered no plan of action for the people to put their affairs into reasonable order.

Kuron also understood for the first time the role that the Church played in the life of the nation. To the leftist belief he had always held, the Church represented the reactionary Poland of old, and had no place in a modern state. But to the people, he realized, the Church was the only institution in Peoples' Poland which had consistently and courageously fought for the conditions of humanity and dignity that he himself was now proclaiming. The intellectuals had forfeited their ancient right to speak to and on behalf of the people. That role had been adopted by the bishops of Poland. The seeds of Jacek Kuron's most enduring work were sown. Several years went by before they were to flower, but on September 23, 1976, fourteen Polish intellectuals at his behest met at 22 Rakowiecka Street, Warsaw. The small, beautifully furnished apartment belonged to a revered and veteran socialist (whose political career had begun at the time of the first Russian Revolution in 1905), Professor Edward Lipinski. At the 1976 meeting the Committee for the Defense of the Workers, better known by its acronym of KOR, was founded. This was a crucial and historic moment in the history of Eastern European Communism. The intellectuals were ready once again to be heard on behalf of all members of society. They had returned, as Kuron himself said to me, to duty.

The immediate reason to establish KOR then was another outbreak of industrial dissent. This time principally at the Ursus factory in Radom, where demonstrators were treated with the utmost brutality by the police. Kuron was determined that this time intellectuals would not stand aloof. The fourteen founding members sent an appeal to the Polish Parliament, the *Sejm*, under a covering note from Jerzy Andrzejewski detailing examples of brutality. "The demonstrators," said the petition, "were kicked, beaten, and arrested on a massive scale. Dismissals from jobs were applied on a wide scale, hitting the poorest families the hardest.

"The use of repressive methods was coupled in most cases with infringements of the law by the authorities. The courts passed verdicts without adequate evidence. The labor code was infringed. The authorities did not hesitate to use force to obtain evidence . . . the victims of the reprisals cannot count on any help or defense from the established institutions, such as the trade unions, which played a deplorable role. The society in whose interests the protesters were persecuted should now take up their cause. Society has no other method of defense against lawlessness except solidarity and mutual aid. . . ." The Speaker of the *Sejm* wrote back to Andrzejewski, returning both his covering letter and the petition with a letter reading: ". . . this text is not suitable for consideration both for formal-legal reasons, and in view of its contents." In others words, the Polish Parliament—legal representatives of the people—disqualified itself from considering the desperate plight of its own working people. The meeting in Edward Lipinski's apartment was embarrassing for the authorities. When Lipinski spoke to some 8,000 students in Warsaw University in March 1981 to commemorate the brutal suppression of the students' revolt of March 1968, he began by saying, "The last time I spoke to such a gathering was probably in the year 1905." Lipinski, one of Poland's most distinguished academic economists, was one of the last survivors of the old left-wing of the Polish Socialist Party from which the Communist Party emerged. In 1905, aged seventeen, he had been fighting for social justice against the Russian czar. In 1976, eighty-eight years old, a member of the Communist Party, he was still fighting the same battles. This great old man, who could easily have been one of the anointed prelates of Peoples' Poland, chose instead to join the opposition, to draw the bow as someone put it, between the 1905 Revolution against the Russian czar and the present revolution against the Soviet Communist system.

The name the committee chose for itself—Committee for the Defense of the Workers—was an even greater scandal. It ensured that Lipinski had to be expelled from the Party to the anguish of the Party itself and everyone connected with it never again ceased to be under police surveillance. Never had there been such a provocation in any Communist country. Who were these men, asked the press throughout the bloc, who dared to suggest that the proletariat needed defending against their own proletarian revolution? But Jacek Kuron and his friends remained secure in the knowledge that they had found a way for Poland's intellectual community to take on the Party where it was most vulnerable—the condition of the working class, on whose behalf Poland's intellectuals themselves had previously argued. The authorities reacted with fury. All over the country KOR workers were terrorized, beaten up, or jailed, but it was not until one was murdered that the whole nation was aroused. Stanislaw Pyjas was a twenty-three-year-old student of philology at the Jagiellonian University of Krakow. On the morning of May 7, 1977, he was found dead from head injuries on the staircase of an apartment building while there seemed to be no valid reason he should have been there at all. He had last been seen collecting signatures for a petition calling for an inquiry into abuses committed by the security services against KOR activists (he, as a student member, was one). To this day no one knows precisely what happened. Officially, according to the press, he "died in a tragic accident unfortunately caused by abuse of alcohol," though the official prosecutor made no mention of drink when he reported that Pyjas "died of choking caused by bleeding from a cut lip and bruised nose." The evidence that he was murdered was circumstantial but I, and no one I ever met in Poland, have no doubt that he was killed by security troops. The only question is whether he was deliberately murdered or whether he was the victim of a beating with an unforeseen outcome. However he met his death, the effect on Poland was stunning. An obituary notice on the bulletin boards of Warsaw University said it all: "Stanislaw Pyjas died because he thought independently."

A young poet, Jan Korwin, wrote "The Wall" which was soon circulating throughout Poland:

> Ah! Accuse no one!
> They have no name,
> They have no face,
> There is no one to point to,
> There is no one to characterize.
> With his head he hit the wall of silence,
> With his head he hit the wall of injustice,
> With his head he hit the wall of violence,
> With his head he hit the wall of ignominy,
> Of treachery and illegality,
> Of crime and servility,
> And he bored through the wall,
> Though only a brick wide,
> And a tiny lump
> From the falling wall
> Killed him
> On that very staircase
> There at the place of murder.
> The keepers patch up
> Yet another breach in the wall
> Which while falling
> Will some day get them.

All of Poland knew it was no longer enough to joke about the system in order to maintain an illusion of freedom, the time was now close for action.

With support mounting daily both from home and abroad, KOR widened its activities so that it had activists in every town and village in the country.

In September 1977, KOR decided to formalize its new status as the principal opposition group in Poland, and to widen its activities. It changed its name to the Social Self-Defense Committee, though still retaining the old acronym "KOR." It summarized its aims as follows:

(1) To oppose reprisals made for political, ideological, religious, or racial reasons and to help those who are persecuted for such reasons;
(2) To oppose violations of the rule of law, and to help victims of injustice;
(3) To fight for institutional guarantees of civil rights and freedoms;
(4) To support and protect all social initiatives made in the cause of human and civil rights.

Its most important function, in a society where news could be defined as that which the authorities chose to publish, was to publish a regular Information Bulletin. An immaculately researched, regular report from all over Poland it documented cases of people, mainly workers, being victimized for curious crimes, like possessing "a negative social stance"; or illegal arrests and secret trials; bad or inhumane working conditions; inept management; and brutal security men. The Information Bulletin was to grow in time into a real newspaper, the *Robotnik* (the "Worker") first the unofficial and then one of the official newspapers of Solidarity, providing Poles for the first time with genuine information about what was really happening in their country. As significant was the formation of the so-called Flying Universities set up under the auspices of KOR in January 1978. Like so much else in Poland, it could trace its origins back deep into history. In 1885 Polish Marxists established what they called a Flying University—a Society of Scientific Courses—because the czarist government had imposed severe political and ideological restrictions on Poland's system of education and left-inclined academics then believed they had a duty to the Polish people to teach courses that the official educational system was either unable or incapable of providing. The sixty-two

Polish Scholars who set up the Flying University in 1978 also called themselves the Society of Scientific Courses in order to "provide advice and information as well as didactic and scientific assistance to all who wish to approach us." In every university town in the country, Flying University courses were held in private apartments, providing not only students but workers as well with a properly organized syllabus of academic instruction, mainly in the social sciences and humanities, and opening the doors to an academic freedom until then unknown in Poland. Meanwhile, as the illegal, independent self-governing unions began forming, established by workers like Lech Walesa, KOR activists were available to every cell to help in technical advice, drafting manifestos, defining the parameters of trade union activity, and last, but far from least, providing financial support. For the whole of 1980, for instance, before Solidarity voted him a salary, Lech Walesa and his large family were completely supported by KOR funds. From all of this emerged an astonishing flowering of Polish culture. Those artists and writers who had been floundering before not only found a voice but a ready-made audience, so that when Solidarity finally was revealed, the cultural and academic community were ready.

Now that self-same cultural and academic community face a period of trial. The myth will be permitted to gain ground that if only Solidarity had been left to "decent workingmen and women," then December 1981 need not have occurred. Men like Jacek Kuron, who suffered because he provided the direction which brought Solidarity into being, will suffer anew because he and his friends will be accused of being the extremists who brought Solidarity into disrepute. Nor is this a view exclusively reserved to the Polish authorities. I heard many Poles say the same thing in the latter half of 1981, when it became apparent that Solidarity was no longer in control of its own house. To some extent they were merely echoing the Polish press, which had sought, from the very earliest moment when Solidarity was officially recognized, to drive a rift between it and KOR. But to some extent too, they were reacting, as human beings will anywhere, to distress by seeking scapegoats for their misfortunes.

It is true that there were elements within Solidarity from the very beginning, such as the Young Poland Movement—a largely middle-class group, anti-Russian and anti-Party—that made contact with the free trade unions long before the strike, and who were in the shipyard throughout the long negotiations leading to the Gdansk Accord and whose ambitions far exceeded those of men like Walesa. Of course, to describe them as extremists is to use the language of their opponents.

If it is extreme to insist upon free elections, then they are extreme; if it is extreme to demand complete national sovereignty, then they are extreme; if it is extreme to insist that the Party give up automatic control of every facet of national life, then they are extreme. Not many outside the Communist bloc would regard this as a particularly obnoxious political program. Nevertheless, these demands—which became more insistent in Solidarity (which never remotely became an homogeneous organization, and with a membership of 10 million how could it?)—were to lead to the final crackdown. Before we all succumb to legend, it is important to exculpate Jacek Kuron and his friends from all responsibility. Not to do so would be to condemn the intellectual movement of social reform throughout the bloc to permanent impotence. Kuron was always clear that the leading role of the Communist Party in Poland, because of the nation's geopolitical situation, could not be reasonably negotiated away. That would come, but not yet, he argued—and for a month in June I was with him almost every day—passionately and strongly within Solidarity and outside, that the purpose of any reform movement must be not to destroy the Party but to make it accountable to the people it sought to serve. Poland's problem, he said, was that the ruling apparatus did not appear, to the people, to have legitimacy and accordingly was greeted with disrespect and cynicism. Communism had been imported into Poland at the barrel of a gun, and the gunsights had never been lifted. Nothing in Poland functioned, because the society rejecting the Party rejected its rules. Thus he advocated a series of "special movements," where pluralism would be accepted in every facet of life, society gradually being democratized from the base upward, until such time as the Politburo would be firmly entrenched at the top, presiding over a series of self-governing institutions, factories and the like, which would not be capitalist in character, though they would not be purely socialist either. It was a "historic compromise" he sought from the Party, and if toward the end he was beginning to flirt with the thought of new political parties, then the explanation for that can only be his despair at the prospect of the Communist Party itself recognizing that its only future lay in its ability to support the aspirations of the working people of Poland.

I last talked with Jacek Kuron on a four-hour drive from Warsaw to Poznan in June 1980. It was on my way out of the country. He was attending the great memorial celebration for those killed in the Poznan riots of 1956. I had picked him up at his apartment and his marvelous wife, Grazyna, was there to see us off. As usual he was running late, tucking in his shirt with one hand as he ran to the car, holding a cup of hot coffee in the other. He slept for part of the way and then talked, not about politics, but about Poland. Everything he had ever done, he said, had been done with Poland in mind. I asked him if he ever wanted to travel (he has never been out of Poland in his life), and he replied that he could not imagine that any place in the world matched Poland for its beauty. His hope for his country was a simple one—that everyone in it should live a dignified life. The dignity that had been denied the Poles for so long was gradually being restored. That, he said, was the justification for everything he had ever done.

I dropped him in the middle of Poznan and watched as this short, barrel-chested man, who had done so much to influence the events of the era in which we live, walk along the crowded street alone and unrecognized. Then I remembered I still had his cup. I stopped the car, held it out the window and shouted, "Jacek, your cup." He laughed. "Bring it with you next time you come to Poland," he called back. And then added with another of his great roars of laughter, "But look after it well." When I heard that Jacek Kuron was one of the first men arrested on December 13, I took his cup out of the cupboard and put it on my desk. It is a plain brown mug with a fluted base—ordinary breakfast crockery. But now Kuron's cup is one of my most precious possessions: a memento of one of the most extraordinary men of our time. As he told me, I will look after it very well, until I meet him again, a free man, in the Warsaw he loves so dearly.

12
The Press

꙳

First man: "I heard on the radio this morning that our standard of living is now higher than Western Europe's. I opened my newspaper and learned that our technology has now surpassed the United States'. And on the evening news bulletin it was revealed that Polish productivity has surpassed that of the Japanese."
Second man: "Jesus, I knew things were bad—but not that bad!"

THE *Gazeta Krakowska* is housed in one of the most fascinating newspaper buildings I have ever seen. As one enters through the main door one is pitched straight into a cathedral of the old print technology. The hall is the well of the building, so that as one stands in it one can look up on either side and see the giant rotary presses and linotype machines in clear view behind glass partitions. It's a thrilling sight for anyone who has ever been involved with newspapers. It may look very antiquated now, but the building was a sensation when it was put up in the 1920s. As you climb the stairs at the far end of the building, you get a unique glimpse into every printing process as you pass by, men hard at work producing the next day's edition of what was for a year or so, before the military crackdown, Poland's most famous newspaper.

My appointment, in June 1981, was with Maciej Szumowski, the editor, whom every journalist I met in Poland insisted I ought to see. I have met many Russian and East European Editors in my time and those from official Party newspapers such as the *Gazeta Krakowska*, come straight out of Central Casting. They tend to be men in their late fifties or early sixties, distinguished-looking, gray-haired, slightly florid, wearing the same squarely cut dark suit, white shirt, and, as a concession to modernism, surprisingly garish tie—in short, the uniform of top Communist officials throughout the bloc. And the editors of Party newspapers like *Pravda* in Russia or *Trybuna Ludu* in Warsaw and their regional counterparts are just that—very top Party officials indeed, ranking in importance only, in many cases, after the

Party Secretary. They are, like Lenin—who was the first editor of *Pravda*—politicians first and newspapermen only incidentally.

Westerners will often complain how boring these papers are, how slavishly they follow the Party line, how tediously they print every word of every speech of a Party bigwig, and how little actual news, which has not been processed through some Party meat-grinder, they print. But this misses the point.

It is a bit like complaining that though a telephone directory may have the bulk, it lacks the literary style of *War and Peace*. Party newspapers were never designed to be newspapers as we in the West understand them. Lenin himself set down the template. The main function of Party newspapers has never been to publish "all the news fit to print," but to act as the propaganda arm of the Central Committee upon which its editor sits as one of the leading ideologues. It is the link between the Committee and the outside world, a kind of company house magazine, whose first duty is to the Party and, only secondarily, to its readers. Thus, if *Pravda* prints in full a speech by Leonid Brezhnev, it is fulfilling its primary function, and the editor, who may well have had a hand in writing the speech in the first place, is fulfilling his duty to propagate the policies of the Party of which he is, one of the principal decision-makers. These days, of course, the official Party press has moved slightly away from the Leninist model. It employs professional newspapermen who report upon events in the wider world outside the Party, but it is the function of the editor to ensure that they do so strictly from Leninist principles.

So when I walked into Maciej Szumowski's outer office, I had a fairly clear idea of what to expect. His secretary stood up, said something in Polish that I didn't catch to a young man leaning against the wall (whom I took to be the office boy or perhaps a reporter), and then opened the door to the inner sanctum. To my astonishment the "office boy" followed me in and took a seat at the head of the conference table. He was Maciej Szumowski. For the first ten minutes or so I barely listened as I studied this extraordinary apparition. Szumowski was wearing a pair of well-faded jeans and a thin, blue round-collared sweater over an open-neck shirt. In his early forties, he has the finely chiseled face of an actor (he is by profession not a newspaperman but a documentary filmmaker). He speaks softly, even nervously, his fingers drumming the table. There are portraits of Lenin on the wall, as there inevitably must be in such an office, but they are the only concession to the old ways. What Maciej Szumowski accomplished in Krakow, unobserved by a world obsessed by Lech Walesa and Solidarity, was as revolutionary in intent and purpose as anything attempted by the Independent Trade Union. *Gazeta Krakowska*, under his editorship, changed from being a dull and predictable organ of the Central Committee of the Krakow Party into the most vibrant and politically exciting newspaper in the country, and certainly in the bloc. Its circulation of 500,000 can be attributed to the national shortage of paper. Szumowski himself believed that if he had more paper, circulation would have risen to 3 million. If this seems exaggerated, then I can report that a paper whose cover price in Krakow is one zloty was selling on the black market in Warsaw for 300 zlotys—an extraordinary situation in a marketplace where traditionally Party newspapers were purchased, if at all, out of a sense of duty rather than any expectation of pleasure or enlightenment.

At the beginning of 1980, the former editor in Krakow went to Warsaw as a political adviser to Prime Minister Jaruzelski. A liberal-minded man, he recommended that Szumowski should take his place, but Szumowski himself was far from sure that he wanted the job. He had a national reputation as a filmmaker. One of a group of young reformers surrounding Andrzej Wajda, Poland's greatest film director, he had enough exciting projects lined up to keep him busy for years. Neither did he want to become involved in the politicking—the canvassing for votes among senior members of the Central Committee, whose newspaper it was and who would therefore be responsible for appointing the new editor. He agreed that his name should go forward "because I realized that this was an important opportunity for advancing ideas which many of us had," but only on the condition that he would not be expected to lobby on his own behalf. It was quite astonishing to everyone who knew him and who understood the system that he was appointed, and for that the Krakow Central Committee deserved great credit.

But even they must have been taken aback by his first statements. He would not, he said, serve on the Central Committee of the Party, for to do so would compromise his independence. The principal newspaper in Krakow should be in a position to criticize the local Party, and how could it if the editor was a member of the Party's governing body. This statement would, to any Western journalist, appear to be unexceptional in its logic, but to the Communist mind it was the most dangerous kind of heresy. The function of a Party newspaper is not to criticize the Party, but to explain it. The function of its editor is not to be an objective observer but a politician with a subjective view of the world. The Krakow Party accepted this anomo-

lous position, thus giving the city of Krakow the first official Party
newspaper in the Communist world (and indeed non-Communist
world, even the editor of the *Morning Star* in England is a member
of the Party's ruling Politburo) that had an editor who was not a
Party official.

It is hardly surprising that by permitting this situation to arise the
Communist authorities in Krakow were suspect. Almost certainly, it
was the principal reason why the whole local Party was suspended—
a remarkable occurrence—during the first week of martial law. Yet,
seen even from the standpoint of the Communist Party itself, the
brave experiment of giving an official Party newspaper the stamp of
independence was one which was to prove wholly beneficial. As one
strongly anti-Communist member of Krakow Solidarity put it to me:
"Under Szumowski, *Gazeta Krakowska* became required reading. I,
and everyone else I know, regarded it as a newspaper that could be
believed, and that is quite something, considering it was, however
liberal, a Communist Party newspaper. If the whole Party had ever
been trusted the way *Gazeta Krakowska* was trusted, then Poland
would never have gotten into the position it did. Szumowski's greatest
contribution to Marxist-Leninism was to prove that it is possible to
be a Marxist-Leninist without being a liar. Unfortunately for the
Party, not enough people learned by his example."

If Poland's intellectual community had long been held in the
deepest suspicion by the ordinary working population, that part of it
which worked for the media—newspapers, radio, or TV—was held in
particular contempt. In Andrzej Wajda's film *Man of Iron*, which
won the Golden Palm Award for the best film in 1981 at the Cannes
Film Festival and is a magnificent evocation of the rise and triumph
of Solidarity, a radio reporter, seen as a frightened puppet of the
secret police, was the villain brought in by the authorities to discredit
the strike leaders at the Gdansk Shipyards. To Western audiences his
role, albeit a principal one, was but a literary device, a method of
giving the film a story-line and a focus which it might otherwise have
lacked. To Polish audiences, however, the message was very clear.
The mass media in Poland, Wajda was telling them, is an arm of the
state, and those who work in it are moral degenerates who have sold
out their consciences to the system. They are not to be believed. If
newspapers, radio, or TV attack Solidarity leaders, he was telling
Poles, who, of course, knew it already, then this is because journalism
in Poland had been corrupted beyond salvation. It was Szumowski's
task, as he saw it, both as a member of the Party and a close friend

and colleague of Wajda's, to show that this was not true. He succeeded magnificently.

Under his editorship *Gazeta Krakowska*, though owing its primary allegiance to the Communist Party in Poland, carried articles highly critical of the government and Party, printed the views of distinguished independent non-Party writers, and was on constant lookout for examples of corruption by Communist Party officials. Of all the papers in Poland, including the surprisingly large number of non-Party papers that, in theory at any rate, ought to have been more independent, the *Gazeta Krakowska* ran more pieces about the excesses of the past than any other, while at the same time being the most vigilant of any newspaper in the country against renewed examples of abuse of power. Two events propelled the paper into the forefront and made everyone in Poland realize that at last an official, not an underground, paper was prepared to deal with the truth.

The first occasion was when Stanislaw Kania, then Party Secretary, went to Moscow in February 1981 to address the twenty-sixth Congress of the Communist Party of the Soviet Union. He proclaimed from the platform that the Polish people were determined to crush anti-socialist elements that were seeking to lead ordinary Polish workers astray. Mildly, *Gazeta Krakowska* pointed out that Mr. Kania was not entitled to speak for the Polish people. He was General Secretary of the Polish United Workers' Party, and it was that party and its 3 million members, and no one else, that he represented in Moscow. For a Communist Party newspaper to explain to the General Secretary of the Party the limitations of both his moral and his legal rights caused a sensation in the country, and overnight *Gazeta Krakowska* became a paper that everyone all over the country who was politically aware, Party members and non-Party members alike, knew they had to read.

The second event confirming that at last the rigidly controlled official Polish press was breaking out of its straitjacket came in March of that year when, after a sit-in strike in the provincial assembly hall in Bydgoszcz, local police stormed the building, dragged out the protestors, and beat up their leaders. Though Bydgoszcz is as far to the north of the country as Krakow is deep in the south, Maciej Szumowski decided to send a reporter to investigate the affair that had become the most explosive in Poland since Solidarity had been born.

"Deciding to send our own reporter rather than rely upon the reports of the official news agency, which is traditionally what the Polish press does on these occasions, was in itself a departure from

the normal way of doing things," Maciej told me. "And having sent
a reporter, I decided we had to print what he wrote, and people were
a little surprised," he went on. That was putting it mildly. The immediate effect was that Szumowski's paper—designed for the purpose
of supporting the regime—ran a series of articles proving that the
Bydgoszcz authorities were almost wholly responsible for what had
happened. In the face of that withering fire from its own lines, the
authorities in Warsaw had no option but to call for a full judicial
investigation.

But the long-term effect, until martial law was to suspend service,
was a good deal more revolutionary. If an official Party newspaper
could actually send reporters into the field and engage in investigative
journalism, why shouldn't other newspapers, especially those not tied
to the Party at all, do the same? For the first time since the war, real
journalism began to appear in newspapers up and down the country.

It was, of course, a short-lived freedom, an exhilarating period when
newspapers could actually become a pleasure to read. Yet it must also
be acknowledged that a profession which, even by the standards of
totalitarian Communism, had permitted itself to become spiritually
debauched, had always possessed in its ranks men and women prepared to risk everything in order that the truth be told. "If, to the
outsider, it seemed as if all Polish journalists had sold out completely
to the system, it was only because a great many journalists over the
years sacrificed their jobs because they tried to write the truth, while
a great many others spent their entire lifetime constructing articles
in such a way that they would escape the watchful eye of the censor,
while providing a coded message to the Polish population," a newspaper editor told me. "Even *Trybuna Ludu,* the *Pravda* of Poland,
once ran an essay on 'Friendship,' which everyone in the country
understood as a brilliantly veiled attack upon the Soviet Union, for
whom friendship means receiving but not giving."

This art was perfected by the editors and writers of *Polityka* under
their editor-in-chief Mieczyslaw Rakowski, who was to become a
Deputy Prime Minister of Poland in February 1981. From the moment it first opened its doors in 1956 right through to the formation
of Solidarity, when all things seemed possible, *Polityka,* a Communist
Party weekly whose senior staff were members of the Party, fought to
maintain an independence of mind and spirit unique throughout the
bloc.

In intellectual circles in Poland today the name of Rakowski is
likely to produce more jeers than applause. Certainly he did the cause

for which he had fought for so long a good deal of harm by insisting on remaining editor-in-chief when he got his job in the government. Much of *Polityka*'s authority dissipated when it was realized that the Deputy Prime Minister was reading the page proofs every week and insisting on alterations. Yet friends of Rakowksi put it this way: "For years he fought and struggled against everything the Party could throw at him to retain *Polityka*'s unique position. Only he knew how difficult it had been, and he simply did not trust anyone else to carry the banner. He knew that things would get difficult again and was determined that *Polityka* would survive whatever happened. Rather arrogantly perhaps—and arrogant he certainly is—he simply took the view that without him the ethic which *Polityka* represented would not survive a catastrophe."

Few Poles, even members of his staff, suspected the extraordinary battle that Rakowski waged all those years with a succession of Party leaders and Politburos. Often, of course, he had to give ground, but each retreat he saw as a tactical maneuver to keep his paper in good shape for the next round. The best journalists in Poland flocked to the paper, where they were given an independence unthinkable elsewhere. Of course, *Polityka* was still a Party paper, and there were rules to be observed, but during the good times these were remarkably flexible, and during the bad, never wholly disreputable.

It can be no accident that those men and women who courageously defied the censorship laws of Poland that clearly and bureaucratically defined what could be published, and kept alive the soul of Poland during some of its most trying years, were to be found in the newsroom of this Communist publication. A young journalist named Jan Walc on the staff of *Polityka* in the autumn of 1976 was asked by a friend, Andrzej Celinski, a KOR activist and one of the organizers of the Flying University, to help arrange a meeting for a group of his students with some of those poets who, because of their outright opposition to the regime, had experienced difficulty in getting published.

It was from that request—from an outright dissident to a member of the establishment press—that the liveliest and most professional *Samizdat* organization in the Communist bloc first went into business.

Walc agreed to help Celinski and organized a first meeting for the poet Stanislaw Baranczak at a community center on the outskirts of Warsaw. But the security forces heard what was planned and banned the use of this public hall. In normal circumstances, that would have been that, but because Baranczak had, after a long and tiring journey, already arrived in the city, Walc felt that he owed him an audience of some kind. So, he changed the venue and borrowed a friend's apartment, which was quickly packed to the rafters. Baranczak's poetry was heard in reverent silence. When he finished pandemonium broke out, as the young people cheered and clapped, a demonstration only conceivable in a country where truth has long since been mortgaged. Walc watched in some astonishment as the students gathered around the poet clamoring for his work, and when they discovered that no copies were available, asked him to repeat his reading, but this time at dictation speed so that they could copy it down.

Another poet, Adam Zagajewski, had been booked for the next meeting, but this time Walc prepared himself properly. He telephoned Zagajewski and asked if he could have some of the poems in advance to have copies made. He was sent seventeen, typed them out himself, and made fifty copies, no mean feat in a country where private possession of copying machines was illegal, and every copy made on an office machine had to be registered.

"I thought the typescript looked rather untidy and in need of binding, so I turned to another friend, a printer, for help," he said. "Luckily, she had a free evening, and with no time to lose, we set to work immediately. We cut sheets of black cardboard into the correct size, and with letters made of rubber we stamped out the author's name and the title of the 'volume.' Moreover, we made a little abstract color drawing on each cover. The booklets were all different, each copy was numbered and carried the writer's signature on the title page.

"Adam Zagajewski's poetry-reading took place in a club belonging to a housing co-operative whose management was unaware that the gathering had not received official approval. Just before the reading ended, I put our booklets on display, leaving the price to the generosity of the buyers. All the copies were immediately sold, and to my surprise, the contents of my hat came to about 2,500 zlotys."

News of the reading and the "books" sold afterwards quickly spread through Warsaw. *Polityka*, which had enough problems of its own without members of its staff openly producing officially disapproved-of material, had no option but to sack Walc, but he, by accident, had discovered the enormous hunger that existed for even amateurishly printed literary publications forbidden by the censorship. From that moment on he never looked back as Poland's underground press grew to phenomenal proportions.

At about the same time, and almost certainly encouraged by Jan Walc's foray into unofficial publishing, a group of writers in Warsaw published the first issue of a new literary magazine called "The

Record" (*Zapis*). There had been earlier attempts to establish *Samizdat* literary magazines, but the *Record* was different. Its editors persuaded writers to publish under their real names—an act of great courage by those who agreed. For they all knew the state publishing monopoly on which they were forced to rely had a sure way of keeping writers in line, by simply withdrawing official recognition and with it the livelihood of any who openly aligned themselves with the dissident movement.

One writer that, for obvious reasons, it would be wrong to name, put it this way: "I received a reputation of being a member of opposition groups in the early seventies and suffered a great deal of privation as a result. Every serious writer knows that he can have a profound effect upon his society through his work and yet also knows that he is among the more vulnerable to outside pressure. A writer who sits on a manuscript that no one will publish is in the same position as a Pole arriving in New York City with 10 million zlotys in his pocket. He knows that what he has is of great worth, but finds himself in a society where its value goes totally unrecognized. He thinks he is rich, and, indeed, on one scale of judgment he is rich beyond compare, and yet on the only scale that matters he is a pauper. My editor, who had dealt with me for years, suddenly sent back a manuscript one day saying he would not be publishing it. Not for a moment did he criticize the political content of my book which, in any case, was implicit rather than explicit, but he criticized its literary merits. I was thunderstruck. I guessed that I was on some sort of blacklist, but it is very easy for a writer to persuade himself that a book which by literary standards is bad is being rejected for some other reason altogether. Ours is after all something of a paranoid's profession. For weeks I just sat at home, I could not think straight, dared not even show my manuscript to other writers for fear that they would confirm the view of the publishing house. I thought it was a good book, but if it wasn't even fit to be published, then my whole world as a writer had collapsed around me.

"Eventually I asked other opinions and was told everywhere that it was not my work that was at fault, but the political atmosphere in which it had been written. I was only half encouraged, tormenting myself with the thought that my friends were merely being polite, but I wrote to my editor asking for a meeting to discuss how he felt the book should be changed. He avoided me, obviously deliberately, until one night I met him in the Writers' Club and pinned him in a corner until I got an answer. Eventually he said that he had been instructed

to turn the book down and suggested a way out of my dilemma: that I
write an article for an official magazine distancing myself from some of
my friends who had taken on the regime in a way I had not, head on.

" 'We don't have Stalinism in this country,' my publisher told me.
'Nobody expects public confessions or denunciations. You are a fine
writer, all that I'm suggesting is that you clarify your own position.'
I can tell you I was often tempted as the years went by. How does a
writer who is not being published provide for his family, not to mention himself? I couldn't even get any 'hack' work. Every editor in the
country had been told that I was officially out of favor, and none were
prepared to run the risk of seeming to give me a platform, even if I
was offering material which could not have been more benign.

"Somehow we managed to keep afloat on savings and then by bor-
rowing money from friends. The funny thing was that I had never
been particularly political before. I was extremely narrow-minded; all
that really mattered to me, and the only thing I protested about, was
literary censorship. But when I was censored myself and bemoaning
my misfortune, a friend patiently explained to me that up till then I
had been a very privileged member of society, that while censorship
was a great crime because it stopped writers from describing the nation's misfortunes, the nation's misfortunes did not disappear because
they were not being described. I opened my eyes for the first time and
became politicized in a way I never was in the past. I'm no longer
looking for a literary reputation, at least that is not the first of my
considerations, everything I write has as its core the issues which confront my country."

Publication of *The Record*, which first saw life as several roneod
typescripts lovingly passed from hand to hand, was to open up new
possibilities for authors on the blacklist, but more significantly, for
their readers, KOR, too, was publishing a bulletin recording the trial,
arrest, and imprisonment of workers involved in free trade unions.

Yet though they had the luxury of a small spirit duplicator capable
of producing 200 copies from one stencil, better than anything else
then available, this hardly met the need for nationwide distribution
which was so essential if KOR was ever to be anything but a self-
indulgent clique of Warsaw intellectuals.

Everyone involved soon realized that a literary manuscript, however
fine, had no independent life of its own until it had a publisher and
a printer. In the West, authors tend to take both for granted, and if
they deign to notice them at all, malign them. However, in Poland
every writer of substance accepts that if it had not been for Mirek

Chojecki, a man with organizational genius but no literary pretensions, their attempts to burst out of the shackles imposed by state control of the arts would have come to nothing.

Mirek Chojecki, once described as "that imp with the face of an icon," was a scientist in his late twenties working in Poland's Nuclear Research Institute when he was peremptorily fired for distributing at the institute the primitively duplicated KOR bulletins. A man of immense energy and humor, always on the go, his ability to instill in others his huge enthusiasm, almost singlehandedly propelled Poland's parlor intellectuals into a mighty political force by providing them with a platform by professionally publishing their works. He also published, in Polish for the first time, foreign authors like George Orwell, Gunther Grass, and Osip Mandelstam, and introduced into the country ideas that had long been unavailable except to those able to read foreign languages. But Chojecki principally addressed himself to Poland's own writers.

Chojecki realized that if Polish writers banned by the regime were to emerge from an intellectual ghetto where their typescripts were handed from person to person (a situation many of them accepted with gloomy fatalism), then one underground organization had to take on the task of printing and promoting their work. So he founded the "Independent Publishing House" (*Niezalezna Oficyna Wydawnicza*) or NOWA as it came to be known. It would be NOWA's job, he told individual writers as well as organizations like KOR, to print and publish their material, everything from full-scale novels to KOR bulletins. All they had to do was give him the manuscript.

Chojecki, extravagantly hirsute with a long beard and shaggy hair, had such a persuasive personality that he was able to convince more sober friends to help, though all must have wondered what this madman had in store for them. He was proposing to publish independently in a country where not only was it illegal in theory, but impossible in practice. Paper, that essential raw material for publishing, was just not available on the open market. Writers who needed it could get it from the Writers' Union, but only in quantities sufficient to write their own books, not to publish them. The state specifically ruled that individuals could not possess their own duplicating machines, photocopying machines, stencils, or even ink.

There were no private printing facilities anywhere and no distribution outlets. To most men these would have insuperable barriers, as they were intended, to independent publishing. For Chojecki they were merely a challenge.

"Matters like publishing policy, editing, or proofreading, normally the major concerns in a publishing house, were minimal compared to the time spent in arranging contacts and materials and throwing the security services off the trail," said Chojecki in 1981. "The first task was to establish a printing base; to learn as much as possible about how to print books without having any legal access to printing presses and paper, under the watchful eyes of the police."

Chojecki and his colleagues consistently refused, even in the high days of Solidarity-won freedom, to reveal how they got their materials. It seems clear that duplicators and the like were either smuggled in from the West or, in some cases, clearly "liberated" from government offices as was paper. In the end, however, it all came down to a network of friends and admirers, often at some risk to themselves, helping out in every stage of production. For example, it would have been folly for the completed pages of a book so laboriously printed to be stored in just one place, in case the police discovered the cache and seized the lot. So, as soon as individual pages were ready, they were ferried out to supporters, who hid them in their apartments until they could be collected again for binding. The printers themselves, often working in dark cellars from which they wouldn't emerge for days on end, snatched very little sleep between shifts. Working on antique equipment that constantly broke down, they are the great unsung heroes of the Polish opposition. Once the book was printed, another group of people organized by Chojecki would arrange distribution. Print runs would be between 1,000 and 2,000 copies per book, not much by Western standards. But each copy of Andrzejewski's *Pulp*, for example, a massive political novel which NOWA published, was read by ten people, which meant that it and books of similar stature could become reasonably well known.

Andrzejewski, now seventy-four years old, was officially banned for twenty years. Published legally in 1981 and now almost certainly banned again, he told me: "My books only started their full existence when they could be on sale in public bookshops with the critics free to talk about them." Nevertheless, without Chojecki they would have had no existence at all. If the stakes had not been so high, Chojecki's life as an underground publisher could be described as romantic. Certainly it was always, with the security services constantly on his tail, eventful.

"The police set about with great persistence trying to detect our network," says Jan Walc, who quickly joined the dynamic Chojecki. "We made it difficult for them by constantly moving from place to place. To begin with, the police concentrated on keeping an eye on the people involved, in one way or the other, with the printing, but as unobstrusive surveillance is hardly possible, we soon managed to compile a considerable dossier of the car registration numbers used by the police agents. If, on the way to the printing works, one of us discovered that he was being followed, we had a whole range of tricks, or rather places, where it was fairly easy to lose them."

When surveillance didn't provide the police with the kind of information they wanted, they sought to infiltrate the organization with their informers. One day a man, not known to dissidents, called on Mirek Chojecki and offered to sell him a spirit duplicator, a piece of equipment desperately needed by NOWA. Mirek suspected him from the beginning of being a police spy, but decided that the bait was too important not to take. Negotiations took place over a long period of time until Chojecki was ready to finalize the deal. As he told his colleagues, "We've got to find a way of getting the duplicator and losing the policeman who goes with it." Eventually Mirek's plans were ready. He arranged a hand-over point, but took the precaution of sending a small group of people, not previously known to the police, all armed with lists of the license plates of police cars that had observed NOWA activists in the past, to check it out. Sure enough most of the cars seemed to be grouped around the perimeter of the area in which the hand-over was to take place. No more evidence was needed that this was a police trap.

Either this was a long-term infiltration exercise by the authorities or, more likely, it was an operation designed to catch Mirek with illegal possession of a duplicator, a crime that could bring a prison sentence. Nevertheless possession of the duplicator was so important that the risks involved in getting it seemed to this remarkable man to be worth taking. Right on time he arrived at the rendezvous point, met his man, and paid over the money, though, knowing that the man was even more anxious to sell the duplicator than he was to buy it, he had bargained with telling effect and had got it incredibly cheaply. He put the machine in his car and drove off, watching from his rearview mirror at what appeared to be the entire police force taking off in pursuit after him. Quickly, a friend in the car got to work. Skillfully he wrapped the duplicator in rags and padding and, as Chojecki suddenly accelerated around a bend so that momentarily his car was lost from the view of the pursuit vehicles, pushed the whole machine out of the window, and two men, apparently changing a tire at the roadside, rushed forward, grabbed it, rolled it into a ditch, and were back hard at work on their tire before the first police car came into view. Meanwhile, Chojecki drove around all that day closely followed by the police until eventually he got home. His house and car were thoroughly searched, but of course, the duplicator was now far away. It had been a marvelous victory, but not as spectacular as one he was to achieve the next time the police tried their duplicator ploy.

The authorities in totalitarian states have a basic weakness—it is difficult for them ever to admit that they are wrong. So the senior security officer who approved the original operation to trap Chojecki —and using a duplicator as bait implied that it must have been approved at the highest level—would not easily have admitted that the whole idea was misconceived. If it went wrong, it was because the junior operatives who had put it into effect had bungled, not because there was anything wrong with the plan itself. So another attempt was made.

Chojecki was approached again by a man he'd never seen before offering to sell him a duplicator, but this time it was a very large machine, not the kind that could be pushed out of a car window. Once again the dealer agreed (after protracted haggling) to accept 20 percent of the price he was originally seeking. It would have been obvious to a child that this was a security operation, and Chojecki was certainly not a child. Friends urged him not to chance his luck and refuse to negotiate, but to Chojecki the machine was so superior to anything he had that he decided any risk was worth taking in order to get it. Carefully he worked out a plan of campaign, and when he was satisfied that nothing had been left to chance, he asked to meet the vendor so that he could make a thorough examination of the machine before committing himself. Carefully he took it to pieces, explaining as he did so that he had to be sure that each part was functioning perfectly, as spare parts were impossible to come by. In fact, what he was doing as he worked was memorizing each detail, so that as soon as he left he could make an accurate working drawing of the duplicator, which would be essential for the second phase of Chojecki's sting. Eventually the big day came. Chojecki had demanded delivery on a Sunday, and when the man arrived with the duplicator in his car in a large crate, Chojecki asked to be driven to St. John's Cathedral in Warsaw where, he said, his car was parked. Off they drove, with what seemed like half the security forces of Warsaw in pursuit. Outside the cathedral, waiting friends took the crate out of the car, walked with it into the crowded church where a service was in progress, and not many minutes later, emerged from another door still carrying the crate which was carefully put into the car and driven off. Once again the chase was on, but this time the police decided to take no chances and after an hour or so overtook Chojecki, forced his car to the curb, and pulled open the doors. There was no duplicator—there was not even a crate. Only Mirek Chojecki, smiling like an angel, asking what all the fuss was about.

The story of the disappearing duplicator became part of Warsaw folklore, but nobody ever guessed how Chojecki had done it. In fact, it had all been brilliantly simple. Inside the cathedral at a side altar was a small army of Chojecki's helpers, all of whom had carefully studied the working drawing that Mirek had made of the machine. As soon as the crate was carried in, it was quickly opened and the machine—every screw of which was now familiar to the people working on it—was dismantled in a matter of minutes. The crate was quickly closed and carried out through the cathedral door while the pieces were divided up among various shopping bags and attaché cases and casually carried out to a central print shop as the Mass ended. As for the crate, it was simply broken up into pieces on the journey and scattered, out of sight of the following cars, throughout the Polish countryside. Later the duplicator was reassembled and did years of useful work for NOWA. Ironically and quite deliberately this gift to the Polish dissident movement by the security service was used by NOWA to distribute an important document called the "White Book," a compilation of cases of legal violations by that same service that had made the machine available.

By the time Solidarity appeared on the scene, NOWA was firmly established as the most important publishing house in Poland, printing 80 percent of all independent literature; student satirical magazines; important literary monthlies; a fortnightly called *Robotnik* ("The Worker"), a KOR publication which reported strikes, stoppages, management behavior, and so on; academic journals handling subjects too sensitive for official publishing houses; as well as a remarkable list of books mainly by Polish writers, including emigrés such as Nobel Prize-winner Czeslaw Milosz, and also foreigners as well.

So well entrenched had NOWA become that it was using five tons of paper a month and it had become fashionable, even in Party circles, to have their publications, which completely undermined the case for censorship as it was being made out by the authorities. What was so astonishing and so refreshing about NOWA for Poles brought up in the rigidly orthodox mold of a Marxist state, was that it proved it was possible to run a publishing house that printed material embracing all points of view. Marxists wrote for NOWA, as did liberals, Catholics, and atheists. The only criterion applied by its editors was whether the material offered was of literary quality worth publishing. In the West that is commonplace, in the East it is positively revolutionary.

Today, as the new Polish government seeks to return to the position that existed before NOWA arrived on the scene to challenge the official state publishing houses, it has to contend with a population that, thanks to Chojecki, has been educated to expect something better. The population knows that the press and broadcasting media lied in the past and is unlikely to be taken in when the media seeks to lie again. Furthermore, thanks to Solidarity publications, it knows exactly how these lies are concocted.

More is known about the Polish censor's office than any similar organization in the Communist bloc, because in 1977 a censor named Tomasz Strzyzewski defected to Sweden, carrying with him 600 pages of a document consisting of "Directives" and "Recommendations" issued by the chief censor in Warsaw for use by censors all over the country. Strzyzewski defected because, in his case once again, the Polish past caught up with the Polish present and delivered it a bloody nose. In the course of his work he came across new directives for how the censors should handle the Katyn Massacre. The directive reminded censors that formerly all references to Katyn of any kind had to be eliminated. However, the chief censor observed, a new edition of the Great Soviet Encyclopedia made reference to Katyn for the first time and told how Polish officers had been killed in Katyn Forest by the Germans in 1941.

Accordingly, said the directive, printed references to Katyn were permitted provided they corresponded exactly with the Soviet interpretation. However, the directive went on, "it would not be advisable to treat the Katyn case extensively in historical works, let alone in the press." Strzyzewski, thirty-two years old, then and there decided to defect and to take his files with him for the understandable reason that his own grandfather, a captain in the Polish Army, had been one of the identified victims of the Katyn Massacre.

The Strzyzewski papers, the authenticity of which there was never any doubt, as subsequently confirmed by another censor interviewed in a Solidarity publication, are important not only for the light they shed upon Poland, but because Polish practice is modeled exactly on the Russian system—one of the Soviet Union's principal exports to every East European country. Thanks to them we have a remarkable window into how the people's democracies manage their press.

The first thing to be noticed is what a remarkable bureaucratic edifice the censor's office is; the second is that no area of life is left untouched by it. One would expect Polish censors to cover politics and international relations but then, as one reads through the directives, one realizes clearly that there is no subject in a Communist country that is not granted considerable political significance by the authorities. So it is that the censor concerns himself with ecology, industrial relations, social affairs, crime, literary criticism, and even the obituary page, right down to paid announcements of death by ordinary readers. The censor's office in Poland has the reputation of being one of the few bureaucratic institutions in the country which works smoothly. Regular directives and recommendations go to offices all over the country and include advice notes on current issues and warnings about new problems likely to come up, as well as deletion of previous instructions thought to be no longer operative. Every fortnight each censor receives a document in a red folder, every quarter one in a brown folder, and occasionally a particularly important one in a yellow folder—all designed to show individual censors "main tendencies in the material withdrawn from all the mass media in the country."

These include long examples of censored copy, both the original text and how it was dealt with, as well as statistics revealing the number of "interventions" by the censor. Thus, for the period March 1 to 15, 1974, there were 616 interventions and 620 in the following two weeks. The interventions are also broken down into subject matter. Thus, during the period May 1 to 15 in the same year, there were 268 interventions in the social-political sphere; 85 in the social-economic sphere; 70 cultural-historic; 36 religious; and 1,125 designed to protect state secrets (clearly a category in which almost anything can be included).

But the important document, constantly being revised, is the one that contains hundreds, if not thousands, of prohibited subjects. It sits on the desk of every censor, it is his Bible, and he neglects to consult it at his peril. Here are some verbatim extracts:

In School No. 80 in Gdansk, a harmful substance emitted by the putty used to seal the windows was noticed. The school has been temporarily closed. No information whatsoever may be published about this subject.

All global figures on labor hygiene and accidents in the economy are to be withheld.

Information about the endangering of life and health of human beings caused through chemicals in industry and farming have to be deleted.

All information about food poisoning and epidemics affecting large groups of people, especially in important plants, and food poisoning in factory canteens, holiday centers, and summer colonies, is banned.

Information and descriptions with instructive character should be eliminated from material about thefts, burglaries, plane hijackings and other terror outrages. *This directive is also to be applied to strikes,* forms and methods of their organization [italics in the original document].

All obituaries, advertisements, and announcements about meetings in cemeteries, at monuments, and memorial sites planned by former soldiers of the Home Army and other right-wing organizations that participated in the Warsaw Uprisings are to be withheld.

Without consultation . . . no criticism of Article 13 of the Customs Law, nor of the relevant activity of the Customs Offices (confiscating some foreign parcels, books, etc.) is allowed. Same ban to be applied to criticism of the Polish Post Office for not delivering such shipments to Polish recipients.

There should be no disclosure about the pollution of rivers flowing from Czechoslovakia, if the pollution is caused by economic activity on our territory. On the other hand, information about the polluting of these rivers can be released if this is caused by economic activity on Czechoslovakia territory.

A book by Adam Schaff, a Marxist philosopher, on structuralism will be published by Ksiaska i Wiedza publishing house. All reviews and comments must be cleared with the office before publication.

Concerning the death of Antonin Slonimski (a great Polish poet and author), the press may publish only the communiques of PAP [the Polish official news agency]; one daily may publish the obituary signed by the Minister of Culture and only one official commentary. The literary press will publish only articles authorized by the Central Committee, and all editorial reminiscences and commentaries must be approved by the Central Committee.

No information is to be disclosed about the special pensions granted by the Prime Minister to certain persons.

No information should be published about the corruption affair in Sandomierz.

No information may be published about the additional purchases of potatoes which are intended for export.

No reference concerning the sale of meat to the Soviet Union is allowed.

No criticism of Soviet oil-drilling equipment used in explorations in Poland may be published. Any reference to suggestions of purchase of such material from other foreign sources must be eliminated.

No information, written in an approving, tolerant, understanding tone about hippies in Poland may be published. Only unequivocably critical references are allowed.

No information should be published about the annual coffee consumption in our country, in order to eliminate all possibilities of calculating the amount of coffee which is re-exported.

All criticism of income and social policies, including wage claims, is forbidden. This also refers to social services such as pensions, grants, leaves of absences, health care, etc.

Absolutely no information is to be published concerning the Katowice mine disasters in which four miners lost their lives.

Information concerning Poland's purchase of licenses from the capitalist countries is to be eliminated from the mass media.

Until verified, no information should be released on General Amin's speech, in which the erection of a monument to Adolf Hitler was announced.

There must be no publication of information concerning possible limitations on the freedom of action of Communist Parties or their leaders in Eygpt, Algeria, the Sudan, Iraq, Libya, and Syria.

No information should be published concerning possible trade with Rhodesia and South Africa or contacts between Polish institutions and South Africa.

In reports of the Polish Exhibition staged in Moscow on account of the thirtieth anniversary of the Polish People's Republic, we should avoid expressing excessive satisfaction with the successes of particular exhibitors, since this may suggest that some Polish products created a furor in Moscow and were not previously known on the Soviet market.

Information concerning price changes of some goods must be deleted from all materials concerning the protocol signed in Moscow about next year's trade exchanges and payments arrangements.

All information about Rumania's initiative with regard to membership in the movement of nonaligned states is forbidden.

But it was the occasion of the Pope's visit to Poland from June 2 to June 10, 1979, which showed Polish press and TV in its most grotesque light. It requires no great feat of the imagination to understand with what ecstasy this Polish Pope was greeted on his return to his homeland. Millions turned out to see him; the country was on an emotional high for the whole period of his visit. No Pole will ever forget it. Before his visit, however, *Time* magazine managed to get hold of Central Committee guidelines for the Polish information media during the visit. Nothing was to be left to chance. "On the opening day of the visit," went the guidelines, "the morning and afternoon press will publish a picture of the Pope, the news of his arrival, a profile and a commentary to be distributed by PAP" [the official news agency]. The party newspapers "will publish no photographs, only a news item, a biography and a commentary provided by PAP." (*Trybuna Ludu*, the official Party paper did print a picture on its front page.) Even headlines had to be provided by PAP and all photographs submitted to the Press Department for approval. As for television, this event transcending even such great national tele-visual occasions as British royal weddings, which probably had no equal for potential impact in the history of the medium, was treated as if it had no special significance at all. Polish national television covered only four events—the Pope's arrival and his reception by Party leaders at Warsaw's Belvedere Palace; the open air High Mass and the laying of the wreath at the Tomb of the Unknown Warrior in Warsaw; the visit to Auchwitz; and the departure ceremony at Krakow. On average, Polish television devoted only about fifteen minutes a day to the visit with only occasional extensions. Regional TV gave additional special coverage when the Pope entered their localities.

Subsequent to the visit, Polish TV cameramen and directors ad-mitted that they had been directed to photograph the Pope so that the vast crowds present wherever he went would be disguised by the camera angle. Everyone, of course, knew that already, and it had be-come a delicious joke. The Pope was always shown from below, so that he appeared to be almost floating in the sky with trees, clouds, and buildings as the only backdrop. Crowd shots were so arranged that the viewer would believe that the only people who bothered to turn out were priests, nuns, and a few elderly people. The fact that hundreds of thousands, sometimes as many as a million, came to see him everywhere he went was never referred to and never shown. The microphones were so placed that only the Pope's words were heard and not the response of his vast congregation, and of course, his words were heavily edited for the consumption of TV viewers.

What a difference there was when, in June 1981, Cardinal Stefan Wyszynski died, and the state, assailed on all sides by the independent trade unions, needed the restraining influence of the Church. Tele-vision, radio, and press rose magnificently to the occasion, with coverage that was honest and caught the emotional temper of the occasion. The difference between media coverage of these two religious occasions, separated in time by only two years, is as neat an illustration as any of how deep the Polish revolution ate into the fabric of the State, radically changing attitudes in a way that astonished those who knew Poland in the old days. It took a revolution to change the system, though the system itself was increasingly a laughing stock among its people.

"During the Pope's visit we always made a point of watching TV," says one Polish student, "just to have the opportunity of watching censorship in progress and of laughing at it. We knew the reality, because we'd been there, and then we would come home and watch what the authorities thought good for us. It was really funny. All of Poland was laughing."

And then there was the occasion when, in the late seventies, a satirical nightclub in Krakow called simply "Cellar" ran into trouble with the authorities, and the local censor's office was ordered to delete all references to it in journalists' stories. The censors took the instructions to delete the word "cellar" all too literally. For a period of several months bemused readers read bizarre circumlocutions for coal cellars or house cellars until the censor's office realized what had happened. But the censors are not content merely to delete; they have also been known to add.

The writer Jerzy Surdykowski complained to an English journalist that in his report on the August events in Gdansk, the censor invented characters saying things like, "People of Gdansk, think what you are doing! No ships are being built; the yards lie idle." But on the whole, if an article or a book bears a tone that the censors don't like, it is simply marked "unsuitable," and that, at least until NOWA appeared on the scene, was that. It simply did not get published. During the sixteen months of Solidarity the censors' position was under constant attack, and though in theory censorship is restricted to the "protection of state and economic secrets," journalists felt that the situation was even worse than before.

"The mice nibble away as much as they ever did," said one prominent journalist in August 1981. "The only difference is that before one knew all the tricks to manipulate the system. When formal censorship goes and is replaced by an informal system, though one equally as harsh, then it is almost impossible to work one's way around it. I am convinced that my bosses are these days given direct instructions which they will never admit to, but the effect is crucifying."

However, at no stage were the mice—the chief censor's office is in a drab building in Mysia Street (Mouse Street), Warsaw, opposite Party headquarters—ever fed to the cats. "When I hear that just one censor has been sacked because there is no longer enough work for him to do, then I will start having some confidence in the future," said the same journalist. "Remember that when the Journalists' Association met in Warsaw to demand changes in the censorship law, reports of the meeting were censored."

Television news was particularly instructive. At no time during the Solidarity era was it ever permitted to be anything but a mouthpiece for the most conservative strata of the Party organization. When the Solidarity leader briefly appeared on television wearing, to the delight of the whole country, a NOWA button badge, it quickly became evident that this was an aberration and would never be permitted to be the norm. In fact, television always treated Solidarity shabbily and was used by the authorities seeking to drive a rift between Lech Walesa and the Solidarity Praesidium. Only he was ever shown, and then only on those occasions when he sought to urge caution upon his followers. The attempt to isolate Walesa by the use of television and the mass media had begun long before the crackdown by the Army. Unfortunately, Solidarity itself too easily fell for it.

I argued strongly with Solidarity people about their refusal to permit state television into any of their congresses, particularly their first nationwide congress in Gdansk in August, on the grounds that democracy is not just a one-way stream. On the other hand, I had some sympathy with them. They knew that TV would distort their deliberations and were determined not to permit this to happen. In any event, Polish TV covered the Congress (and distorted it) but, greatest of ironies, had to rely on pictures supplied by Western European television services. This was not revealed by Polish commentators to their viewers.

Mouse Street is now back in business, and the ludicrous attempts by Polish TV to show, in the early days of martial law, that the military takeover had the general consent of the population proved that the Polish authorities had learned nothing from the past. And there were valuable lessons to be gained for anyone, even in the highest reaches of the Party organization, who wished to sit up and take notice. The most important lesson was that in a country where the press is fully censored, people will simply not believe it, even when it is telling the truth.

The Polish writer, Adam Szczypiorski put it well when he wrote, "Contemporary reality, as supplied by the Polish mass media, is not only truncated but emerges as an astonishing and incoherent miasma of falsehoods, half-truths, and vague innuendoes—a world of illusion and wishful thinking that bears little resemblance to real life.

"Misconceptions about the West are directly attributable to propaganda and the censor. If the Polish press say that the West is suffering from a continual recession, then there is no doubt in people's minds that the Western economy must be thriving; when Polish television recites unemployment figures for the USA (or West Germany or Great Britain), this must mean that unemployment is inconceivable. No one will even hear of abuses or terrorism in some countries of the so-called free world. Foreigners thus sometimes find Poland to be a country of bizarre reactionaries who refuse to believe the crimes of the Chilean junta, are sceptical about the problems of terrorism in Italy, reject as untrue reports of racial segregation in South Africa, approve of the Berufsverbot in West Germany, and so on. A mind fed on garbage becomes poisoned."

All of this is true because the press cannot be believed, and yet people feel the need to believe something, so every kind of rumor can emerge as fact. Three years ago, in the center of Warsaw, a gas main blew up inside a bank near the Forum Hotel killing several people. The rumors which have circulated about this kind of tragedy, which can occur anywhere, are remarkable. There are several different versions of Russian involvement: of a secret police operation that went wrong; of a gang of Polish terrorists on the loose, and so on. The simple truth that a gas main blew up was simply not believed by many people.

Unable to believe their own newspapers, the Poles can believe the most unlikeliest of scenarios with an almost fanatical determination. When I suggested to a group of young Solidarity members that the government had a point when it urged people to work harder because the country was bankrupt, my remark was greeted with derisive laughter.

"Of course we're not bankrupt," they said. "That is put about by the Government to make us come to heel." "But," I persisted, "even the Western press accepts that Poland has taken out loans on which it can barely afford to pay the interest." "Ah," they said, "that is not the first time that the West has been taken in by Communist propaganda."

There was hardly a Pole, during the period of the most acute food shortages, who did not believe that there was ample food to go around, but that the government was storing it in order to turn the population against Solidarity. And when the Russians moved in with cash loans and food supplies, Poles, though reading about it in their newspapers, dismissed it out of hand as another propaganda exercise. The rule, in fact, appears to be—if it's printed in the press, it can't be true.

Censorship, in short, has proved to be totally counterproductive, unless its primary aim is to persuade the leadership of a totalitarian government that it is loved by the population at large, its policies are provably producing results, and that its critics abroad are operating for the basest of reasons. "Do not dismiss that theory too lightly," says a Polish friend. "There is a lot of evidence to suggest that our leaders lay down the guidelines of what the press may say, and then somehow manage to fool themselves into believing when they read what they have caused to be printed.

"I know of a Regional Party Secretary who wrote virtually every word of the panegyric to himself on his sixtieth birthday in his local Party newspaper, after he had angrily rejected the one specially written for the occasion. After publication of his article, he had it framed and hung it in his home, where from time to time, close to tears, he would read it to friends. Somehow he managed to block out the fact that he had written it himself."

But to some thoughtful Poles the lies they are told about conditions today are not as important an issue as the distortions which they are forced to accept about their past. "We must save history from political manipulation," said Maciej Szumowski, explaining why his *Gazeta Krakowska* ran a series, one of the most popular and most widely read of any ever to appear in a newspaper in Communist Poland, called (and no explanations are necessary) "Blank Pages in the History of Poland."

"Poles," he told me, "want to know what actually happened in their past, not what the official histories tell them happened."

"How can the average Pole come to a coherent conclusion about, for example, the country's relations with the Soviet Union," said a historian, "if they do not know our history or do not believe what they are taught. We have been turned into a nation of cynics because our past has been taken away from us."

Szumowski puts it another way: "A country with a fraudulent history can hardly call itself a country at all."

Or, as a member of the Krakow Central Committee said: "Polish history does put a appalling weight upon our shoulders. But that burden is increased unbearably because my Party tried to pretend it didn't exist at all. I now believe that if the Polish people could be trusted with their past, they would learn more readily to trust the present. Unfortunately, I can find few people in a position to do anything about it who will agree with me. There you have the root of the Polish tragedy."

13

The Burden of History

FIRST CHILD: *"My daddy is related to the first Polish king."*
SECOND CHILD: *"My daddy is related to the First Secretary of the Polish United Workers' Party and he's never heard of the first Polish king."*

BEFORE THE DAWN OF TIME, three brothers, Lech, Russe, and Czech, from the family Slav, seeking land on which to establish their dynasties, found themselves in the middle of a vast plain in a countryside that was both fertile and beautiful. There they decided to part— Russe to the east, Czech to the South, while Lech, wondering where he should go, suddenly saw a White Eagle rise high in the red sky, a symbol of power and freedom. There and then he decided that this was where he would settle, on the land that was to become Poland.

"Poland," says an eminent Polish historian, "has been troubled by a history in which myth is as potent a brew to the Polish imagination as fact. There is not an event in our current travails that cannot find some echo in our history.

"But because that history is constantly distorted by the authorities, it is also distorted in a completely different way by the public. Because the Party is so terrified by the past, ordinary people cling to it with a passion that is terrifying. We have become a people who can live only in the imagination of what we believe to be the glorious past. When the present is too painful to contemplate, then we seek solace in our national folklore."

In fact, Poland's history requires very little gloss to give it a glorious patina in which the present is constantly reflected. It is, as every Pole will say, impossible to understand the country without knowing something of its history.

When, in 1386, the thirteen-year-old Polish Queen Jadwiga married Jagiello, Grand Duke of Lithuania, he agreed, as part of his marriage vows, to bring Lithuania into union with Poland and to permit its people to be converted to Roman Catholicism. Poland entered a golden age that was to last for three hundred years, and it became one of the most powerful nations in all Europe. A great power had been created, albeit at the expense of a young and innocent girl. Jadwiga was forced by the barons and bishops of Poland, as well as her own mother, to enter into a union that she hated. Jagiello, three times her age, didn't even speak her language; he changed his pagan name to Wladyslaw and took the religion of his wife.

Thereafter, while he managed the state, she devoted the rest of her short life—she died when she was only twenty-four years old—to the poor. Her cloak, which she'd used to cover a coppersmith who had drowned in the river, became the banner of the coppersmith's guild, and the whole of her fortune she willed on her death to poor students. But Poland prospered, both spiritually and materially.

The ancient University of Krakow, already one of the oldest in Europe, but which had fallen into neglect, was rebuilt and renamed the Jagiellonian University, a name that it still carries today. Polish scholars were sent to all parts of Europe, to return and make Poland a center of learning and scholarship, and for all its subsequent vicissitudes, this is a reputation it has never entirely lost.

The great battle of Grunwald and Tannenberg in 1410—perhaps the greatest clash of medieval arms—in which the Polish king defeated the Knights of the Teutonic Order, until then the most powerful military force in Europe, settled Poland's new-found stature as a great power. The Polish crown ruled a mighty empire, stretching from the Baltic in the north, including Prussia, which was a fiefdom of the Polish crown, to the Black Sea in the south, while to the east it stretched to within 200 miles of the gates of Moscow, and was a permanent threat to the state of Muscovy. At the height of its glory, Poland's wealth came from the magnificence of its agriculture, making it the breadbasket of Europe.

Always plagued by a lack of natural frontiers, Poland's position on the map of Europe put it at the very crossroads of the continent. If you draw one line from the northernmost tip of Norway down to the southernmost tip of Malta, and another from the most western peninsula of France through to Orsk, the most Eastern city of European Russia, you will see how the lines cross in the very heart of Poland. It became not only the natural prey for ambitious neighbors but also a strategically vital crossroads upon which every military power in the area cast envious eyes.

Poland was so powerful a state that it could have resisted foreign aggression but for that fatal inability of Poles to agree among themselves around a national purpose in times of peace. Poland had a kind of democracy long before anywhere else in the world. The country was ruled by the gentry—the *szlachta*—who had been granted privileges by successive monarchs in order to raise local detachments to fight invading armies of Swedes, Tartars, Russians, Hungarians, and Turks. There are some rooms in Wavel Castle in Krakow where one can see, with permission of the caretaker, one of the most extraordinary and valuable museum collections ever assembled anywhere. In magnificent, almost pristine condition, the richly decorated tents and pavilions of Turkish pashas now stand fully erected, carpeted with rugs of incalculable value, all seized when the Polish Army, under King Jan Sobieski in July 1683, marched to Vienna to raise the siege of the city by Vizier Kara Mustafa who commanded 138,000 Turks on a campaign designed to destroy the Holy Roman Empire and Christendom itself. The king arrived with 30,000 men to add to another 46,000 sent by the princes of Europe, and took command of the Christian Army. Europe and its civilization was saved on September 12, 1683, when King Sobieski led a charge from the heights of Wienerwald outside Vienna, broke the Ottoman Army and put it to flight. The king of Poland entered the gates of Vienna as the savior of Christianity, and one of the great passages of arms of the Middle Ages was over.

Yet Polish historians say that even as this decisive battle was being fought, internal conflicts in Poland had made the state virtually ungovernable—a situation which was to lead to the extinction of the Polish state.

While Poland's neighbors were ruled by powerful monarchs sustained by the doctrine of the absolute right of kings, government in Poland had been made all but impossible by the power and privileges of the gentry. They insisted that not only should Poland's kings be elected by them, but once the monarch ascended the throne, his power would be considerably circumscribed by a Parliament made up of members of the gentry who either attended directly or voted for delegates to represent their regions. Astonishingly, the gentry class consisted of about three quarters of a million people, or 10 percent of the population. Some were great barons—called "Magnates"—with estates and untold wealth. Others scratched a precarious living from the soil. It was difficult sometimes to tell the difference between them and the peasants alongside whom they worked, save for the fact that while one possessed power over king and country, the other had none at all.

And it is no exaggeration to say that the gentry, even the poorest, did have that power. Poland's Parliament had developed over the years a unique system whereby any legislation could be voted down by a single member of Parliament, who had merely to sit in his seat and declare "I disapprove." Not only that, but each member was entitled by his one vote to dissolve the *Sejm* at any time, and in so doing nullify all acts passed during its sessions. The assumption behind this *liberum veto* was that all nobles were equal, and that each possessed in his person the well-being of his nation. In practice, of course, the concept that nobility conferred upon its holder an almost saintly disregard for his own interests was not, as one might expect, exactly justified by events. Between 1652, when the *liberum veto* was first used, and 1764, when King Stanislaw II August Poniatowski (reputedly Catherine the Great's most successful lover) attempted in vain to make constitutional reforms, forty-eight out of fifty-five sessions of the *Sejm* fell under the *liberum veto*. Usually members objected to the raising of taxes to fight off yet another foreign interloper, but often invading foreign armies themselves found a member to bribe, to ensure that he used his veto to frustrate Poland's ability to defend itself. Even before the Battle of Vienna, the Cossacks in the Ukraine who had previously paid tribute to the Polish king changed sides and put their armies at the disposal of the Czar of Russia, changing forever the balance of power between these two great neighbors. With Cossacks on the loose, with the Polish Army itself often in revolt because the *Sejm* had not voted the money to pay its salaries, the country was wide open to attack, and the Swedes and then the Russians made the most of the opportunity.

The periodic election of Polish kings provided new excuses for outside intervention as Poland's neighbors fought to promote their own candidates, while the nobility—always squabbling between themselves —consistently failed, because of *liberum veto*, to agree about anything. August Stanislas's belated attempt to force through constitutional changes led to virtual civil war as a section of the Polish nobility, desperate to protect its ancient rights, refused to give way, even though what amounted to the whole Russian Army was camped on the grounds of the Russian ambassador. In the end, using the fate of Russian Orthodox churches in Poland, supposedly persecuted by the Catholics, as a pretext, Catherine the Great marched into Poland. Austria and Prussia, determined that Russia should not become too powerful, also moved, and the Polish *Sejm*, most of its members bribed by one or another of the competing parties in 1772 voted in favor of the First Partition of what was once their mighty nation. About 30 percent of the country was carved up among the three countries, leaving Poland considerably reduced in size, within frontiers even more difficult to defend than hitherto, and with a population bitter and divided.

At last, and too late, a group of Magnates and members of the minor gentry realized how their squabbling and insistence on their privileges had led to the dismemberment of the nation. They were determined, within the area still left to Poland, to give Poland a real constitution and the necessary energy to withstand outside pressures and reestablish its former prosperity. So, on May 3, 1791, in a carefully organized plot, timed to coincide with the moment that reactionary members of the *Sejm* were out of town, the liberals voted through the Parliament a new constitution, the first written constitution in Europe, and the second in the world—after America's, upon which it was closely modelled.

Known and revered throughout Poland today as the 3rd May Constitution (in 1981 Solidarity demanded that May 3 be celebrated as a national holiday rather than the Communist holiday of May 1), this document was nothing short of revolutionary. It provided for the country advanced social and political forms unknown elsewhere, in the immediate area. But to Poland's neighbors—like the Gdansk Accord signed almost 290 years later—this Constitution was perceived as a direct threat to their interests. If it were allowed to go unchallenged, this Constitution could disaffect their people and give Poland a political stability enabling it to resist their insistent demands. An eminent Prussian politician declared, "The Poles have given the coup de grâce to the Prussian monarchy by voting a Constitution much better than the English. . . . How can we defend our state against a numerous and well-governed nation?" Catherine the Great swore her determination to stamp out "the French plague" in Warsaw, and as has so often happened in Polish history, she found influential supporters inside Poland whose wealth and power depended upon the old ways being preserved.

It is almost uncanny how Polish history is fated to repeat itself. The events of 1980–1981 so echo the events 1791–1792 that the scenario seems to have been written by the same script-writer. Grossly betraying Poland, the Conservatives (the Russian Party as they were known) went to St. Petersburg and signed an Act of Confederation with Russia, blaming the "monarchal and democratic revolution" which had taken their country by storm. They called for Russian troops to put down the democrats, and on May 18, 1792, two weeks after Warsaw had celebrated the first anniversary of the Constitution, they crossed the frontier with Catherine's army behind them. Though the Polish Army fought courageously, it had no hope against numerically superior opponents. Poland was partitioned for the second time, as the Russians and the Prussians grabbed huge sections of Poland and promulgated for the first time the concept of Poland as a buffer state, "a barrier between the powers," as Catherine put it, but with the Russian ambassador in Warsaw as effective ruler.

Two years later in 1794, Tadeusz Kosciuszko, leading an army of peasants demanded national self-rule, abolition of the monarch, equal civil rights for all citizens, freedom for the peasantry, and a limited (though for those days, remarkable) franchise based on property qualification. With reckless courage that won the admiration of all Europe, he took on Russia and, when it intervened, Prussia too. Despite several victories won against great odds, the Poles were finally defeated before the gates of Warsaw and their leaders fled into exile, principally to France. For the third time Poland had to submit to the terrible indignity of partition, but this time the three occupying powers were determined that this troublesome nation should be wiped off the map, and they divided up what was left of the country among themselves. According to legend, Kosciuszko shouted, "Finis Poloniae!" when he fell from his horse in the final battle of the war, and in the partition treaty, the three powers vowed: "In view of the necessity to abolish everything that could revive the memory of the existence of the Kingdom of Poland, now that the annulment of the body politic has been effected . . . the high contracting parties are agreed and undertake never to include in their titles . . . the name or designation of the Kingdom of Poland, which shall remain suppressed from the present and forever. . . ."

But the Poles were far from finished. "Poland is not lost while Poles still live," still sung to this day, was during these dark hours the anthem that kept alive the dreams of a Poland reborn. The lyrics represented the aspirations of a people denied a homeland of their own. It was the 120 years of Polish history, between the third partition and eventual independence in 1918, that set the mold of the Polish character as we know it today. The options were limited—either fight or go under—and they decided to fight. This was the national will, and nothing that has happened since has weakened it. It was during this period that these courageous people became suffused with the kind of hopeless romanticism, nationalistic to a fault, even the victims, if you like, of a grand passion for Poland which has been both ennobling and destructive.

The world reacted to the Polish tragedy 200 years ago much as it did when General Jaruzelski imposed martial law on the Polish population in December 1981. In America, Thomas Jefferson spoke of the "crime" and the "atrocity" of the partition; "to post-Revolutionary Frenchmen, the spectacle of Poland writhing under Europe's most repressive monarchies seemed a horror almost beyond historical precedent"; while in England societies were established to keep alive the name of Poland and Polish civilization. Extraordinarily, this was a time of a flowering of Polish culture—romantic but magnificent. It was the time of Chopin, who evoked memory of an eternal Poland through his music; Adam Mickiewicz whose twelve cantos of *Pan Tadeusz*, Homeric in their scope, recounted the historical tradition of a great people. Zygmunt Krasinski and Juliuz Slowacki regarded Polish suffering as an almost mystical event, basis for a philosophy of self-sacrifice and ideals of liberty from which the Polish people have never departed. A nation, they said, could survive the destruction of the state provided that its people remained true. It is a lesson no Pole has ever forgotten, and it ensures that, whatever else may happen, in the end Poland will somehow survive.

The attempts by the partitioning powers to crush the Polish spirit were brutal beyond compare. Nonobservance of the laws of the partitioning powers, particularly the Russians, meant certain death or exile to Siberia, a route taken by thousands of Poles, yet the spirit of resistance never died. In 1815 the Congress of Vienna ratified the partitions but established the tiny kingdom of Warsaw as a sop to Polish pride and then undid that by placing it under the czars.

In 1830, in what Poles know as the November Insurrection, young men from the School of Cadets in Warsaw led by a sub-lieutenant rose against the Czar and held out for a year. In January 1863, this time with no army, not even officer cadets to call on, the people rose again with few expectations. As a Polish writer has put it, ". . . this act of despair has left a memory sacred to every Pole. No sacrifice for the national cause had, in fact, ever been so disinterested and of so moving a nature.

"Never had such large classes of the population rallied to a movement that, unlike that of 1830, did not possess even the skeleton of a regular army."

The Russians reacted with predictable fury. The kingdom was finally removed from all their maps and became Vistulaland. Polish was replaced by Russian in government and commerce; Russian became mandatory in every school; while the Polish nobility, the natural

leaders of the nation, were pauperized as their land was removed from
them. In Prussia, too, attempts were made to destroy Polish influence
once and for all. Only German could be spoken at public meetings,
Polish place-names were changed to German, Poles were heavily discriminated against, and yet, as the policy of Germanization increased,
to the puzzlement and then the anger of German officials, the Polish
national consciousness seemed to grow still stronger. Only in Austrian
Poland where the Poles were given autonomy in 1870 were things
better, and it became a haven for revolutionaries of all political per-
suasions escaping from persecution elsewhere. Life for everyone was
pitifully hard under their foreign masters. Well over 2 million Poles,
mainly peasants, could take no more and emigrated, principally to
the United States, but all over Europe and Latin America too. The
gentry went abroad to study, many never to return. Yet even as
Poland was being drained of its people, a loss no nation can afford
and remain whole, even as the very heart of the country seemed to
be dying, wherever they met Poles talked of independence, and
schemed and plotted to achieve it. The tragedy was they spoke in
different tongues.

The leader of one faction was Jozef Pilsudski, a remarkable man
in an age that was to produce many remarkable men. Because of
Poland's subsequent history, Pilsudski, in the 1920s and 1930s a
well-known name throughout the world, is remembered, if at all, as
a shadowy figure of our recent past. Yet few statesmen had quite
such a romantic early life as he. Pilsudski, the child of a fanatically
nationalistic Polish family, was born in Zulow in Russian Poland
(now Lithuania) in 1867. At the age of seventeen he joined the
illegal Socialist Party, not, apparently, out of any great sense of conviction, but because by joining the left-wing, he could demonstrate
in the most dramatic way then possible his hatred of the Russians.
On March 1, 1887, three young students were picked up by the
police outside the Winter Palace in St. Petersburg and were found
to be carrying Browning pistols and homemade bombs. Yet another
attempt to assassinate Czar Alexander II had been discovered in time.
Seventy-four socialist students throughout the empire, all friends of
the would-be assassins were picked up, including Jozef's brother,
Bronislaw and Lenin's older brother, Alexander Ulyanov. Bronislaw,
who had lent money for the plot, was sentenced to fifteen years hard
labor, Lenin's brother was executed. Jozef Pilsudski, because he was
related to Bronislaw, was sentenced to five years' exile in Siberia. On
his release Pilsudski edited and printed the Socialist Party's illegal

newspaper, *Robotnik* ("The Worker") (a name that was revived in similar circumstances by Jacek Kuron's KOR in the 1970s), and Pilsudski became one of the most influential people in the left-wing underground.

In 1900, after six years of precarious freedom during which he had managed to keep just one step ahead of the Czarist secret police, he was arrested again, his identity established, and he was sentenced to the Warsaw Citadel, one of the most notorious prisons in the whole of the Czarist empire. But Pilsudski was nothing if not resourceful. To the horror of his jailers, slowly at first and then with increasing vehemence, he took on all the appearances of a madman. He refused to eat anything except boiled eggs—still in their shells—because he claimed that all other food had been poisoned. He alternately raged or cringed in the corner of his cell when his warders entered. Eventually a doctor diagnosed him as psychotic, and he was transferred to the prison hospital of St. Nicholas the Miracle Worker in St. Petersburg, where he was put in a ward with fifty other madmen. On May 13, 1900, in the company of a Polish doctor who had come to see this interesting case of schizophrenia paranoia, Pilsudski simply walked out of the hospital a free man, his acting career over. His subsequent exploits became legendary in a Poland desperate for local heroes, especially for those who tweaked the noses of the Russians. Though not particularly popular among fellow socialists, whose constant plotting bored him, Pilsudski was asked to form a terrorist organization, the *Bojowka* or "Fighting Organization" to attack Czarist officials wherever they could be found.

Pilsudski saw his role differently, and with his small band of followers, became a kind of Polish Robin Hood, robbing banks and Czarist freight trains, and releasing political prisoners from jail. In September 1908 he hit the jackpot—a train traveling under military escort was raided by Pilsudski and his gang in a brilliantly conceived operation. When the looters counted the money they discovered to their astonishment they'd collected over $100,000, an unbelievable fortune in a country that had been beggared by its occupiers. Pilsudski put the money to good use. In Austrian Poland, where the authorities were only too glad to have a quiet life, Pilsudski with his newfound wealth set up a "Riflemens' Association" that was, in fact, the embryo of a new Polish Army that Pilsudski vowed he would use to set Poland free.

Not everyone in Poland approved of Pilsudski. To some he was still regarded as a "Red," though he wore his socialism lightly. To others, including the brilliant leader of the second important political faction, the nationalists, Roman Dmowski, he was simply an irrelevance. Dmowski, head of a party known as the National Democrats, was also working for Polish independence, but he prided himself on his "realism."

Poland, he declared, had been destroyed by a series of romantic gestures doomed to failure. There was no future for the country if it did not throw off the past, forget its history, and accept the realities of its geographical situation. Germany, he decided, was the real enemy of Poland, and Russia, whatever its past misdeeds, was Poland's only natural protector. Thus Poland, if it were to sustain independence, could only do so closely allied, politically and economically, with Russia.

Ironically, perhaps, in view of Poland's subsequent history, Pilsudski, who utterly rejected this concept, was on the left. Dmowski, whose party was middle-class and supported by the Roman Catholic Church, was quite definitely on the right. That argument raged in pre-independent Poland, and still rages today, and will probably never be satisfactorily resolved.

Poland achieved independence in 1918 at the conclusion of World War I, though its frontiers were not officially delineated until the Treaty of Versailles in 1920 and the Conference of Ambassadors in 1923. Before that Pilsudski took the law into his own hands, confronted the new Bolshevik government in Russia, took over land that was traditionally Polish, and then, in 1920, dealt the Red Army a decisive blow by defeating them on the outskirts of Warsaw and driving them back into their country.

The Polish–Soviet War, which began in 1919 and ended with an armistice on October 12, 1920, and the Treaty of Riga on March 18, 1921, is still a subject of controversy. The war was misunderstood by contemporaries and has been subject to dishonest Soviet historiography. Insofar as it is mentioned at all, the war has been completely misconstrued by most modern historians. The myth widely promulgated throughout Europe at the time was that General Pilsudski and the Polish government chose to fight on the side of the Whites during the Russian Civil War, against the Reds. The Red Army went on the offensive, driving deep into Poland, because of the continued harrassment by the Poles, determined to assist in the destruction of the revolution. So assiduously was this version of history planted at the time that dockers in England, France, and Czechoslovakia refused to load ships bound for Poland, because they felt the country wanted to restore Czarist rule. The facts are quite different. General Pilsudski himself sided with the Bolsheviks against the Whites—not solely for political reasons, though he was by temperament and upbringing a leftist. He was sure that while no restored Czarist regime would honor Polish independence, he thought the Bolsheviks could be taught to respect the independence of its neighbor. Nothing in Leninist dogma or the Marxist manifesto suggested that a Communist Russia would be an imperialist power. Pilsudski's policy was honored in the observance, for when the Whites expressly requested the assistance of Polish units, Pilsudski refused to help, despite the private urging of Britain and France.

The Poles went to war for one reason, and one reason alone: to restore to Poland land that had historically belonged to it, and that still had large Polish populations longing to be returned to the Motherland. Wilno and Minsk were two such cities that Pilsudski seized, but on March 10, 1920, the twenty-seven-year-old General Mikhail Nikolayevich Tukhachevsky (he was put to death by Stalin in 1937) won an international reputation for himself when he grouped a huge army of 700,000 men and launched a massive offensive that, despite some early setbacks, soon had him on the road to Warsaw, with the ringing declaration, "To the West! Over the corpse of White Poland lies the road to worldwide conflagaration." So quickly and brilliantly did he maneuver that the governments of Europe woke up, far too late, to realize that a huge Russian Army was poised to make a decisive breakthrough into Western Europe at a time when the war-weary armies of continental Europe were in no fit state to face an enemy freshened by a bout of revolutionary zeal. The spectre that their armies might actually join in on the side of the Soviets also haunted Western leaders as "Hands off Russia" became a worldwide cry aimed against the Poles at the very moment that the Russians were camped on the outskirts of Warsaw. Lord D'Abernon, the British ambassador, could not understand why the people of Warsaw did not take their peril closer to heart.

He wrote in his diary: "July 27. The Prime Minister, a peasant proprietor, has gone off today to get his harvest in. Nobody thinks this extraordinary.

"August 2. The insouciance of the people here is beyond belief. One would imagine the Bolsheviks a thousand miles away and the country in no danger."

And on the day, August 13, that Marshall Tukhachevsky opened his assault upon Warsaw itself, the ambassador records:

"There is singularly little alarm. The upper classes have already left town, in many cases having placed their pictures and other valuables in charge of the museum authorities. Warsaw has been so often occupied by foreign troops that the event in itself causes neither the excitement nor the alarm which would be produced in a less experienced city."

(It seems to be very much a Polish characteristic not to panic in the face of impending military catastrophe. Before going to Poland in June 1981, I had official advice in London and through friends in Washington about the likelihood of a Russian invasion, a possibility much discussed in the newspaper. The concensus of opinion was that invasion was imminent. In Warsaw I discovered the authorities had placed all hospitals in the country on alert by sending home all non-urgent bed cases, refusing to admit new patients, and turning specialized clinics into field hospitals. They estimated a death toll of 1,000 in the first week and ten times that number wounded. However, though this news worried me, the ordinary people of Warsaw displayed such extraordinary calm that it seemed almost lunatic. People to whom I expressed my concern dismissed my talk as "alarmist." While the embassies were sending hourly situation reports and their military attachés busily collecting information on Soviet troop maneuvers, the people of Warsaw packed the cafés and nightclubs in an atmosphere of total unconcern. Yet if the invasion had come to pass, they would have fought—and magnificently so.)

In 1920 events justified the incurable and romantic Polish optimism. First, Warsaw's defenses held, as Tukhachevsky launched his attack. In a series of brilliant maneuvers Pilsudski and his citizens' army (that had paraded before him only days before—armed with staves and scythes, some of the middle class workers in boaters and winged collars), went on the offensive. Within days Pilsudski's army had totally encircled the Soviet Army.

A hundred thousand Russian soldiers were taken prisoner, three entire Soviet Armies wiped out, and the remainder harried and chased back into continental Russia. During fighting on the way, at Komarov near Zamosc, on August 31, the last great horse cavalry battle in European history, was won decisively by the Poles. D'Abernon called the Battle of Warsaw, which the Poles themselves call the "Miracle on the Vistula," the eighteenth most decisive battle in the history of the world. "If Charles Martel had not checked the Saracen Conquest at the Battle of Tours, the Koran would now be taught at the schools of Oxford, and her pupils might demonstrate to a circumcised people

the sanctity and truth of the revelation of Mahomet. Had Pilsudski
. . . failed to arrest the triumphant advance of the Soviet Army at the
Battle of Warsaw, not only would Christianity have experienced a
dangerous reverse, but the very existence of Western civilisation
would have been imperiled."

The Russians were forced to sign a humiliating peace treaty which
gave Poland most of what it wanted, but the defeat was never forgotten by the Red Army.

However glorious a moment this was, it did not give Poland much
of a breathing space. Few Poles can look back to this first experience
of independent nationhood with anything but a sense of despair. They
had dreamed of this moment and wrote of it in their literature, their
popular songs, and their hymns. When it came, the intransigent
factionalism of its politicians destroyed any hope for national unity
as they scrambled for power. In bleaker moments, Poles see this
period of history as confirmation of their deep suspicions that Pole
will always quarrel with Pole, that something intrinsic in the national
character makes unity impossible, that Poland, as one gloomy historian told me, doesn't need external enemies, it will always self-
destruct. Certainly, the question first posed by one of Poland's internationally known historians, Joachim Lewewel (1786–1861)—*Polska
tak, ale jaka?* ("Poland yes, but what sort of Poland?")—has been
raised in every debate on Polish nationalism since then. The period
between the wars was not one of great and glorious achievement; it
would be surprising if it had been. The chances of this new nation,
albeit one reborn, immediately becoming a model of Western democracy—the ideal of its supporters outside Poland—were small. In 1981
a Polish diplomat in London, talking about Solidarity, said to me in
some exasperation: "The trouble with them is that they speak about
democracy and do not understand the word." "If that is true," I said,
"whose fault is that?"

When Poland gained full independence, it had suffered political
and psychological turmoil. It does not seem to me that the fault for
this lies in any intrinsic flaw in the Polish character. For over a hundred years Poland had been divided into three parts which had little
contact with each other, and which absorbed the administrative,
political, and cultural values of three distinct partitioning powers.
Principally for this reason, the newly independent Poland, though it
had managed to unite in the war against Russia, never stood a chance.
The 1931 census showed that only 68.9 percent of the population
were ethnic Poles. It was a country of minorities. The Ukrainians who

had settled along the length of the Carpathian Mountains, where they served as a constant threat to Polish sovereignty, had their own demands and were the largest group. Yiddish-speaking Jews, many of whom spoke no Polish at all, comprised 8.7 percent of the population as a whole, but in many major cities were either in the majority or close to it. And the Germans were another prosperous national grouping, particularly in the West. A country that had been divided into three isolated parts could hardly be expected to operate as a homogeneous whole, despite the yearning of its people to achieve it. Poland became independent with six currencies, four official Army languages, eighteen registered political parties, railway gauges of different sizes, three legal codes, three disparate codes of social behavior, and regions (such as industrially important Silesia) with administrations separate from the central authority.

There was nothing wrong with the new Constitution planned for the republic. It promised a government as advanced as any in Europe, more radical in many respects than most countries have today. Far from being a nation of unreconstructed conservatives, the image prewar Poland has had ever since, the main political parties, including the rightist National Democrats, put forward extremely leftist concepts of land reform and industrial reconstruction.

However, the harsh truth was that though Poland had sought independence for so long, it was singularly unprepared for it. The country had been spectacularly robbed of its wealth by the partitioning powers, and now it faced the future virtually bankrupt. The politicians who had labored for the cause of freedom had neglected to consider how it was to be maintained once it had been won. Pilsudski was created Poland's first head of state, but he hated the detailed work that the position entailed. In any case, he believed that Poland should be governed by a parliamentary democracy. The task of achieving that proved more difficult than he had imagined. "I thought," he wrote later "that together with her physical resurrection, Poland would also achieve a spiritual rebirth." In point of fact it did, but not politically so.

The first Prime Minister he appointed was Jedrzej Moraczewski, regarded as a moderate socialist, but he turned out to be so radical that within six weeks Poland was gripped with rumors that the right was preparing a coup against him. He was dismissed and replaced by Ignacy Paderewski, one of the most famous concert pianists in the world. Throughout the First World War, Paderewski had toured America to sell the concept of Polish freedom, using his name as a calling-card. Exceptionally gifted musically, he proved to have an even more finely honed talent as a publicist, a gift that he used first on his own behalf and then on Poland's. He was instrumental in persuading Woodrow Wilson to include the cause of Polish independence in his famous fourteen points, and he returned home a national hero.

Once established as Prime Minister, however, Paderewski turned out to be a disaster. Dominated by his wife Helena, Paderewski deferred to her constantly. She had acted as his business manager while he had been a successful concert pianist and saw no reason why this arrangement should not continue now that he was Prime Minister. When ministers came to see him, she intervened constantly, disagreeing frequently with her husband and sulking when she didn't get her way. As for Paderewski, eccentricities which are lovable in a concert pianist can be infuriating in a Prime Minister. He refused, as a matter of principal, to use the telephone, which he regarded as an outlandish instrument. He had never had to wake up early before in his life and saw no reason why he should do so now, arriving at his desk at whatever hour happened to suit him. If friends called, they were granted precedence over ministers on the grounds that they were likely to be more amusing. But criticism in Parliament and the press finally proved his undoing. As an internationally celebrated pianist he had never been subjected to such harsh treatment. He was destroyed by it and, after less than a year in office, left Poland for Switzerland.

From then on Poland's political fortunes went into a downhill spiral. In 1922 Pilsudski resigned as head of state—he called the office a "gilded cage." A vicious campaign to elect his successor resulted in a narrow victory for Gabriel Narutowicz, a friend of Pilsudski's who managed to mobilize the Peasant Party, the Parliamentary left, and minority nationalities, like the Jewish parties, on his side. "Narutowicz—President of the Jews" was the cry from the right on his inauguration. Only five days later, making a ceremonial appearances at the official opening of the annual winter exhibition of paintings at the Warsaw Palace of Fine Arts, he was assassinated by a mentally unstable, extreme right-wing nationalist painter.

Poland had its independence, but it seemed merely to have exchanged one form of wretchedness for another. Unemployment was staggeringly high. Polish rural poverty was one of the most distressing spectacles of Europe. There were strikes and lock-outs, there was corruption and a political system so unstable that it had little hope of dealing successively with any of these desperate problems. So, in

May 1926, Marshal Pilsudski, who had been sweating and fuming on the sidelines for years, staged an armed insurrection. He believed his authority in the Polish Army was so strong that when he marched on Warsaw with barely a thousand men, no unit would stand in his way. He was proved wrong, and the coup was far from bloodless, but it left Pilsudski the virtual dictator until his death in 1935. So General Jaruzelski was not the first Polish general in recent years to take over political power.

To his contemporaries, Pilsudski appeared to be just another of the fascist dictators with whom other European democracies were then flirting. Yet when university students in Poland in 1980 began sporting Pilsudski badges, to the astonishment of visitors to the country, they were aware of the less savory aspects of the Pilsudski regime. Oppositionists both on the extreme left and extreme right were arrested and kept in special internment camps, and parliamentary democracy was severely curtailed. Yet, what Pilsudski promised and delivered, and what students in 1980 were looking for, was *Sanacja* (his regime was known as the Sanacja), which can be translated as a moral political cleansing. General Sikorski, who achieved renown in the Second World War as Prime Minister of the Polish government in exile and commander-in-chief of the Polish Army, was bitterly opposed to Pilsudski. He characterized Pilsudski's regime as "drawn from a clique of colonels, who head one of the most stupid and harmful dictatorships imaginable." That was a gross exaggeration. Another remark at the time likened the May Coup to "an attack by bandits on a lunatic asylum"; this comment was probably as near the mark as any.

The situation in Poland before the coup was so desperate that Pilsudski, whose loyalty to Poland was never in question, who wore the soubriquet Father of the Nation without embarrassment, who had fought for its independence valiantly and with little regard for his personal safety, and who had taken for his pains little in the way of material rewards, was justified in believing that he alone could save the country.

Pilsudski's Poland, by the standards of the countries that surrounded it, was almost a haven of liberalism. He fought the anti-Semitism of the right as vigorously as he fought the revolutionary ambitions of the left. The economy, in such disarray when he took over, began to pick up, while Polish experimental art took off into the far reaches of the imagination. The avante-garde, assiduously suppressed in Russia and Germany (and mocked in Britain), possessed in Poland an exuberance that could only be compared with what was going on in Paris.

"We do not pretend that Pilsudski never made terrible mistakes or attempt to justify his coup," said one historian in Warsaw last summer. "We do say he was a man of principle. Throughout his life he was moved by one consideration—the preservation of the sanctity and the independence of Poland. Before the May coup Poland was lapsing into anarchy. Whether he was justified or not in moving against the parliamentary institutions which he himself created, history shows that Poland was a more stable, more prosperous, and more just society after May 1926 than it had been before."

No doubt, Poland's generals would say much the same today, but there are several crucial differences. Pilsudski acted against the politicians, not against the people. He acted on behalf of Poland, not on behalf of a foreign power. He had consistently fought for parliamentary democracy—as distinguished from his opponents. After the coup he did not abolish the *Sejm* as he certainly could have done, and he constantly proclaimed his belief in parliamentarianism "because it is the basis of democracy."

Poland, he believed, was being weakened by the rancorous squabbling of its political parties and by the inability of its governments to function in the face of opposition for the sake of opposition. As he grew older he became impatient with the Parliament that he had supported for so long, as it continued its noisy and intemperate harrassment of the government—often with good reason. Always an authoritarian, in one of the most disgraceful episodes of postwar Poland, he imprisoned some sixty members of the center and left opposition, including the distinguished Wincenty Witos, who had three times been Prime Minister of Poland. By the standards of the time, in a Europe of emerging Fascism, Pilsudski's Poland never even came close to the barbarism that had become commonplace elsewhere. He hated Fascism, and in 1934 he moved against the crypto-Fascist parties that were establishing themselves in the country. He declared them illegal and threw their leaders into a concentration camp he had established at Bereza Kartuska.

Pilsudski died on May 12, 1935, mourned by the whole nation, and he left a void that could not be filled. He had been a unique figure—an adventurer, a soldier, a patriot, a democrat, and a dictator, and he never ceased to be any of these things. The dictator never subdued the democrat, and the democrat never wholly convinced the dictator. But, because he was unique, Pilsudski's political party without Pilsudski soon degenerated into everything that he despised, a right-wing, militaristic, incompetent, and mildly anti-Semitic government that was to misrule Poland until the terrible war that the German Chancellor launched on September 1, 1939.

Poland had been allowed only twenty years to rebuild a strong and proud nation. History's harsh verdict is that it failed.

Perhaps it did. But Poles have the right to argue that the rest of the world, having willed the resurrection of the Polish state, then failed to help sustain it.

The West left it alone to confront its enemies—Germany and Russia—and overwhelmed by its own economic problems offered no help to a country that had few resources of its own.

And so Poland entered the war with little left of that high energy of purpose that had seen it through the bitter years of partition. All that remained was patriotism, but that was to prove enough to sustain the Poles in the terrible trial that followed.

14
The War

At war's end, an outraged woman got up at a public meeting being addressed by a Russian officer on the glories of socialism. "I want to tell you," she said, "that during the war the Germans hanged my son. And now the Soviets have shot my husband...."

"I understand your distress," said the Russian. "Believe you me, I do. But we socialists, in this new world we are creating, have got to learn to live with and embrace the new technology."

AT 4:17 A.M. on September 1, 1939, without any declaration of war, the German warship, the *Schleswig-Holstein* on a "courtesy visit" to Danzig (now Gdansk), which had, under the Versailles Treaty, been granted the status of a Free City (neither belonging to Poland or Germany) opened fire with fifteen-inch guns on the Polish fort of Westerplatte. At 4:45 A.M. the German Army crossed the Polish frontier at several points with fifty-three divisions under the command of General von Brauchitsch, and within a few hours the fragile Polish defenses were overwhelmed. World War II had begun. It was a titantic struggle in which millions died, both innocent and guilty, until, 2,194 days later, an exhausted world returned to an uneasy peace. It was in Poland that this terrible war reached the full expression of its savagery.

Add the casualties suffered by Britain, which fought so valiantly from the very beginning, and whose cities were devastated by German bombs, to those suffered by the gallant Americans who once again came to the rescue of European civilization. Take that figure, and add on the civilian and military casualties suffered by the French and the Belgians, the Dutch, the Greeks, and the Canadians. Keep that figure before you, and then add on the deaths (both civilian and military) of Germany's three allies, the Italians, the Austrians, and the Rumanians, and for good measure, enter in Yugoslavia's war victims, which included well over 1 million civilian casualties alone. And once you have that terrible death roll add one more figure—the number of military and civilian death that Japan suffered, a nation devastated by two atomic bombs. Now, and only now will you have reached that figure of 7 million who were killed in Poland between 1939 and 1945. In sixty-three heroic days alone, that glorious if ultimately futile expression of Polish arms, the Warsaw Uprising in 1944, as many Poles were killed as the United States lost during the whole of World War II.

Germany's intentions toward Poland were clear from the start. The bombing of the small Spanish town of Guernica by the German Air Force had been the world's first awesome experience of massive aerial bombardment against civilian targets. It was a dress rehearsal for the real thing.

The bombings of Warsaw and other cities in the opening days of World War II demonstrated the devastation that an enemy air force could inflict on poorly defended civilian targets. The Poles fought heroically against the brilliant maneuvering of three Panzer commanders, Generals Guderian, Hoeppner, and von Kleist, whose tactics revolutionized the art of war—tactics which, in due time, won most of Europe and Russian until the sheer weight of numbers deployed against them by the Allies wore the Germans down.

At the outset, the Germans were unstoppable. They surged through the Polish countryside, operating tank squadrons in a new way, not like mobile fortresses to protect infantry, but as strategic weapons in their own right, moving in columns at speed, outstripping their own infantry, punching great holes in enemy static defenses, and then enveloping them before they could regroup. Against this new kind of mobile warfare, the Poles could only pitch a few antiquated tanks, some artillery, an air force whose planes were almost all completely out of date and their fierce courage. Time and again the Poles held out stubbornly, then fell back on one defensive line after another. They mustered counterattacks too, leading to heavy German loss of life. Against the tanks, the Poles launched their cavalry.

This gave rise to one of Poland's golden myths. During the dark hours of the German assault, the Polish cavalry, the finest sons of the nation, mounted their charges, raised their lances into the attack position, and rode at full gallop at the German tanks. It didn't quite happen that way at all. It was neither quixotic still to use cavalry—as the Russians were subsequently to show against the Germans—in this kind of terrain, at this stage of the war, nor were Polish commanders so careless of the well-being of their men that they would deliberately pit man and horse against machine. Nevertheless, these cavalry charges were typical of the selfless bravery of the Polish Army fighting for its homeland.

On two occasions cavalry units were trapped. The men had two choices—break out or surrender. The Poles chose to break out, and in the process, to the astonishment of German tank commanders, seemed to be charging them. Not many cavalrymen got out, but those who did gave their countrymen something to cheer about.

Any hope of prolonged Polish resistance collapsed on September 17 —a day of great infamy. Warsaw was under siege when the Russians, claiming that Poland had "ceased to exist," crossed the eastern frontier and rapidly occupied half the country. Only then did the rest of the world know that a secret protocol existed in the Ribbentrop-Molotov Pact, signed on August 23, 1939, under which Germany and Russia agreed to carve up Poland between them. The Polish Army, fighting a desperate rearguard action against the *Wehrmacht*, reeled hopelessly as they were attacked in the East by the Red Army.

At the time the Poles were given little credit for their conduct in defense of their homeland. In their view, as well as that of the rest of the world, their collapse appeared to be humiliating. An army that had held staff exercises to discuss an invasion of Germany only a few months earlier had capitulated in thirty-five days, leaving the Germans and the Russians masters of Poland. The British Army's Chief General Ironside summed up this view when he said to the head of the British Military Mission in Warsaw: "Your Poles haven't put up much of a show, have they?"

By the time everyone realized what a magnificent weapon of war the Nazis had forged, the Poles and their fight had been forgotten. So perhaps now it is time to acknowledge the glorious resistance of the Polish Army.

The Poles lost 60,000 men in the fighting, some 140,000 were wounded and there was an enormous number of civilian casualties. But they had not gone down lightly. They killed over 10,000 German soldiers and wounded over 30,000. The war was over in thirty-five days; after the intervention of the Russians, further resistance was useless.

It is worth pausing for a moment to compare this campaign with the German attack on the Western Front, launched on May 10, that took the *Wehrmacht* through the Netherlands, Belgium, and into France. After five days the Dutch Army capitulated; after seventeen days a defeated British Expeditionary Force commenced the evacuation from the beaches of Dunkirk; after eighteen days King Leopold of the Belgians signed his country's surrender and the Belgian Army ceased to exist; after thirty-four days Paris was occupied, and on the thirty-fifth day Marshal Pétain, the new French Premier, instructed his Foreign Minister to ask the Germans for an armistice. It took the Germans, with help from the Russians, thirty-five days to conquer Poland, and thirty-five days to sweep the floor with Holland, Belgium, France, and a formidable British Army. The Poles seem to have put up a pretty good "show" after all.

Poland was to enter the period of its greatest trial, its Golgotha, as one historian has put it. For as long as Poland exists the Second World War will never be forgotten by its people. I know of no family that did not lose one, and in most cases considerably more, of its members during this terrible period. Those who try to understand Poland without first knowing something of this period of suffering will abjectly fail.

As soon as formal fighting came to an end, Poland was divided into three parts. The northern and western areas of the country were annexed by Germany to become part of the Reich. The Polish inhabitants living there were either driven out or used as slave labor by the Germans who came to settle on the land. The central and southern areas, which included Warsaw, Krakow, and Lublin, became known as the General-Gouvernment and were ruled from Wawel Castle in Krakow, the ancient seat of Poland's kings, by the Governor General and Hitler's lawyer, Hans Frank. And finally, there was the Soviet zone, where conditions were as harsh as they were in German-occupied Poland. Poland had been partitioned once again.

The story of the suffering of the Jews in German-occupied Poland has been told many times before. Herded first into ghettos, they were finally transported to the extermination camps, to be slaughtered in the millions.

It is not in any way to diminish the suffering of the Jews to suggest that the terrible privations of non-Jewish Poles has been less sympathetically documented. The Slavs, particularly Polish Slavs (though not "vermin"—a term exclusively used for the Jews), were categorized as *unter-menschen* by their conquerors and had one function—to slave for Germany and to be treated without pity when they shirked. Behind the *Wehrmacht* came the dread Nazi *Einsatzgruppen* (Special Actions Groups) whose job it was to terrorize the Polish population into submission.

The first mass killings in Poland were not of Jews but of Polish intellectuals. Most of the professors and senior lecturers of the Jagiellonian University in Krakow—teachers, civil servants, academics from other universities, and writers—were herded into Dachau, Buchenwald, or Sachsenhausen, and thousands were shot. Nearly a million Polish peasants were forced out of their homes at gun point, not permitted to take a single possession, and driven from land they had farmed for centuries so that Germans could settle in their place. Thousands died as they were force marched to the General-Gouvernment. Blond, blue-eyed children were snatched from orphanages and then from the arms of parents to be taken to Germany to be brought up as good little Aryans. Radios were forbidden, so was education beyond primary school level. All laws were rescinded other than those arbitrarily fixed by the Occupation authorities. Poles were shot on sight simply because they looked suspicious. The slightest infraction of the rules led to a bullet or a concentration camp, sometimes by way of a Nazi torture chamber.

If the Poles in the West were suffering, so were those in the East. The NKVD quickly moved into their new territory to remove all "undesirables." The list was formidable. It included all members of pre-Revolutionary Russian political parties; all members of contemporary political parties, including students belonging to student organizations; all members of the police force; all officers or ex-officers of the Army; everyone ever to have been dismissed or who had resigned from the Communist Party; refugees and political emigrés from Russia; anyone who had ever traveled abroad; people who were Esperantists (which had taken a hold in Poland); or those who collected stamps(!); Red Cross staff; clergymen and active members of religious communities; aristocrats; landowners; wealthy merchants; industrialists; and hotel and restaurant proprietors. In fact, so long was the list that it was impossible to process everyone, so people were just picked up from the streets, assigned to one or another of these categories, and shipped off to the Gulag Archipelago. After having been formally sentenced either to hard labor or penal exile, 1½ million Polish citizens were shipped, in conditions of indescribable horror, in unheated cattle cars during the hard Russian winter, on a journey of six thousand or so miles to the Gulag Archipelago, where they were put to work, and where they eventually died from exhaustion, hypothermia, or malnutrition.

"The conclusion is unavoidable," writes the British historian Norman Davies. "At this stage, the USSR was seeking to prevent the resurrection of an independent Poland in any form whatsoever. Stalin was outpacing Hitler in his desire to reduce the Poles to the condition of a slave nation incapable of ruling itself.

"There is little doubt that if the Nazi-Soviet Pact had lasted much longer, the goal of the two participants with regard to Poland would have been achieved. By 1941 the Nazi extermination machine was moving into top gear. The Soviets needed no encouragement. Isolated from all outside help, the Polish nation could not conceivably have survived in any recognizable form. Fortunately for them, the vagaries of war turned in their favor. The Poles were saved by the German attack on Russia. Although four long years of horror remained, the Germans were to prove incapable of annihilating Poland single-handedly. The Soviets, who for two years had acted as Hitler's chief accomplices, turned for Polish assistance. The Poles were spared total annihilation."

When Germany invaded Russia on June 22, 1941, Poland and Russia instead of being the deadliest of enemies, became allies. General Wladyslaw Sikorski, who had set up a Polish government in exile in London, launched a campaign for the release of those Poles held in Russian camps. On July 30, 1941, Stalin declared an amnesty for Polish prisoners. The camp gates were opened and most, though far from all of those still serving, were permitted under General Anders to leave Russia by way of Tashkent, into Persia, to form a Polish Army that fought valiantly on all fronts of the war under British command.

Among those pathetic people—about half of those who had been arrested and tried on trumped-up charges eighteen months earlier— was the future Prime Minister of Israel, Menachem Begin. More precious to me, was a bewildered little girl whose skin was so tightly pressed over her diminutive frame that one could trace every bone in her body. She was seriously ill, and not expected to live, let alone, in later life, become a well-known pop-singer, then a lecturer in one of London's best-known art colleges and a painter of repute. Her name is Inka, and today, I am proud to say, she is my wife.

The German invasion of Russia unleashed still further the blood-lust of the German occupying authorities in Poland. It has been said that because of the terrifying nature of the Occupation, no decent German officer was prepared to serve in Poland, thus leaving the territory free for every kind of sadist or psychopath. Personally I find this unconvincing. What seems more likely is that in a society that encourages bestiality, that withdraws sanctions from those who violate normal moral codes, that permits every kind of excess, that treats life itself with total indifference, in such a society those who administer these policies themselves become dehumanized. Some Poles relate stories of Germans behaving decently, of individuals seeking to mitigate the distress of those under their charge. But these are so tragically rare that one can only assume that every German soldier was in the grip of some outside force that permitted him to see and yet not see. Walk around any Polish town or village today, and on every street corner there are little shrines, still lovingly tended, to men and women shot on the spot. Germans committed terrible crimes elsewhere, but in Poland they acted with particular savagery.

For example, when SS General Reinhard Heydrich, Protector of Moravia and Bohemia (probably the ablest man in the whole Nazi hierarchy, considered by Hitler himself to be his natural successor), was assassinated by the Czech Resistance working under the orders of British Intelligence, the Nazis, by way of reprisal, razed to the ground the village of Lidice and killed its 142 male inhabitants.

In Poland such reprisals, though on a greater scale, were conducted by the Occupation authorities as a matter of course. Lidice has become something of an international shrine, but who has heard of any one of the five hundred or so cases of mass executions conducted on Polish territory during the same period.

For example, 215 were murdered in Skloby on April 11, 1940; 232 in Borow on February 2, 1944, and 370 in Lipniak-Majorat on September 2, 1944. Those not shot were transported to the concentration and extermination camps where thousands of Poles were set to work under the most inhumane conditions, and hundreds of thousands died. In six years of war, nearly 3 million non-Jewish Polish civilians were killed by the Germans—about 10 percent of the population of the country. The same number of Polish Jews were slaughtered, representing, of course, virtually the entire Jewish community.

It was in this abattoir that the Polish Resistance operated. Men and women of all classes and beliefs, from the day the Germans invaded to the moment of their defeat, organized a Resistance movement that was the largest, most sophisticated, and, in the end, most successful in all of Occupied Europe. Even in Auschwitz, the Polish Resistance movement operated effectively, helping some 600 people escape, snatching hundreds of others from the gas chambers, and by bribing guards, keeping alive thousands of others who would otherwise have died. Compared to the millions who died there, these figures may seem of little consequence, yet the Auschwitz resistance movement was of immense psychological importance to the prisoners, restoring humanity and hope to those who had lost touch with either.

In September 1940, when rumors of what was happening in Auschwitz reached the terrorized population of Warsaw, a young Polish officer, Witold Pilecki, agreed to be arrested so that he could be deported to this place, mentioned only in frightened whispers, and either escape or smuggle out a report to the Resistance movement on the truth of these rumors.

Deliberately he walked into one of the mass round-ups that were a commonplace feature of Nazi rule of Poland. With false papers in the name of Tomasz Serafinski, he embarked on an act of such courage that his story would be unbelievable if there were not so many witnesses to his deed; he became Auschwitz's only voluntary inmate. That he survived the first few weeks was little short of a miracle. He recounts his journey from the railway station to the camp:

"On the way, one of us was ordered to run to a little post just off the road, and immediately after him went a round from a machine gun. He was killed. Ten of his casual comrades were pulled out of the ranks and shot on the march with pistols, on the ground of 'collective responsibility' for the 'escape,' arranged by the SS-men themselves. The eleven were dragged along by straps tied to one leg. The dogs were teased with the bloody corpses and set on to them. All this to the accompaniment of laughter and jokes."

At this time Auschwitz was for Polish prisoners only, several thousand of whom were set to work to build Birkenau, which became the main extermination camp of the Jews. Pilecki had gone to Auschwitz as an active service soldier on duty, and immediately established in the camp a network called the "Union of Military Organization" under his command. The Union of Military Organization operated in Auschwitz until the camp was liberated by the Russians. Many of its members were caught and tortured hideously, but never once was the network destroyed. Ex-inmates remember, for example, Helena Plotnicka, the wife of a Polish coal miner and mother of five who had joined the Resistance, had been arrested on May 19, 1943, and sent to Auschwitz. She joined the Auschwitz Resistance but was caught trying to smuggle messages out of the camp. She was taken to the notorious Block Number 11, the Gestapo torture chamber. She was tied up with her hands behind her back, red hot oil was poured into her nose, her teeth were driven from her jaws, her finger nails torn out, she was starved and given nothing to drink, yet she refused to reveal a single name. Eventually she was released to her block in the women's camp in Birkenau, where she died of typhus. In one of the most moving ceremonies in the history of Auschwitz, her fellow prisoners, somehow acquiring a clean sheet, lovingly wrapped her body in it and laid it on a "few green spring branches to honor her great sacrifice before her remains were engulfed in the fire of the crematorium."

As for Pilecki, he had become convinced that despite the reports he had smuggled out, the world was not taking the tragedy of Auschwitz seriously, for otherwise surely the Allies would have bombed the railheads to stop the terrible deportation trains, and the Polish Resistance would have launched a full-scale attack on the camps to release the thousands of prisoners.

So, this remarkable man determined to escape, and in April 1943, with great daring, got out through the bakery and made his way to Warsaw. He was listened to sympathetically, but an attack on Auschwitz by the Resistance was ruled out because it was in Reich territory from which the Polish population had been deported. Even if such an attack had been feasible, it would have been impossible to move the prisoners to safety before more German reinforcements arrived. What the Resistance did do, and never ceased in their efforts, was to keep London fully informed about conditions in the concentration camps, the gas chambers, and the extermination of the Jews. Initially they were not believed, and when finally they were, the Allies decided that bombing the railheads did not accord with the strategic war aims of the Western alliance.

If a resistance organization could be established in such forbidding territory as Auschwitz, then for the Poles nothing was impossible. The saga of the Polish Resistance is one of the most remarkable stories to emerge from World War II. They did the obvious things brilliantly. The main marshalling yard in Warsaw was blown up on October 8, 1942; in the same year the Communist Resistance movement blew up an officers' club in reprisal for the murder of fifty of their members; prisoners were rescued from the hands of the Gestapo; a bank was raided to provide funds when they were low; Jews were spirited away into hiding; armed columns of German troops were ambushed; and major engagements were fought with German units in the countryside. But the Polish Resistance had other tasks of equal importance at a time when they were occupied by an enemy determined to turn Poland into a slave market for the greater glory of the Reich.

Education at secondary and university levels was forbidden, so classes were conducted clandestinely. Over a million children were taken through all stages of their schooling in secret classes that never ceased functioning despite heavy losses among the teaching staff. Amazingly, too, every university course continued uninterrupted, in private homes in the main, but also in establishments whose real purpose was disguised. Students took examinations and got their degrees in between taking part in military actions against the Occupation authorities. Most astonishing of all, though over 5,000 Polish doctors died during the Occupation, 4,000 students studied medicine and pharmacy in clandestine circumstances, so that by 1950 the number of doctors per 1,000 of the population was actually greater than it had been in prewar Poland. In Warsaw, the Poles managed to convince the Germans for a time that a medical school was only an establishment training medical orderlies. This illusion was helped by the advertisement seeking candidates for admission with "at least elementary school education." The first director, Professor Stefan Kopec, was arrested and executed by the Gestapo. Thereafter, despite several alarms, the school managed successfully to teach a three-year course in two, before sending students to hospitals for clinical training. Students were hired officially as ward orderlies, stretcher bearers, cleaners, etc., while all the time, under the eyes of this ruthless occupying force, they were moving toward medical qualifications that were accepted after the war. The boast of these underground medical schools, that whatever the circumstances their standards did not drop, was to prove justified.

The medical faculty at Warsaw University continued medical education in the tragic conditions of the Warsaw Ghetto, under the cover of an institution (set up with the permission of the Germans) called Courses for Sanitary Action for Fighting Epidemics, which was, in fact, the medical faculty of the ghetto. It existed right up until July 22, 1942, when mass evacuation to the German death camps began. In halls without electricity, so dark and cold that students were obliged to bring their own candles or carbide lamps, with a few illegally mimeographed textbooks, young Jewish students did their first two-years' study before being taken off to Auschwitz. After the war hundreds returned to have their examinations successfully verified.

Elsewhere too the Poles were making a mockery of the German boast that Poland was completely pacified. Not permitted their own newspapers (in the rest of Occupied Europe *listening* to foreign broadcasts was a punishable offense; but in Poland mere *possession* of a radio was punished by death or the concentration camp) the Resistance printed its own. Books, magazines, and leaflets of all kinds were constantly distributed among the population. Most people had bogus identification papers making administration difficult, if not impossible. Bogus ration cards, travel documents, birth certificates (for Jews), all beautifully forged, were in constant circulation. "The whole Nazi Occupation machine depended upon physical administrative terror. The theory was only too simple. Known malcontents would quickly be eliminated. The rest of the population would be kept in subjugation by ensuring that they could do nothing without a piece of paper issued by the German authorities," says one ex-Resistance fighter. "Thus if you wanted a ration card and with it the chance for food, you had to have a registered address and a registered place of employment. In theory, therefore, the Germans would know where you were at any time, who your friends were and whom you associated with. Certainly the system was designed to make it impossible to move around the country. A Warsaw ration card, for example, was no good anywhere else. In practice, my problem was quite different. I had so many sets of documents, because my job was to move around the country coordinating Resistance groups, that I had some difficulty in remembering exactly who I was."

It was in Occupied Poland that the Poles learned the art of running a black market. "Even in the worst days of the war," says my friend, "most things were available somehow. The ration gave us bare subsistence living, but most families managed to supplement their diet with recourse to a black market that flourished under the German noses, and in many places, of course, thanks to substantial pay-offs, with their connivance. Nevertheless, it is still one of the great miracles of our time how the peasants managed to bring food into town, food which ought to have gone to the occupying authorities. I remember once when the whole block I was living in was surrounded by German troops on a search-and-destroy operation. However many times one had been through these, they were always terrifying. German rule was so arbitrary that one could be taken off to Auschwitz simply because some young officer didn't like the look of your face. Suddenly, there was a loud hammering on my door. I had hidden anything that could incriminate me, but I was only too well aware that anything more than a cursory examination would reveal them. So with a sickening sense of dread, I opened the door, but instead of the Gestapo, there was my supplier from the black market, a small farmer from the outskirts of Warsaw, with a small box of eggs in his hand. 'You idiot,' I said. 'What on earth are you doing here? Didn't you see the Germans? They've got the whole place surrounded.' He drew himself up to his full height. 'My dear sir,' he said. 'Chickens may stop laying for God, but never for Germans.' "

There was more important work being done too. The Resistance discovered that the Germans were building rockets (the famous V-1's and V-2's that caused so much destruction to London) in Poland—far away, the Germans imagined, from any chance of British Intelligence's discovering what they were up to. In fact, slave workers passed information to the Resistance, that in turn informed London. But the extraordinary courage and resilience of the Polish Resistance assisted them little when the tide of war turned, and the Germans were forced back on the defensive. It became clear to the Polish Government in exile, in London, that as the Red Army pushed the Germans out of territory that had been Polish until 1939, they treated this land as if it were their own. Tragedy was now heaped upon tragedy.

Members of the Resistance, who had eased the path of the Red Army by acts of daring sabotage against the Germans as the front-line drew closer, found themselves under arrest when the Russians finally arrived. Denounced as subversives, these men who had escaped Auschwitz were instead shipped off to the death camps in the Gulag. In Vilna and Lvov, the Resistance, having decided to stay its hand and husband all its resources until it could act as the advance unit of the Red Army, harried and harrassed the retreating *Wehrmacht* in a full-scale military uprising. In Lublin, the Resistance actually cleared the city before the arrival of the Soviets. That was the last anyone has ever heard of them. They were arrested and interned, and nobody, save for the Russians themselves, know to this day what happened.

The Polish Government in exile and the Resistance movement in Western Poland were now faced with an agonizing choice. They had not fought with blind indifference to their own safety for an independent Poland simply to swap one form of foreign domination for another. General Tadeusz Bor-Komorowski, commander-in-chief of the Resistance forces in Poland, knew that Warsaw's only chance of emerging from the war as a sovereign state, was if the people of Warsaw, rather than the Red Army, liberated the city. In a message to London on July 22, 1944, he outlined his priorities.

1. Not to stop our struggle against the Germans even for a moment.
2. To mobilize the entire population spiritually for the struggle against Russia.
3. To crush the irresponsible activity of the ONR (Extreme Right-wing Nationalists).
4. To detach from the Soviets as many as possible of the Polish units already standing at their disposal.
5. In the event of a Soviet attempt to violate Poland, to undertake an armed struggle against them.

After a Radio Moscow appeal to the people of Warsaw to rise up against the enemy, with the words "For Warsaw, which did not yield but fought on, the hour of action has arrived," Soviet tanks moved toward the Vistula. "Operation Tempest," the general uprising in Poland, and the great Warsaw Uprising itself began on August 1, and continued for sixty-three days until October 2. Citizens of the brave city fought from street to street, house to house, even in the sewers, in one of the most heroic engagements of the war.

The Germans responded to the Uprising with savagery. They were not fighting a well-trained and -equipped army, but a group of young insurgents who rarely had enough rifles to equip a full platoon. Yet they responded with long-range heavy artillery, reducing whole sections of the city to smoldering ruins. Dive-bombers screamed in to attack insurgent strongholds. Hostages were seized from the streets and tied to German tanks in an attempt to stop the Resistance firing at them; women and children were herded in front of infantry units as they advanced through the streets towards the insurgents' line. After some early successes, the old city was evacuated, as 1,500 survivors, carrying 500 injured on stretchers, made the four-mile journey through the sewers in waist-deep sewage to safety. The 4,000 who surrendered at Ochota were murdered. The stench of death was everywhere. But for the Poles, it was easier to bear death than betrayal.

While Warsaw was being crushed, the Russians remained on the opposite bank of the river. Not only did they refuse to come to Warsaw's aid, but they also refused landing rights to Allied planes that could have made supply-drops from France, if they had the range for the return journey. It must be said that it was not only Stalin who stood by. The Allies, for reasons of their own, also bear responsibility.

On August 17, the American Ambassador in Moscow, Averell Harriman, cabled Washington: "I recommend that the President send immediately a strong message to Stalin and instruct me to deliver it personally provided he is in Moscow, otherwise to Molotov. . . . In making this recommendation I assume that I am not so out of touch with American opinion but that I reflect your views in believing that we cannot, repeat not, accept the Soviet position when they allow the Poles fighting in Warsaw to be killed without lifting a hand and arbitrarily prevent us from making efforts to assist.

"My own feeling is that Stalin should be made to understand that American public belief in the chances of the success of the world security organization and postwar co-operation would be deeply shaken if the Soviet Government continues such a policy. . . ."

The President authorized Harriman "to make personal representations." A day later Winston Churchill cabled Roosevelt "the refusal of the Soviets to allow the US aircraft to bring succour to the heroic insurgents in Warsaw, added to their own complete neglect to fly supplies when only a few score of miles away, constitutes an episode of profound and far reaching gravity. If, as is almost certain, the German triumph in Warsaw is followed by a wholesale massacre, no measure can be put upon the full consequences that will arise. I am willing to send a personal message to Stalin, if you think this wise and if you will yourself send a separate similar message. Better by far than two messages would be a joint message signed by both of us. I have no doubt we could agree on the wording."

In this Churchill was mistaken. Secretary of State Cordell Hull cabled Harriman that the Americans were not prepared to go as far as the British "in attempting to force Soviet cooperation or participating in sending aid to the Underground. . . . Our chief purpose has already been achieved as a result of your representations."

But Harriman was not prepared to wash his hands of the situation, even given this transparent opportunity to do so. "I do not see how it can be considered that 'our chief purpose has already been achieved' and I feel strongly that we should make the Soviets realize our dissatisfaction with their behavior."

A joint message from Roosevelt and Churchill did go to Stalin, but it had no affect, so on August 25 Churchill again cabled Roosevelt. "We do not try to form an opinion about the persons who instigated this rising which was certainly called for repeatedly by Radio Moscow. Our sympathies are, however, for the almost 'unarmed people' whose special faith has led them to attack German guns, tanks and aircraft. We cannot think that Hitler's cruelties will end with this resistance. On the contrary, it seems probable that this is the time when they will begin with full ferocity. The massacre in Warsaw will undoubtedly be a very great annoyance to us (sic) when we all meet at the end of the war. Unless you directly forbid it, therefore, we propose to send the planes."

Roosevelt replied coolly: "I do not consider it advantageous to the long range general war prospect for me to join with you in the proposed message to U.J. (Uncle Joe)."

And there the matter rested. On September 1, the Polish commander-in-chief General Sosnkowski addressed his own troops in Order of the Day Number 19. He recalled how Poland, with British encouragement, had resisted the German invasion. That resistance had never slackened, and Polish units scattered throughout every theater of war had fought for the common cause. Yet, now in Warsaw, the *Armia Krajowa* (Home Army) was left "alone" and "abandoned."

It was, he said, a "tragic mystery that we Poles cannot fathom, particularly in view of the technical preponderance of the Allied Forces . . . Warsaw is waiting. Not for empty words of recognition, not for words of appreciation, not for assurances of compassion and solicitude.

"Warsaw waits for weapons and ammunition. [Warsaw] does not beg, like an impoverished member of a family, for crumbs off the table, but demands the means to fight, in recognition of the duties of the Allies and our agreement with them.

"If the population of this capital . . . have to perish under the ruins of their homes because of lack of assistance, passive indifference or cold calculation, it will be a sin of unbelievable magnitude and without precedent. . . . Your heroic commander [Bor-Komorowski] is being charged now with not anticipating the sudden halting of the Soviet offensive at the gate of Warsaw. Only the judgement of history will be able to present a verdict in this matter. And we are quite confident about that verdict. The Poles are . . . blamed for not coordinating their initiative with operational planning in Eastern Europe. When it becomes necessary we shall prove how many times our attempts to achieve that coordination was fruitless. For the past five years the Armia Krajowa has been systematically charged with passivity and feigned fighting against the Germans [by the Russians and no one else]. Today [the Armia Krajowa] is being blamed for fighting too intensely and too well."

His message ended with two lines from a Polish poet: ". . . perfidy, and lies [here dwell], I know it, I know it, I know it too well."

Eventually, and far too late, Allied planes began making drops from Italian bases. Many were shot down, most dropped their supplies into German hands. Some that landed with the insurgents contained surprises. "We don't need money," the Armia Krajowa commander despairingly radioed London. He could also have radioed that they didn't need wooden bullets, of a type used for training exercises, that were found in one container. The help was too little and far too late. Those brave airmen, all volunteers, who made the journey simply added more dead to the tragedy.

Churchill was still deeply troubled and once again urged Stalin to help, but on September 5, he had from Roosevelt a message notorious for its hypocrisy, ". . . I am informed by my office of military intelligence that the fighting Poles have departed from Warsaw and that the Germans are now in full control.

"The problem of relief for the Poles in Warsaw has therefore unfortunately been solved by delay and by German action, and there now appears to be nothing we can do to assist them.

"I have long been deeply distressed by our inability to give adequate assistance to the heroic defenders of Warsaw, and I hope that we may together still be able to help Poland be among the victors in this war with the Nazis. Roosevelt."

In fact, the insurgents did not capitulate for another three weeks.

One of the last messages broadcast from Warsaw indicated the feelings of betrayal of the Polish people: "This is the stark truth. We were treated worse [by the Allies] than [the Allies treated] Hitler's satellites, worse than Italy, Rumania, Finland. May God, who is just, pass judgement on the terrible injustices suffered by the Polish nation, and may He punish accordingly all those who are guilty.

"Your heroes are the soldiers whose only weapons against tanks, planes, and guns were their revolvers and bottles filled with petrol. Your heroes are the women who tended the wounded, and carried messages under fire, who cooked in bombed and ruined cellars to feed children and adults, and who soothed and comforted the dying.

"Your heroes are the children who went on quietly playing among the smoldering ruins. These are the people of Warsaw.

"Immortal is the nation that can muster such universal heroism. For those who have died have conquered, and those who live on will fight on, will conquer and again bear witness that Poland lives while the Poles live."

"All that is necessary," said Edmund Burke, "for the triumph of evil is that good men do nothing." The Warsaw Uprising was the enactment of that well-known aphorism.

And so the Battle for Warsaw was over. An unexpected concession by the *Wehrmacht* accorded the insurgents the status of combatants and took them into prisoner-of-war camps, a decision that undoubtedly saved the lives of thousands of Poles. But the *Wehrmacht* could not save the civilian population. Over half a million were despatched to concentration camps and about 150,000 to forced labor in the Reich. As for Warsaw, on Hitler's orders, house by house, block by block, it was systematically razed. When eventually the Red Army arrived, not a single person was living in a city that at the start of the war had housed 1,289,000 inhabitants. Even as the Red Army arrived as liberators, another war began. The Communists who had ridden in with Stalin's tanks were determined to seize their opportunity, and the remnants of the old Armia Krajowa were determined that they should not. Men who had been hunted by the Germans were now hunted by the Russians. And more poignantly, the only nation in Europe that never produced a Quisling to side with the occupying forces, now produced a large number prepared to help the Russians establish their law on Polish soil.

Sixteen leaders of the Home Army were invited to Moscow for talks and were immediately arrested and sentenced as "saboteurs and subversionist bandits." All over the country, men and women who had successfully fought the Germans and somehow evaded arrest now, when they came out of hiding, were picked up and sent to prison or work camps. Can one imagine the bitterness of Kazimierz Moczarski, who had fought heroically on behalf of the Jews in the Warsaw Ghetto Uprising and found himself after the war sharing the same prison cell as SS-*Brigade-Fuehrer* (Major General) Juergen Stroop, who commanded the operation that led to the destruction of the Ghetto?

All over Poland the same scene was being repeated. Men and women who had valiantly fought Fascism emerged from the cellars of their war-torn cities, confident that they would receive the rewards of their heroism. Instead they were arrested and excoriated as Fascists by their captors. The cup of bitterness overflowed.

It was only in 1956 that old combatants of the Armia Krajowa were vindicated and only in 1981 given their just dues and made to feel confident enough to wear the lapel pins of their units. "My brother was picked up by the Nazis, most horribly tortured, and then killed," one doctor told me. "How did anyone expect me to give my loyalty to the regime that ruled us ever since when it forbade me the luxury of publicly mourning him?"

"I imagined everything during the war," said another excombatant. "I imagined what it would be like to be under torture. I imagined what one would feel as one stood before a firing squad. I imagined how I would respond if my mother were arrested as a hostage for my insurrectionary activities, and I imagined how I would behave once the Nazis were defeated. What I never imagined was that after a war in which the Allies were victorious I would be under suspicion, my career prospects blighted, and my life narrowly constrained, because I had chosen to fight for my homeland. I think I could have borne all of those other things more easily than I can bear what happened to me and to those with whom I served."

In 1981 I asked a young member of the Committee of the Warsaw Region of Solidarity what the war meant to him. He was born ten years after it was all over. By the time he was old enough to sit up and take notice, most of the physical scars had been healed. Carefully I wrote down his reply:

"Every Pole living, of whatever age, has lived through the war. If we were not involved, our parents and our grandparents were. This country has never fully recovered. A whole generation was traumatized and we of the next generation are not indifferent to that. A collective memory is at work. Even though I was not alive, I feel that their fight was also mine.

"And, of course, the battle continues. Under conditions of undescribable terror, my parents' generation kept alive the concept of Polish independence and freedom. We who follow can do nothing less. Many brave men have appeared in postwar Poland and many more will appear yet. They are all the heirs of the Polish Resistance movement of World War II. This movement of ours, Solidarity, owes its existence to the national will to resist, and it was our fathers who taught us that.

"But the war also taught Poland its most important lesson. We can expect no help from any quarter. What we achieve we will achieve by our efforts. We have friends and yet will always be friendless. To be a Pole is to know what it is to be alone."

15
The Jews

"It's all the fault of the cyclists and the Jews."
"Why the cyclists?"
"Why the Jews?"

AFTER THE ARMY COUP at the end of 1981, the press under Stefan Olszowski, a member of the Politburo and Russia's best friend in Warsaw, used all of the old anti-Semitic slurs that have so disfigured the image of Poland abroad to attack the so-called extremists in Solidarity. Today a country where once lived 90 percent of the Jews of Europe has barely 10,000 left—it is all but, to use the language of Nazi Germany, *Judenfrei.* A policy of anti-Semitism without Semites is a considerable achievement, even for a country like Poland where anti-Semitism has existed for as long as anyone can remember. It is true—though it has gone unreported—that shortly after the Minister of Religious Affairs, on the express orders of General Jaruzelski, called in leaders of the Jewish community to apologize for these slurs and to ask them to report to him any examples of reoccurrence.

Depending upon whom you talk to in Poland, there are alternative reasons why anti-Semitism remains. Members of the nationalist wing of the Communist Party, led by General Mieczyslaw Moczar, say that after the war the Communist Party was dominated by Jews who sold out the Party and the country to the Russians, at the expense of those seeking the "Polish Road to Socialism." Members of the right pro-Soviet wing say that Jewish Communists want to introduce liberal, internationalist theories that fly in the face of pure Marxist-Leninism. And both wings agree that KOR, and perhaps Solidarity too, has been dominated by Jews who led ordinary working people astray. While I was last in Poland, a whispering campaign was making the rounds that Tadeusz Fiszbach, the reformist Party Secretary in Gdansk (he was sacked after martial law), was a Jew though there is no evidence that he is. A poem chalked on a wall in Warsaw even denounced Lech Walesa as being of Jewish origin.

[305]

Ugly incidents of a similar nature have distressed those who value the good name of Poland.

One might see a Solidarity poster marked with the Star of David. A document, subsequently repudiated, emerged from the Supreme Chamber of Control (run by Moczar) which suggested that Karol Modzelewski, one of Solidarity's national leaders, though brought up as a Catholic, was a Jewish foundling. In Warsaw a group gathered to commemorate Polish patriots "tortured, sentenced and executed by the Zionist clique" during the days of Stalinist terror in the 1940s and 50s. Party members in the extreme right-wing Confederation for Independent Poland, a political movement that was making some progress until the coup, laid all of Poland's ills on the Jews, that "alien, cosmopolitan, Bolshevik creed." As for ordinary working-class Poles who would not think of themselves as being anti-Semitic, many are likely to let slip the insult Zydokomuna ("Commie Jew") at the slightest provocation.

Whenever there is a crisis in Poland, the anti-Semites crawl out of the woodwork to wreak their mischief. Poland, so goes the perceived wisdom, is the most anti-Semitic country in the world. Whether that is true or not is another matter altogether. The case for the prosecution, however, seems formidable.

The war was hardly over, the stench of the gas chambers still in the air, when on July 5, 1946, forty-five Jews were murdered and another forty-five seriously wounded in Kielce in what, at least until now, was the last medieval style pogrom in history. Before the war, the Jewish population of Kielce was 50,000, of whom only 850 were left as the mobs smashed their way into their homes. The pogrom began when a nine-year-old boy reported visiting the Jewish quarter to deliver a message. He said he had been grabbed by a Jew and thrown into a cellar where he had seen the bodies of fifteen Christian children before he had managed to escape.

As news of this outrage spread around the town, hundreds gathered to seek revenge. For several hours a huge mob ransacked the Jewish quarter, plundering, looting, and killing, until the authorities were able to bring the situation back under control. An investigation that led to the trial and execution of nine people, including two militiamen, found that the boy who began it had been coached what to say by a local anti-Semite. Most disturbing was the readiness with which the local population, so soon after the horrors of the Holocaust, was prepared to believe in the ancient superstition of Jewish ritual murder. Neither did the Church acquit itself well. The local clergy waited twenty-four hours before doing anything to help, despite requests by the authorities for the local bishop to appeal to the mob to stop. Eventually, the clergy acted, but it was too late. The primate of Poland, the late Cardinal Hlond, hardly calmed Jewish fears when he described the pogrom as "highly regrettable," but explained that it had occurred "not for racial but for religious reasons" (a remark which, to say the least, was double-edged) and then became the first Pole publicly to justify Polish postwar anti-Semitism using words, variants of which have often been heard since:

"The condition [of the Polish Jews] is deteriorating because the Jews who today occupy leading positions in Poland's governments endeavour to introduce a governmental structure that the majority of the people do not desire."

To his credit, Wladyslaw Gomulka sought to make no excuses. "The crime committed in Kielce," he said, "holds all Poland up to shame."

Most Poles, however, did believe that the Communist government that Stalin imposed on Poland after the war was largely Jewish in composition. From this it was easy to extrapolate the thought that he chose Jews because "decent patriotic Poles" could not be found to do his dirty work.

The truth, of course, was quite different. Before the war, the Polish Communist Party, like most Communist Parties throughout the world, had a significant Jewish membership. Between 22 percent and 26 percent of the Party organization was of Jewish origin, a significantly high proportion in a country where the Jews represented 10 percent of the population. During the war, Jewish Communists fled to the East, where they had a chance of survival, while in the West, under the Nazis, they had none. Non-Jewish Communists, remembering Stalin's purge of the Polish Communist Party in 1938, tended often to stay in the West, calculating initially that they stood a better chance to stay alive under Hitler than Stalin. To most of the Communist Jews, what mattered was the proletarian revolution not their sense of Jewishness. As Communists they had quite specifically renounced religious, racial, and, in the early days at least, national aspirations in favor of the Internationale. Thus they, together with Polish Communists, plotted against prewar Polish governments, welcomed the arrival of the Army in the Eastern Territories on the outbreak of war as liberators, and fought vigorously against any Pole—Jew or Christian—who opposed them. The fact that they were Jews was, to most of them, supremely irrelevant. And if Jewish Communists tended in the early days to be Stalinists, then this was only because of the historical accident of their long residence in the Soviet Union during the war. However, if some ministers and senior officials in the first Communist government to take power after the war were Jewish, the Jewish population in Poland derived no benefit from this whatsoever—contrary to popular imagination. It has been shown that Jews recovered more slowly at the end of the war than did the rest of the population, unemployment among their number was higher than general, and hunger and malnutrition more severe.

In 1946 a delegation from the Party's Jewish Bureau saw Gomulka and sought to persuade him to stop the mass emigration of Jews from Poland to Palestine because their skills were needed to help build the country. Gomulka refused to do so. Building socialism, he said brusquely, was complicated enough without attempting to solve Jewish-Polish relations. In 1947 Gomulka approved a suggestion by the Minister of Public Security to open files on Jewish employees within the administration in order to replace them with "true Poles." From 1949 and onward the appointments and promotions of Jews to responsible positions discontinued, and Jews were gradually, albeit systematically, moved out of important posts. In 1950 a special government commission decided that all Jewish institutions should be taken over by the state, and that Jews should be accorded the right of emigration to Israel. Indeed they were encouraged to go, and by the end of the Stalinist period in 1954, only 45,000 Jews, 1 percent of the prewar population and one fifth of the number remaining at the end of the war, were all that was left of Poland's once mighty Jewish population. In the early fifties there were three Jews among the thirteen members of the Politburo and eleven among the seventy-seven members of the Party's Central Committee. A number of top officials were also Jews; Jacub Berman, in charge of security and ideology, and the eminence grise behind the Polish government, was certainly the most sinister of all the top Party officials. Conversely, the Minister of Industry, Hilary Minc, also Jewish, was probably the most decent.

The truth is that wherever their loyalties ultimately lay, to Poland or to Stalin's Russia, they did not feel they owed anything to Judaism. They were militant atheists, intent on destroying the power of the Catholic Church but not because they were Jews. Communism was the all-consuming religion to which they and their non-Jewish colleagues, always greater in number than they, subscribed, and Stalin was their god.

When in 1968 a section of the Party launched an anti-Semitic campaign as part of an extraordinary play for power, hundreds of young Poles, many of whom still live in Poland, discovered for the first time that they were Jews. Their parents had not deliberately concealed their Jewishness from them, but regarded their origins as being of such little importance that they had not thought it worth mentioning. They were Communists first, Poles second, and nothing else mattered. Today, some people believe that the official figure of 10,000 Jews remaining in Poland is a ridiculous understatement. There are, it is said, thousands of Jews still left—some who don't know they are Jews, and some who know but wish to conceal it. As one Pole told me, "Show me an urban Pole who doesn't have Jewish blood in him somewhere, and I'll show you the most boring man in the country."

I began my research into the anguished history of Jewish-Polish relations in the old Jewish Cemetery in Warsaw, several acres of land in the heart of the city that are decently looked after by a population supposedly endemically anti-Semitic. Warsaw, of course, was once the greatest Jewish center of religion, learning, commerce, and politics in the world. Poland itself, before the war, had a larger Jewish population than Israel has today. One can go further back still to the seventeenth century, when it is estimated that four fifths of the Jewish population of the world were then living in Poland. Tombstones in a cemetery are the markers of history, and old Szenicer Pinkus, the official caretaker, was pleased to show me around.

"Look, there is Professor Dr. Maier Balakan." You expect to see an old gentleman sitting on a bench, but he's pointing to a handsome tombstone. "Did you know him?" "Professor Dr. Maier Balakan? He was a professor at Warsaw University. How should I know a professor at Warsaw University?" "Chaia Bersohn—1855," reads another inscription. I know a Bersohn living in London who has always managed to give the impression that he came over with the Conqueror. I make a note to tell him that the reason he so likes my wife's cooking is that there is borscht somewhere in the bloodstream. Rachel Lande—1909; David Cohn—1874. The name Cohn is in my family, and I put a flower on the grave.

Like all old cemeteries the Jewish Cemetery tells the story of those who rest there on the gravestones. Here is a family, that you can see by the quality of the graves, went in three generations from poverty to even great wealth. And here is another family that went in the opposite direction. Here is a family of rabbinical scholars with one black sheep buried close, but not too close. "Ah," says Szenicer Pinkus, "they weren't too proud to take his money to bury the rest. But when it was his turn—into the back row with him!" And there they all lie, the dates matching up from the seventeenth to the nineteenth century, beneath those curious iron tombs which once symbolized modernity and progress but now are sadly rusted, and then the twentieth century, each generation following on, every year accounted for, until we come to the 1940s. "Regina and Josef Dobrzynsey: They died from Hitler's hand in 1943." The stone is not unique—but extremely rare. That is the extraordinary gap in this sad and beautiful place.

From the evidence of this graveyard one would be entitled to deduce that between 1942 and 1944 hardly a Jew died in Warsaw. But we know that they did. They were murdered, hunted down and killed when they fought back in the heroic Ghetto Uprising in 1943, and then those still left were shipped off to die in the most foul and hideous circumstances that we have somehow sanitized with the use of the word Holocaust. With the Jews of Warsaw went the Jews of Lublin and Krakow, of Radom and Lodz, of all the Jewish communities of this country where they'd sheltered for so long, becoming a nation within a nation, speaking their languages of Hebrew and Yiddish, the representatives of a great culture that has disappeared forever and not even Israel can replace. The Jews of the Diaspora are different from the Jews of Israel, and the Jews of the Polish Diaspora were most different of all.

With those Jews died a part of Poland, for Poles and Jews, though often disliking each other a great deal, had a close relationship that would be impossible to deny. Few subjects are more sensitive in Polish circles than the mention of Poland's relations through the years with her Jewish minority. And among Jews, few remarks are more calculated to earn one lasting enmity than to suggest, as I once did, that an anti-Semitic Pole is likely to be friendlier to the Jews than a pro-Israeli Englishman.

Today Poland is the kind of country it is both because of and in spite of its Jews. To an outsider like me, the similarities between the two peoples are so striking that knowing both of them so well, I find myself talking about Polish problems to Jews and Middle Eastern affairs to Poles as though being a Pole and being a Jew were virtually synonymous. Whether the Poles inherited more from the Jews or the

Jews from the Poles, I cannot say, but the resemblance seems obvious. And if that remark is not calculated to win me friends either in Warsaw or in Tel Aviv, then it is because this is a family squabble, all the more bitter and irrational for that.

Jews lived in Poland in large numbers since Casimir the Great who ruled from 1333 to 1370 and gave them sanctuary from persecution in Spain and brought them under the protection of his throne. They performed vital and necessary economic tasks for Casimir and his successors as tax collectors and merchants, administrators of great estates and so on, all functions that the Polish gentry, the only people in the country educated sufficiently to handle, steadfastly refused to have anything to do with. The Catholic Church forbade lending money for interest, so the Jews became bankers. The gentry refused to leave their estates, and Jews filled the learned professions like medicine and law, as well as being artisans, tailors, and jewelers. Under the benevolent eyes of the kings of Poland, the Jews lived with safety and prosperity knowing that any occasional outbreak of anti-Semitism would be dealt with by the authorities. The whole country became a sanctuary for Europe's hard-pressed Jewry, the "Jew's Paradise," it was called. The situation changed radically with the partitions at the end of the eighteenth century. Russia, of course, was virulently anti-Semitic and treated the great number of Jews in its enlarged empire with all the savagery it devoted to its own Jewish population. After the assassination of Czar Alexander II in 1881, the Jews of Russia were mercilessly harried, "systematically impoverished, terrorized, and deprived of every right and privilege." Part of Poland, though still under czarist rule, did have a measure of autonomy, and Jews from all over Russia fled there. Almost overnight the nature of Polish Jewry changed. From being the educated merchant class, it was forced to assimilate hundreds of thousands of Jews "the most impoverished, the least educated, the old and sick of Russia's Jews," crowded into the already tightly jammed Jewish quarters in Polish cities, altering forever the character of great cities like Warsaw, 30 percent of whose population was now Jewish.

Most of the Jews were desperately poor—peddlers, small shop-keepers, and factory workers. What united them was their strong religious faith, which they expressed in their traditional garments and their language. For the majority Hebrew or Yiddish was their first language, and a great many didn't speak Polish at all. Meanwhile Jews in the country districts held the traditional jobs of tax collector, horse and cattle trader, and owner of the local store. When

times were harsh—and they often were—these people appeared to
Polish peasants to be the very representation of the evils that beset
them. They were the ones who foreclosed on mortgages or refused
credit or demanded taxes. We know now that most of them were as
poor as the Polish peasants they worked among, though it is understandable why, during a period of appalling rural poverty, anti-
Semitism grew on ground well prepared to nourish it. There was, in
fact, a perfectly respectable case to be made out in preindependent
Poland for discussion of Poland's minority problem once independence was achieved. That there was a problem there can be no doubt.

According to the 1931 census, 9.7 percent of Poland's population
was Jewish, and 8.5 percent regarded themselves as Jews rather
than Poles; 2.4 percent were Germans, all of whom regarded themselves as Germans rather than Poles; 3.1 percent were Byelorussians;
no less than 13.8 percent were Ukrainians who wanted their own
country; and there was a substantial number of Russians, Czechs,
and Lithuanians. Many of these minorities, including a large number
from the Jewish community, regarded themselves as belonging to
nationalities separate from the Polish nation—a view hard to accept
for the Poles who had struggled so long to regain their independence.

It is from the time when Poland achieved independence that the
history of Poland and its Jews becomes such a complex, often bitter,
story, relieved at time by acts of personal courage and self-sacrifice.
Unfortunately for Poland and its subsequent reputation, and for
Poland's Jews and their consequent well-being, the wrong people
tended to be in the wrong place at the wrong time. In Versailles
where the shape of the postwar world was negotiated, Poland was
chiefly represented by Roman Dmowski, a cold, hard, nationalistic
politician who saw the Jews of Poland as his country's greatest problem. Asked by an American official about Poland's position vis-à-vis
its minorities, Dmowski replied brutally, "Jews form at least ten
percent of our population, and in my judgement this is at least eight
percent too much. Where there is only a small group of Jews in our
villages, whether they are grasping storekeepers or avaricious money-
lenders, as they often are, everything moves along smoothly; but
when more and more come, and they generally do come, there is
trouble and at times small pogroms. . . . Unless restrictions are imposed upon them soon, all our lawyers, doctors, and small merchants
will be Jews." From statements such as this one, Poland, along with
Czechoslovakia, was internationally branded as anti-Semitic and

forced to sign a treaty giving special rights to minorities and imposing obligations upon the government to protect them.

Of course, being forced to sign such a humiliating document had precisely the reverse effect of what was intended. All over the country incidents occurred—usually small-scale, though highly unpleasant— as Poles sought to assert their sovereignty at the expense of what they regarded increasingly as an alien and threatening body in their midst. The first government after independence, greatly influenced by Dmowski's party, the National Democrats, did legislate against them. It was difficult for Jews to get into the civil service and a *numerus clausus* existed in many universities, a quota system under which the level of Jewish students was artificially held down to 9.7 percent, equalling the proportion of Jews in the country. Laws, innocuous on the surface but deliberately designed to harrass the Jewish population, were enacted. In some districts a Sunday-closing law was passed. It hit small Jewish shopkeepers hard—they closed on Saturdays and regarded Sunday as their most important trading day. Compulsory examinations were introduced before certain artisans could practice their trade, but the exams were held in Polish, thus effectively depriving thousands of Jewish craftsmen who could only speak Hebrew or Yiddish of a living. Many of the old czarist laws specifically designed to make life difficult for Jews, especially in rural areas, were retained.

Politically, too, the Jews were under suspicion. The Polish Communist Party, like the Russian Party, had a large Jewish membership. All of Europe trembled before the new menace of Bolshevism. Poland, on the very border of Russia, from which it had just won its independence, had a Communist Party that actively opposed Polish sovereignty, and the nation was positively paranoic. Thus, any radically inclined Jew in Poland became the object of official hostility, while the Church, more reactionary than it is now, equated Bolshevik atheism with Judaism and pronounced both anathema.

Yet the issue of anti-Semitism was not quite as straightforward as it may appear today. The great majority of the Jews differed from the Poles in language and in dress. In the depression years as Poles sought to discriminate against Jews in an attempt to alleviate Polish poverty and unemployment, so did Jews discriminate against Poles. They did business only with each other, employing only other coreligionists. As one Israeli friend born and brought up in Krakow told me, "It is true that the Poles did have the government on their side, which sometimes made things difficult for us. On the other hand, we had tradition on our side. In the big cities Jews tended to have significant trading advantages for the simple reason that they had been at it longer. I went to Polish school, but though my father was by no means a wealthy man, I was certainly one of the better-off boys. It is also true that though my father was assimilated, all the executives in his factory and ninety percent of his workers were Jewish. I remember once my mother, who was something of an intellectual, challenging him about this, telling him that he was being discriminatory. He said he felt easier working with Jews and that was all there was to it."

Politically, too, the Jews divided themselves as sharply as did the Poles. Vladimir Jabotinsky's Zionist Revisionists were powerfully supported. The sight of Jewish students, like a young man called Menachem Begin, strutting through the streets in their paramilitary uniforms seemed to many—Jews included—as chilling a sight as right-wing Poles dressing up in the uniforms of the far-right organizations that were beginning to put in an appearance.

Despite all of this, the Jews in Poland during this period suffered no greater hardship than the Poles themselves. Once Marshal Pilsudski came to power in 1926, all official anti-Semitism ceased, and Polish Jews again enjoyed the kind of official protection they had traditionally received from Poland's kings.

If most lived in dire poverty, then so did most Poles. When Pilsudski died, the Jews lost their friend and protector, and in the last years before the war, the plight of the Jewish community in Poland became desperate. Faced with the rising menace of German Fascist militarism, Polish right-wing semi-Fascist parties grew stronger. Although a leading member of the government said: "The promulgation of racial hatred is foreign to the Polish spirit," Poland, under pressure from the right, became more and more anti-Semitic. The facts are indisputable. All over Poland posters went up exhorting people to "Buy only in Polish Shops," or more directly, "A Poland Free from Jews is a Free Poland." Cardinal Hlond wrote in a pastoral letter to be read out in all churches ". . . it is a fact that Jews fight against the Catholic Church . . . constituting the advance guard of a godless life, of the Bolshevik movement, and of subversive action . . . It is a fact that the Jews are embezzlers and usurers and that they engage in the white-slave traffic." In a country faced with such "facts" in a sermon in which the cardinal set out to condemn violence against Jews, it is hardly surprising that more violence ensued.

In the universities Polish students insisted that the *numerus clausus* be adopted and that Jews sit on separate benches, that came to be called the "ghetto" benches. The effect of that was that fewer Jews went to the university and those that were there became politicized —attending their classes standing up rather than sitting on the "ghetto" benches, or becoming more and more involved in the activities of the illegal Communist Party or in militant Zionist organizations. The deep and lasting split between the communities that had lived together for so long with remarkable harmony was widening to the point where it could never be wholly repaired. Economically, too, the Jews suffered severe deprivation. Local councils and the Church encouraged professional and economic boycotts by forcing all shops to place the name of the proprietor in a prominent position outside, so that non-Jews could be sure which were Jewish stores. "Markets without Jews" were established in villages throughout the country: these were market days during which the traditional Jewish trader was kept away. Restrictions were placed on kosher butchers, while all trading licenses on goods that the Jews had traditionally sold were withdrawn and then only reissued to gentiles, thus depriving thousands of Jews of their livelihood at a stroke though, as the Poles were to say at the time, providing thousands of Poles who didn't have a livelihood with work.

It must be said that the majority, the best elements of Polish life—the Pilsudskiites, the liberals and the socialists—were deeply opposed to anti-Semitism and bitterly ashamed of it. Polish Jews who were assimilated in business or in most of the learned professions (save for law) felt no direct effect of the government's anti-Semitic measures. The irony was that while relatively poor Jews suffered, the wealthy remained almost wholly unaffected. But the situation wasn't entirely bleak for the remainder either. Though Menachem Begin today speaks ill of Poland, the country in which he was born and brought up, the fact is that of all the countries in Europe, the Poles were the most helpful in issuing passports to Jews to enter Palestine illegally, while providing arms and training for the Irgun fighters, most of whom were Polish, in Poland waiting to go to Palestine. Itzhak Shamir, who in 1977 became Speaker of the Israeli Parliament, has an uncharitable explanation. "It was a political agreement. They helped us for anti-Semitic reasons. We explained to them 'if you want to get rid of the Jews, you must help the Zionist movement.'" But another distinguished Israeli takes a more balanced view. "They saw us as the fighters for the freedom of our people. And they thought that Zionism would be an end to Polish anti-Semitism. They believed there would always be anti-Semitism in Poland as long as there were 3 million Jews in Poland."

Boguslaw Miedzinski, a member of the Polish Parliament in 1936 who had a Jewish wife, summed up the attitude of most Poles when he said: "Personally, I love Danes very much, but if we had three million of them in Poland, I would implore God to take them away as soon as possible."

One event, above all, received widespread publicity at the time. Both its cause and effect have been hopelessly confused. This event confirmed the image the world still has of Poland as an endemically anti-Semitic nation.

In October 1938, the Polish government announced that all Poles living abroad had to take their passports to a Polish consul prior to November 15 of the same year for revalidation. It was rumored that the purpose of this law was to deprive the large number of Polish Jews living in Germany of their Polish citizenship, and force them either to stay where they were or emigrate to America or Palestine. What the Poles did not foresee was the violent reaction of the Nazi government. Immediately, some 17,000 Jews of Polish origin were rounded up, put into cattle trucks, and dumped with their meagre possessions on the Polish border. One of the deportees, called Grynszpan, wrote to Herschel, his seventeen-year-old son studying in Paris, telling him of their suffering. Maddened with rage, Herschel went to the German Embassy and shot a young Third Secretary dead. It was precisely the kind of incident the Nazis had been waiting for. They used it as the excuse to unleash the full horror of what became the Holocaust. Two days after the murder of the German diplomat (ironically an anti-Nazi), the Nazis went on a rampage. Throughout Germany thousands upon thousands of shops were smashed and looted, synagogues torched, and twenty thousand Jews arrested, most never to be seen again, and dozens killed on the spot. It was known as *Krystal-Nacht* from all the broken glass, and from that moment on, the Jews of Europe were doomed.

Poland suffered too. Though wholly innocent of the greater crime, it became involved by association with one of the great and terrible chapters in the history of the twentieth century which largely took place on Polish soil.

No country other than Israel has been more affected by the Holocaust. It was in Poland where most of the main extermination camps lay. Names like Auschwitz, Treblinka, Chelmno, Belzec, and Sobibor, all in Poland, are names that hang heavy on the conscience of the world. Millions of Jews—mostly from Poland, but also from all over Occupied Europe—met their terrible deaths in the camps. So did over a million Polish Christians. If the Jewish people have not yet ceased to suffer the consequences of the Holocaust, then neither have the Poles.

It has often been said by Jews that the Polish nation either did nothing to assist the suffering Jewish minority or, even worse, assisted in its extermination. Some Poles, through either racial hatred or fear, did assist the German occupiers. Such people existed in every country in Occupied Europe, and one can be sure they were represented in Poland, too. I have been told stories of some Polish peasants hunting for Jews that had escaped from Treblinka. I have heard of people hiding Jews in return for money and then denouncing them to the Gestapo. I have heard stories of Poles standing by laughing as Jews were led away to the deportation trains. I have no doubt that these things happened. But to leave it at that, to condemn the whole Polish people because of the behavior of a few, is to do a brave people an immense injustice.

Israeli Prime Minister Menachem Begin said on Dutch television in 1979: "I will never put my foot on German soil. I shall also never visit my native country, Poland. What concerns the Jews, the Poles have been collaborating with the Germans. Of the thirty-five million of Poles, only at most one hundred people have been helping Jews. Between ten and twenty thousand Polish priests did not save even one Jewish life. All these camps of death were (therefore) established on Polish soil." It was a disgraceful statement in which Begin dishonored himself and dishonored his own people.

When the Germans completed their conquest of Poland, their first target for extermination was not the Jews at all, but the Polish intellectuals. Long before the ghettos had been set up, thousands of Polish university teachers, lawyers, and the like, the intellectual strength of the nation, were rounded up and sent to concentration camps. Contrary to what I imagine that 99.9 percent of the world believes, Auschwitz was originally built to house and murder Poles and not Jews. Reichsfuehrer-SS Himmler's "General Eastern Plan" allowed for the virtual extinction of the Polish nation once the war was won, and he began on this policy the moment Poland was occupied, leaving the fate of European Jewry far less sharply defined, at least during those early stages. As the ghettos began to go up, the policy of unrestrained terror against the Polish population was still unabated. Whole districts suspected of being disloyal were razed to the ground, and their populations executed; constant blockades, street roundups and document checks leading to arrests on the flimsiest of pretexes, reduced the population to a state of helpless despair. The Army had been defeated and languished in prisoner-of-war camps; half of Poland had been taken by the Russians and its people apparently lost forever, the political leadership had fled from the country and the intelligentsia capable of taking its place was either already dead, in German custody, or being harried with no less vehemence than were the Jews.

"Of course I knew that the Warsaw ghetto was going up, and soon we heard that conditions inside were pretty terrible," one Polish lawyer told me. "But they were pretty terrible for us too. As a matter of fact, I can remember thinking that the Jews were rather better off than we were. They seemed, somehow, safe inside the ghetto, policing themselves, looking after their own problems, while we were under constant threat of Gestapo actions. One day I missed one of these by a hair's breadth when going to a meeting to discuss an appeal to the Polish underground from the ghetto for help. My section voted to give the ghetto one pistol, and a message was sent to the ghetto for it to be picked up. A few nights later, a Jew broke out of the ghetto, met me, and I gave him the gun.

"He looked at it in disbelief. I could see what he was thinking. 'These anti-Semitic Poles. One pistol is all they'll give us to defend ourselves.' I was about to explain when we heard a German patrol, and we both had to dive into the shadows, and I never saw him again. But it always haunted me that I was unable to say to him: 'My section has two pistols and one hand grenade—that is all the arms we possess. We voted to give you one of the pistols. We decided that we should have the hand grenade because we believed that we were in greater danger.'"

About that time the Nazis promulgated a law in Poland unique in all of Occupied Europe; it formally established that any Pole helping a Jew would automatically receive the death penalty. Not only was that the law, but it was ruthlessly and unfailingly enforced to the letter by the Germans. A Pole who gave so much as a glass of water to a Jew outside the ghetto was liable to be shot. A Pole who failed to report to the authorities knowledge of a Jew in hiding was unfailingly deported to a concentration camp. But if Poland was the only country in Occupied Europe where helping a Jew required the courage of men who are prepared to die for their fellows, it was also the only country in Europe where, from the beginning of the war to the end, a full-scale secret organization existed for the sole purpose of spiriting as many Jews as possible to safety.

And what is particularly impressive is that help came from every section of the population. The Church behaved with extraordinary courage, even though nuns and priests were not immune from prosecution by the authorities. It has been established that virtually every convent in Poland had some dealing with Jews in its locality, hiding thousands, principally women and children. Many orders, like the Congregation of Franciscan Sisters of the Family of Mary, made it mandatory on their houses throughout the country to do all in their power to assist Jews. So, too, did the Ursuline Sisters acquit themselves with honor, as did the nuns of the Benedictine Samaritan Order of the Holy Cross, the Sisters of the Order of Resurrection, the Franciscan Sisters, the Sisters of Charity and the Sacré Coeur Congregation in Lvov, the Sisters of the Lady Immaculate, and the Sisters of Charity.

Monks, too—the Congregation of Father Missionaries of St. Vincent de Paul, the Congregation of the Most Holy Redeemer, the Salesian Order, the Association of Catholic Apostleships, the Congregation of Marist Friars, Franciscans, Capuchins, and Dominicans.

The individual acts of heroism by members of the clergy are almost too numerous to list. There was Father Andreas Gdowski in Vilna who not only hid Jews in his church but provided a room suitably camouflaged to use as their synagogue. Father Urbanowicz of Brzesc-on-Bug was shot by the Germans in June 1943 for helping Jews; the Rector of the Clerical Academy in Warsaw was sent to Majdanek Concentration Camp, where he died by torture in October 1943, for the same "crime"; the Deacon of the Grodno Parish and a prior of the Franciscan Order were both shot for helping Jews. So much for Begin's slur on the Polish clergy. Even more remarkable is how many instances there were of members of the old, strongly anti-Semitic National Democratic Party who behaved with the most extraordinary courage in defending those whom once they had vilified. Witol Rudnicki, a commander of one of the Home Army units, was a pre-war nationalist politician of some fame. After the German policy of extermination of the Jews became clear, he heard that Polish peasants were blackmailing Jews hiding in the village of Pustelnik, near Warsaw, and threatening to report them if they didn't pay, he ordered the peasants' immediate execution. His apartment in Warsaw became a haven of sanctuary for Jews escaping from the ghetto and his unit the principal link between the Jewish Underground and the Home Army.

Poland's prewar lawyers had proved to be among the most extreme anti-Semites in the country. In 1938 the Union of Polish Lawyers disgraced itself by expelling all Jewish barristers not merely of Jewish worship, but following Germany's Nuremberg Laws, those of Jewish blood. Once war began, these same lawyers behaved quite differently. When the German authorities asked the Polish Bar Council to strike all non-Aryans from the roll of lawyers, the Bar Council, though made up almost exclusively of members of the Union of Polish Lawyers, coolly entered a submission to the effect that such an act was contrary to the fundamental laws of the Polish state, and that under the Hague Convention of 1907 the Germans had no right to insist upon it. Only one member of the Bar Council declined to go along with the majority, all of whom, apart from that one renegade, immediately lost the right to practice. The Germans then decided that each lawyer in Warsaw had to personally submit to questioning about his attitude on the Jewish question before being permitted to practice. As a result the Germans were able to split the lawyers into three categories. The first, between eighty and a hundred, argued that the Occuptaion authorities had no right to impose German legislation on Poland. The second group, in which there were nine, refused to say anything at all. The last group confined themselves to stating that they belonged to nationalist groups or the Union of Polish Lawyers. They refused to say anything else. The last two groups were permitted to continue working as lawyers. But the first group was immediately arrested and taken to the notorious Pawiak Prison in Warsaw and then transported to Auschwitz. Of these, many were members of the anti-Semitic Union of Polish Lawyers and two were nationally known for the virulence of their anti-Semitism. Jerzy Czarkowski was a brilliant, ambitious young lawyer-politician who had used anti-Semitism as a potent weapon before the war. Now he preferred to go to Auschwitz rather than accept the German thesis that Jews were less than people. Jan Mosdorf, who belonged to the same group, was also a famous nationalist jurist and writer. He was killed in Auschwitz by the Germans, because even though he and his friends were hardly well fed, nevertheless they smuggled food to the Jewish compound because it seemed to him that the suffering there was even more terrible.

The Communist and socialist Resistance movement was never

anything but splendid, and there were always workers and peasants throughout the country who risked their lives on behalf of the Jews.

At the beginning of the Occupation, a German soldier got on a Warsaw bus and chased Jews off. An elderly gentleman observing this stood up too. "If the Jews leave," he said, "so will I." He left the tram and all the Poles present followed. Of course, overt acts of this kind became impossible as the Germans with increasing fury applied their terrible law of death to anyone who helped the Jews. Yet the fact is that at war's end some 200,000 Jews were discovered to have survived, 90 percent of whom could only have done so with the help of Poles. It has been calculated that probably up to a million Poles were either directly or indirectly involved in relief activity.

Poland's enemies reply by saying that a great many Poles did help, and probably a good many more than the nation has ever been given credit for, but these still comprise a minority of the population. This is, of course, true, but it is equally true of every nation that the Nazis conquered, and also ignores that no country, except those areas of Russia taken by the Germans, suffered quite so badly. This was a population driven to penury and serfdom, demoralized, defeated, and humiliated. Its leaders were either dead or thousands of miles away, its thinkers and intellectuals imprisoned, its cultural inheritance under extreme pressure. It is astonishing to me not how little help was forthcoming in these circumstances, but how much. Just three excerpts from the Bulletin of the Central Commission for the Investigation of Nazi Crimes in Poland are worth quoting:

"December 6, 1942. Ciepielow Stary district of Ilza. Twenty-three persons, twenty names of inhabitants of Ciepielow Stary identified (three families including twelve children aged from seven months to fourteen years). Burned alive by an SS unit, billeted in Ciepielow Gorki on suspicion of harboring Jews. Thirteen victims were burned in a one-room cottage and ten in a barn. The remnants of charred bodies were burned in the field."

"December 6, 1942. Rekowka near Ciepielow, district of Ilza. Ten persons from Rekowka (including six children aged from three to thirteen years, two women, one aged sixty-six, and two farmers—names identified. Burned alive in the farm by an SS unit billeted in Ciepielow Gorki on suspicion of sheltering Jews. The remnants of charred bodies were buried in a field."

". . . for hiding Jews in the village of Szarwark, district of Tarnow, the Germans shot on August 5, 1943, the entire Mendel family, composed of seven persons and burned down their homestead."

Maybe Poland could have done more for its Jewish population (though I doubt it), but then so could every country of Occupied Europe. The record shows, I believe, that the Poles did more than most. Certainly Polish diplomacy never forgot its duty to its Jewish population.

Only the Poles throughout the entire war constantly and repetitiously (to the fury of the Allied leaders) insisted that the Germans were committing the crime of genocide against the Jews. It was a Polish Foreign Minister who first passed the full story of these atrocities to the world in 1942; Polish diplomats begged the allies to bomb the Auschwitz railheads. It was Poland that sought to remind the world of the Nazi's policy of racial extermination. And it was Poland, alone of all the nations of Europe, that set up a special unit of the Resistance movement specifically charged with helping the Jews, and its record was a glorious one.

Yet once the war was over, all of the old anti-Semitic slurs surfaced once again.

"In a curious way," says one Polish commentator, "Jews are a kind of ritualistic scapegoat in Poland as Communists are in the West. Before the war 'Jew' was shorthand for rich banker; after the war the word was used to describe a Russian or a Party man; now it is used to describe an intellectual. The classic illustration occurred during the war itself, in the middle of the Holocaust, when nationalists of the far right actually claimed in their newspaper that the Jews were working hand-in-glove with the Germans to destroy the nation.

"Yet it is interesting that though the Poles have often been verbally anti-Semitic, seldom has this ever spilled over into any kind of direct physical action against the Jews, collectively or individually. In the thirties, despite their privation, the Jewish community was well enough off to pay 30 percent of the nation's taxes; after the war Jews were prominent in government and in the seventies they remained a significant force in our artistic and intellectual life. The one exception to this rule was the great purge in 1968. On that occasion anti-Semitism was used as a weapon by one political group against another. It got out of hand, and I do not know a man in Poland who is not ashamed of it. The whole battle was conducted in the higher reaches of government, and the ordinary Pole was simply too mystified by the whole thing ever to get involved.

"But I tell you one thing, during the Six Day War the whole country, and I mean the whole country, was 100 percent behind the Israelis. We sat in our homes and coffee houses delighting at the spectacle of so many Polish Jews defeating the Russian's Arabs. And I tell you something else, even though he may not like us very much, if Poles had a vote in Israel, Menachem Begin would never need to worry about being reelected ever again."

My friend went on: "The Jews have brought out the best and worst in every Pole. Yet I can tell you this. I have traveled the world, and outside Poland, it is only in Tel Aviv that I really feel at home.

"I think most Poles would like to hold out the hand of friendship to Israel and to the Jewish people of the world. We are afraid to do so, because it is likely to be bitten off. We understand how our un-reconstructed anti-Semites make any kind of reconciliation difficult. But the Jews are so much a part of our history that their memory will forever haunt us. What a tragedy it is that two peoples that fought and died together, and often selflessly for each other, today cannot live together. That is just one more modern Polish tragedy."

16
The Young

A young man being taken on for his first job in a Warsaw factory was asked to sign his name on a job application form.

"Unfortunately, I can't write," he said. "Can I make my cross?"

"Fine" said the interviewer when he'd finished. "But why the second cross?"

"Ah," said the young man, "that's for my Ph.D. in Marxist-Leninist studies."

ONE COUNTRY IN THE WORLD where it is difficult, if not impossible, to learn the truth about Polish history is in Poland itself. No nation, not even Russia, is as frightened of its past as is Poland. The taboo subjects run into legends, while the deliberate falsification of historical fact is a scandal that few teachers attempt to excuse.

Poles have always been taught in school that a student uprising in Warsaw in 1905 supported the abortive Russian revolution of that year. It was nothing of the sort. It was against enforced Russification by the czarist government that had prohibited lectures in Polish at the university. Marshal Jozef Pilsudski, who led the war against the Russians in 1920, has been consistently presented by teachers as a Fascist, which patently he was not.

The role of the non-Communist Resistance during the war has been downplayed, while the much smaller and less significant Communist Resistance movement was glorified. The Molotov-Ribbentrop Pact is so fudged that, as one student told me, the trick to writing an essay on that period is "to give three paragraphs to the pact but to say nothing that makes any sense whatsoever." Katyn, of course, cannot be mentioned at all, while modern history, from the Stalin era until today, presents such a series of embarrassments that committed members of the Party beg their department heads not to be asked to teach it.

Care has to be taken even over the teaching of the revolution of 1791, with its obvious parallels to Russian-Polish relations today. "One of my students wrote an essay about 1791," one teacher told me, "and I quickly realized that he had artfully framed it, so that by changing names and dates, it became a scathing commentary about the situation in Poland now. I called him aside and told him that another teacher would have made sure that his academic career was over forever. You just don't joke about that sort of thing."

In fact, most children have heard the truth from their parents and learn early on how to differentiate between history and current affairs as taught at school and the facts.

"This has two appalling consequences for the nation," says a member of the Academy of Sciences responsible for setting the school curriculum. "Firstly, it has bred a generation of cynics—if children are taught not to believe what their teachers tell them, then no one ought to be surprised if they grow up not believing what the authorities tell them. At examination time children faithfully transcribe the authorized version of events as presented in their textbooks, knowing perfectly well that they are writing lies. How can those children be expected subsequently to treat their society—which they know from their personal experience is built on lies—with respect? Secondly, it has made this a society whose historical memory is based mainly upon myth and undigested half-truths. If what they are taught at school is nonsense, what they are taught informally at home or from their friends is likely to be equally unscientific. The cult now surrounding Pilsudski is a classic example. He is eulogized by the young, his tomb at Wawel Castle in Krakow is covered with votive offerings, and students wear badges carrying his portrait. At school they are told he was a Fascist. Their parents tell them that he was a great patriot and a man of the people. If they had textbooks that examined his life honestly and objectively, they would not accept either analysis. They probably wouldn't condemn him as the authorities would like. But they certainly wouldn't glorify him the way they are now."

Thanks to the nucleus of an heroic staff, universities, if only privately, have managed to retain something of their academic purity. Students who express an interest have usually been able to find professors or lecturers prepared to run private seminars under the guise of tea parties in private homes, where they teach what they call "outdoor" history, that is, history outside the hothouse of the official curriculum. The effect upon the students is not what the authorities might expect.

"Once I learned the truth about prewar and wartime Soviet-Polish relations, I became more sympathetic to the Russians, rather than less so. When I heard my parents talk, and they influenced me enormously, they were only able to see things from a Polish perspective, through the distorting prism of their personal experiences. I'd been brought up to hate the Russians, but when I had the chance to see things more objectively, I understood that the Russians had problems too. They often behaved very badly, but the Poles have not always been perfect either. So why do the Russians have to be so defensive now about their previous record, so frightened of our knowing the truth? Do the British feel they've got to constantly apologize to the Indians? Of course not. Everyone accepts those were different times and different people."

During the period of liberalization ushered in by Solidarity, the Academy of Sciences set up a committee charged with preparing a new set of guidelines for the teaching of history in schools—the most significant educational reform proposed in any Communist country since the war. Recent information from Poland suggests that this work is being allowed to continue, though whether it will be permitted to come to fruition through the syllabus only time will tell.

"We want teachers to be able to tell the truth in class," said a member of the committee. "That must be the first step in restoring political health to this country. Until schools once again become places of genuine learning, reforms in every other sphere are irrelevant."

Education has always been the diamond in the crown of the Communist system, and Poland is no exception. In Poland at the end of World War II an estimated 2 million or 10 percent of its people were illiterate, today the nation possesses an educational system in which it rightfully takes pride. Children who started their first year of school on August 21, 1978, will have ten years' compulsory schooling. Sophisticated educational techniques sort out early on the academically gifted from the rest of the children who receive specialized courses in crafts and industry as well as a good general education.

Poland's success in producing an educational system as academically rigorous as any in the world was one of the principal reasons for the spectacular progress made by Solidarity during its short sixteen months of freedom. I, and everyone else who visited Poland in 1980 or 1981, was immediately struck by the extraordinary youth of so many of Solidarity's leaders, many still in their twenties. They were ordinary workingmen who were widely read, politically and socially sophisticated, and supremely articulate. After meeting dozens of them, I came to the view that, in many instances, their wholesale condemnation of the socialist system under which they lived was in reaction to the sense of personal frustration to which the system has condemned them.

Under this system the kinds of middle-level jobs that require personal initiative and that can be filled by academic underachievers with vocational skills untestable in formal examinations are non-existent. In such jobs ambition and industry are more highly prized than rigorous intellectual training. Because there is so little private business, there is not much opportunity for an independent-minded young man to set himself up in a small way, with the hope that one day he might command a mighty industry. There are few jobs for salesmen in a system that allows for no competition. Poland has produced many great poets, but what about that huge army of graduates with a literary bent who, in the West, find gainful, agreeable, and socially acceptable employment working in publishing houses as book editors or advertising copywriters, all with the potential of making it to the top. Some jobs simply don't exist at all—like that of realtor or car salesman. Others are so restricted that they provide employment for very few.

Because there are only a few publishers, there are very few jobs for book editors or jacket designers. Because there is only one state fashion industry, the chances of becoming a fashion designer are severely limited. There are plenty of lawyers, of course, but the wide range of services they provide in the West, giving necessary employment to many law school graduates, are simply not necessary. Accountants exist, but only to do the books for the big industrial enterprises. The concept of a tax consultant is unknown. Poland has plenty of journalists, but for a young man, unable to get a job on a publication, to work freelance for a period is desperately difficult. Secretarial or receptionist jobs are few and far between, without the myriad of companies that exist in the West all requiring ancillary services to support them.

"Any society," says an English friend, "that has managed to dispense with three quarters of its lawyers, eighty percent of its accountants, all of its hucksters, as well as the whole substructure of jobs that keep them afloat, can't be all bad." But like Party doctrine that decrees that jobs that are nonproductive have no place in a socialist society, this is elitism run mad. Polish experience shows its ultimate folly. While in Poland I had to have my car serviced, and the only way to ensure that it was done was to spend the entire day at the garage. Eventually I got into a discussion with the two mechanics

—both in their thirties. One was a graduate in mathematics from Warsaw University, and the other a graduate in physics. What, I asked, were they doing working as garage mechanics. They explained. Neither had first-class degrees permitting them to pursue academic careers or to enter industry at a high enough level. They were condemned, they said, to a life as little more than clerks within the state system, earning the average national wage of 5,000 zlotys a month. Each had been offered jobs that were boring, far beneath their intellectual abilities, and wasteful of the knowledge that they had so painfully acquired.

Instead of working for very little money at a repetitive job that had little hope of promotion, they decided independently of each other to work in this privately owned garage, where they could at least expect to earn between 15,000 and 20,000 zlotys a year. "It broke my father's heart," said one. "He is a workingman with little education, and it was the proudest moment of his life when I was accepted by Warsaw University. He simply cannot understand how it is that I am not doing a pleasant white collar job with the academic qualifications I have, and why it is that I have chosen to revert, to become like him, a workingman." Nor are these two untypical. All over Poland men and women have dropped out of the system. They work as repairmen and the like in the stunted private sector because they are not sufficiently qualified for the jobs they would like, and overqualified for the jobs they are offered. All modern societies, with their emphasis on equal educational opportunities, produce young men and women educated but unemployable in the level to which they aspire. In Poland—and the rest of the Communist bloc—that situation is enshrined in the system.

Poland has found one unorthodox way out of the dilemma and that is by exporting the problem. At this time there are probably a million young Polish men and women all over Europe working illegally, without work permits, as waiters and waitresses, dishwashers, builders and decorators, and mechanics—all jobs that they expect to do for one to three years before returning home and starting life for real. A young Polish economist, currently a waiter in a London coffee shop, explains: "I've got a reasonable degree which, if I had Party membership, would probably get me a senior position in one of the planning ministries, but Party membership is vital, otherwise my road would become very quickly blocked. It is unfortunately not a good enough degree to get a top academic post, so I, together with 80 percent of my graduation class, have come to work abroad. I live very frugally so that I can save as much money as I can, so that when I go back to Poland I will be economically self-sufficient for some time.

"I will probably end up at a tedious government job for which my qualifications will not be of much value. With the money I'll have earned in the West, I will be able to buy a reasonable apartment and a car, and live very well in People's Poland. The basis of my wealth will come, however, from the generous tips my customers give me here in Kensington. I will have an easy job and, because I'll have money, an easy life."

A Polish engineer described his personal frustration to me several years ago when I met him in Egypt, where he had been set by his government as part of an aid project to build power stations. "I quickly realized," he said, "that Western engineers without half my qualifications had double the responsibility, and of course, a hundred times the pay. Eventually I had to admit that they were no less capable. The reason was that they had come out of universities and technical schools and had taken jobs right away with a wide variety of engineering firms, where they got on-the-job experience at an incredible number of large and small projects. I came out of the university and was put to work on power stations; that is all I have ever done and ever will do. I am an expert, but my life is really not my own. If I told my people I wanted to move, they'd be shocked. I'm 'Mr. Power Station' and always will be."

Total lack of flexibility is the hallmark of a planned economy. It creates precisely the kind of economic and human wastefulness it is specifically designed to avoid. Thus, while I was last in Warsaw, a lecturer in architecture at the university for the past seven years announced that he felt he had now repaid the education the state had given him, bought himself some greenhouses, and went into the commercial production of carnations. He found himself in good company. Greenhouses are among the few Polish industries in which the private sector is permitted to compete with the state on more or less equal footing. Nearby greenhouses were being run by ex-doctors, ex-dentists, ex-schoolteachers, and ex-engineers. All had this in common: They had been put through a high-pressure school system, but could only find jobs that lacked status or challenge. Of course this happens in the West too, but a corporate executive who is bored by his work at least has the compensation of a salary and a lifestyle to go with it.

In Poland the average members of the professional middle class—

not those who have joined the *nomenklatura* or those who have risen to the top of their particular disciplines—are given salaries considerably lower than those of top industrial workers, yet they have middle-class values to support. "It is not snobbery that says that I like to go to the theatre or to a concert once a week, when the average worker is happy at home watching television," says a Polish doctor. "It is not snobbery that I like to buy books that the average worker wouldn't dream of wanting. It is not even snobbery to suggest that I like an expensive style of furnishing while the worker is happy with something cheaper. These are the tastes acquired through my education. My father doesn't understand or even approve of them. It doesn't make me a better person than he is, it merely makes me different. The motivation that drives people to work hard in order to acquire possessions to support their tastes cannot operate in this country. It is either sublimated, which leads to a lack of personal fulfillment, or it is channeled into another direction altogether. In this country that tends to mean joining one of the groups in opposition to the regime. By doing that people may not be earning money, but they at least feel they are living for a purpose, albeit a dangerous one."

Of course the professionals are still fortunate. The dream of everyone in a worker state is to be anything but a worker! However, just to become an office clerk a certificate of some kind is essential. The pressure that puts on children is enoromus. Children first go to school at the age of six, or even seven, and though in theory they should have at least one year in nursery school beforehand, reality does not match promise and there are not enough places to go around. From the moment they enter school, children are on an educational treadmill that leaves little time for the out-of-school activities considered important in the West for helping to develop character as well as the intellect. Every year there are examinations to be passed. The child will progress to the next class if successful or else be put on a different track—to the so-called vocational schools.

To be a sales assistant in a shop, headwaiter of a restaurant, restaurant chef, secretary or hotel receptionist, stationmaster, ticket clerk, decorator, electrician, or anything, a Pole needs a certificate from a vocational school. No amount of natural flair or willingness to prove oneself on the job will do—the certificate is essential. The vocational schools, which have had a stultifying effect, began with the best of intentions. A headwaiter, it was reasoned, is no less important a human being than a lawyer. His job requires specific skills that need to be taught. So why should the headwaiter not be granted his own institution, his own graduation ceremony, and his own scroll to show the world that he is a professional worker? In fact, as any headwaiter will tell you, only someone with an exaggerated idea of the importance of his own professional qualifications is likely to want a formal diploma that can only be a meaningless scrap of paper to do a job that requires so much intuitive skill and finesse. There are vocational schools all over the world, and they fulfill an important need, but in Poland they are mandatory. Without the necessary certificate, one simply cannot get the job. The old idea of a kitchen hand ending up as a great chef; the copyboy as a newspaper editor; the assistant stage manager as a great actor; the bricklayer as the manager of a great construction complex; the lighting cameraman as a film director; the switchboard operator as a director of the firm—all of this is simply not possible in Poland, because the law decrees it. One cannot be a film director unless one has taken a course as a film director in a film school, though to be fair in this case, the Polish film school in Lodz, whose graduates include Wajda and Roman Polanski, is probably the finest film school in the world.

One cannot be an actor unless one is registered as an actor and has gone through stage school. A switchboard operator will always be a switchboard operator, however brilliant, unless he or she manages to go to night school and take a parttime diploma. A friend, a graphic designer, wanted to buy a plot of land in the country where he could work in peace and grow a few vegetables. But because the plot he had in mind was designated for agricultural use, he wasn't allowed to buy the land, even though he proposed to cultivate it, because he didn't have a certificate. So he went to night school to learn about pig-breeding—the only course available. After six months he got his graduation certificate and was permitted to buy his plot. Since then, of course, no pig has ever been near it; nevertheless the state and he are both satisfied, and the vegetables he grows are magnificent.

It was only when I realized how pervasive was the vocational school system in the Communist bloc, did I understood why it is a restaurant in Krakow serves food virtually identical to the food in an equivalent restaurant in Warsaw; or a hotel restaurant in Leningrad has precisely the menu, prepared in exactly the same way, as a hotel restaurant in Moscow. The answer is not only that the state decrees the sizes of portions and the price for each dish, but more importantly, the chefs have been through the same school system, operating on a common syllabus, laid down by the appropriate ministry. Every family in Poland will have its own secret recipe to make pierogi, a delicious dish of stuffed dumplings. Every, or nearly every, Polish restaurant has only one way—the way taught in the state kitchens.

The elite among the young go to the universities, for which there is ferocious competition, and the word "elite" is used advisedly. In this theoretically classless society, the class differences among Polish youth are no less than they are in America. This appears to be due to a variety of reasons, all endemic to the system. In a society that lays such stress on education, those who have the ability to pull strings and have "shoulders," are likely to benefit disproportionately over those who don't. The favored ones are children of middle-class families (especially the *nomenklatura*) that have the money to pay for private tuition for their children during their school days, that have the pull to get them into schools renowned for their academic excellence, and finally, that use their influence on university professors and rectors to gain them admission.

Once at the universities even those students heavily involved in student politics prove to be considerably more conservative than they realize. I was shocked to discover that one of the principal demands of Polish university students during their strike in 1980, which led to the formation of an Independent Students' Union, was that all students should be exempt from the two years' national military service. The students never got their way, but fewer felt a genuine sense of grievance that the authorities did not grant the demand and continue to this day to press for its implementation. I explained to students I met that this request was wholly unreasonable and undemocratic, that in any Western society that has ever had national service, all students could expect was deferment from the draft until they'd completed their studies, but then they had to go like everyone else. Students were, in any case, a privileged section of society, in receipt of state funds to further their education; why then should they escape the obligations to the state that ordinary workers could not avoid? This didn't go down at all well. If Polish medical students were exempt (which they were not in Britain during its days of National Service), so other students should be, too, I was told. Students, they portentously explained, were trained to serve society in other ways. In manner and dress the student population, particularly at Kracow University (which is to Poland what Harvard is to the United States or Oxford and Cambridge are to Britain), take pride in being different from their contemporaries. Rather like young men from the great public schools of England, they believe they have the right to lead society as a consequence of their background and education, and they are contemptuous of those who do not possess their advantages.

This kind of elitism doesn't sit well with the rest of Polish youth. Many more than the government will ever acknowledge are permanently estranged from society. "They are constantly told that they live in a classless society with opportunities available to all," says a Polish sociologist. "What is more, they tend to believe it, treating any evidence to the contrary as an unimportant aberration. But this creates a psychological problem for a great many young people. They have lost all alibis for their apparent failure. If they haven't made it to university, then the fault must lie within them. They were given an opportunity equal to everyone else's, so they believe, and yet they failed to grasp it."

Losing all sense of their own worth, they turn to drinking and drug-taking—which the official media has at last acknowledged as a major social problem in the country—to juvenile crime and hooliganism on a scale no less than in the West, or when it was possible, they went abroad to return with financial means to speculate on the black market. Others, believing themselves pariahs in their own society, become part of the state's instruments of repression, the police or security forces, knowing full well that by doing so they cut themselves still further off from their fellow countrymen. A form of self-hatred makes them do it, says the same sociologist. They feel rejected by normal society, so they join an elite with its own privileges, one which has considerable power over the rest of population which they believe discarded them. No wonder they can be so easily persuaded to take up arms against their fellow countrymen.

It is a fascinating commentary on modern-day Poland that many social scientists believe that the educational system in this Communist society, far from destroying class barriers, has made them more acute. "In a pluralist society, the 'have-nots' are represented through the political parties at national level, and efforts are made—if only for electoral reasons—to alleviate their lot," says the sociologist.

"In our society this class is constantly told by the mass media that the government and Party represent their interests above all others. In fact, the government and Party machine represent only their own interests at the expense of the rest of the community, particularly of the economically disadvantaged. It becomes very difficult for an ordinary workingman and the young people, who have been brought up with no other ideology, to understand the enormous disparities in people's standards of living, which they can see with their own eyes, while at the same time they are being constantly told that the guiding philosophy of the system is one of equality."

A social survey conducted by a Polish sociologist, Elzbieta Otawoka, in 1975 showed that only 57.8 percent of Polish skilled workers believed that social distinctions in Poland were less apparent today than they were before the war (13 percent thought they were greater), which means that nearly 30 percent believed that nothing had changed after thirty years of indoctrination. The same survey, however, shows that 69.1 percent of nonmanual workers and 66.9 percent of the intelligentsia—in other words, those who have derived direct material benefit from the system—thought there was greater equality now than there was in the past. In a society that is supposedly based on egalitarianism, it is disturbing to discover that a sizable number of its citizens believe that class differences are as great today as they were before the war, when their own propaganda tells them their country was ruled by a Fascist oligarchy. Despite the fact that the whole nation was almost literally turned upside down in the revolutionary process, a significant number of the working class believe that they have benefitted so little from the system. Millions feel cheated by a system that has claimed so much and provided so little.

One of the leaders of the Warsaw branch of Solidarity, a skilled lathe operator, described how he had been a rebel at school, consistently failing exams that others, whom he regarded as less bright than he, passed comfortably. However, when he left school, he realized the class differences between himself and the children of middle-class families. "Even those who did less well than I at school managed to get good, white-collar jobs while I, coming as I did from a working-class family, had no alternative but to go to work in a factory." The point is not that this is a phenomenon unique to Poland, but that Poland prides itself on having eradicated the problem that this man complains of. The gap between ideology and practice is so wide that it has led to a disillusionment with the present system so deep-seated, it seems as though nothing but a different kind of revolution can ever heal it.

It is generally, if sadly, acknowledged in the highest reaches of government in Poland that if it were not for compulsory national service and for the fact that so many young people leave Poland to find menial but hard-currency-earning jobs in the West, the country would be in the grip of an explosive youth problem. As long ago as 1952, Polish newspapers were sufficiently alarmed to print what was happening. According to one paper, street gangs had been formed called the "Bikinis," the "Pheasants," with their ladies "The Kittens," also known as the "Stankas"; the "Colorado Beetles"; and the "Babkas" or grandmothers. One Polish reporter wrote: "I saw a gang of hooligans trying to break into a nightclub. A cordon of guards could hardly hold back the surge of the eighteen-year-old Bikini boys and Pheasants. Finally the invaders smashed the sinks, destroyed a telephone, and wrecked the elevator."

Another newspaper, using rather heavy satire, described a typical Pheasant as follows: "Although not the normal pheasant of the Gallinaceous family, he scratches among the secondhand clothes in Rozycki flea market for loud neckties, short stove-pipe trousers, sacklike jackets, and high collars. His coiffure is a fantastic crest which he calls a 'mandoline' or 'swallow,' but which really looks like a duck's behind. He lives on the offal of transatlantic culture. In winter he changes his plumage, wearing an outer garment which is a cross between a sugar bag and a monk's cowl fastened with wooden pegs. The Pheasant is a typically pugnacious cock and starts fights on the least provocation." Eventually, even *Trybuna Ludu,* the official Party newspaper, joined in and called upon the entire population to help "combat the type of ruffian disturbing the peace of the street and public places."

Another newspaper gave a graphic description of Kittens. "A Kitten is, in appearance, a kind of hen-pheasant—a cross between a demimondaine and a pick-up girl. In Lodz she is called 'Babka' and on the coast 'Stanka.' Kittens associated with Pheasants use, as do Pheasants, coarse language for its irresistible charm, worship vodka, cigarettes, fights, and nightclubs. It is Kittens who tell Pheasants how smart they look and are enchanted by them. Kittens love their vulgar nonchalance." So much for the theory: Juvenile delinquency is an improbable phenomenon in a Stalinist society.

These articles—remarkably frank in their description of a major social problem—were part of a campaign in the fifties to shield Poland from the excesses of the Western youth culture. They were designed to mobilize public support for the state's attempts to ban Western popular music and fashions at a time when the young were beginning to clamor for them. In this they were entirely unsuccessful.

One of the strangest nights of my life was spent in Warsaw in

1965, when the Rolling Stones came to give their first, and to date only, concert behind the Iron Curtain. The performance itself was a disaster. Seats had been taken up by the *nomenklatura* and Party officials for themselves and their children, who behaved not as if they were at a rock concert but at a recital of a string quartet. Outside the hall, however, rioting continued all night as angry Polish youth, denied admission, took out their frustration on the police, in what was probably the most serious street rioting seen anywhere in Eastern Europe. After the concert, the Stones, my wife Inka (also in Warsaw —at that time appearing as a singer on television), and I sat up all night in the basement nightclub of the smart Europeski Hotel, drinking vodka and trying not to listen to the occasional sound of crashing glass or the 1930s-style palm-court orchestra music being played over the public address system. The late Brian Jones, who had earlier stunned onlookers by turning up in clothes that were as near as possible to a drag outfit without quite being one, retired to his bed, ill. Charlie Watts talked longingly about giving the whole thing up and becoming a full-time farmer, while Mick Jagger, who impressed me by his wide knowledge, his willingness to listen, and his ability to articulate serious thoughts, talked politics until dawn, when the mob dispersed. His publicist, the delightful Les Perrins, downing more and more vodka, would clutch me by the sleeve every so often and say, "Listen to him, he's intelligent isn't he?" rather in the way, I thought, of a proud dogowner showing off his pet's latest trick. Said Jagger that night as the young of Warsaw took to the streets, "You see, rock 'n' roll can conquer the world." "Perhaps it can," I replied, "but would it be wholly desirable if it did?" "I think," said Charlie Watts, "it would be pretty terrible." To which we all, Jagger included, intoned Amen to that.

It would be nonsense to suggest that this was the night that the rock 'n' roll culture arrived in Poland, for if it had been there would have been no pressure to get tickets. But it certainly was the night that Polish youth first took to the streets to protest against the authoritarian nature of their government. For if rock 'n' roll was taken up in the West as a socially and culturally liberating force by young people determined to break from the stultifying traditions of their parents, in the East, as Jagger sensed that night, it was primarily a political weapon. The Russian press, at first dutifully followed by their Polish and Eastern counterparts, took up the cudgels against this "neanderthal music," so it became almost the political duty of the young to support it. If "I Can't Get No Satisfaction" was taken in the West as a cry for sexual liberation, in Eastern Europe it was the anthem of the politically dispossessed.

One young man told me that he couldn't understand why for a time at his high school he was suddenly, for no apparent reason, frozen out by his friends. Eventually he got to the truth of it, when he was accused to his face of being either a Russian or a police agent. When he protested his innocence, he was asked to explain why he had told his classmates that he didn't care for rock music!

Rock is discussed in Poland among the young with a seriousness worrying to a Western visitor who has difficulty telling the difference between Punk and Heavy Metal, let alone the philosophic abstractions of individual bands. How can one respond to the student who claimed that he understood Jean-Paul Sartre for the first time after listening to The Who? Rock is valued more for its supposed message than its music. The majority of young people simply do not have access to Western literature or thought, and even if they did, the language barrier would be an insuperable problem. Rock, on the other hand, indubitably Western in origin, is accessible to everyone. It breathes defiance, it has the virtue of being detested by the authorities, and it is sufficiently elusive to permit quite astonishing intellectual theories to be built around individual songs or bands. Unfortunately, Polish rock groups—some of whom are very good indeed—find that any attempts to give rock a Polish dimension are totally rejected by their audiences. If they are to be successful, it is mandatory for them to be derivative. Only rock music that is indubitably Western has any chance at all.

Poland was the first country of the Eastern bloc to accept the Western youth culture. It began producing its own rock music, which is in much demand throughout Eastern Europe and Russia—where it has the advantages of availability and faithfulness to the real thing. Equally, after a hesitant start, Poland's state fashion industry began in the early seventies to produce a stream of products for the youth market, acknowledging what the Russians seem quite incapable of doing, that there is no reason why a socialist country needs to be gray and utilitarian.

Central Planning being what it is, the Poles never quite succeeded. Thus long after the Western youth had discarded platform shoes and bell-bottom trousers, they were still being churned out by Polish factories unable to cope with a fashion switch to straight-legged pants. This became such a serious problem that, to their bewilderment, magazine editors were requested to print old pictures, supplied by Polish embassies abroad, showing Western street scenes with young people wearing bell-bottoms and captions implying that the photos had been taken that week. No one was fooled for a moment, of course. Polish youth's obsession with the West is so strong that they are as up to date with the latest trend—they take with almost canonical seriousness—as the most fashionable young blade in London, Paris, or New York.

One of the most important effects of international interest in Poland following the Gdansk Accord was that this obsession with even the most meretricious of Western products began to weaken. It was not only the world that discovered Poland, Poland discovered Poland too. Given a chance, I believe, the effect of this national self-discovery would have produced the kind of patriotic response to the economic problems that the government was rightly insisting upon. In the summer I was sitting in a Warsaw restaurant with some students, and I was wearing a military-style olive-green bush jacket. One of the students admired it extravagantly and offered to buy it from me for 5,000 zlotys. "I'll sell it to you," I said, "but you might do a bit better if you went to Moda Polska (a department store in the middle of Warsaw) where I bought it this morning for 1,200 zlotys." He had the good grace to laugh, and we then went on to discuss the damaging assumption that most Poles, particularly the young, have: that Western products, Western lifestyles, and Western ideas are automatically preferable to anything locally produced.

"Our system of government has managed to remove from us any sense of our own worth," he said. "We see the shabbiness around us, the lies that kept our government afloat, and compare that with what we imagine life to be like in the West. Of course, we come off badly in the comparison.

"But then all of a sudden we had a Polish Pope, a Pole winning the Nobel Prize for literature, and we had Solidarity. *Time* Magazine or *Newsweek* would come in, and we'd see page after page about Poland written by people who obviously were impressed by us and our country. When we traveled abroad, we'd suddenly discover that people were eager to talk to us. To be a Pole for the first time in generations meant that you were someone.

"Borrowed ideas are no longer attractive. We are creating our own society—a specifically Polish society from which in due time the rest of the world will wish to come and take. For the moment we are working out the ground rules of that new society; it is obviously a painful and sometimes even counterproductive period, but as soon as we have established them, you will find Poles eager to work and work hard for the new society we are creating. You see, we are at last proud to be Polish."

To successive Party leaders, all of this has been bewildering. It would be unfair not to acknowledge that the Party tried hard to educate its people and always invested heavily in its educational program against the most appalling difficulties. In 1945 a school census revealed that out of 7 million children then in school, no less than one in three had lost his or her parents during the war. Nearly 3 million children and young people had to be looked after in state orphanages, some of whom didn't even know their names or where they came from. This was a huge burden, but the state honored its commitment, it educated them and fed them, with the result that Polish children today are healthier and better schooled than ever they have been in their history.

Youth organizations like the Polish Socialist Youth Union that are derided in the West as instruments of pure brainwashing, have made a positive contribution to enlarging the horizons of young people. The Youth Union, for example, boasts of 8,700 artistic groups of one kind or another—music, dance, cabaret, and theatrical. It organizes holidays of exceptional quality, comparing more favorably with American camps for young people, and sets standards of civic and social responsibility for which no country need feel ashamed.

Yet the response of youth has been, in the eyes of the Party at least, one of blatant ingratitude. No statement angered the Party more in recent times than a Vatican broadcast in June 1979 to Yugoslavia. The Communist Party in Poland, said the Vatican, could no longer be regarded as "the guiding force of the nation" because it had "lost the battle for the hearts and minds of young people." The Vatican was speaking nothing but the truth. Brought up in a strictly atheistic school system, sent to summer camps where religious observance is often forbidden or mocked, the children of Poland, nevertheless, have never been more devout than they are today.

Taught to respect and understand their Constitution, they wish nothing less than to tear it down and begin all over again. Forced to learn Russian as a compulsory second language, few can construct even a coherent sentence when they try to speak it. Provided with lessons on the basics of Marxism, they deride it whenever they have the opportunity. Presented with a bleakly grim portrait of Western society, they assume that the West represents a kind of earthly paradise.

I believe that one can draw a straight line to the total collapse of the Communist system in Poland from that moment (whenever and wherever it was), that the first Polish teacher told the first deliberate lie to his pupils in a Polish classroom. Truth is not just an abstract virtue. Truth is what binds a society together. General Jaruzelski complained about anarchy spreading in Poland before he took over so brutally in December 1981. A state of anarchy is the natural result of a system of falsehoods. When you have the one, the other must, one day, automatically follow.

17

Women

The government decided to open a new striptease show in Warsaw in order to attract foreign currency and appointed a trusted figure to run it.

When the accounts were settled at the end of the first year's trading, it was clear that it had been an absolute disaster.

"I can't understand it," said the manager, when the authorities remonstrated with him. "I chose only the very best girls—they were all Party members in good standing for at least thirty years."

"I DON'T WANT TO READ in your book any nonsense about Polish women not being liberated," said my friend Halina—and she won't.

Life has always been too hard and serious for Polish women to permit themselves the luxury of sitting back and contemplating the role of women in society.

Of all the thousands of articles written about Poland over the past few years, many have distorted the complex reality of day-to-day existence in Poland. This has not been for any sinister reason, but because the Western mind has enormous difficulty in comprehending the people of any Communist country, never mind one so infuriatingly complex as Poland. But of all these, the only article that Poles have drawn to my attention, with some acerbity, was a brief interview printed in the London *Sunday Times*, in the autumn of 1981, with left-wing British journalist Denis MacShane, who is now an official with the International Metalworkers Federation.

MacShane had just published a perfectly straightforward book on the rise of Solidarity. In the interview, however, MacShane permitted himself to be drawn into discussing the role of women in Poland. They possess, he said, a "third class position" in Polish society, "the desire to be equal has not yet come," and "the enormous leap forward for the trade union movement and the people of Poland over the last year takes little account of the role played in society by women." Part of his evidence was that every time Lech Walesa meets a woman, he bows and kisses her hand, and then MacShane went on to say: "I talked to any number of Polish women about equality—they looked at me blankly. To them it is irrelevant." Which, of course, states the case exactly, though not quite in the way MacShane, taking all of his Western preconceptions as part of his baggage to the East, imagines.

On the surface the charge that Polish women have fallen behind women in the West appears valid. At the time of writing there is only one woman in the Politburo. The very top leadership of Solidarity (membership of its inner cabinet was a dozen) had no woman among its number, and women, of course, have no top places in that other great center of power, the Church.

There have only been a few women to reach ministerial rank and, at the time of writing, only one woman in the whole of the Polish diplomatic service has reached the rank of Counsellor. Yet ask any Pole, male or female, whether women have power in Poland, and they will consider the question naive and ignorant. Even before the war, in intellectual circles (unlike in the West), women were given the status and respect their important contributions deserved. For every one Virginia Woolf, there were ten remarkable Polish women writing and publishing, deeply involved in the Polish literary scene and accepted on the basis of complete equality. On the revolutionary political scene, women made a formidable contribution. Rosa Luxemburg at the age of twenty-three was a Polish delegate to the International Socialist Congress held in Zurich in August 1893. She went on to become one of the most significant socialist thinkers of her day, one of the founders of the Polish Social Democratic Party. Far to the left of Lenin, whom she normally bested in argument, she quit the country for Germany, because she believed the revolutionary impetus there was greater and more likely to succeed.

Wanda Wasilewska, daughter of a distinguished Polish socialist and for some time a close friend and collaborator of Pilsudski, secretly embraced Communism before the war. In Soviet-occupied Lvov in 1941, she became co-editor with another woman, Helen Usiyevich, of a literary and political monthly called *New Horizons*, around which formed the nucleus of a group called the Union of Polish Patriots that eventually took over Poland after the liberation in 1944.

Male Polish gallentry—the hand-kissing by Lech Walesa is an example—delights most women and has obstinately refused to die away. Those who are infuriated by it need to work hard to explain why it is in any way offensive. "Of course, I do not feel patronized when a man kisses my hand," says Halina. "I feel desired, and surely that is only unacceptable on the wildest fringes of the women's liberation movement. One of the greatest crimes men committed against women in the Anglo-Saxon world was to deny them their sexuality. That never happened in Poland, and the kiss on the hand I believe to be the ancient demonstration of our right to love and be loved."

Maybe it is hard to have too much sympathy with the Polish noble-men who propelled the beautiful Countess Maria Walewska (with the initial agreement of her husband) to the attention of the Emperor Napoleon in 1806 in order to secure his support for Polish aspirations, though history shows that, once established, she became his most accomplished, as well as his most loyal, mistress, even visiting him in exile on Elba.

But Polish women (remember Madam Curie?) were never regarded as simply pretty ornaments. In every revolt against the Russians during the partitions, Polish heroines proved that even during periods of extreme terror there could be no doubting the courage and strength of the so-called weaker sex. In our time, the Warsaw Uprising showed them at their greatest. It has been said that without women the Polish Resistance movement could not have existed. In a Poland occupied by the Nazis, between 35,000 and 40,000 women took the Polish soldiers' oath to protect the Constitution. In 1943 a special decree of the President of the Republic proclaimed that women soldiers had the same rights, but also the same obligations, as men. A letter written to the historian of the Uprising by one of the principal participants states:

They (women) undertook many functions of high responsibility. A woman was the chief of liaison and communications on the staff and headquarters of AK [the Home Army]. A woman reorganized liaison and communications with the Eastern territory. For some time a woman was responsible for liaison and communications with the West. A woman was deputy commander of the Women's Sabotage Officers' School, which had 120 women instructors. The superior of the couriers' exchange points was a woman, as was the chief of all insurgent magazines and storage points during the Uprising.

On the women rested the responsibility for operational liaison, coding and decoding, contacts with Polish prisoner-of-war camps, and the medical department. [They were responsible for] watching places possibly endangered [by German surveillance], guarding the clandestine meetings and radio stations [and for the] transport of money, weapons, and printed material.

Women also [arranged] contacts with concentration camps, intelligence parties and units [and planned] diversion and sabotage. . . . Within the AK alone, 35,000 women underwent military training; [of this number there were] 5,000 in para-medical training, 700 in liaison and communications, 550 in military administration and 500 in military escort and guard."

"Yes," said a British feminist, when I read this passage to her, "but notice how few women were placed in active service units." "Do not," I replied, "should you ever go to Warsaw, repeat that there." The fact is that the whole city was the front-line. Nurses and soldiers faced exactly the same dangers and required the same courage as a man or woman on the barricades. Every place seized by the insurgents was under constant German air and artillery bombardment, or in direct line of sniper fire. And, of course, many of the women, who made up one seventh of the fighting strength of the Poles, did take part in actual combat. There are many stories of individual heroism (a woman was parachuted from London into the thick of fighting). Veterans remember the fourteen-year-old girl who singlehandedly attacked and burned out two German tanks, or the eighteen-year-old girl who blew up the door of a German police station, enabling her unit to storm and capture the building.

One of the most dangerous jobs of all was to act as a unit or battalion messenger crossing a city constantly strafed by withering German fire. Weapons were in desperately short supply; there was certainly not enough for the messengers, who were forced to move out of the usually illusory safety of their dugouts and out into the terror of open space with nothing for protection. In one battalion 50 percent of the messengers, all women, lost their lives and yet there was never a shortage of volunteers.

A special group of girls were messengers in the dark, terrifying sewers of the city, linking groups of insurgents cut off by the Germans. Small girls were preferred, because the dank and foul passages were often desperately narrow.

Some girls made journeys that could take up to six hours, carrying ammunition and supplies, and emerged at their destination only to collapse from sheer exhaustion. Some went into the sewers and were never seen again. Colonel Niedzielski remembers asking his platoon, which had fought heroically, street by street, in one sector of the city, to pull out by going through the sewers. Young men who had risked everything for several days refused. Death in the open was one thing, the unknown and unseen terrors of the sewers was something else altogether. Then a sixteen-year-old girl, her hair in long braids, stepped forward, opened the manhole cover, and went down. Shamed by her example, the platoon followed.

Nurses could not operate in safe hospitals far from the front line. They were attached to each unit or working in field hospitals which, to be of any use at all, had to be right in the center of the combat zones. Again there are many examples of women acting with the greatest heroism. On September 3, 1944, in Warecka Street, three nurses, one after the other, tried to recover the body of an AK soldier cut down by enemy fire in front of the German position. The first and second were shot in the attempt, but the third recovered him. A woman messenger reported: "While attacking the university building, we had several wounded who were left on the street under direct German fire. Five Catholic sisters . . . ran into the open . . . and approached the wounded. They were dressed in their habits, they had Red Cross bands, and they carried stretchers. The Germans opened fire on them. They could, of course, have withdrawn. Instead, they started to give assistance to the wounded. All of them were shot, one after another. During the night we went after them, and were able to bring back one of them. She had many machine gun bullets in her body. Her name was Pulaska. I don't know whether she survived."

Another insurgent reports: "The private apartment of a woman [messenger] was frequently placed at the disposal of the underground. She could never be allowed out of sight, had to live where she could be found easily, and was not allowed to change her name or address without permission. As long as she was active, she could not be permitted to go into hiding or to lose contact with us. To do this meant breaking the contacts between members and branches of the Underground. . . .

"She was therefore in constant danger. All the details of her life were known to many people; this in itself is undesirable in underground work. She constantly carried incriminating documents. Her movements were of the kind that aroused suspicion and her presence was necessary at many (dangerous) places. The average 'life' . . . of a [messenger] woman did not exceed a few months.

"They were invariably caught by the Gestapo in incriminating circumstances and were treated with bestial cruelty in the Nazi jails. Most of them carried poison and were under orders to use it without hesitation when the need arose. It was almost impossible to get them out of prison, and the AK could not take the risk of their succumbing to torture. It can be said that of all the workers in the Underground, their lot was the most severe, their sacrifices the greatest, and their contribution the least rewarded. They were overworked and doomed. They received neither rank nor honors for their heroism."

At war's end, Polish women may have been less content than they were previously to return to home and kitchen, and were backed in this determination by a government that was committed to the concept of sexual equality. That they should work there was no question at all, and today about 40 percent of the work force is made up of women. Though economic conditions were such that few households could get by on one salary alone, this was not the only motivation for Polish women going to work. There was the feeling that as women had fought for Poland, now they should be given the opportunity of rebuilding it. Today any Polish woman who does not work, however well-off her husband, is very much frowned upon. A woman without children who doesn't work is an almost unheard-of phenomenon.

Yet Polish women, having been tested on the battlefield and shown to be the heirs of the same heroic traditions as their men, simply do not possess the same, sometimes chilling need to prove themselves. "The front-line is a great equalizer," says Wanda, who fought throughout the Uprising. "I saw people flinch under fire, and I know that some people during the Occupation behaved badly, but never did anything occur that permitted one to make the normal kind of generalizations about the sexes.

"Men and women were in equal measure heroic and afraid. In my unit a young boy literally froze under battlefield conditions. At the time I felt a great contempt for him. Now I wish I had been more understanding. The fact is that war robs everyone of his or her sensibilities."

The survivors had a perspective different from that of middle-class women in America or Britain whose only struggle has been to get on equal terms with men. "I commanded men," says Wanda, "in conditions where only the ablest and the fittest had the right to demand equality with me. Women won that right and have never lost it." Oddly, however, to Western feminist sensibilities, Polish women, having achieved equality during the war, voluntarily failed to capitalize on the fruits of their victory. Those women who survived the war seemed driven by some mystic imperative to restock the nation that had lost so many of its sons and daughters.

"After the war," says Wanda, "all women could talk about was having babies. The most independent-minded women I knew, those who had previously scorned the thought of pregnancy and being tied down by children, were desperate in their determination to become mothers. A lot of women during the Uprising ceased to menstruate, probably because of the strain, and I know several who assumed that they would never have babies. But as soon as the war was over, they were back to normal—and a look at the population statistics for those days shows them to have been fertile. Though I had a chance for a political career, I too had only one desire—to live at home with my husband and have lots of children. All three are now leading lights in the opposition movement. They are my answer to those who may think I wasted my opportunities." Wanda was far from unique. Though there had been a tradition of women serving in senior positions within the illegal Communist Party, once it took power few Polish women took an active interest in politics, despite the Party's going to great lengths to urge them to do so.

Even despite this, women's representation in the Polish Parliament is higher than for most parliaments elsewhere—about 21 percent of the Deputies (nearly 100 members in all), and at local level, in the People's Councils, women take up nearly 30 percent of the seats. Educationally they do well, too. In the 1977-1978 school year (the last year for which complete statistics are available), girls accounted for 71 percent of secondary school pupils and 50 percent of those attending higher educational institutions. Twenty-four percent of all students in technical subjects were women, 42 percent of law students, 64 percent of medical students, and 76 percent of those studying the humanities. Women in Poland also do well in fields where they are hardly represented in the West at all. Of all Poland's architects, 30 percent are women, as are 38 percent of the country's building engineers. Out of a total of 501 professorships conferred in 1978, sixty went to women, not many fewer than the total number of women professors in the whole of Great Britain. There are very few Polish women who do not believe that they have equality and that the best jobs are theirs for the taking. There is a small women's liberation movement, based mainly at Warsaw University, but not many women take it seriously. It is regarded by those who know about it (and not many do), as being a pale imitation of the Western Movement, owing its existence entirely to the need of some Poles to ape the latest Western fad. This may or may not be fair, for clearly the women's movement has outgrown its original purpose of seeking equal opportunities in a man's world. If that were its only platform in Poland, it would have even fewer members than the few dozen it now possesses.

But Western women, especially those who insist upon imposing their ideas upon other cultures, would find much in Poland to disturb them. All the evidence suggests that not only are Polish women given educational opportunities equal to men, but actually manage to make better use of them. Women currently employed in Poland make up 70 percent of those with general secondary education or higher. Though women are employed in offices in senior executive capacities far more than in the Western world, Polish women have not made the breakthrough, save for a very few cases, into the very top positions.

Feminists will argue that Polish men use the women's talents only as far as it suits them to do so, but then shut them out when it comes to the top decision-making posts. This would not be the view of Polish women, however. "When you have the opportunity of true equality," says my friend Wanda, "then you have the luxury of wondering whether you really wish it for yourself. After my war experiences, I was sixteen at the time of the Uprising, there was no boy in all of Poland who would have dared question my right to share in the fruits of victory, to take what was rightfully mine. And for a period at the university, a group of us did decide that men had successfully managed to misrule the world, and now women, who had suffered, should take the initiative. 'A world ruled by women,' we argued, 'would be a world of peace.' But then I fell in love, married, and had children. My skills were badly needed by the state, and so there was no problem about crèche facilities and nursery schools, as there certainly are for some mothers, and I carried on working. But more and more I questioned whether I wanted my career or whether I wanted my children. And I came to the view that I wanted my children. Of course, I work, but my work very much takes second place to my home."

I heard similar stories time and again from women in Poland. And the choice they were making was an honest one, unencumbered by the economic arguments that make it more difficult to decide these matters in the West. It is far from uncommon in Poland for a wife to be earning more than her husband. Traditional role reversals have become so commonplace that they are hardly ever commented on. In Wanda's own case, it could certainly have been argued at the time, that if her husband had chosen to take a less demanding job, and spent more time at home looking after the children, the family would now be much better off on her earnings, with her qualifications, than on his. And, of course, there are families where this occurs. But by and large, the women, given the choice, fairly and with no outside pressure of any kind, chose the family.

The importance of the family in Poland cannot be emphasized enough; it is one of the most vibrant forces binding the nation together. This sense of family has always existed, but today with both state and Church working on this issue (without realizing it) in perfect alliance, it has taken on a cast that is as agreeable to observe from the outside as it is unique.

The state, by giving equal opportunities to women, has removed the fear of so many Western women that somehow they are being cheated of the good things in life. If a middle-class Polish woman spends a lot of her time with her children and in the kitchen, it is nearly always because she has chosen to do so. But the state also organizes the day so that parents and children can spend a lot of time together. School starts early, especially in the summer, and lets out at 2:00 P.M., while parents can often be home from their offices by 4:00 P.M., by which time homework should have been done, and the family can spend the long summer evenings enjoying each other's company.

The Church emphasizes the role of the family in its teaching, disallows divorce, and strenuously opposes contraception. The state permits both and also, against the bitter hostility of the Church, free abortion on demand. Most Poles I know receive considerable comfort from both doctrines. A doctor friend put it this way: "If two people aren't getting on, inevitably the question of divorce comes up. In most countries these days, no sooner is divorce spoken of, then it is done. Here there are no barriers to divorce erected by the state. But there are moral barriers built into our society by the Church, and they give people pause for thought; make them agonize over what is surely one of the most important decisions they are ever going to have to make. If the situation becomes unbearable, then they divorce, and that's that. But when there is still a spark left, they are encouraged to go on trying, and I can vouch that very often the results are spectacularly successful. It is the same with birth control. There is pressure from the Church on people to have children, and I don't know many women who have ever regretted giving birth. But then they have to make a choice. In some countries the Church is so powerful that this choice hardly exists. Contraceptives can't be bought openly, and the whole thing becomes rather unpleasant. In other countries nobody gives a second thought about birth control, and the population starts shrinking alarmingly. Here we have the perfect balance. Contraceptives are available openly, and yet they are not used lightly. And finally, speaking for myself as a doctor, I don't think that I could perform abortions in a country where there is not a powerful moral imperative against it.

"Here women who positively don't wish to have the child can have an abortion. But the doctor who performs the procedure knows that his patient, in coming to him, has overcome great moral and spiritual pressures in reaching her decision. That is our guarantee that this is what she really wants."

But Polish family life would hardly be possible if it were not for the presence of what can only be described as a special breed of very short, very round, bespectacled women, known to everyone in Poland as "Babca," or Granny. Babca (pronounced Bab-cha) keeps the whole nation going. Without her the large number of women able to hold down full-time jobs would be drastically reduced. Babca is responsible for the oral tradition of the nation—passing stories on from generation to generation, keeping alive even in the darkest moments folk memories that are the soul of the country. You see them everywhere. They queue for the family for hours on end. They take the children to school or the parks to play. At home they sit in a corner knitting or, as one I know is apt to do, keep up a daily furious quarrel with the television newscaster, shouting him down, contradicting everything he says, laughing ironically, and when the news is over, turning to her family with a self-satisfied smirk saying, "I told him that time."

I have long since learned to accept that the greatest mistake a visitor can make is to permit the Babca of any home he visits to exclude herself from the conversation and retire to her own room. It is difficult to get them to talk about their past, perhaps because they are aware how precariously they lived, but more probably because in nearly every case they are reminded of some terrible tragedy. Making conversation once with an old lady while momentarily left alone with her, I asked her to take me through, one by one, the pictures on the mantlepiece. "That was my husband," she said, "he was shot by the Gestapo." I should have stopped there, but somehow I couldn't. "And her?" "She was my daughter. She was killed in the Uprising." "And him?" "He was my eldest son. He just disappeared somewhere in Russia."

But what lives so many of these women lived. There was the lady from one of the great families of Poland for whom life before the war was a series of great balls, who brought out faded photographs of splendidly dressed Polish officers and their ladies in each of which she is in the middle, the most ethereally beautiful of them all. Then suddenly the photo album flicks over to another page and there is a skeleton, just a pair of great luminous eyes staring out of a skin stretched taut over the bones. "Ah, that was me," she says almost gaily, "after Auschwitz. I was working in the Underground and was caught and spent three years there. But you see I was lucky, I survived." "Can you tell me about Auschwitz?" I asked. "It was a terrible place. I don't let myself think about it. Let's talk about what life in Warsaw was like before." But her son told me that she isn't really so flippant —that once a year she goes back to Auschwitz where she kneels and prays in memory of all the people she knew there who were not so "lucky."

"I remember," says another Babca, "our independence, when the students of Warsaw University hauled Marshal Pilsudski into Warsaw on a gun carriage. After that I was in trouble. I joined the Socialists so my father threw me out of the house. If that's the way he wants it, I thought, he can get it and so I joined the Communists. I spent most of my time hiding from the police. Twice they caught me, beat me up, and threw me into prison. But we didn't mind. We knew, or thought we knew, that history was on our side. When the war began I made my way to the East to escape the Germans, and the Russians sent me to Siberia. I spent two years there before I was let out and then became a nurse with General Berling's Army. Believe you me, the Poles who fought with the Western Allies had it easy. We didn't have enough food or clothing or anything. Neither, to be fair, did the Russians. They fought on nothing but a patriotic love for their country.

"After the war I came back to Poland. I was forty-two years old, I had a university degree but had spent five years of my life in prison, two more years in a Russian labor camp, two years in the Army, and the rest of the time on the run. I also wasn't too fond of the Russians, and I made this known. What happened? Two more years in prison. I used to infuriate my jailers by saying things like 'Didn't I meet you here in 1938? I must say the rubber truncheon you then used was of far superior quality.' Eventually they let me out, and I was given a low-grade clerical job that I kept until retirement. During all of that time the only thing that made me angry was when my son tried to get into Warsaw University and was told unofficially that though his grades were good enough, it was unlikely that he would succeed because his mother was 'politically unreliable.' That was too much. All the suffering and hardships I endured, I had willingly endured, because I always felt that I stood on a moral plane, far higher than those who persecuted me. But now I found that this state, that I had worked so hard for and sacrificed so much for, was persecuting my son, and that I could not bear. I went around to the local militia, screamed and ranted at them like a woman possessed. I told them what I thought about them and their rotten system. To do them credit they were quite nice. 'Okay old woman,' one said, 'you've got it off your chest, now go home, have a vodka and write to Comrade Gomulka.' He was joking, of course. But that's what I did. I wrote Gomulka a fifty-page letter in which I told the story of my life and what had happened now to my son. Well, let me tell you this. I never got an acknowledgment, but ten days later my son received a letter from the rector of the university, saying that a mistake had been made in rejecting his application, apologizing for the error and informing him that he had been enrolled as a student of special merit. Some people say harsh things about Gomulka today. Never me. Never me."

The heroes of yesterday are the Babcas of today. But the experiences they went through personally and collectively cannot fail to have marked them. It is part of Communist orthodoxy that religion will die with the old people who keep it alive. Certainly the Babcas are very religious, but in many cases they are more politically aware than their rather apolitical offspring, having detailed and often personal knowledge of the great political traumas of Poland's recent past which affect the country today. The only balanced, detailed, and accurate account I got in Poland about the years from 1944 to 1947—the story of consolidation of power by the Communists—came from a woman who is now in her seventies. Babcas really came into their own after the war, when the country slowly and painfully began the task of rebuilding.

The great cities of Poland had been reduced to rubble, so there was no question of married couples being able to leave their parents' homes, if they still existed, to set up housekeeping; or if the homes were destroyed, couples could not refuse to take in one or both sets of parents to live with them.

Initially this situation caused considerable hardship and was the direct cause of many marital breakups. However, as the years went by, what started as a necessity became a custom, and both sides derived benefit. While in the West the nuclear family was breaking-up, in

Poland it was increasing in number, to the point where now I cannot see it ever changing again. The advantages to both sides are obvious. Grandparents are kept constantly involved and busy with the lives of their children and grandchildren. The latter benefit from the strength of a large family unit around them, the former have the freedom to pursue their careers and outside interests, secure that their children are being well cared-for.

"It can only work today, because it was made to work in the days when there was no alternative," says a friend, who herself benefits from a great-grandmother looking after her daughter. "One doesn't often hear of problems with 'Granny' as often as one does in the West, because we have devised an informal code of behavior to which we all subscribe without actually realizing that we are doing so."

"Babca goes with us everywhere," says another friend. "We wouldn't dream of going on holiday without taking her. It's not a question of tolerating her. She is central to our whole family life. But our Babcas are different from your Grannies. It is a cultural thing. Nobody in Poland would ever dream of telling a 'mother-in-law' joke. They just wouldn't understand them; wouldn't know what you were talking about."

Babcas are a universal Polish experience—as evident in working-class homes as they are among the middle classes. But working-class women don't have an easy time of it. They work in the factories alongside their menfolk, and then hurry home, and if there is no Babca, look after the children and cook the family meals. They earn equal pay and in some cities like Lodz, the center of the Polish wool industry, they can earn more bonuses than their menfolk and become the principal wage-earners of the family.

Lenin wrote, "To effect [woman's] complete emancipation and make her the equal of men, it is necessary to be socialized and for women to participate in common productive labor. Then women will occupy the same positions as men." Though great evidence is placed in East European countries on the dignity of labor—and rightly so—the fact is that factory work is hard and monotonous, and most men, given the opportunity, would willingly escape from it. No wonder then, working-class women feel that they have the worst of all worlds.

A woman dockworker in Gdansk, the home of Solidarity, put it this way: "Equality of work has meant, for many of us women, equality of misery. Working in these yards during a cold winter is, believe me, no picnic. If it were to be suggested to me that I should leave my work and stay at home and look after my husband and my children, I would jump at it, and if that meant that I became a little less equal than the breadwinner of the family, though I do not think that would inevitably follow, I would be quite content to trade. The trouble is that under our system it is absolutely impossible. No individual, certainly not here in the dockyards, earns enough to support a wife and a family. Both parents must work. Women before had a choice. Now they have none."

Like men, women suffer from the fact that in a socialist economy many jobs are simply not available for secondary-school-educated girls. There are some secretarial jobs, but very few compared to the West, few beauticians or manicurists, few jobs in boutiques or sales in general, advertising, or the like. It is not surprising that thousands of young girls are leaving the country because they lack qualifications for the few interesting jobs that the system provides, or that others, with fewer scruples, enter a profession that ought to have disappeared in socialist Europe years ago. In and around the big hotels in Warsaw, especially the Forum, but also the Hotel Victoria, probably the most attractive prostitutes in all of Europe ply their craft. Their reputation is such that Finns and Austrians (who before the state of emergency didn't need visas for Poland) came just for the weekends to enjoy the pleasures that these girls offer. I once met a West German steelworker in the American bar of the Forum Hotel who told me that he frequently came to Warsaw where "the girls were the best and the cheapest anywhere."

Germany's vast army of "guest workers" from the poorer Mediterranean countries also, while the borders were open, put on their best suits, and once a year came to Warsaw to live for a fortnight like Arab sheiks. The girls' presence is always very noticeable. Seldom do they seem to suffer any police harrassment, suggesting to some experts on the East European scene that (like many of their sisters in Moscow) they are employed by the security services to entrap visiting Western businessmen or diplomats in a snare known as a "honey pot." Whether this is so or not, only the security police themselves, or perhaps some unfortunate businessmen, can say. On the whole, it seems unlikely. Why spoil one of the most profitable businesses in Warsaw by mixing it up with politics. Instead, according to well-informed gossip (only in Poland is it possible to have "well-informed gossip"), the girls get by through a wide variety of pay-offs to police and hotel doormen.

Not quite prostitutes, because they do not offer their services indiscriminately, are an even larger and even more beautiful collection of girls, centered almost exclusively in Warsaw, known as "foreigners' girls." Their ultimate aim is to marry a rich foreigner, and leave the country, to live in what they consider to be a life of luxury abroad. Ten years ago, almost any foreigner who entered Poland flashing expense-account dollars appeared to be an attractive catch, and many a Polish girl would end up, hardly speaking the langauge, in some small suburban community with little money and certainly none of the bright lights she had always aspired to. These days the "foreigners' girls" are considerably more knowledgeable. They are prepared to be the mistresses of Westerners working in Poland and to enjoy the standard of living than those who have access to hard currency are able to enjoy. But they will marry, on the whole, men who have real money and can give them a lifestyle commensurate with what they enjoy in Warsaw. What is undeniably true, is that it is better to be at the top of the heap in a city like Warsaw, than at the bottom in a city like Paris. So one meets the "foreigners' girls" everywhere. I have come across them in London, dressed in the most up-to-date and expensive fashions in Nice and Monte Carlo, shopping in the most exclusive precincts in Munich, in New York on Fifth Avenue, and in Hollywood by the fashionable swimming pools. Few are married, but all are trading Polish beauty for the good things of life. There are too many of them not to regard them as a social phenomenon, or to regard their plight as anything but a desperate one. They have rejected absolutely the three most potent influences on the life of any young Pole—the Church, the state, and Polish patriotism. In a country where female emancipation can be regarded as having run its full course, they are a throwback, permitting themselves to be sexually enslaved in return for a life they could otherwise not hope to achieve. In a sense they are examples of a lost generation, doomed by a system that has failed to live up to any of its promises and conceits. A girl I know in London, certainly not a "foreigners' girl," left Poland determined to find work in the West, and by working hard, she made a success of a new life; she tells me that Polish women, even more than men, feel betrayed by the system.

"We were constantly reminded at school and at the university of the benefits of the socialist system, and there are many. But women, perhaps more than men, sometimes require to be surrounded with beautiful things, to live in an environment that is gentle and non-aggressive. In an extraordinary way that is quite difficult to explain, People's Poland sometimes gives me the impression of being a society designed by men who do not like or understand women and women's needs. It became a joke in my family that one day my mother said to my father that she wanted a new dress. 'You've got a dress,' he said unthinkingly, but then had the grace to laugh at himself. But that's Poland, and what I know of the Soviet Union too. They are countries designed by men who would say 'you've got a dress already.' The state recognizes that people need furniture, so it produces furniture—one piece exactly like another. It sees we need shoes—and six lines providing virtually no choice suddenly appear in the shops. It believes that luxuries like a very special box of chocolates or a silk blouse or a pair of superfine nylons are manifestations of a bourgeois way of life and have no place in a Communist country. And, of course, it is difficult to argue to the contrary. A silk blouse is clearly impractical, superfine nylons will go in no time, and fine chocolates have no more nutritional value than ordinary chocolates. Yet anyone who understood women would also understand that their nature is such that practical considerations are not everything. We know that ordinary working-class women with little money will save hard for a very special dress and then enjoy and savor it. We now know enough about human psychology to understand that women don't buy fashionable clothes, or make themselves up, or decorate their homes pleasantly, because they are vapid of self-indulgent or vain, but because built into their nature is a desire to surround themselves with things that are attractive and pleasing. Dear Mr. Marx and Mr. Lenin only ever understood production values, not that these values must sometimes be expressed in terms of sheer beauty."

I suspect that my friend has put her finger on it. For all the emancipation and the liberation implicit in a Communist society and enshrined in the constitution of every Communist state, the basic ethos is essentially, masculine, in a way that is impossible in a capitalist society, where producers are forced to bow to the whims of their customers, a large number of whom are women. In Poland, women respond to this challenge either by being extremely masculine in dress and speech, aggressive and businesslike, or by making enormous efforts, quite out of proportion to any gain they might be expected to achieve, in order to become excessively feminine. Western fashions are purchased on the black market at enormous cost and self-sacrifice. They are reacting to a society where male values predominate, and yet one in which, ironically, the sexes have complete equality. As a result, Polish women, contrary to the experience of Western society, are even more radical in their demands for political change than men.

Women factory workers were among the first to join Solidarity and proved to be the fastest on the trigger during the subsequent calls for strike action. Yet when approached by management, their demands tended to be generalized in the extreme, persuading many that their grievances ran considerably deeper than those of the male population. Though many Western women—particularly Europeans —who are feminists are also socialists, the Polish experience suggests that feminism and socialism are not natural bedfellows.

In the West women are unequal in a world designed with women in mind. In the East they are equal in a world that has yet to note their existence.

18
The Plan

***

❀

*When America was in trouble during its war of independence, we Poles
sent them two generals, Kosciuszko and Pulaski. Now we're in trouble they
should send us two generals back—General Motors and General Electric.*

HANIA ABRATANSKA is a joy, a bubbly, laughing redhead who refuses
to give her age but ought not feel any need to be coy. Whether she
is thirty-five or forty-five doesn't matter, because she cannot be less
vibrantly attractive now than she was at twenty-five. We're sitting in
Hania's little apartment, just one room and a kitchen, neatly and
inexpensively furnished. She makes tea, offers vodka, and opens a
small tin of caviar. When one watches her in Wrangler cords and
bomber jacket as she prepares the snack, it is difficult to believe that
she belongs to a small, unique, and courageous group of people in
Poland, the private business community. Hania produces makeup.
One can hear machines in the room next door, where six girls prepare
and pack that day's production: the face powder, rouge, and eye
makeup, most of which she herself mixed in the morning. She admits
that the quality is not quite what she would like, but the reason is
that a vital ingredient, adherol, that helps fix cosmetics is simply
unavailable in Poland for love or money. But the colors are beautiful,
somehow both suble and striking, and the cases that she designed
herself are as attractive as any produced by the great perfumeries of
the West. She is the citizen of the country that gave the world Helena
Rubenstein, and if the world had any sense, it would now take up
Hania Abratanska.

What Hania does with little money, few facilities, and sheer un-
relenting guts, is a small miracle. Hania is an oddity—a capitalist in
a Communist country, a private entrepreneur, allowed to operate
only under the most rigid control and under a tax structure weighed
so heavily against her, it is a wonder that she bothers. Her products
have to be tested and passed by no fewer than six state commissions
before they can be put on the market. Her prices are fixed absolutely
by law, and she is taxed on sales rather than profits. In order to buy

[367]

vital ingredients in the West not available in Poland, she is officially
permitted a dollar account, but the state assumes she purchases a
dollar for 80 zlotys (in 1981), when in fact a dollar costs three or even
four times that amount when I met her, over ten times that now.

In order to persuade anyone to come and work for an enterprise
that is outside the state system, and is unable to offer the advantages
of job security, sanitoriums, and other benefits of a state factory,
she has to pay more than double the going salary. Her employees can
earn 12,000 zlotys a month, nearly as much as a coalminer and about
the same as the editor of the *Gazeta Krakowska*. Hania has failed and
started up again twice, though on one occasion it was a husband
rather than the government that caused the problems. Nevertheless,
undeterred by the hardships, she is in business again, determined to
become a success in a system in which by rights she had no place
whatsoever. How can she, with the dice loaded against her, possibly
make a profit?

"The point in favor of my little factory is that it is efficient, while
factories operating within the state sector are not. The factor of
efficiency in my favor more than compensates for the factor of controls that are imposed on me. My workers earn a lot of money, but
they have to work hard for it. I provide good wages, I am a caring
employer, and the girls are my friends. But they must work. In the
end they are satisfied and so am I."

Hania's factory is a large white house near Praga, on the bank of
the Vistula opposite Warsaw, the place where the Russian Army
stopped its advance on Warsaw at the time of the Uprising. When
you go to Praga, you can see just how close it is to the city. Hania
occupies the top two floors, taking a small area for her living space,
leaving as much room as possible for the factory itself. The two
floors below she rents to another private entrepreneur who makes
sunglasses.

Poland permits a certain amount of private industry, provided that
it is on a small scale, which means, generally, not employing more
than fifty people. What is astonishing is how many people like Hania
are prepared to risk everything and try a private business. By and
large the population is committed to a socialized economy. An opinion poll of unquestionable validity taken in 1978 showed that a large
majority of young people were against any industrial enterprise over
medium-size (employing over 100 people) being held in private
hands.

I found very few people, even among those most hostile to the

Party, who were in favor of a system of free enterprise, or even a mixed economy on the British or French model. Though a majority (not an overwhelming one) of those polled were in favor of small industrial enterprises like Hania's (53 percent in favor, 38 percent against), the business climate in which she operates is hardly propitious. Yet her products are of unquestioned quality and in great demand throughout the country. The possibility that consumers benefit from a competitive, rather than a monopolistic (state or capitalist) business framework, is not one that the Poles appear to be aware of.

Despite this, the Polish private economy has produced thousands of zloty millionaires (a million zlotys, even at the official exchange rate is worth just over $30,000) and a few dollar millionaires. But 90 percent of them operate in a strange and uniquely Polish outgrowth of the agricultural industry. It all began with one of the most delightful Polish customs, the giving and receiving of flowers. I defy anyone to stand on the street of any town and not see within the space of a few minutes someone hurrying along carrying a bunch of flowers. To turn up at someone's home without a bunch of flowers for the host is unthinkable. Poles present flowers when they meet friends at airports or trains. They present flowers at name-days, birthdays, and anniversaries. A mother seeing her child's teacher at school will bring a bunch of flowers. A man arriving for a business appointment might well bring flowers for the secretary. It is part of Polish folklore that the moment the guns were silenced after the liberation of Warsaw, and people came out to look at the devastated old city, not one building of which was intact, as they looked across this bleak landscape they suddenly saw a small patch of color—an old woman had opened a stall, selling bright red carnations, the first shop to be doing business in postwar Warsaw. The central flower market in Warsaw is today one of the great sights of the city—a vast area of blooms of all colors and sizes, a spectacular discovery in a city that, for all its beauty, puts a sombre face to the world. The postwar planners applying, as sensible men will, common sense to the problems of a ravaged economy, laid down the template for the new society. Everything was thought of, food, industry, housing, and even recreation—everything but flowers, for which most Poles would sacrifice any of these things.

When a few owners of small plots around Warsaw asked permission to build greenhouses to grow flowers commercially, the requests were instantly granted. After all, how could a small nurseryman threaten the integrity of a socialist state? Fly into Warsaw today and look out the window. Half the country seems to be under glass; most of it is private, and a good deal is devoted to flower-raising. It is a tribute to the capitalist impulse, that during the worst of the terrible shortages to hit Poland these last two years, one thing never in short supply was flowers.

Pani Ewa is a typical flower-grower. She owns about ten acres, all under glass. The business was started by her late husband, a qualified doctor who, in his late forties, decided that the attractions of medicine had waned with his inability to earn more than a living wage through its practice. "He was often offered money on the side," says his widow, "in order to push people to the top of hospital waiting lists, or provide a service that was regarded as illegal, but he felt it was immoral to make money this way. At the same time he was resentful that he couldn't make it honestly. So he left medicine and started growing roses. He eventually died of cancer, but his greatest comfort as he lay desperately ill was that he had been able to leave me this." "This" is now one of the biggest businesses of its type in Poland. Ewa won't say how much money she makes, but experienced eyes looking over her property put her income at several million zlotys a year. Certainly she gives every appearance of wealth. She is elegantly dressed ("all my clothes come from Polish dressmakers, I don't see why I should use dollars so precious to this country just to buy clothes"), drives a smart Volkswagen Golf ("I wanted a Polish car, but without bribing someone I couldn't get any promise of delivery"), has by all accounts one of the most elegant apartments in Warsaw, a cottage in the woods nearby, and a holiday home in the Mazurian Lakes in the north.

Producers like Ewa kept strictly to flowers in the early years, but in the mid-fifties when the pressure to collectivize Polish agriculture eased off, they began raising tomatoes and salad vegetables, then fruits and other vegetables which they sold in the so-called peasant or free markets around every city. They made an immediate killing in the winter because Poland, like the rest of Eastern Europe, still relies very much on seasonal produce. Thus, anyone who likes strawberries is advised to go to Poland in June, when on every roadside in the country children sell vast pannets of the most delicious strawberries I have ever eaten for ridiculously small sums of money. Everyone knows that in a few weeks they will disappear altogether, and not another strawberry will be seen in Poland until the following year. So when the "glass" millionaires began branching out from flowers and arrived at markets with their off-season tomatoes and salads, they were greeted with exultation by a populace weary of stores carrying only the basics. The state itself tried to get into the greenhouse business. Though it now has a lot of acreage under glass, one official in the agricultural ministry sadly admitted to me that just as in the more traditional farming economy where the state simply cannot hope to compete with the private sector, so it can't in nursery production. Another private "glass" millionaire provides the probable explanation: "I get up at 4:00 A.M. every day," he said, "and often work through until 11:00 at night. I am my own gardener, bookkeeper, tax adviser, and storekeeper." No state-salaried employee, however dedicated, is ever going to match that.

Since the mid-seventies the state, far from cracking down on the "glass" millionaires, actively began to encourage them. Certainly their taxes were high, but they were permitted to keep a proportion of their income reasonable enough to make the enterprise worthwhile. Despite initial reservations, most were persuaded to become part of gardening cooperatives that have turned out, in practice, to be copy-book examples of how state and private initiative in a socialist economy can work together for the ultimate good of the community as a whole. The cooperatives, of which some 150 exist all over the country, own research institutes that advise members on technical matters such as new growing methods and pesticides. The cooperatives run some 3,000 stores throughout the country that are outside the state system and purchasing centers that buy a fixed percentage of the produce for resale to the state itself or for export.

These hothouse farmers differ from the rest of the farming community in that the prices they charge are not arbitrarily fixed by the state, but are properly negotiated between the chairmen and committees of the cooperatives and the food ministries. Of course, these are not negotiations between equals, and some of the hothouse farmers complain that they are consistently forced to accept too low prices for an unacceptably high proportion of their crop. On the other hand, some Polish newspapers from time to time complain about the lavish and conspicuous consumption of the "glass" millionaires and demand that the state tax them still further.

"I suspect that Pani Ewa pays more to her hairdresser and manicurist a week than I earn a month," said the mutual friend who introduced us, but this was said without rancor, because my friend knows how hard Ewa works for her money. Hania Abratanska—"I've never been to the West, and I won't go until such time as I can afford

to stay at the best hotels. I refuse to be anyone's poor relation"—
accepts that resentment of the private sector in Poland stems from
the fact that few Poles understand how hard those who live off their
own resources and wits have to work anywhere in the world, but
especially in a country where their activity is very much on sufferance.

Nevertheless, for the moment at least, privatization is very much
"in." Because of the greenhouse cooperatives, an increasing number
of greengrocers in the big cities are private businesses. The state rents
or sells stores to enterpreneurs and then shares profits with them.
There are innumerable boutiques in Warsaw that are privately
owned, and even though the owner cannot employ even a seamstress
who doesn't have an official licence from the vocational school, some
owners are beginning to make a lot of money. The better restaurants
are now private, and obviously so the moment one walks in. The
waiters and waitresses are actually courteous and helpful. The Hotel
George, just outside Warsaw, for example, was purchased when the
proprietors inherited some religious paintings which they assumed to
be valueless, but in fact netted them 1½ million zlotys. The hotel's
food is excellent, and its proprietors appear to have the gift of getting
supplies from some secret source when every other restaurant in
Warsaw appears to be short. "But there's no mystery to that," said
the owner of another private restaurant.

"Please don't quote my name, or I'll have difficulties with my
license. The point is that we're prepared to work that much harder.
I was a member of a state restaurant for years, and I did my work, I
thought, as conscientiously as I could. Now I know that's not true.
Today when I've run out of materials and can't get them from my
normal suppliers, I drive around all night if necessary until I find
someone who can supply me. When beer first began running out
here, the state supplied its own restaurants first and left us at the
back of the line. Well, you see the result. This restaurant has beer
while the state restaurants in Warsaw don't. And I don't buy on the
black market either. I couldn't afford to. I have to hustle. State
restaurant managers wouldn't dream of it. It really is as simple as
that."

A popular Polish saying goes: Poles are prepared to fight for their
country but not work for it. This is not an entirely new phenomenon.
The Germans have had a saying for years: *"Polnische Wirtschaft,"*
which they apply to a situation they wish to describe as an utter
shambles. It is true that the Poles are not a naturally disciplined
people, but the widely held view, shared by Western bankers, most

commentators, and General Jaruzelski, that the Poles have got themselves into their current predicament because they are not prepared
to work for a living requires some examination.

I have before me as I write an official government information
bulletin issued in 1980, before the events in Gdansk. It makes impressive and—in the light of what has happened since—quite staggering reading. The 1975 gross national income per capita (at 1980
prices) was estimated at $2,325 more than Spain's at $2,051 and only
slightly less than Italy's at $2,563. Poland with 0.8 percent of the
world's population, contributed, I read, approximately 2.5 percent of
the world's industrial production, which put her in tenth place "as
to volume of industrial production." From 1976 to 1978, Poland's
annual average rate of growth of 8.3 percent was higher than even
Japan's and West Germany's. If one allows for a lower starting point,
this appears to have been an impressive achievement.

Her raw material production was equally impressive. Coal extrac-
tion amounted to 7.7 percent of world production and placed Poland
in fourth place after America, Russia, and China. Poland was the
world's fifth-largest producer of lignite, a mixture of peat and coal
sometimes known as brown coal, and after the U.S.A. the world's
largest producer of sulphur. Poland also became one of the world's
most important producers of copper ores, and occupied eighth place
in world production of refined copper (at a time when copper prices
were going through the roof). Her power industry ranked tenth in
the world. She ranked ninth in the world in crude steel production,
ahead of such countries as Sweden and Belgium.

Poland was one of the world's largest producers of fishing vessels
(second place) and specialized merchant vessels. Her chemical industries were also booming. She contributed 2.8 percent of the
world's production of sulphuric acid, 3.1 percent of nitrogenous
and 3.2 percent of phosphatic fertilizers, and 1.6 percent of non-
cellulose artificial fibers. It occupied tenth position in the production
of cement, sixth in the production of wool yarn, and seventh in the
production of cotton yarn. Even in agriculture she seemed to be
doing well. Polish agriculture contributed approximately 2 percent
of the world's food production and about 4 percent of food production of the temperate zone. She held second place in the world in
the production of wheat, fifth in the production of oats, second in the
production of potatoes, sixth in the production of sugar beets, and
fourth in the production of rapeseed and agrimony. She ranked
twentieth in the production of milk, and twelfth in the production

of eggs. One can only read these statistics with open-mouthed astonishment, because despite these impressive figures here is a nation that
is literally bankrupt, no longer able to feed its people. One can see
why Western bankers, asked to lend money to help the rapid industrialization of the country, saw Poland as "a dream investment." And
so it must have seemed. But what went wrong?

These statistics seem to dispute the notion that the Poles are constitutionally indolent—after all, coal doesn't dig itself, ships don't
just grow, and chemicals don't simply appear. A Polish-born economist who has studied the Polish economy and Polish economic literature states:

". . . economic growth which *disregards* [his italics] human welfare
is self-defeating not only politically, ideologically and socially but
also economically. . . . The lack of faith [by ordinary people] in the
rationality, feasibility or usefulness of the required plan targets, existing regulations, obligatory norms, etc., is *in itself*, an important ob-
stacle to efficient performance."

Orthodox Polish economists will argue, and many Western political analysts will agree with them, that it was vital if Poland were to
rebuild in 1945 from the devastation of war that she take as her
model what is known as the Soviet command economy.

Oskar Lange, the world-famous Polish economist, said in Belgrade
in 1957: "The process of industrialization requires such centralized
disposal of resources for two reasons. First, it is necessary to concen-
trate all resources on certain objectives and avoid dissipation of
resources on other objectives which would divert resources from the
purpose of rapid industrialization. . . . The second reason . . . is the
lack and weakness of industrial cadres."

Today, Polish economists say that the economy fell apart because
it proved unexpectedly difficult to break from the rigid, though historically necessary, Stalinist-style command economy, to a system,
while essentially socialist in character, that was also flexible enough
to meet the ever-growing complexities of a modern economy. For
the Polish authorities and the Western banks that invested so
heavily in the country, this explanation has a seductive charm. After
all, if nothing is basically wrong with the Polish economy that the
judicious application of a few extra levers into the system cannot
cure, then (provided there is labor discipline) in the end the economy
is bound to respond.

Yet the evidence by now is overwhelming that the economies of
Russia and Eastern Europe grew in the 1950s in spite of, and not

because, the Stalinist system of control. The waste was incredible, masked only by an undeniable and impressive record of economic growth. How both could be achieved simultaneously is explained by the fact that during Poland's first Six Year Plan, no less than 32.6 percent of the national income went into economic investment. Manpower increased substantially, while wage costs were kept down to an annual increase of 0.66 percent during each year of the plan. A crash program of this order had to produce some results, but how did these compare with the results of countries that allowed at least some proportion of their national wealth to percolate directly through to its citizenry. Polish growth (from a much lower base) during this period, was roughly equal to that achieved in the slow-growing economies of the United Kingdom and the United States, but the difference is that their economies relied on half the investment put into the Polish economy, permitting their citizens to enjoy the fruits of their labor. Other economies, Japan and Western Germany, did spectacularly better. Poland's dash for growth at all costs, as shown by its excessive rate of investment during this period, actually produced "negative marginal efficiency of investment," or in layman's terms, for every extra dollar pumped into the economy, the economy produced less than a dollar's worth of goods.

Virtually all of the targets laid down in the first ambitious Six Year Plan were missed. The Nowa Huta steel mill near Krakow, in which the state invested enormous financial, as well as political and even emotional resources (this was to be the symbol of Poland's industrial rebirth as a Communist state), reached only 42 percent of its planned capacity in time, electric generating only 56 percent, cement 74 percent, and bricks 68 percent—all items which the planners gave top priority. Even if part of this shortfall occurred because the plan itself (and all subsequent plans) was wholly unrealistic, this cannot be the entire reason. The first Six Year Plan estimated that raw materials and fuel imports would fall by 0.2 percent, when in fact they rose by 23 percent, producing, says one economist, "probably one of the most drastic deviations between plan and performance in the history of planning!" It is not true, as is sometimes imagined, that planners in Communist countries grab a figure out of the air, double it, and then present it, as if it had already been achieved, to a delighted Party congress. A friend who works in one of the key sectors of the Polish economy tells me that virtually his entire work is devoted to help write the plan for the industry for which he is responsible.

This involves, he tells me, a huge army of highly trained professionals: economists, sociologists, demographers and, of course, the managers and support staff of the various enterprises involved. "There may have been occasional cases of a planning staff producing unrealistic projections in the hope of currying temporary favor, but from the very beginning, the tendency among planners and managers is to present as pessimistic a picture as they can possibly get away with. The ideal that everyone involved strives after is to come up with a realistic projection, let us say of a growth rate of 5 percent, and then halve it, so that the official plan as published allows for a 2½ percent growth rate. This gives industry 2½ percent to play with, so that even if things go awry with their private projections, managers still have a chance of equaling or even beating the published plan and all that means in terms of personal advancement."

My friend tells me that one of Poland's most illustrious industrial chief's whole career was built on his days in the mining industry, when he managed to conceal from the Ministry of Mines the fact that his engineers had discovered a new and highly productive coal seam. The plan was drawn up without taking cognizance of this find, and so the results, when eventually they came, were spectacular. He was decorated and highly publicized as the man who could get Polish industry moving and now holds great responsibility, when he is actually just a man who has learned to manipulate the system—to make figures on a balance sheet jump to the dirge of the funeral of the economy he is helping to bury. But he is no more guilty than those who fall short of the plan and then doctor the books to conceal the deficit. The effect of that on the economy as a whole is, if anything, even more disastrous.

My friend from the Planning Ministry explains: "Let us say for the sake of argument that the plan allows for the manufacture of 1,000 tractors a year. In a centrally planned economy, once it is agreed that this is what shall happen, it ceases to be merely a pious hope, but becomes an essential factor within the equation of the central plan itself. On the assumption that those 1,000 tractors exist, all sorts of other decisions will be reached. The Ministry of Finance will draw up its budget on the basis that 500 of those tractors will be exported to the West, 250 to Comecon countries, and 250 provided for Polish farmers. The Ministry of Technology may be told that it will be given the hard currency that the 500 tractors destined for the Western market will earn, and it uses this to import some advance technology that it believes Poland requires. The Ministry of Agriculture draws up its assumptions about agricultural productivity on the grounds that it will be able to distribute 250 tractors to its farmers, while Comecon countries export food products to Poland in exchange for the tractors they've been promised. And so on . . . an enormous labryinth of economic decision-making is reached on the basis of what is still, after all, only a scrap of paper. What happens when the plan falls short of target? If the industry admits the shortfall immediately, then something can be saved from the wreckage by scaling down activity across the whole economic spectrum that had been colored by the original planning target, or more normally by, in mid-course, diverting money designed for one purpose to another. When that happens, the plan, which is at best a delicate instrument, ceases to have any meaning at all. The constant adjustments that become necessary multiply to the point where the plan simply disappears, and all that is left is a polite fiction that no one believes for a moment.

"It is far more damaging, however, when managers of enterprises, fearing the consequences of failure, manage to conceal the fact that they have not reached their planning targets. It happens all the time. Take the tractor example. The plan calls for 1,000 tractors. The factory produces only 500, but claims it built 750, which doesn't look too bad. The Ministry of Finance will immediately demand 500 for export to the West. Foreign exchange is vital. But ministers dealing with the Comecon countries will advance socialist machismo as the reason why Russia and Eastern Europe need to be supplied, too. The Minister of Agriculture will passionately plead the cause of his farmers. So a compromise will be struck. The West will get 300 tractors, the East will get 200 tractors, and Polish farmers, because everyone recognizes the problem of rural unrest, will get the 250 they were promised. But, of course, as there are only 500 and not 750 tractors to distribute, the farmers will get none at all. They protest about the lack of mechanization on the farm, figures will be produced that ministers believe to prove that, contrary to what they say, tractors are increasingly becoming available. And when agricultural productivity does not improve, this will angrily be put down to the natural conservatism of the peasantry, who have failed to take advantage of the modern tools with which the state has provided them."

I asked my friend if he was not exaggerating the problem. If anything, he said, he was underestimating it. The Polish economy was built on an enormous backlog of myths that are almost impossible now to sort out. So many lies were told during so many plans by so many people, great and small, that today there is not a single economic statistic, either for external or internal consumption, that can be seriously relied upon. The first task of any program of economic reform must be to cut through years of obfuscation, strip the economy bare, and get at the dry rot underneath.

It is against this background that the Polish worker must be judged. He sees around him important investment decisions being made, none of which he benefits from directly or, as he sees it, money being criminally wasted, knowing that in the end he will pay for it out of his own pocket. He will read in his newspaper or see on television, certainly right up to the end of 1980 when the truth could no longer be concealed, that Poland was daily becoming more successful and its people increasingly richer. He either believed the figures and resented the apparent anomaly, that he was the only man in Poland not to share in the general sense of well-being. Or he didn't believe them, and became increasingly disillusioned with a society that he knew to be built on a pyramid of lies. What is certainly true is that the morale of the Polish worker sank lower and lower as, in some unfathomable way, the "Poland" described by ministers and the media had very little to do with the Poland he recognized.

It would be unfair to say that the state has willfully sought to depress its working class. Poland's labor laws are as advanced as any in the world. The ideology insists that just as there must be central planning of the means of production, so does it insist that in a socialist state there can be no such thing as unemployment. That, too, has had its catastrophic consequences.

Hundreds of thousands of Polish workers are paid to do nothing in factories working far below capacity, and thousands more work at a snail's pace to keep an already incompetently organized enterprise barely moving. "There is no incentive to work in this country," says a friend. "A man who earns regular bonuses doesn't have anything to spend them on, because the economy is unable to meet even normal consumer demand. Everyone in Poland knows that the decision to return to Saturday working is nonsense.

"Under normal conditions of productivity prevalent elsewhere, there is not enough work in our factories for three-day weeks, let alone six. Most factories don't even have the fuel to keep them going that long."

He then added: "There is much talk here about the so-called dignity of labor, without anyone's giving too much thought to what the expression actually means. The act of laboring is not in itself dignified, otherwise it could be held that slaves have dignity, which clearly they do not. Labor confers dignity on a man only if, through it, he is able to purchase independence by providing for his family needs and comforts, by alleviating his poverty through his own efforts, and providing a style of life, or at least the prospect of which, is consistent with what are regarded as normal decent civilized standards. All the Polish economy has been able to provide is the bare minimum for most of its people most of the time. No wonder then, that the work ethic has all but disappeared."

In its place has come petty pilfering and thieving from factory and office premises on a gargantuan scale. The attitude seems to be that if people can't earn the money, then they will simply take the products.

All of this has come as something of a shock to Western bankers, who plunged so recklessly into financing the Polish economy in the seventies, apparently with as much faith in the great National Plan as did the men who wrote it. It wasn't until April 24, 1980, a few months before the wave of strikes that led to the formation of Solidarity, that the first doubts began to creep in. Fifty Western bankers met at the vast, elegant Victoria Hotel in the center of Warsaw to listen to the Poles seeking to raise a further $500 million on top of the $550 million they'd raised the year before. Bankers then realized that Poland needed this money, not for investment in its industry, not even to invest in the social well-being of its people, but merely to help repay loans that they'd already made to refinance, in effect, the country's vast $20-billion hard-currency indebtedness. Though no one wanted to say it, the bankers knew that unless new money was forthcoming Poland could even default on its payments.

No Communist country had ever formally asked for its debts to be rescheduled, and Poland had no desire to be the first. The bankers told the Poles that they had to make massive adjustments to their system of paying huge subsidies for meat, sugar, and milk—all costing the Polish government about $6 billion annually. The Poles accepted these conditions, and when the new loan (not as much as they'd hoped) was set, the government immediately doubled the price of sugar, raised meat prices, and made it plain to the already hard-pressed Polish consumer that more changes in Poland's pricing structure were in the pipeline. Once again the ordinary Polish worker was punished for the profligacy of his government and its incompetent management of the economy. The carelessness of the Western banking community in lending money to a country because it was prepared to pay premium interest rates and, it was thought, was protected by the Soviet umbrella, contributed a great deal to the subsequent collapse of the economy. As a result of those price rises, the first strikes in the summer of 1980 began, picking up steam as they spread, until eventually they led to the gates of the shipyards in Gdansk, the arrival of Lech Walesa, the emergence of Solidarity, and sixteen months of freedom and hope.

That movement was eventually crushed because, like the Western bankers, the Polish authorities assumed that economic reform could be introduced without political changes. One of Solidarity's economic advisers told me only a few days before martial law was declared: "What we are trying to explain to our critics both inside and outside Poland is that the nation's political problems and its economic problems are indivisible. The men who wrote the plans are still in place, still in charge of our destiny. They are the people who brought this country to the point of utter ruin. Men will not work if common sense tells them that not only will they not benefit from their labor, but neither will the nation. Until there is a program of complete political reform, this country cannot be put back on its feet economically."

Long before Solidarity was ever heard of, a Pole replying to the "Experience and Future Group" wrote: ". . . we are faced with sham planning and the sham implementation of plans, and even the over-stepping of plan guidelines, sham accomplishments in industry, science, the arts, education, the sham declaration and fulfillment of pledges, sham debates, sham voting and elections, sham concern for social welfare and the appearances of government, sham socialism and social work, sham freedom of choice, sham morality, modernity, and progress, the opening of ostensibly complete factories and social facilities with great pomp and circumstance, the sham struggle against wrongdoing, and the sham contentment of all citizens, sham freedom of conviction, and sham justice. The playing of this game of appearances for appearance sake has become so widespread that no one—not even at the highest levels of government—can distinguish any longer between what is real and what is unreal."

Soviet-style socialism turns out to be a system mostly preoccupied with coping with the problems of its own creation. Poland is the classic textbook illustration. After thirty years of a highly organized and planned socialized economy, this important European nation has been reduced to the status of a third-world country, reliant on loans and handouts from its friends as well as its foes. All one can wish for Poland now is that austerity be piled upon austerity. There is no other way out. It is estimated that ninety-two cents in every dollar of Poland's export earnings go to pay interest and principal on the country's hard-currency debt. If Poland sells a ship for $40 million only $3,200,000 go back into the economy. Put it another way: In 1972 Poland's export earnings stood at $3.5 thousand million (at current prices), and in 1978 this had risen to $14.1 thousand million. Though export earnings have shrunk significantly since, let us assume that Poland is able to get back to her performance in 1972, regarded by the Polish government at the time as inadequate to meet the requirements of a modern state. In 1973 after repaying her debts, Poland had about $3.1 thousand million in hard currency to redistribute around the economy. Today, earning the same, Poland would be left with less than $3 million in pocket. That is the measure of the Polish collapse.

In his book *The Russians*, Hedrick Smith states: "Month in and month out the pressure of The Plan has undoubtedly forced Russian workers to disgorge a greater volume of output than would have emerged without Plan deadlines." This is a highly questionable assertion. In Poland just as in Russia, the plan is given an almost mystical importance, with posters everywhere exhorting workers to honor the targets they've been given. The result has led to less rather than more, and certainly shoddier, production.

Jan, a manager of a medium-sized enterprise, was remarkably frank about his problems. "We were manufacturing components for switching gears under the last Gierek Plan, but it soon became apparent to us all that we were on the wrong lines, that Western technology made what we were doing appear very primitive indeed. But it was quite impossible so late in the plan to alter it without altering all kinds of other aspects of the plan as well.

"So on we went, producing goods that were worthless, working not for our enterprises, not for Poland, but for the plan. The plan has become an end in itself. Productivity in Poland came to mean simply a measurement of individual output within a given period of time. What no one took into consideration was the effectiveness of that output—whether the goods when they were produced were actually wanted by anyone!"

Capitalist countries get by with no national plan. They operate on what has been described by their critics as "the animal law of competition." Party members wax eloquent when they describe the maladies of our system. Competition leads to overproduction and therefore to waste. Two or more competitors fighting over the same product leads to bankruptcies and unemployment. Lack of control over the economy from the center leads to scarce resources in manpower and material being employed on unworthy objects, mere tinsel. All of this, socialism vowed to avoid. Hence the plan. It was all so simple and obvious that it is a wonder no one thought of it before. Production would be planned; goods needed by the community for itself and for export—no more, no less—would be manufactured. There would be no waste. Why have competition if experts can sit down and discuss between themselves rationally what the people require, and then go ahead and produce it? The precise amount of investment capital would be channeled into the precise enterprise that would then produce the precise number of products required. With no waste there would be no spare capacity or shortage of investment, therefore no unemployment. The country would become rich, and the well-being of its citizens assured.

The problem, apparently unforeseen, is how to decide in advance what it is that people want, and also who should do the deciding.

At a fairly trivial level, who is to decide that women will want to buy more red shoes than blue shoes, when anyone who has been shopping with a woman knows perfectly well that, though she may well have set out determined to buy a pair of red shoes, prepared to fall back on a pair of blue shoes if absolutely necessary, in the event, once in the shoe shop, she will be absolutely knocked out by a pair of green shoes.

At a more serious level, ought coal production to assume that the next three winters are going to be exceptionally cold, exceptionally mild, or average for the year? In 1979, one of the coldest winters in Polish memory, Warsaw's central heating system only worked intermittently because of a shortage of coal in one of the great coal-producing countries of the world. And if it is possible to decide these matters, who ought to be doing it? Should this be done at local level, or at Central level? If it is to be done at local level, then while it is more likely that realistic targets will be advanced by those who have actually some first-hand ideas of market conditions, it is also highly unlikely that managers of local enterprises will have any concept of national economic goals. If it is to be done at national level, then it will be in the hands of men who are well able to understand the macroeconomic needs of the country, but their knowledge of conditions down on the shop floor is all but nonexistent.

With the aid of computers, the central planners do the best they can. Every conceivable bit of data, whether it be accurate or the absurd figment of the imagination of some incompetent factory boss down the line, is fed in, to produce at the end of the day a remarkable hodgepodge of figures that are shown to be wholly meaningless the moment anyone seeks to translate them into reality.The proof of this is in the marketplace. There are few products in Polish stores. Those that are there are of inferior quality. The world outside is not exactly clammering for Polish exports. The people subsist on low wages, and the so-called social wages, free facilities such as medicine and education, are not noticeably better than elsewhere and, in far too many particulars, considerably worse. The budget runs an enormous deficit, and the balance of payments is in a woeful predicament.

Lenin predicted that it would be in the sphere of productivity that the real competitive battle between socialism and capitalism would take place.

Who can doubt that, by his own definition, capitalism has won a great victory.

19
The Future

General Jaruzelski went to his Chief of Economic Planning and asked for a realistic yet optimistic projection of what would happen in Poland in ten years' time.

"For a start," said the Minister, "every Pole will have his own individual airplane."

"That sounds fine," said Jaruzelski, "but what for?"

"They'd come in very useful," was the reply. "When someone is in Warsaw and he hears that some potatoes are on sale in Krakow he'll be able to. . . ."

EVERYONE whom I and, judging from news reports, every Western reporter met in Poland, sooner or later came out with the phrase, almost the anthem of post-Solidarity Poland: "Nothing will ever be the same again." Momentarily, when General Jaruzelski proclaimed martial law and the paramilitary police, the ZOMO, took their revenge on the workers who had so humiliated them for sixteen long months, my confidence in a statement I took to be unchallengeable was shaken. But after a few days when the shock had worn off, when I'd had the opportunity to reread some Polish history, when I went over again my notes on the dozens of people I'd interviewed—from people high in the Party apparatus to the lowliest peasant—I saw with a clarity which it actually required Jaruzelski's coup to endorse, that the People's Republic of Poland, as we have known it since the end of the war, had passed into history. What follows now may have the same label on the bottle, but the contents will be even more dramatically different than seemed likely when Lech Walesa and his quarrelsome Praesidium seemed to be carrying all before them.

A mass movement like Solidarity, which at its peak represented 90 percent of the Polish work force, cannot be simply wished away with the wave of a general's baton. In order to be able to work and be able to feed their families, people may well sign forms disassociating themselves from the movement, but they will do so, like naughty

children telling lies, with their fingers crossed behind their backs.
There may be no badges or banners, no congresses and no factory
committees. Solidarity, as a free trade union, owing its authority to
the will of its membership, may have been driven underground, but
it is insane to believe that the spirit that brought it into being, that
motivated it throughout the great crisis months of its existence, and
that was brutally put down on December 13, 1981, does not still live
on in the heart of every Pole. On the contrary, the mere fact that its
leaders were arrested and that its operation declared illegal, ensures
that the movement will take on in the minds of Poles an even greater
significance than it had when it was fully active. Even now those who
opposed it from the beginning, who sought to put roadblocks in its
way throughout its sixteen short months of life, and who cheered on
General Jaruzelski when he finally moved with such efficiency and
dispatch, have realized they've been touched by Solidarity in a way
that they never knew. For Solidarity was not just a trade union, which
it always pretended to be, or an opposition political party, which its
opponents claimed it had become, but something unknown in the
lexicon of political phenomena since the days of the medieval Church,
a mass movement of political and economic reform that encompasses
the entire nation-state without actually being the nation-state itself.
Its light shone into the darkest corners of modern Poland. It im-
pinged into the very highest echelons of the Party apparatus, the
Politburo itself.

One source who, alas, must remain anonymous, for to mention
his name would speak volumes, told me several months ago that
debate within the Politburo had, since the advent of Solidarity, taken
on a completely new dimension. Previously, though disagreements
existed over many issues, an unnatural sense of decorum always existed
in debate. There were defined limits past which no one ever dared
stray. If one faction wished to attack another, they would often
choose a trivial issue with which to face down the other side. Members spoke in a coded language of their own—saying one thing, when
everyone there knew they meant something else altogether. But as
this source reported, when people in the country bgan speaking freely,
so, quite unexpectedly, did members of the Politburo. Suddenly debate
became real. People who had known each other and worked together
for years would look at each other in astonishment and say: "I didn't
know you thought like that!" It happened in the Politburo, it happened in the Central Committee, it happened in the *Sejm*, the Polish

Parliament, and it happened in meetings of the Council of Ministers. And if it happened in these exalted circles, imagine what was happening down at the grassroots.

"I found all of my old friends absolutely fascinating," a doctor in Warsaw told me. "I stopped going to the theater or the cinema for months simply because the greatest pleasure I could contemplate was to be among people, many of whom had been friends since university, and hear them talk. It was a revelation. Even though we Poles are not terribly well disciplined, nevertheless, despite all the political jokes we made, all the fun we had at the expense of the authorities, we had been taught to keep a curb on our tongue.

"I don't think any of us really realized how insidious this process was. I had always thought of myself as a man not afraid to speak his mind. It was only, however, when all inhibitions had been swept away that I realized that I had been lying to myself, that always when it came to it, I had been very circumspect indeed. In 1981 I heard my fellow Poles speak freely for the first time in my life. It was an exhilarating experience."

Another friend told me about the "loneliness" of living in a land where freedom of speech is denied the people. "You seethe inside at the incompetence and injustice that you see all around you. You know there is an Opposition movement, but it takes a particular breed of person to be prepared to commit social and professional suicide by openly siding with the enemies of the regime. So you shut up and say nothing, and imagine that you are all alone, or at least a member of a small minority. Imagine then, what it is like to wake one morning and discover that everyone in Poland sees things as you see it. Imagine what it is like to open one's brain when for years the only sensible course was to try to close it."

It is part of the apparatus of control of all totalitarian countries, be they of the right or the left, to deny their people free access to their own minds. George Orwell brilliantly grasped this truth in his book 1984, in which he gave his security services, his tool of repression, the name "Thought Police." A censored media and a secret police on the lookout for "anti-socialist elements" can eventually persuade people that the evidence of their own eyes can no longer be relied upon. Truth is not a commodity that is generally available.

"I once spoke abroad at an international congress on trade unions," a member of the old official trade union, who quickly joined Solidarity, told me, "and was given a speech to deliver by a senior officer in

the union about trade unionism in Poland. I was curiously schizo-
phrenic about it. I knew that it was objective nonsense, but nevertheless seeing myself as a representative of Poland, I thought I had
a duty not only to deliver it but to improve upon it by adding some
hyperbole of my own. I had no conscience about it whatsoever. I
thought I was doing my duty."

But truth has a curious quality all of its own. It is possible to
suppress it for years. But once it emerges into broad daylight, it can
no longer be unlearned. For sixteen months the Polish people had
access to the truth. They learned that the Party they had been taught
to respect as the guiding light of the nation, was corrupt and incompetent. They learned that the Soviet Union, which they'd been
told was their protector and friend, was a frightened bully interested
only in its own power and prestige. They learned that the press and
television didn't even pretend to report the news but were the cynical
instruments of a rotten bureaucracy that distorted everything it
touched. Poles had gone to the cinema and seen films like Andrzej
Wajda's *Man of Iron*, which told the story of the birth of Solidarity,
and more importantly showed how frightened little men, in this case
a radio reporter, were browbeaten into submission by the security
apparatus in order to defame worker-leaders who had risen up to
challenge the system. In every Polish city they had gone to lectures
given by the most famous historians in the land who told the truth
about the methods used by the Stalinists to seize power in Poland
after the war. They had traveled by car, coach, and train to attend
the great memorial services for the workers, killed in Poznan in 1956,
and dockers, killed in Gdansk in 1970, by the security police, because
they had dared to rise up against a repressive state. They had opened
their newspapers and read articles that told in scathing detail about
the economic mismanagement of their country that led to their current suffering. They bought books of their own writers, previously
forbidden them, men like Jerzy Andrzejewski, Kasimierz Brandys,
Wladyslaw Broniewski and Slawomir Mrozek, and now have them on
their shelves. They learned about their security police, not just a
collection of whispered rumors, but a collection of hard facts that the
authorities hardly bothered anymore to deny. From the end of February
to the middle of May 1980, KOR recorded the following cases:

Warsaw: Wiktor Karpinski and Krzysztof Lachowski, students of
the Warsaw Polytechnic, beaten and tortured at the Warsaw Police
Headquarters; Sergiusz Kowalski, mathematician, beaten in the face
at the Warsaw Police Headquarters; Tomasz Michalek, photographer,

kicked down the stairs at Warsaw Police Headquarters and afterward stripped naked and beaten, also on the head; Aleksander Hall, historian, hit in the nose for refusing to give evidence; Jerzy Godek, student of musicology, beaten and then jailed for thirty days with two homosexuals who molested him; Janusz Gwozdziewski, beaten and stifled at Warsaw Police Headquarters to make him agree to cooperate with security forces; Janusz Jarosz, beaten and dragged into a police car; Marek Respond, kicked and karate-chopped and his beard and moustache set on fire; Marek Kozlowski, male nurse, beaten in the kidneys and liver; Zenon Palka, seriously beaten while in police custody.

Gdansk: Bogdan Borusewicz, historian, beaten during detention; Piotr Bystrzanowski, student, Maciej Grzywaczewski, student, Janusz Karolik, Miroslaw Rybicki, and Tadeuz Szczudlowski, historian, all brutally beaten and kicked after attending an illegal celebration of the anniversary of 3rd May Constitution of 1791. Bystrzanowski was afterward beaten in a police car and threatened with death, then left unconscious, abandoned in the suburbs. After the same celebration, Nina Milewska was also beaten and her eight-year-old son dragged by the hair.

But a complaint filed with the public prosecutor by one Roman Wojciechowski, an active KOR worker, on December 29, 1978, is also known by Poles, many of whom, thanks to KOR, possess a copy. It is worth quoting here in full as an eloquent tribute to the work of the security forces.

"On December 28, 1978, I was summoned to Police Headquarters in Warsaw as a witness in case No. DS 96/78. I was questioned by Inspector Kabala from 10 A.M. to 12:15 P.M. in a manner conforming to the law. After the evidence was given and the record signed, Inspector Kabala wanted to see me out. In the hall we were approached by a security officer who said that I was required for explanations in a different matter.

"He did not reveal his name. I remembered him from a search of my home in which he had participated together with Inspector Andrej Zakrzewski. He led me to a room and addressed me as "Mr. Grochowski." I explained that my name was not Grochowski, but Wojciechowski. The security officer smiled and said that it was not very nice for a police collaborator to refuse to acknowledge his pseudonym. He then asked whether I denied collaborating with the police. I said that such, indeed, was the case. In reply, he put on the desk photocopies of several texts that ran as follows (I quote from memory).

" 'Warsaw, 9/1/69. I acknowledge receipt of 1500 zlotys for information given to the police. The money was handed over to me personally by Inspector Stefan Zbiciak.' Another photocopy contained an almost identical text, but mentioned 500 zlotys instead of 1500 zlotys. The handwriting was exactly like my own, although I never signed such receipts.

"After this introduction, a five-hour-long session of blackmail followed, which I will try to relate here as faithfully as possible. The security officer informed me that in writing (together with Miroslaw Chocjecki) the text entitled *The Citizen and the Security Service*, I had challenged them and must suffer the consequences. The only hope there was for me was to agree to collaborate with the Security Services. I refused and this, in his opinion, condemned myself to death. He mentioned a dozen names, of which I remember a few: Golaszewski, Wnuk, Korzen. These people, according to the security officer, are perverted hooligans. They will be informed by the security people that I helped the police to reveal their crimes. They will do me in. He described to me in vivid detail how they would cut my throat, how the blood would gush forward while I lay twitching and struggling. In answer to my question, if he was aware of the fact that planning a murder is a crime, he said it was all my own fault because I refused to cooperate and, besides, a wise commander will always sacrifice an individual to save his unit. He assured me that no legal action would be taken against him for organizing my murder because the whole thing would be staged in such a way that it would seem to be a settling of accounts between criminals. The end would be preceded by a nationwide propaganda campaign against the Social Self-Defense Committee, KOR.

"The materials in possession of the security services would be published in the mass media. On the one hand, members of the Social Self-Defense Committee (KOR) would be defamed as agents paid by the CIA, while on the other, my death would be presented in such a way that people would be led to believe that the murderers, my own colleagues, had cut my throat because I was an informer paid by the police. All these facts put together would inevitably give the public the impression that the Social Self-Defense Committee (KOR) consists partly of degenerate criminals and partly of agents manipulated by foreign intelligence services (I am still quoting from memory the words of the security officer). After this propaganda prelude, reprisals on a mass scale would take place: 200 people, for whom arrest warrants had been prepared a few months ago, would be im-

prisoned within two hours. He told me to get acquainted with articles
122–126 of the Penal Code, since my friends and colleagues would be
tried on the basis of these articles only. All the time I was being
insulted with terms such as: paid traitor of the country, foreign agent,
collaborator with thieves, instigators, and agents, imperialist lackeys,
etc. My friends and acquaintances were insulted and accused of grab-
bing over 10 million zlotys and informing on people for money. At
one stage, the security officer asked whether I loved my seven-year-old
daughter. I did not answer. He started then to talk in detail about the
Golaszewski brothers who will very likely want, after having murdered
me, to 'have fun' with my daughter. He asked whether the awareness
of the fact that my little daughter would fall into the hands of per-
verts did not induce me to cooperate with the security service and
thus ensure safety for myself and my family. I demanded to be taken
immediately to his superior to whom I wanted to complain about the
lawless behavior of my tormentor. He told me that the boss was very
busy then, just as the police would be busy when the criminals were
'finishing me off' and torturing my child. I was not even allowed to
go to the toilet, despite the fact that I had been sitting in the interrogation room from 10 A.M. to 5:40 P.M. I was only allowed to use the
toilet by one of his colleagues around 5 P.M.

"At the end (for the last three hours I had said not a word) the
security officer said that in the next few days searches would take
place in the homes of my acquaintances and friends, where security
men would drop some copies of the texts I have quoted above. This
would compromise me in the eyes of the members of the Social
Self-Defense Committee (KOR) to such an extent that I would
have to face the criminals condemned and completely alone.

"He warned me not to attempt any legal defense, because if I did,
I would be accused by the security service of insult, slander, and attack
on state officers, and put in prison, where criminals, already briefed
about me in a special way, would find me. At an earlier stage of the
interrogation, he mentioned that I had been lucky last spring, when
unidentified men had beaten me up in a café, breaking four ribs and
a hip, that I did not publish the fact in the underground press. Had I
done so, I would be sitting in prison now with a five-year sentence
for slander. The security service know who did it, but as a harmful
individual I am outside police protection.

"The security service ordered me to report on January 3, 1979, to
the Permit section of the Police Headquarters in Warsaw, where he
would leave my name and telephone number. If I accepted collabora-

tion with the security service and supplied the required information
—he did not specify what information—he would in return give me
the compromising papers and would also refrain from a slandering
campaign against me in the mass media. If I refused, however, I
would put myself at the mercy of criminals and bring defamation
upon my head . . ."

Poles now know that story and hundreds like them. Can they ever
take the authorities who permit these things seriously ever again?
Can they believe their newspapers when they attack the West?

Thousands of Poles have now traveled to the West to discover
supermarkets abundant with food. A Polish taxi driver told me that
when his father came over on a visit to New York and went shopping
for the first time, he just burst into tears.

Equally, it was a chastening moment for a leading Communist
editor on a visit to London when I produced for him the evidence
that an unemployed British worker has a standard of living roughly
equivalent to twice that of one of his coal-miners, the aristocrats of
Polish labor. So how can things ever be the same again?

It is certainly true that in normal circumstances the majority in
any society will opt for the quiet life—will support the status quo,
be opposed to revolutionary change, learn to live with even a dis-
agreeable system rather than place their own comfort and safety in
jeopardy by supporting wholesale change. The astonishing achievement of Solidarity, and the crash course in democracy that it gave the
nation, was that it broke through this natural inertia of society to
create a new society, the final form of which was never completed, but which promised new hope not only for Poland but for
the largely discredited socialist ideals that had motivated the founding fathers of Polish Communism in the latter half of the nineteenth
century.

In 1944 when the Communists first arrived and showed their
determination to take power, they were given the willing support of
large sections of the working class and the intelligentsia that believed
that Marxism was the philosophy of the future; that social justice
could only be attained through Communism; and that Russia was
the only possible guarantor of the sovereignty of the nation. Today,
the Party (which, it is no exaggeration to say, lost power in August
1980), insofar as it still rules at all, does so with the acquiescence of
nobody. Marxism is seen as belonging to the past, the Communist
Party as the political arm of the security police, and Russia as the
colonial overlord.

The Party is now very different. It is as small as it has ever been—with a membership certainly well below 2 million. It has lost many of its worst elements—the openly corrupt and the blatantly dishonest careerists. But it has also lost many of its finest ornaments, men with open minds who saw that the alternative to treating as equal partners with Solidarity was repression on a Stalinist scale, and they were not prepared to lend their names to that. Most of all it has lost any residual goodwill that it once might have had. And that is the significant difference between 1944 and 1982. Those were the days of innocence. Communism in Poland possessed an ethical and philosophic appeal that was very attractive to many. As it happens, I am not one of those who believes that General Jaruzelski is a "Russian agent"; neither do I doubt, from all the evidence available to me, that he is well-intentioned. He was close to tears on one occasion when he met with a group of academics, begging them to understand why he acted as he did, pleading for them to give him a fair chance: Martial law had caused severe deprivations; good people were locked up; the human dignity of thousands assaulted. Yet, almost perversely, General Jaruzelski, the man who called martial law, has been more responsible than most in mitigating against its severest effects. When in the early days there were reports of internees being beaten up, it was Jaruzelski who personally saw to it that militiamen responsible were removed and punished. It was he who insisted that internees should be entitled to receive food parcels from outside and it was he who on a great number of unreported occasions intervened to ensure that a large number of people remained unmolested. And it was General Jaruzelski, too, who has insisted time and time again that, whatever the setbacks, negotiations with the opposition should continue, officially or unofficially, in the hope of reaching some kind of modus vivendi. Nor—seen from the perspective of his office—is the deadlock entirely of his own making. It was clear to a great many people—inside Poland and out—that the very structure of Solidarity created the problems which made martial law inevitable. Here was a national trade-union movement, split up into regional rather than craft groups, able to call upon the entire membership at a moment's notice to harry the authorities. Inevitably this gave it an extra-parliamentary power which no country—in either the East or West—could tolerate for long. Of course, as I told my Polish friends, in the West such problems were easily solved—by the calling of free elections. This meant that the power of the people was transmitted through Congresses or Parliament and did not need to be expressed through the unfettered use of union power.

By the Autumn of 1981 it was clear to everyone, including General Jaruzelski, that the only way out of the Polish dilemma was through elections or martial law. The General, because he knew that the former was unthinkable, opted for the latter.

And that leads this volume to its natural, logical, and only conclusion, by answering the three questions that have been dealt with only by implication. These are: Did Solidarity, through poor discipline of its central Praesidium and a lack of true leadership qualities in Lech Walesa, overstep the mark? Did Solidarity, through the extremism of some of its members, acquiesce in its own destruction? Did Solidarity seek to push too hard and too fast, and thus force a reluctant government to act against it?

I do not believe that anyone who has read this book will be able to give anything but a resounding *"no"* to these questions that have become serious charges, heard both in Poland and the West. It is of vital importance now, to the Poles themselves and to every opposition group in the Communist bloc, as well as to the Western alliance and its future attitude to Russia and the Warsaw Pact, that these questions be faced head-on.

It is true that Solidarity had political ambitions—not necessarily to take over the country (most thought that an impossibility), but to revolutionize the way the country was managed.

Almost everyone of any note in Poland, outside the police wing of the Party, had concluded that as long as all of the levers of power remained where they were, Poland would continue to stumble from crisis to crisis. Poland's problems could not be solved by tinkering with the mechanism of economic reform. They could not be solved while the old *nomenklatura* remained in place. They could not be solved while every remedy had first to be judged against the very ideology that had led the country to its parlous plight.

Why does Poland with its rich farmlands not have enough to eat? The government accuses the farmers of not producing enough, or of hoarding their produce, when everyone knows that Poland came close to starvation in 1981–1982 because in 1977, in yet another attempt to force collectivization, the authorities deprived private farmers of essential fertilizers and farm machinery.

Just ten years ago, a leading Polish economic journal, *Zycie Gospodarcze*, pointed out that in 1973 farmers had purchased 46,000 horse-drawn ploughs, 61,000 horse-drawn barrows, and 36,000 horse-drawn seeders—all fit, said the writer, for a museum. That equipment is still around, witness to the incompetent mismanagement of Polish agriculture by the central authorities.

Why do Polish workers produce so little? The government accuses them of not working hard enough, when everyone knows that the nation is bankrupt because the economy has been deliberately steered to produce goods for the Eastern bloc, where it cannot earn hard currency, rather than the Western bloc, where it can.

A Yugoslav Marxist, Svetozar Stojanovic, has most neatly summed up the dilemma of all workers in a modern socialist country, a system that he defined as "oligarcho-statis." "The name statism," he wrote, "should be given to a system based on state ownership of the means of production and state control over production and other social activities. The state apparatus represents a new ruling class. As the collective owner of the means of production, it employs labor and exploits it. The personal share of a member of the ruling class in the distribution of the surplus value is in direct proportion to his position in the state hierarchy."

As for the working class, "it is more than subordinate and exploited. Not only does it not control production and the distribution of surplus value, but it does not even possess the rights it secured for itself in a developed bourgeois-democratic system; it cannot choose its employer, nor can it bargain for working conditions and the level of wages. The proletariat has no independent organization of its own which can represent and protect its rights."

What is more, the basic tenet of Marxism—that in a socialist system each individual would receive a share in the total wealth of the community directly corresponding to his contribution to it—has been falsified by experience. As one Western academic and expert on Poland, Peter Raina, has put it in *Political Opposition in Poland 1954–71*: "The worker in a socialist enterprise still does 'necessary' or 'paid' labour as well as 'surplus' labour for which he is not paid. The surplus value, which in the capitalist system of production is owned by the capitalist, is, in state socialism, owned by the central authorities. Even small compensations [premiums or bonuses] for extra labour which the factory worker puts in to fulfill the general plan of the enterprise is no reward for his surplus labour. Profit of the product sold is cashed by the state, and very often the state dumps the finished product in capitalist markets at a price far below its production costs. The socialist worker is thus frequently exploited: once by his employer, the state, which does not adequately pay him for his 'surplus' labour, and secondly through dumping, because of which the worker suffers loss on the 'necessary' labour invested in the production of goods. Thus, the unjust distribution of wages and wealth causes alienation of the proletariat."

A Polish worker made the same point to me, though in less academic, Marxist language. "All my working life I have been urged to work for the plan, for the greater glory of socialism, and for Poland. And I have worked hard, in the beginning because I believed the propaganda, and afterward because I thought that my country needed my hands and muscle. But everybody wants a fair return for his labor. I worked in terrible factory conditions, I ruined my health, and all I have ever got is just enough on which to live, a tiny flat so small that my wife and I can't fit into the kitchen together, and a new set of slogans every week urging me to work still harder yet. A few years ago I went on holiday to the Mazurian Lakes and a German-Polish couple were staying there as well. He had this wonderful car; I made a detour every day just so that I could admire it. I didn't dare approach them because I assumed that anyone with a car like that must be very grand indeed. But he must have noticed me, and one day stopped and chatted, and asked if I'd like to take a ride. I then discovered that he was a steelworker just like me. I knew then how I had been cheated by our so-called socialist system."

As the great Polish philosopher Leszek Kolakowski said in an Oxford press conference on August 22, 1980: "The Poles are fed up with the rule of the lie. The workers of the Baltic coast have presented political demands which they regarded as a minimum condition for economic recovery. From the sixteen demands on their list, we should like to quote just one so that you can see what the top state functionaries mean when they label them as 'hostile' and 'anti-socialist.' The workers are asking for 'realistic steps toward leading the country out of the crisis by giving the public full information about the socioeconomic situation and by making it possible for all classes and sections of the Polish community to discuss the program of reforms.'

"It is in search of this aim that they are invoking the right of free election of representatives from the shop floor, the right to independent trade unions, the demand for access to the mass media, etc.

"But the question has been raised: Are such demands realistic in a country ruled by Communists? We believe that they are, since a proper solution to the socioeconomic crisis that has engulfed Poland is in the interest of everyone, including the Polish authorities, the West, and the Soviet Union, and there is no other way to such a solution than that set out in the workers' demands. Without granting society minimal control over the activity of the state, any program of reform that the Party leadership may announce in the hour of crisis will remain a paper proposal only—just as happened in the past."

And, of course, this is precisely what those who claim that Solidarity went too far have in mind. Solidarity was not merely demanding higher wages and better conditions, the normal trade unions' concerns, but with the wholesale reform of their political system. It did so, however, because without political reform they saw there could be no economic reform. The grand old man of Polish socialism, Professor Edward Lipinski, said that . . . bad economic decisions were "reached in a closed circle of the Party leadership, without proper preparation and without wider discussion. To a great extent they are haphazard and stem from definite myths, such as the myth of the primacy of production, particularly in heavy industry; the myth of the accelerated growth strategy, and so on. *This proves that without political reform, without democratization and decentralization, there is no way of correcting the economic system, which is glaringly irrational*" [author's italics]. Lipinski then added—and he was writing in 1978—". . . one needs a certain amount of both internal and external competition: otherwise monopolies rise which, making use of their power, act against the consumer and disregard technological progress."

The answer then to the universal charge that Polish workers don't work hard enough is that the system doesn't allow them to.

It is, of course, clear that the Polish people were demanding more than what Alexander Dubcek the Czech Communist Party leader in 1968 called for with his "Socialism with a Human Face," and which was so brutally denied by the Soviet Union when they invaded his country to crush this movement of reform. The Poles wanted a new kind of socialism altogether. When Poland's rulers accused Polish workers of ruining the economy by their incessant strikes, the workers laughed. There was nothing they could do to worsen Poland's economic situation that had not been done already by the men who were their accusers. "When a plane is crashing, it is a fairly pointless exercise for the crew to go on strike for more money," said a Warsaw intellectual. "If, however, they know the plane is going down because of the incompetence of the captain and his officers, they may well be persuaded that these are not the best people to organize their rescue, and may well, in those circumstances, insist upon some say in how matters should be arranged in the future."

Poles were beginning to take matters into their own hands in a way that went largely unreported in the West at the time, perhaps because they lacked the drama of strikes. All over the country factories were in the hands of Solidarity members who began organizing production themselves. They dealt directly with clients and suppliers, ignoring completely the official channels that have effectively gummed up the works for so many years. Although I met no one who could say with any authority that there were gains in efficiency and productivity, it would have been surprising if it had been any other way, with the state determined to crush the local revolutions by denying them whatever materials it controlled. The government was discussing with Solidarity and its experts ways in which enterprises could be more independent, with a greater degree of worker involvement in management. Solidarity itself agreed that rationalization would mean unemployment—not the attitude of a trade union that many charged lacked responsibility and was prepared to make no sacrifices. These negotiations, for the bare minimum that Solidarity required to ensure that the dreaded grip of the *nomenklatura* could be loosened from the economy, dragged on, month after suffocating month, always close to agreement but never quite getting there.

It has been alleged subsequently that all the time the government and the Party were playing a clever hand. They hoped to wear Solidarity down and to turn the population against it, until finally the Party could absorb it into the system, where Solidarity might retain its name but lose its independence. Another, even more sinister, theory, is that Jaruzelski was marking time until he could spring his coup. The truth is less dramatic. Agreement between the government and Solidarity was impossible, not because of the "extremist" demands that Solidarity was making, but because of internal Party disagreements. Time and time again, when the ruling elite was about to agree on a peace formula, they fell apart into warring factions. Of course, Solidarity was also often divided between moderates and so-called extremists, but these divisions were nothing compared to those among Poland's ruling class.

Some were unable to escape from the ideology that had held them in thrall all these years; others were genuinely convinced that concessions would lead to a Russian invasion, while a third group and the largest of them all were concerned about not losing the privileges their power had given them.

It is no coincidence that Jaruzelski did not inform the Politburo of his intention when he acted. He had lost patience with them as much as he had with Solidarity itself. As for Solidarity's extremists, there were some who coupled their demands for economic and social reforms with generalized attacks on the Soviet Union. Such gross folly, though it may have reflected the general view of many Solidarity members, never came close to reflecting the official policy of the union. Indeed Solidarity and all of its principal supporters constantly went out of their way to reassure the Russians that they had no desire to disturb Poland's external relations, or to campaign for a withdrawal from the Warsaw Pact, or to seek the neutrality that some Western observers were urging.

But, of course, the "Russian question" was always uppermost in people's minds throughout Solidarity's legal existence as a free trade union and in the days and weeks following the coup. The whole world, East and West, suffers from serious misconceptions about the nature of the Soviet threat. General Haig in Washington appears to be convinced that he is fighting the Communist menace. It is nothing of the kind. If, by some extraordinary miracle, the czar were to return to the Winter Palace in Leningrad (quickly renamed St. Petersburg) on Sunday, the new Russian government would be making territorial claims on Poland on Monday, reaffirming its right to hold Afghanistan on Tuesday, and press for Mediterranean anchorage on Wednesday. Russia is an imperial power and always has been one. It was Stalin who subsumed czarist foreign policy for himself, and it is czarist foreign policy that remains the dynamic force in Soviet Russia today. When Russia today uses the language of revolutionary socialism to justify its imperialistic adventures, it is being as cynically hypocritical as it is when it locks up its dissidents, using every pretext to do so, but never admitting that the great sin committed by these people is that they are telling the truth.

To attack Communist imperialism, when it is Russian imperialism we should be assaulting, merely sows confusion in the minds of the Russian people, among the most patriotic on earth, and in the peoples of Eastern Europe, who have long since accepted, albeit reluctantly, that they will never escape from beneath the Russian military banner.

"Western propaganda," says one Polish friend, "causes problems for us all. The rhetoric of a U.S. President or a Mrs. Thatcher makes it easy for our government to allege that those opposed to the system are opposed to the nation. One ought to be able to accept the big-power status of Russia, grant her the respect that is her due, and yet dissent from the form of government the Communists have imposed on the Russian people. I, for one, accept Russian protection but reject her political system. One day, I pray, Russia will accept that this position is compatible with her interests."

Most Poles believe that it is to the direct benefit of the Soviet Union to have on her border a friendly power that offers no threat, either explicit or implicit, that is relatively prosperous and with a contented citizenry. It must be obvious that such a country has to be free to choose its own system of government. If it cannot, its people, regarding their status as that of a subject race, will react with hostility to any system imposed on it, even the most benign.

"I visited Ghana while it was a British colony and visited it again a few years after independence," says a Polish academic. "It was impossible to escape from the conclusion that the average Ghanian was better off and certainly more fairly administered while the British were there. Yet who can doubt that, given the chance now to vote either for continued independence or to revert to its previous colonial status, 99.9 percent of the people would vote for independence. In Poland we all assume that if we were able to control our own destinies, our society would be materially and politically better off. I do not see, judging by our past history, that this would necessarily happen. But we would be spiritually free, and that by itself would inject into the Polish bloodstream an energy and dynamism that would give us the strength to face up to all the new problems we would inevitably create for ourselves."

"Our relationship with Russia," said a Party member, "has been distorted by history. The tragedy is that the Russians are so paranoically obsessed with their notions of security that they do not understand that the way they treat Poland actually undermines their security. They have in this country 36 million people who hate and despise them. I say this as a Communist and it pains me to have to admit it."

Some Poles, by no means orthodox Party men, yet close to senior politicians and army men in the country, are convinced that the Russians, or perhaps more accurately some Russians, in the Politburo and Central Committee of the Soviet Communist Party have realized for years that there must be a shift in relationships if Poland is ever to be relied upon as a loyal member of the Warsaw Pact and Comecon. "It was only in about May 1981 that the Russians really began throwing their weight behind orthodox hardline members of the Party," said one insider. "But from after 1956, when they tried unsuccessfully to stop the Politburo from electing Gomulka as Party

Secretary right through to the Spring of 1981, they consistently backed the liberal, reformist wing of the Party. They were clearly embarrassed by the purge in 1966 and would like to have got rid of Gomulka then as he became more and more authoritarian, but were blocked by the right, who cleverly concocted their anti-Zionist nationalist campaign, which was also principally a cleverly concealed anti-Russian operation which few seemed to realize. Immediately, the Russians began looking around for a successor and lit upon Edward Gierek in Silesia. In the West, because he spent some time in a Belgian coal mine during the war, he was regarded as being Western oriented and was thought by many to be the man to prise Poland away from the Soviet Union. In fact, from his base in Silesia from 1966 and onward, until he became Party Secretary in 1971, Gierek made a number of unscheduled, unannounced, and unpublicized trips to the Crimea, away from the limelight, where the policies that he was quickly to adopt once he took charge were first worked through. The enormous borrowings that Gierek made in the West to finance his program, because they were so misconceived and maladministered, led to the final ruination of the country. They could not have been negotiated without the full approval of the Soviet Union."

"Gierek's economic policy," adds a top Polish politician, "was absolutely revolutionary as was his program of liberalization. He carried through both because Russia was behind him and not against him."

As for 1971 itself, it is well known that Gomulka ordered General Jaruzelski, then Minister of Defense, to put down the Gdansk uprising by force and that he refused to do so, thus precipitating Gomulka's collapse and his removal from office. "It is inconceivable to imagine that Jaruzelski could possibly have survived such a gross act of disobedience unless he had been acting on instructions of the Russians," says the same man. "We know that Gomulka asked Brezhnev for direct assistance, but this was rather brusquely refused. It is impossible to escape from the conclusion that Russia wanted Gomulka, who had become too stern and unbending, out, and the new, flexible, and pragmatic figure of Edward Gierek in."

It is also clear that, ten years later in August 1981, the same thing happened. Gierek was out of favor with the Russians because of the evident failure of his economic policy. His attempts to mobilize opinion in the Party and the Army (General Jaruzelski was the Minister) to crush the Gdansk workers proved to be as unavailing as had

Gomulka's before him. Desperately he sought to retain control by throwing all his supporters in the Politburo to the wolves and accepting some of his most vehement critics in their stead. But the squeeze was now on and he no longer had the power to resist. In one of the most extraordinary scenes ever enacted inside a Communist country, Gierek alternately weeping and issuing contradictory instructions, finally appeared to crack. On either August 24 or 25, he ordered Stanislaw Kania to go to the palace of the primate of Poland, Cardinal Wyszynski, and beg him to attend him at his residence. An astonished Wyszynski agreed to go, as he put it, not as primate but as the First Secretary's parish priest and confessor. Gierek implored Wyszynski "to save the nation" by intervening, for otherwise the Russians surely would. But Wyszynski, who proceeded to hear the broken man's confession, told him that the episcopate and the whole Church was on the side of the workers whose "cause was just."

Gierek's obvious successor was Stefan Olszowski, who had recently been brought back from East Berlin, where he had been sent in disgrace as ambassador for criticizing Gierek's economic policies. He was known to be an orthodox Communist who had served his country as Foreign Minister and was by far the most experienced potential leader at hand. However, the Russians appear to have persuaded him not to seek election and advanced the relatively unknown Stanislaw Kania who, to the disgust of Party oldtimers, was evidently told that there would be no objections from Moscow if he came to a reasonable compromise agreement with the workers. Once again the Russians, though this time they were to regret it, clearly took the view that the Poles were such a peculiar and difficult people, the rules that applied elsewhere in the empire could not be made to apply to them.

Unfortunately for the Poles, the Kremlin, though apparently understanding that the Poles must be treated differently, has lacked the courage to permit this great truth to be translated into a policy that would permit Poland to regard the Soviet Union as its protector not its oppressor. "I can remember," said one Polish journalist, "being taken by my parents to throw flowers before the French and British embassies when France and Britain, honoring their treaty obligations to us, declared war on Nazi Germany on September 3, 1939, forty-eight hours after the German invasion began. We stood there in the thousands, singing Polish patriotic songs, the "Marseillaise," and "God Save the King." I think that everyone in the crowd believed that both Britain and France would launch a massive strike immediately against Germany, and that the war would be over within a few days. I remember being surprised that the RAF was not flying in the skies above us.

"Of course, nothing happened, at least for a very long while, and it took another five years for Poland to be liberated—by the Red Army. There is an indelible lesson in that for all Poles. We may think of ourselves as being Western Europeans but, whether we like it or not, we are too far away for the great Western powers to be able to have any real influence on our affairs.

"We are East Europeans whose nations must group together in alliance, and logically it is to Russia that we must look for our defense."

There are naturally enough a good many Poles—and probably more now—whose hatred of Russia is such that the very suggestion of any voluntary alliance comes as anathema to them. But there's no one I have met in Poland, either in the Party or in any of the main opposition movements, who does not accept that Poland and Russia are condemned to political unity for as far ahead as it is possible to imagine.

"There would be no real argument in the country," said one principal opposition leader, "if any new democratic constitution, guaranteeing us freedom over our own affairs, also guaranteed the Soviets that Poland would remain as a soverign state, part of the Soviet military alliance, and would pursue foreign policy objectives compatible with those currently being pursued by the Kremlin. Solidarity brought to light a number of hitherto unknown people during its few months of active life, but hardly a one challenged Poland's foreign policy or Poland's military alliances. And this was not just caution either, for as you know, on every matter caution was swept to the winds fairly quickly. It was because, I believe, the great majority of Poles, though critical of the Russians, believe that the fates of both countries are so interwoven that it is impossible to imagine one without the other.

"It is our misfortune that the West has failed to comprehend this. Western reporting of Solidarity gloatingly rubbed the noses of the Russians in the predicament they were facing. Western politicians constantly spoke of our movement of reform in terms of the Cold War. Those members of the Politburo who argued that Russia's only guarantee of Polish friendship rested on Russia's willingness to cut the cord, were constantly undermined by those in the West who did not seem interested in Poland, but only in how they could show Poland was humiliating the Soviet Union. Tell a proud nation like Russia it is being humiliated, and it will respond like a stung bear.

"If only Washington politicians like General Haig had tried harder to persuade the Soviets that they were not trying to roll back Yalta, that never would Poland become the forward base for NATO missiles, that the NATO countries accepted that the balance of power in Europe rested on Russia's having secure access to its interests in East Germany, then perhaps, though only perhaps, the debate within the Kremlin would have been clearer cut. As it was, ideological hardliners were able to employ geopolitical arguments to advance their cause, and effectively defeat any faction prepared to support liberalization and reform. It will be a long time before the West has another chance to see inside the Communist bloc an advanced form of liberal democracy, with the long-term implications that would have for everyone, East and West."

Poland now is once again left to its fate. Its internal institutions and contradictions will permit it only occasional bursts of temporary and illusory prosperity. Its administrative apparatus—supported entirely by the security services—will constantly block and frustrate any reform that could clip its powers. Movements towards democracy initiated by the regime, however well intentioned, will collapse into sour disillusion. A man manacled to a rock by one foot may be better off than a man manacled by two, but when it comes to trying to walk, there is little enough difference between them.

No one can possibly predict exactly what will happen next in this extraordinary saga. Yet some things are quite certain in this uncertain world. Poland will never forget—not for another thousand years—the men and women who built the independent, self-governing union, *Solidarnosc*. The name of Lech Walesa, which so inspired not only his fellow countrymen but the whole world, will go down in Polish history, to be passed on like a talisman from generation to generation, to be coupled with that other heroic figure of eternal Poland, Tadeusz Kosciuszko. His comrades, whatever happens to them now, will be revered forever. Those who died or were imprisoned will be added to the list of those martyred for their country. The underground movement, already quite formidable, will become stronger and stronger still. The jokes, bitter and contemptuous, that uniquely Polish form of passive resistance, will flow uninterruptedly, constantly undermining by ridicule the pretentions of the authorities to govern in their name. And then one day the dam will burst again: There will be another explosion, perhaps more dead, and once more the flickering of hope.

For Poland is a very special country, inhabited by a very special people. The Poles have many great virtues—their humor, their sense of self-sacrifice, their concepts of honor and decency—all of which, though sometimes betrayed, have never failed to shine through even in the darkest moments. When set against the heroic qualities of the majority, what does it matter, in the last resort, if a few corrupt, greedy officials got to the top? What does it matter that petty bureaucrats have temporarily taken control, when the country still produces so many great men, some described in these pages, of such humanity and vision? And what, when set against such a stormy but heroic history, is martial law but a mere hiccup in time? The Poles are, above all else, a people of courage and dignity. These are the qualities, so rare in the modern world, which will see them through this time as they always have in the past.

The spirit of Poland, that national will for redemption, has always triumphantly survived the most terrible of trials. It has not and cannot ever be extinguished. Those who seek to do so today will assuredly be devoured by it tomorrow.

Jean-Jacques Rousseau, as long ago as 1771, on the eve of the partitions told Poland: "You will never have an offensive force, and for a long time you will never have a defensive one. But you already have . . . a preservative force that will protect you from destruction, even in bondage, and will protect your government and your freedom in their only true sanctuary—in the hearts of the Poles."

It was true in 1771, and it remains true today.

Years later in August 1980, during the Gdansk sit-in which led to the formation of Solidarity, a vast memorial was erected by the strikers to commemorate those workers who had died in the earlier riots of 1970. On it was pinned a sheet of paper, decorated with the national colors of Poland, a picture of the Virgin Mary—the "Queen of Poland"—and a stanza from a poem by Lord Byron translated by the great Polish national poet, Adam Mickiewicz. Those words are now inscribed on the heart of every Pole—the most precious words in the language

> "Battle for freedom
> once begun,
> bequeathed by father
> passes to the son.
> A hundred times crushed
> by the foe's might
> still it will be won. . . ."

and so, it will.

Notes

Chapter 1

Basic statistics in this chapter and throughout the book have been taken from the officially published "Facts about Poland" from Polska Agencia Interpress. The problems of alcoholism in Poland are discussed in *Survey*, Winter 1980, Volume 25, No. 1, and an article in *Polityka* in July 1978 by Halina Malinowska, "Extent and Effects of Alcoholism in People's Poland." Quotations from Lenin are taken from Professor Leszek Kolakowski's magnificent three-volume study, *Main Currents of Marxism*, which I used extensively for background reading. I consider it the most accessible account of Marxism—it's history, philosophy, and current practice—available anywhere. It will also be evident to specialists that I have made considerable use throughout this volume of *Poland: The State of the Republic* published by Pluto Press Ltd. in London, and simultaneously in the United States by M. E. Sharpe Inc., New York. This is a translation of two reports prepared by a group of Polish intellectuals, ironically enough initially brought together by the Party in 1978 to prepare a critique of the economic performance of the nation, but which ended up as a sustained and well-documented polemic against the social, political, and economic policies of the People's Republic. The group called itself *Doświadczenie i Przysztość* (Experience and Future) and is commonly referred to as DiP. Unfortunately, official statistics, which are all we have, cannot be absolutely relied upon. They show, for example, that 94 percent of Polish households own washing machines, which simple observation would seem to disprove.

As I make clear in the foreword to this book, recent circumstances in Poland have forced me to remove the names of all my Polish sources. Unnamed quotations are generally unsatisfactory, and there are many in this volume. I am convinced, however, that the decision to remove the names that would have figured in these notes is justified. I have limited all chapter notes to a minimum, in view of the fact that as I cannot name my primary sources, it doesn't seem to me that my secondary sources can be of much interest. The general reader won't be interested, and the specialist will recognize them immediately.

Chapter 2

Thanks to my Polish researcher, I have been able to take cases of corruption entirely from the Polish press. Friends in Poland gave me many more examples, some remarkably dramatic, but I decided that the only way to ensure that this chapter could not be faulted by Polish authorities was to rely entirely on their own publications, most of which were overlooked in the West. These stories were published in *Gazeta Krakowska* (17/3/81; 20/3/81; 21/3/81; 22/3/81; 20/1/81; 27/4/81; 2/12/80; 7/1/81; 3/12/80). *Trybuna Robotuize* (28/4/81; 7/4/81; 28/4/81). *Kurier Polski* (15/11/80; 16/11/80; 1/3/81; 22/5/81; 24/5/81; 9/4/81; 27/4/81; 13/3/81; 14/10/80).

The point has been made to me that some of the allegations made in the press against named officials were exaggerated in the sometimes overheated atmosphere during the reign of Solidarity. But I spoke to some of the editors and journalists involved in these stories, and I am convinced that whatever may be said now, at the time they erred on the side of caution, as indeed one might expect them to have done.

Chapter 3

It is impossible to prove that the state sells directly to the black market. The theory, however, is not mine, but was explained to me by an official well versed in these matters. Jacek Kuron is the source for the story of Richard Kowalski, whom he met while they were both serving prison sentences. This chapter contains some quotations from DiP. Polish officials, incidentally, will swear that Cepelia prices are genuine. It depends what you mean by "genuine."

Chapter 4

This chapter is based largely on talks with private Polish individuals in Warsaw and other Polish cities.

Chapter 5

A full list of *nomenklatura* appointments was published in "Revue Française de Sociologie," Number 2/April–June 1979. Published quotations in this chapter come from DiP; Leonard Schapiro's magnificent review of *The Rise of the Gulag: Intellectual Origins of Leninism* by Alain Besançon, Continuum Books (New York) 1981, published in the "New York Review of Books," September 25, 1981; also from the British historian, Richard Davy, writing in the *Times*, October 6, 1981.

I discussed the *nomenklatura* with virtually everyone I met in Poland, both in the Party and outside. I met no one who approved of the system. Even members of the *nomenklatura* themselves would say that while they were individually doing useful work, there was very little evidence that anyone else was!

Chapter 6

Published sources include M. Rakowski, *"Dobry Fachowiec ale Bezpartyjny," Polityka,* July 3, 1971; *Political Opposition in Poland* by Peter Raina; *The Authoritative Communist Party of Poland* by M. K. Dziewanowski; Jan Szczepanski, *"Rozwazania o Rzeczypospolitej"* (Warsaw 1971); /"The False Policy of Zaremba and Zulawski" by B. Drobner (*Naprzod Forward*), March 11, 1947; "How Long can Poles Walk the Tightrope," an article by Mark Bonham Carter in the *Times* of London February 18, 1981; Neal Ascherson's *The Polish August.*

Chapter 7

The story of the burial of a Communist partisan is quoted almost verbatim from *Nothing but Honour,* the story of the Warsaw Uprising 1944, by J. K. Zawodny, quite the best account of this epic engagement. There is no difficulty in finding people in Poland prepared to talk about Russian-Polish relations—the difficulty is in sorting out fact from fantasy.

The story of Poland's economic relations with Russia comes from a speech delivered on May 16, 1981 in Warsaw by Marian Rajski, when he was a delegate to the city's Party Congress. It was reprinted in Polish in *Kultura* (Paris) No. 11/410 1981.

Chapter 8

I know of no serious work discussing the relations between Church and state in Poland, surely a subject that would be immensely rewarding. Much of my information comes from sources inside the Church who made it a condition not to be quoted, even before the present crackdown. The Church has been around for too long to be too easily taken in by sudden bursts of liberalization!

Chapter 9

The story of Kuron's imprisonment during the Gdansk strikes came from Kuron himself in a series of long conversations with the author. Though I have said I would not name the sources of my quotations, I believe it legitimate to make an exception in Kuron's case, principally because there is nothing I can write here that would surprise the authorities in Poland, but also because I believe the security authorities in Poland have consistently misrepresented his position, to his detriment. It will be a surprise to many in Poland to learn that at the time of Gdansk he was a "moderate," opposing the concept of a free trade union. Neal Ascherson's book, *The*

Polish August, which is likely to remain for some time the best book about the early months of Solidarity, was published too late for my initial writing, but was nevertheless a useful source during the final editing of the manuscript, although there was no difficulty in finding Solidarity leaders and activists prepared to talk about their experiences.

Chapter 10

Father Sadlowski being in the same position as Kuron, I do not believe that these direct quotes can in any sense harm his position. Though not well known in the West, his fight on behalf of Polish farmers from the mid-seventies on has been one of the most inspiring stories of recent Polish history. Statistics in this chapter come from official sources.

Chapter 11

The lyrics of Panufnik's "Song of the United Party" come from *12 Polish Composers* by B. M. Maciejewski. The quotation from Kasimierz Brandys comes from his superb book *A Question of Reality*. I abstracted Leszek Kolakowski's speech from *Political Opposition in Poland* by Peter Raina. This chapter is based principally on a series of interviews conducted with writers and painters, of whom perhaps 5 percent accepted the general thesis that the mass of the population believed that they had been betrayed by the intelligentsia for many years. Jan Korwin's "The Wall" was originally published in *Kultura* (Paris), No. 6/1977. This translation appeared in *Political Opposition in Poland* by Peter Raina. The quotation from Slwomir Mrozek comes from Norman Davies's *God's Playground* as being an infinitely better translation than the one available to me.

Chapter 12

The story of the *Gazeta Krakowska* comes from an interview with its editor, which there is little point in concealing. Mirek Chojecki's story comes from personal interviews and from an article by Jan Walc in "Index on Censorship," November/December 1979, Vol. 8, No. 6. "Index on Censorship" proved a valuable source during the writing of this book. Anyone writing upon Polish censorship is indebted to Tomasz Strzyzewski, who defected to the West with censorship documents from his desk, all of which were subsequently printed in two volumes in Polish in London. I have used a translation in "The Bureaucracy of Truth," by Paul Lendvai, which also deals with TV coverage of the Pope's visit to Poland.

Chapter 13

It was not until January 1981 that a decent history of Poland became available in the English language. Norman Davies' two volumes of *God's*

Playground, A History of Poland is an outstanding work, even though it is skimpy on modern history. Unfortunately, it came out too late to be of more than marginal use to me; however, I was able to check my conclusions against it. *Bitter Glory: Poland and its Fate 1918–1939*, by Richard M. Watt, was also immensely useful for the period he covers. However, I am mainly indebted to a professor of history at Warsaw University who took valuable time to lead me patiently through the history of his country.

Chapter 14

Everyone in Poland over the age of fifty has some extraordinary stories of the war years, some of which I have incorporated into this chapter. The story of the resistance movement in Auschwitz comes from *Fighting Auschwitz* by Josef Garlinski. The story of the Warsaw Uprising and the diplomatic exchanges between Roosevelt, Churchill, and Harriman from *Nothing but Honour* by J. K. Zawodny. "Clandestine Medical Studies in Poland 1931–1945," by Professor Witold Rudowski and Ryszard Zablotniak, in the *Journal of the Royal College of Surgeons*, Edinburgh, Vol. 23, July 1978 was immensely useful.

In the mid-seventies a high-powered Polish delegation led by a Deputy Prime Minister visited Iran, where they were entertained at a sumptuous banquet by the Shah. After many toasts, one of the Shah's aide-de-camps rose to his feet and said that during the war he had been honored as a young officer to be one of the liaison officers between the Persian and the Polish Armies. Every day, he said, he visited the Polish encampment, where he was treated royally by his Polish opposite numbers. He always remembered the Polish words of the toast they drank to him with vodka, and now on this emotional occasion, when the Poles had returned, he would like to drink it to his sovereign. The whole company rose while he intoned *Zdrowie Tego Pieprzonego Beduina*. *Zdrowie Tego Pieprzonego Beduina*, the whole company repeated to the pleased Shah. If the Shah noticed that his Polish guests were not the same thereafter, he was too well mannered to say so, but he did ask for a translation. "God bless this great country," said the Deputy Prime Minister quickly, a politer version of the real translation—good health to that fucking Bedouin.

Chapter 15

The story of the 1967–1968 anti-Zionist campaign has been well documented in an unpublished thesis by Wlodzimierz Rozenbaum. The stories of Polish help to Jews during the war is told in *Righteous Among Nations* by Wladyslaw Bartoszewski.

Chapter 16

This chapter is based entirely on personal interviews with young Poles over a long period of years.

Chapter 17

This chapter is also based almost entirely on personal interviews.

Chapter 18

I wondered whether to remove Hania Abratanska's name from the text; she was the only owner of a private enterprise who had no objection to seeing her name published.

Though conditions have changed since she gave me permission, I have decided to keep her name in, not only because she is entirely apolitical, but because I hope that this book can serve as an advertisement for her products. Poland badly needs foreign exchange and, as I suggest in the text, anyone retailing cosmetics could do worse than fly to Warsaw and seek to set up a partnership deal with her. The statistics in this chapter come from official sources. I was helped enormously in this chapter by an official from the Central Planning Office.

Chapter 19

The stories of police repression come basically from KOR documents which have been reprinted in English by Peter Raina in *Independent Social Movements in Poland*. The complaint filed by Roman Wojciechowski is reprinted in its entirety from Peter Raina's excellent translation. The quote from Svetozar Storianovic comes from Raina's earlier book *Political Opposition in Poland 1954–1977*, one of the most valuable books written by a Western scholar about conditions in any East European country.

Bibliography

Ascherson, Neal. *The Polish August: What Has Happened in Poland*. London: Allen Lane Penguin Books Ltd., 1981.

Bartoszewski, Władysław, ed. and Lewin, Zofia. *Righteous Among Nations*. London: Earlscourts Publications Ltd., 1969.

Bethell, Nicholas. *Gomulka: His Poland and His Communism*. London: Penguin Books, 1972.

———. *The War Hitler Won*. Allen Lane, London: The Penguin Press, 1972.

Blazyński, George. *Flashpoint Poland*. Oxford: Pergamon Policy Studies, 1980.

Brandys, Kazmierz. *A Question of Reality*. London: Blond & Briggs, 1978.

Central Commission for the Investigation of German Crimes in Poland. "German Crimes in Poland." SW. *Wojciecha Pod Zarz.* Poznan: Panstw W. Pozaniu, 1947.

Ciechanowski, Jan. *The Warsaw Uprising of 1944*. Cambridge: Cambridge University Press, 1974.

Cienciala, Anna. *Poland and the Western Powers 1938–1939*. London: Routledge & Kegan Paul Ltd., 1968.

Czerny, Zofia. *Polish Cookbook*. Warsaw: Panstwowe Wydawnictwo Ekonomicznc, 1976.

David, Janina. *A Square of Sky and a Touch of Earth*. New York: W.W. Norton & Co., Inc., 1965.

Davies, Norman. *God's Playground: a History of Poland*. Volumes I & II. Oxford: Oxford University Press, 1981.

Dawidowicz, Lucy S. *The War Against the Jews 1933–1945*. New York: Holt, Rinehart & Winston, 1975.

de Madariaga, Isabel. *Russia in the Age of Catherine the Great*. London: Weidenfeld & Nicholson, 1981.

Dobbs, Michael (with K.S. Karol and Dessa Trevisan). *Poland: Solidarity: Walesa*. Oxford: Pergamon Press, 1981.

Dziewanowski, M. K. *The Communist Party of Poland*. 2nd ed. Cambridge, Mass.: Harvard University Press, 1976.

Garliński, Józef. *Fighting Auschwitz*. London: Julian Friedmann Publishers Ltd., 1975.

Giertych, Jedrzej. *In Defence of My Country*. Published by the author. London: 1981.

Gieysztor, Aleksander (with others). *History of Poland*. Warsaw: PWN-Polish Scientific Publishers, 1979.

Halecki, Oscar. *A History of Poland*. London: Routledge & Kegan Paul, Ltd., 1978.

Hiscocks, C. R. *Poland: Bridge for the Abyss?* Oxford: Oxford University Press, 1963.

Howe, Sonia, E. *A Thousand Years of Russian History.* London: Williams & Norgate, 1915.

Index on Censorship. Volume 8/No. 6. London: Writers and Scholars International Ltd., 1979.

Index on Censorship. Volume 10/No. 1. London: Writers and Scholars International Ltd., 1981.

Interpress. "Facts About Poland." Warsaw: Wydawnictwo Interpress, 1980.

Iranek-Osmecki, K. *He Who Saves One Life.* New York: Crown Publishers Inc., 1971.

Jarociński, Stefan. *Polish Music.* Warsaw: PWN-Polish Scientific Publishers, 1965.

Kolakowski, Leszek. *Main Currents of Marxism.* Volumes 1–3. Oxford: Oxford University Press, 1978.

Kuron, J. and Modzelewski, K. *An Open Letter to the Party.* London: International Socialist Publications, 1969.

Lemnis, Maria and Henryk Vitry. *Old Polish Traditions in the Kitchen and at the Table.* Warsaw: Interpress Publishers, 1981.

Lendvai, Paul. *The Bureaucracy of Truth.* London: Burnett Books, 1981.

Leslie, R. F., ed. *The History of Poland Since 1863.* Cambridge: Cambridge University Press, 1980.

Levytsky, Boris. *The Uses of Terror: The Soviet Secret Service 1917–1970.* London: Sidgwick & Jackson, 1971.

Lewis, Flora. *The Polish Volcano.* London: Secker & Warburg, 1959.

Maciejewski, B. M. *12 Polish Composers.* London: Allegro Press, 1976.

MacShane, Denis. *Solidarity: Poland's Independent Trade Union.* Nottingham: Spokesman, 1981.

Massie, Robert, K. *Peter the Great.* London: Victor Gollancz Ltd., 1981.

Miłosz, Czesław. *The Captive Mind.* New York: Vintage Books, 1953.

———. *Native Realm.* London: Sidgwick & Jackson, 1981.

Miynarski, Bronislaw. *The 79th Survivor.* London: Bachman & Turner, 1976.

Nichols, Peter. *The Pope's Divisions.* London: Faber and Faber, 1981.

Ostaszewski, Jan, ed. *Modern Poland Between East and West: Six Essays.* London: The Polish School of Political and Social Science, 1971.

Piłsudski, Jozef. *Year 1920.* New York: Piłsudski Institute of America, 1972.

Raina, Peter. *Political Opposition in Poland 1954–1977.* London: Poet and Painters Press, 1978.

———. *Independent Social Movements in Poland.* London: London School of Economics and Political Science, 1981.

Rozenbaum, Wlodzimierz. "The Anti-Zionist Campaign and Student Demonstrations in Poland 1967–1968." Unpublished thesis submitted to the graduate faculty of the Virginia Polytechnic Institute and State University. Blacksburg, Virginia, 1972.

Singer, Daniel. *The Road to Gdansk.* New York: Monthly Review Press, 1981.

Smith, Hedrick. *The Russians.* New York: Quadrangle/The New York Times Book Co., 1976.

Survey. "Poland from Inside." Part I. Volume 24, No. 4 (109), Autumn 1979. Oxford University Press, 1980.

Survey. "Poland from Inside." Part II. Volume 25, No. 1 (110) Winter, 1980. Oxford University Press, 1980.

Vale, Michael, ed. *Poland, the State of the Republic.* London: Pluto Press, 1981.

Watt, Richard, M. *Bitter Glory: Poland and its fate, 1918–1939.* New York: Simon and Schuster, 1979.

Zawodny, J. K. *Nothing but Honour.* London: Macmillan London Ltd., 1978.

Zielinski, J. G. *Economic Reforms in Polish Industry.* Oxford: Oxford University Press, 1973.

Index

abortion, 355
Abratanska, Hania, 367–368, 369, 371–372, 413
Academy of Sciences, 328, 329
Act of Confederation (1792), 269
alcoholism, 13–16
Alexander II, Czar, 272, 311
Andrzejewski, Jerzy, 220, 230, 250
anti-Semitism, Polish:
  explanations of, 305–306, 313
  as government policy, 314
  Krystal-Nacht killings and, 316
  in legal profession, 320
  in post–Second World War period, 304, 322–323
  in preindependent Poland, 312
  in press, 305
  prevalence of, 305, 306, 312–313
anti-Semitism, Russian, 311
Armia Krajowa, 299, 301, 319–320
Armia Ludowa, 140
Army:
  cavalry in, 286–287
  under Jaruzelski, xvii
  during martial law, xvii, 20
  in Second World War, 286–287
  Soviet officers in, 148
artists, 217–219, 228
Ashes and Diamonds (Andrzejewski), 220
Auschwitz camp, 291–292, 293, 317
Authors' Association, 220

Babcas, 356–359
Baltic Free Trade Unions, 191
bankers, Western, 374, 378–379
Baranczak, Stanislaw, 245–246
Barszcz, Edward, 39
bartering, 75–76, 77
Baziak, Archbishop, 157
Begin, Menachem, 290, 314, 315, 317
Bek, Zdzislaw, 105
Berling, Zygmunt, 121
Berman, Jacub, 122, 308
Besançon, Alain, 95

Bierut, Boleslaw, 122, 123, 141, 204
Birkenau camp, 292
Black Madonna, cult of, 157, 159, 160–161
black market, 48–67
  deliveries in, 50–51
  economic effects of, 50, 51–52
  for food, 48–49, 50–51
  for health services, 57–58
  for money, 60–61, 62, 64, 65–67
  during Nazi occupation, 295–296
  official prices vs. prices in, 49
  "shoulders" in, 57–58, 59–60
  smugglers in, 53–54
  social inequalities created by, 52, 66–67
  state's role in, 49–50, 64–65, 67
  in tourist trade, 62–65
  for Western products, 53–54
Bojowka, 273
Bor-Komorowski, Tadeusz, 296–297
Brandys, Kasimierz, 221
Bratkowski, Stefan, 20
Brezhnev, Leonid, 144, 145, 149, 150, 190
Bujak, Zbigniew, 192
Burke, Edmund, 301
businesses, private, 368–372
  attitudes towards, 368–369
  flower-raising as, 369–371
  state cooperation with, 371
  stores as, 84–85, 372
Byrnes, James F., 118

Casimir the Great, 311
Catherine the Great, 268, 269, 270
Catholic Church, 152–171
  anti-Semitism in, 313, 315
  Black Madonna cult in, 157, 159, 160–161
  Communist move against authority of, 157–161
  conservatism of, 168, 169
  family emphasized by, 355
  under martial law, xviii

Catholic Church (*continued*)
  in mediator's role, 156
  nationalism in, 156, 157, 159, 168
  Pax's relations with, 164–165, 166
  popular criticism of, 167
  power of, 155, 168–169
  in pre–Second World War period, 162–
    163
  during Second World War, 163–164
  Solidarity's relations with, xviii, 156,
    168
  state infiltration of, 164–165
  Znak's relations with, 165, 166
Celinski, Andrzej, 245
censorship, 254–257, 258–262
Central Commission for the Investigation
    of Nazi Crimes in Poland, 321
Cepelia shops, 63–64
Chojecki, Mirek, 248–254
Chopin, Frédéric, 5, 271
Chorobski, Ryszard, 35
Churchill, Winston, 298–299, 300
Ciesiolkiewicz, Zdzislaw, 104
coal mining, 25–26, 373
Coal-Mining Industrial Building Company
    (PBPW), 27
Comintern, 76, 121
Commercial stores, 82–83
Committee for the Defense of the
    Workers (KOR):
  aims of, 175, 233
  farmers included in, 208–209
  Flying Universities established by, 233–
    234
  founding of, 230, 231
  in Gdansk strike, 177
  Information Bulletin published by, 233
  Jews in, 305
  persecution of members in, 231–232
  security police actions recorded by, 390–
    391
  as Social Self-Defense Committee, 233
  Solidarity supported by, 234
  underground publications of, 248, 249,
    253
Committee of Farmers' Self Defense, 209
Committee of National Liberation, 117
Communist Party, 108–132
  agents in, 109, 118
  arrests of members in, xvi
  Central Committee of, 90, 91, 103, 114,
    128, 257
  coal miners in, 25–26

collapse of rule by, 132, 394–395
collective psychosis in, 125
Control Commission of, 41
corruption in, 27–43, 123–124
Democratic bloc election of, 117–118
discord in, xviii, 120, 121–122, 400
as elite group, 123–124
expulsions from, 32, 105, 123
Home groups in, 121–122
horizontalism in, 127–131
intellectuals' relations with, 215, 217–
    220, 225, 229, 231
under Jaruzelski, 42, 43, 126–127, 131
Jewish membership in, 307–309, 313
during liberation of Poland, 117–118,
    121
under martial law, xvi, xviii, 132
mass base lacking for, 115–116
membership of, 109, 110, 115–116, 123,
    127
Mickiewicz play closed by, 225–226
Muscovites in, 121–122, 141
new constitution installed by, 165–166
new debates in, 388–389
nomenklatura in, 90–91, 100–101, 103–
    104, 105
police wing of, 122–123
Politburo of, 90, 91, 110, 118, 126–
    127, 142, 178, 388
popular resistance to rule by, 19, 116
in post–Second World War period,
    118–120, 122–123
in pre–Second World War period, 120–
    122
rebuilding of, 124–126
reform movement within, 110–114
Solidarity members in, 110
Solidarity's relations with, 32, 41, 42,
    43, 101, 105, 125, 126
Soviet Union's relations with, 109, 112,
    117, 118, 119, 140
Stalin's role in, 118, 119
Western assumptions about, 109, 110–
    111, 130
women in, 348, 353
youths' relations with, 342
Confederation for Independent Poland,
    306
Constitution, May 3rd, 269
contractors, foreign, 36
Cossacks, 268
Council for Mutual Economic Assistance
    (Comecon), 54

crime, 129–130
currency:
  exchange rates for, 60–61, 62
  in government stores, 83–84
  import and export of, 61–62
  shortage in hard forms of, 62, 64
  two-tier system of, 65–67
Czarkowski, Jerzy, 320
Czechoslovakia, 8, 13, 110, 312–313
Czerniak, Boleslaw, 38

D'Abernon, Lord, 275–276
Davies, Norman, 289–290
democratic centralism, principle of, 129
divorce, 355
Dmowski, Roman, 274, 312, 313
Drobner, Boleslaw, 116–117
drug abuse, 336
Dubček, Alexander, 399
Durbacz, Stanislaw, 38–39
Dzierzynski, Felix, 19, 120

economy, 366–383
  black market in, 50, 51–52
  collapse of, 380–381
  debt rescheduling in, 379–380
  export earnings in, 381
  flexibility lacking in, 332
  under Gierek, 81–82, 98–99
  growth of, 375
  oversights in planning for, 80, 98–99
  plans in, 375–378, 381–383
  popular discontent with, 71
  problems in, xviii, 374–375
  "shoulders" in, 57–60
  Six Year Plan for, 375
  socialism as favored form of, 368–369
  Soviet command model for, 374–375
  statistics on, 373–374
  two-tier price system in, 81, 82–83
  unreliability of statistics on, 377–378
  Western investments in, 99, 374, 378–379
education:
  achievements in, 329, 342
  class barriers in, 336–337
  as compulsory, 329
  corruption in, 40–41
  employment arising from, 330–331
  historical events falsified in, 327–329
  levels of, 3
  reform in, 329
  "shoulders" in, 58–59, 335

as treadmill, 333
in vocational schools, 333–335
for women, 353, 354
Einsatzgruppen, Nazi, 288
Esperantists, 289
Eve of our Forefathers, The
  (Mickiewicz), 225
Ewa, Pani, 370, 371
export earnings, 381

Falanga Party, 119, 164
families:
  extended, 358–359
  importance of, 354–355
farmers, 197–211
  as anti-socialist, 199–203, 206
  black market and, 48–49, 50–51, 207
  in gentry class, 201–203
  under Gierek, 81–82, 206
  historical pauperization of, 201–202
  hothouses used by, 370–371, 372
  investment program for, 206, 207
  KOR organization of, 208–209
  land valued by, 203
  Peasant Party for, 204–205
  as "peasants," 200, 202–203, 204–205, 206
  as political power bloc, 199
  private vs. collective, 206–207
  productivity of, 197–198, 207–208
  Rural Solidarity organized by, 210–211
  Sadlowski's work with, 198, 199, 208, 209–210, 211
  standard of living of, 198–199, 204, 208
  strike by, 204
  taxes levied on, 206
  technology and, 98–99, 396
  urban migration of, 200
  as worker-farmers, 207
Fascism, 105, 164, 281
Fascist Party (Falanga), 119, 164
fashion, 340–341
Financial Times, 208
Finder, Pawel, 121–122
Fiszbach, Tadeusz, 176–177, 305
flowers, popularity of, 369
Flying University, 175–176, 190–191, 233
folklore, political, 146
food, attitude towards, 47–48
food subsidies, 208, 379
Frank, Hans, 288
Frederick the Great, 201

Gajowniczek, Francisek, 170
gangs, street, 338
Gazeta Krakowska, 240–244, 368
  government criticized in, 243–244
  history articles in, 262
  offices of, 239
  revolutionary changes in, 241, 243–244
  Szumowski as editor of, 239, 242–243
Gdansk, 7
Gdansk Agreement, 103, 177
Gdansk strike of 1970, 188–189, 190, 191, 216
Gdansk strike of 1980, 175, 176–178, 191–192
Gdynia strike of 1970, 189–190, 216–217
gentry class, 201–203, 267–268, 269, 272, 311
Germany, West, 13, 223
Gierek, Adam, 28–29
Gierek, Edward, 28, 92, 137–138
  appointment of, 190, 216
  as corrupt, 29–30, 40–41
  economic expansion under, 81–82, 98–99
  end of rule by, 403–404
Glazur, Adam, 34
Godlewski, Marceli, 163
Gomulka, Wladyslaw:
  Catholic Church's relations with, 159, 160, 161, 162
  collective farms dissolved by, 206
  as Home group leader, 122, 123
  intellectuals' support for, 222
  on Jewish emigration, 308
  Kielce killings condemned by, 307
  Muscovites rejected by, 227
  in persecution of Jews, 228, 229
  resignation of, 190, 216, 403–404
  rise to power of, 141–143, 159, 222
  Soviet relations with, 137–138, 144–145
Grass, Gunther, 249
Grudzien, Zdzislaw, 27–29, 40
Grunwald and Tannenberg, battle of, 266
Grunwald Patriotic Union, 104–105
Grzyb, Zofia, 185–186
Grzybek, Stanislaw, 34
Guardian, 208
Gulag Archipelago, 289

Haig, Alexander, 401
Harriman, Averell, 298
health services, 57–58
Heydrich, Reinhard, 291

Himmler, Heinrich, 317
Hirszfeld, Ludwik, 163–164
Hitler, Adolf, 301
Hlond, Cardinal, 307, 314
hoarding, 74–75
Home Army, 299, 301, 319–320
horizontalism, 127–131
Hull, Cordell, 298
Hungarian Revolution, 143

Independent Student Union, 335
intellectuals, 215–236
  Communist Party's relations with, 215, 217–220, 225, 229, 231
  as elite group, 219–220
  Gomulka supported by, 222
  impotence of, 220–221
  isolation of, 221–222
  in KOR, 230
  in media work, 242
  Nazi killings of, 288–289, 317
  women as, 348
  workers turn against, 215–217
International Herald Tribune, 109–110
investments, foreign, 99, 374, 378
Irgun fighters, 315
Ironside, William Edmund, 287
Israel, 310, 316
Iwanov, Zbigniew, 128–129, 131

Jablonski, Henryk, 155
Jabotinsky, Vladimir, 314
Jadwiga, Queen, 265–266
Jagger, Mick, 339
Jagiello, Grand Duke of Lithuania, 265–266
Jagiellonian University, 266
Jagielski, Mieczyslaw, 191–192
Janta, Alexander, 118
Jaroszewicz, Piotr, 36
Jaruzelski, Wojciech:
  Communist Party under, 42, 43, 126–127, 131
  martial law imposed by, xvi, xvii–xviii, 41, 271, 343, 387, 400
  as Minister of Defense, 403
  nomenklatura's relations with, 100, 103, 105
  Party corruption attacked by, 42, 43
  Rakowski appointed by, 113
  on Rural Solidarity, 211
  Soviet Union's relations with, 149
Jefferson, Thomas, 271

Jews, Polish, 278, 288, 291, 292, 293, 294, 295, 304–323
  Church's war aid for, 163–164, 319
  in Communist Party, 307–309, 313
  Communist Party persecution of, 215, 226–228, 309
  emigration encouraged for, 308, 315
  isolation of, 313–314
  Kielce killings of, 306–307
  legislation passed against, 313
  Nazi extermination of, 310, 317, 319, 321–322
  numerus clausus for, 313, 315
  pauperization of, 315
  Pilsudski's protection of, 314
  Polish fight against extermination of, 318–322
  in preindependent Poland, 311–312
  in pre–Second World War period, 314–316
  Resistance movement's aid to, 320–321
  Russian Jews merged with, 311
  after Second World War, 308
  see also anti-Semitism, Polish
Jews, Russian, 311–312
John Paul II, Pope:
  accession of, 153–155, 169
  as Cardinal, 154, 166, 170
  political role of, 154–155
  press coverage of visit by, 257–258, 259
John II Casimir, King, 157
John III Sobieski, King, 267
jokes, Polish, 8–13
  in America, 8
  political content of, 8–9, 11–13, 18
  during Second World War, 9–11
Jones, Brian, 339
juvenile delinquency, 336, 338

Kaczmarek, Bishop, 157
Kafel, Bronislaw, 35
Kaim, Franciszek, 35
Kania, Stanislaw, 103, 131, 155–156, 166, 210, 243, 404
Katowice, 25, 26
Katowice Forum, 125
Katyn massacre, 135–138, 144–145, 254
Khrushchev, Nikita, 142–143, 144–145
Knights of the Teutonic Order, 266
Kolakowski, Leszek, 17, 225, 226, 398, 409
Kolbe, Maxmillian, 169–171
Komar, General, 142

Kopee, Stefan, 294
KOR, *see* Committee for the Defense of the Workers
Korwin, Jan, 232
Kosciuszko, Tadeusz, 270, 406
Kosciuszko Division, 121
Kowalski, Richard, 54–55
Krakow, 5–6
  Communist Party of, 241–242
Krasinski, Zygmunt, 271
Krystal-Nacht, 316
Kulpinski, Jan, 38
Kuron, Jacek, 158, 175–176, 177, 186, 187, 222–225, 230, 234–236, 410, 411

Lange, Oskar, 374
Lejczak, Wlodzimierz, 39–40
Lenin, V. I., 18, 120, 348
  democratic centralism promoted by, 129
  on emancipation of women, 359
  nomenklatura based on writings of, 95, 127
  as *Pravda* editor, 240
  on productivity, 383
  on revolution, 132
  on working class, 16–17
Leopold, King, 288
Lewewel, Joachim, 277
liberum veto, 268
Lipinski, Edward, 230, 231, 398–399
literary magazines, 246–249, 253, 348
London *Sunday Times*, 347
London *Times*, 219
Luxemburg, Rosa, 348

MacShane, Denis, 347–348
Malenkov, George, 92
malnutrition, 52
Mandelstam, Osip, 249
Man of Iron (Wajda), 15, 242, 390
Markov, M. D., 136
Martial Council for National Redemption (WRON), xvi, xvii–xviii
Marx, Karl, 18
Marxism, 74, 90, 95
Michelet, Jules, 175
Mickiewicz, Adam, 225, 271, 407
Miedzinski, Boguslaw, 316
Mieloch, Roman, 34
Mikolajczyk, Stanislaw, 204
Milosz, Czeslaw, 219, 221, 253
Minc, Hilary, 308

Minex company, 37
Moczar, Mieczyslaw, 227–228, 305
Moczarski, Kazimierz, 301
Modzelewski, Karol, 186, 187, 306
Molotov, V. M., 138
Moraczewski, Jedrzej, 278
Morning Star, 242
Mosdorf, Jan, 320
music, popular, 339–340
Mustafa, Vizier Kara, 267

Narutowicz, Gabriel, 279
National Democratic Party, 278, 313, 319
New Horizons, 348
New Left, European, 185
Niedzielski, Colonel, 350
Niezalezna Oficyna Wydawnicza
    (NOWA), 249, 251, 253–254, 259,
    260
1984 (Orwell), 389
NKVD, 118, 136, 289
nomenklatura, 90–105
    appointments to, 90, 91
    chaos in, 97–98
    Communist Party's relations with, 90–
        91, 100–101, 103–104, 105
    Grunwald movement in, 104–105
    isolation of, 94–95
    under Jaruzelski, 100, 103, 105
    language of lies in, 95–97
    Lenin's blueprint for, 95
    mediocrity in, 91–92
    mismanagement in, 98–100
    police wing of, 104–105, 109, 114, 227
    popular hostility toward, 101–102
    posts created in, 90–91
    privileges granted to members of, 93,
        94, 101
    as social class, 89–90, 101
    Solidarity's relations with, 101, 104,
        105, 109
    Western bureaucracies vs., 93–94
November Insurrection (1830), 271
Nowotko, Marceli, 121

Ochab, Edward, 228
Odnowa, 131
Olsowski, Jerzy, 35–37
Olszowski, Stefan, 92, 105, 148–149, 305,
    404
Orwell, George, 249, 389
Otawoka, Elzbieta, 337
Ozdowski, Jerzy, 167

Pacis, E., 34
Paderewski, Ignacy, 278–279
Palestine, 315, 316
Pan Tadeusz (Mickiewicz), 271
Panufnik, Andrzej, 219–220
Paris Match, 116
Pasternak, Boris, 180
Patriotic Party Cadre, 227
Pax organization, 164–165, 166–167
Peasant Party, 204–205
Pekao stores, 84
Perrins, Les, 339
Pétain, Henri, 288
PEWEX stores, 83–84
Piasecki, Boleslaw, 164
Pilecki, Witold, 292, 293
Pilsudski, Bronislaw, 272
Pilsudski, Jozef, 138, 163, 272–275, 276,
    278, 279–282, 314, 327, 328
Pinkus, Szenicer, 309, 310
"Pledge of Youth" (Panufnik), 220
Plotnicka, Helena, 292–293
Poland:
    boundaries of, 7–8, 266, 274
    cities of, 5–6, 7
    countryside of, 4–5, 197
    1830 November Insurrection in, 271
    ethnic divisions in, 277–278, 312
    falsification of historical events in, 327–
        329
    first constitution of, 269
    first partition of, 268–269
    Germanization policy in, 272
    golden age of, 265–266
    history as central to, 265
    as masculine society, 362–363
    1918 independence for, 274, 277–280
    1926 coup in, 279–280
    Russia's historical domination of, 270,
        271–272
    second partition of, 270–271
    Soviet war with, 274–277
    third partition of, 288
Polanski, Roman, 334
Polish Bar Council, 320
Polish-Soviet War, 274–277
Polish United Workers' Party (PZPR),
    118, 121, 165–166, 178, 186, 219–
    220, 243
Polish Workers' Party (PPR), 118
Political Opposition in Poland 1954–71
    (Raina), 397
Polityka, 14, 113, 228–229, 244–245, 246

poverty, 52
Poznan riots, 140–141, 159, 222
Pravda, 130, 143, 239–240
press, 239–262
 anti-Semitism in, 305
 censors' office for, 254–257, 259–260
 editors of, 239–240, 241
 infiltration of illegal work in, 251–252
 during Nazi occupation, 294–295
 Pope's visit covered by, 257–258
 popular attitudes toward, 241, 254, 261
 as propaganda arm, 240, 241
 reporters in, 243–244
 revolutionary changes in, 243–244, 258–259
 Solidarity covered by, 259, 260
 Soviet model for, 254–255
 underground printing in, 245–253
 Wyszynski's funeral covered by, 258
production:
 in agriculture, 197–198, 207–208, 373–374
 in industry, 373
 of raw materials, 373
prostitution, 360–361
Pulp (Andrzejewski), 250
Pyjas, Stanislaw, 231–232

queues, 71–75
 causes of, 74–75
 etiquette of, 71–72
 social function of, 72, 73–74

Raina, Peter, 397–398
Rakowski, Mieczyslaw, 112, 113–115, 228–229, 244–245
Rapacki, Adam, 228
rationing, 52
Rawkowski, Franciszek, 34
Record, 246–247, 248
Resistance, 291–295
 in Auschwitz camp, 291–293
 classes conducted by, 293–294
 Communists in, 293, 327
 Jews aided by, 320–321
 medical schools established by, 294
 publications by, 294–295
 during Soviet invasion, 296–297, 301
 women in, 349–352
Ribbentrop-Molotov Pact (1939), 121, 136, 287, 327
Robotnik, 233, 253, 273
Rokossovsky, Konstantin, 142, 143

Rolling Stones group, 338–339
Roosevelt, Franklin, 118, 298, 299, 300
Rousseau, Jean-Jacques, 407
Rudnicki, Witol, 319
Rural Solidarity, 210–211
Russian Orthodox Church, 159, 268
Russians, The (Smith), 381
Rzessuta, Jerzy, 35

Sadlowski, Czeslaw, 198, 199, 208, 209–210, 211, 411
Samizdat organization, 245, 247
Sanacja, 280
security police, 390–394
Sejm, 230, 268, 281, 388
Self-Ruling Trade Union for Individual Farmers, 210–211
Shamir, Itzhak, 315
shortages, 74–80
 behavior affected by, 74, 76–77, 85–86
 of consumer durables, 78–80
 hoarding as cause of, 74–75
 of paper, 241, 249
 prices during, 77
 professional shoppers created by, 78
 of repairmen, 80–81
 "shoulders," 57–60
Sikorski, Wladyslaw, 290
Slavs, 288
Slowacki, Julius, 271
Smith, Hedrick, 381
Sobien, Inka, ix–x, 339
Socialist Party, 220, 231, 272–273
Socialist Youth Union, 342
Social Self-Defense Committee (KOR), 233
Society of Scientific Courses, 233
Solidarity, 174–193
 achievements of, 178
 arrests of members of, xv–xvii
 Catholic Church's role in, 156
 Communist Party's relations with, 32, 41, 42, 43, 101, 105, 125, 126
 conservatives in, 185–186
 discord in, xviii, 183–186, 187–188, 400
 educational reforms under, 329
 Gdansk strike for, 175, 176–178
 government negotiations with, 400
 horizontalism and, 129, 130, 131
 individuals represented in, 179
 intellectuals in, 233–234
 internal debates on role of, 184–186
 Jews in, 305–306

Solidarity (*continued*)
  KOR support for, 233–234
  leaders of, 329–330
  under martial law, xv–xviii, 19, 387–388
  membership of, xviii, 180
  as national crusade, 180, 388
  New Left support for, 185
  nomenklatura's relations with, 101, 104, 105, 109
  outspokenness encouraged by, 183, 389
  popular impact of, 390, 394
  power expressed by, 180–181
  press coverage of, 259, 260
  as pressure group, 184
  publications of, 254
  as response to economic discontent, 71
  rise of, 18–19, 21, 177–178, 191, 379–380
  Soviet issue in, 401–402
  student union in, 182
  women in, 348, 363
"Song of the United Party" (Panufnik), 219–220
"Song to the Virgin Mary" (Panufnik), 219
Sosnkowski, Kazimierz, 299–300
Soviet Union:
  agents placed by, 109, 118
  currency exchange in, 61–62
  democratic centralism in, 129
  German invasion of, 290
  imperialism of, 401–402
  in Katyn massacre, 135–138, 144–145
  Orthodox Church in, 159
  Poland invasion prepared by, 147–148, 149
  Poland's present relations with, 147–148, 404–407
  Poland's war with, 274–277
  Polish Communist Party's relations with, 109, 112, 117, 118, 119, 140
  Polish enmity against, 138–140, 147, 148, 405–406
  and Polish martial law order, xvii, xviii
  Polish October defiance of (1956), 143–144
  post–Second World War Poland controlled by, 140–143
  satellites of, 145
  Warsaw Uprising and, 139
Spychalski, Marian, 122
Stalin, Joseph, 18, 300, 401
  Poland controlled by, 140

Poles persecuted by, 138
Polish Communist Party and, 118, 119, 121
  during Second World War, 290, 298
Stanislas II Poniatowski, King, 268
Staruch, Stanislaw, 33–34
Stojanovic, Svetozar, 397
Stomma, Stanislaw, 166
Stroop, Juergen, 301
Strzyzewski, Tomasz, 254
student protests, 215, 216, 225, 226, 327, 335
Surdykowski, Jerzy, 259
Swieckici, A., 14
"Symphony of Peace" (Panufnik), 220
Szczepanski, Jan, 115
Szczepanski, Maciej, 29–31
Szczypiorski, Adam, 260–261
szlachta, 267
Szumowski, Maciej, 239, 240–244, 262

television, 258, 260
Time, 257
Tolkarz, M., 14
tourist traps, 62–64
Treaty of Riga (1921), 274
Trybuna Ludu, 105, 239–240, 258, 338
Tukhachevsky, Mikhail Nikolayevich, 275–276
Tyranski, Kasmierz, 37–38

Ukrainians, 277–278, 312
Ulyanov, Alexander, 272
Union of Artists, 181
Union of Military Organization, 292
Union of Polish Lawyers, 320
Union of Polish Patriots, 121
Union of Polish Writers, 215, 226
universities:
  academic purity of, 328
  conservatism of students in, 335–336
  for elite, 335–336
Urzad Bezpieczenstwa, 100–101
Usiyevich, Helen, 348

Versailles Treaty (1923), 274, 312
vocational school system, 333–335
vodka, 13–14, 15, 66–67

Wajda, Andrzej, 15, 241, 242–243, 390
Walc, Jan, 245–247, 250–251
Walentynowicz, Anna, 191
Walesa, Lech:

arrest of, xvi
background of, 188
Baltic Free Trade Unions established
by, 191
as Catholic, 156, 193
as heroic figure, 406
Jagielski's debate with, 192
KOR support for, 234
male gallantry of, 347, 348
in 1970 Gdansk strike, 188, 189, 190
in 1980 Gdansk strike, 176, 177, 191–
192
press coverage of, 260
as Solidarity leader, 186, 187, 188,
192–193
Walewska, Maria, 349
"Wall, The" (Korwin), 232
Warsaw, 6–7
Warsaw University, 215, 294, 353
Warsaw Uprising, 139–140, 286, 297–
301, 310, 349
Wasilewska, Wanda, 121, 348, 352–353,
354
Watts, Charlie, 339
Who's Who, Polish, 40
Wilson, Woodrow, 279
Witos, Wincenty, 281
Wojciechowski, Roman, 391–394
Wolski, Wladyslaw, 118
women, 346–363
as Babcas, 356–359
childbearing by, 352–353
in Communist Party, 348, 353
education for, 353, 354
equality for, 347, 348–349, 352, 353–
354, 355, 359, 362
family valued over careers by, 354–355
in government positions, 348, 353
as intellectuals, 348
in liberation movement, 353
male gallantry accepted by, 348–349
as prostitutes, 360–361
in Resistance movement, 349–352
in role reversals, 354
in Solidarity, 348, 363
in work force, 352, 353, 354, 359–360
worker-farmers, 207
workers:
certificates required for, 333–335
charges against, 399
as illegal aliens in Europe, 331–332

intellectuals alienated from, 215–217
low morale of, 378
as over-educated, 330–331
survey on attitudes of, 337
underemployment of, 378
as women, 352, 353, 354, 359–360
Workers' Councils, 222
World War, First, 120
World War, Second, 285–302
Allies in, 298–300
death toll in, 285–286, 291
extermination camps in, 316–317
Katyn massacre in, 135–138, 144–145
liberation of Poland after, 117, 121
Nazi exterminations during, 288–289
Nazi Germany in, 136, 286, 288, 290–
291, 297, 301
Polish cities bombed in, 286
Polish Resistance in, 291–296
rebuilding after, 6–7
Soviet invasion of Poland during, 287,
296, 301
writers, 19–20, 217–218, 226, 229, 247,
249, 253
Wrzaszczyk, Tadeusz, 34–35
Wyszynski, Stefan, 155, 156, 157, 159–
162, 165, 169, 198, 258, 403

Young Poland Movement, 234
youths:
Communist Party's view of, 342
delinquency among, 336, 338
in gangs, 338
protests by, 339
self-hatred among, 336
Western culture adopted by, 340–341
see also education; universities

Zagajewski, Adam, 246
Zareba, Tadeusz, 126
Zasada, Jerzy, 124–125
Zawieyski, Jerzy, 165
Zielinski, Andrej, 187
Zionism, 227, 315–316
Zionist Revisionists, 314
Znak organization, 165, 166, 167
Zolnierz Wolnosci, 105, 227
ZOMO, xvii
Zycie Gospodarcze, 396
Zymierski, Michal, 118–119